ARCHITECTURAL CULTURE IN BRITISH MANDATE JERUSALEM, 1917–1948

ARCHITECTURAL CULTURE IN BRITISH MANDATE JERUSALEM, 1917–1948

Inbal Ben-Asher Gitler

EDINBURGH
University Press

Edinburgh University Press is one of the leading university presses in the UK. We publish academic books and journals in our selected subject areas across the humanities and social sciences, combining cutting-edge scholarship with high editorial and production values to produce academic works of lasting importance. For more information visit our website: edinburghuniversitypress.com

© Inbal Ben-Asher Gitler, 2020, 2022

Edinburgh University Press Ltd
The Tun – Holyrood Road
12 (2f) Jackson's Entry
Edinburgh EH8 8PJ

First published in hardback by Edinburgh University Press 2020

Typeset in Trump Mediaeval by
Servis Filmsetting Ltd, Stockport, Cheshire

A CIP record for this book is available from the British Library

ISBN 978 1 4744 5749 1 (hardback)
ISBN 978 1 4744 5750 7 (paperback)
ISBN 978 1 4744 5751 4 (webready PDF)
ISBN 978 1 4744 5752 1 (epub)

The right of Inbal Ben-Asher Gitler to be identified as author of this work has been asserted in accordance with the Copyright, Designs and Patents Act 1988 and the Copyright and Related Rights Regulations 2003 (SI No. 2498).

Every effort has been made to trace the copyright holders, but if any have been inadvertently overlooked, the publisher will be pleased to make the necessary arrangements at the first opportunity.

Published with the support of the University of Edinburgh Scholarly Publishing Initiatives Fund.

Contents

List of Figures vi
List of Abbreviations xi
List of Digital Archives xii
Acknowledgements xiii

Introduction 1

1 A Holy City for the Twentieth Century: Urban Planning during the British Mandate 20

2 Appropriating Multi-histories: The Palestine Archaeological Museum 55

3 Americans Imagining Jerusalem: The Jerusalem YMCA Building 101

4 Constructing Palestinian Identity: The Palace Hotel 145

5 Constructing Zionist Identity: The Zionist Executive Building 181

Conclusion: Buildings, Communities 214

Bibliography 228
Index 240

Figures

Abbreviations used in Legends

ABHC Avie and Sarah Arenson Built Heritage Research Center, Technion Institute of Technology
ACM   American Colony Photo Department, Jerusalem. Library of Congress, Washington, DC, G. Eric and Edith Matson Collection, http://www.loc.gov/pictures/collection/matpc/
CZA   Central Zionist Archives, Jerusalem
IAA   Israel Antiquities Authority
IGPO National Photo Collection of Israel, Photography Department Government Press Office
KFYA Jerusalem YMCA Records, Kautz Family YMCA Archives, University of Minnesota Libraries
NKU   Mehmet Nihat Nigizberk Collection of Architectural Drawings and Photographs, © Suna Kıraç Library/Koç University

I.1	Work at the building site of the Palestine Archeological Museum, 1930s	xvi
I.2	Henry Kendall, The 1944 Scheme: Zoning Plan	3
I.3	Panorama of Jerusalem facing Mamilla Cemetery and southeast Jerusalem	17
I.4	American School of Oriental Research and Olivet from St George's Cathedral Tower, Jerusalem, detail	17
1.1	Jaffa Gate with the Ottoman Clock Tower (erected 1901, demolished 1924), c. 1898–1914	27
1.2	William McLean, Jerusalem Town Planning Scheme No. I, 1918	29
1.3	George S. C. Swinton, John A. Brodie and Edwin L. Luytens, Urban Plan of New Delhi, 20 March 1913	31
1.4	Patrick Geddes, Jerusalem Town Planning Scheme No. 2, 1919	32
1.5	Charles Robert Ashbee, Jerusalem: Zoning Plan, 1922	34
1.6	Kampala 1919 Scheme	40

FIGURES

1.7	Richard Kaufmann, Plan for Janjirieh Garden City [Rehavia]	41
1.8	Clifford Holiday, Jerusalem Town Planning Scheme, 1930	43
1.9	Henry Kendall, The 1944 Scheme: Zoning Plan	47
1.10	Henry Kendall, 1944 Survey: Distribution of the Population	50
1.11	Henry Kendall, The 1944 Scheme: Grouping of Neighbourhood Units	51
2.1	Austen St Barbe Harrison, Palestine Archaeological Museum, Jerusalem, 1928–35	56
2.2	The Archaeological Museum at 'Way House', Jerusalem, 1921–35	61
2.3	Austen St Barbe Harrison, Palestine Archaeological Museum, ground plan, 1928–35	67
2.4	Austen St Barbe Harrison, Palestine Archaeological Museum, south gallery	68
2.5	Austen St Barbe Harrison, Palestine Archaeological Museum, central court facing tower	69
2.6	Austen St Barbe Harrison, Palestine Archaeological Museum, section, 1928–35	70
2.7	Austen St Barbe Harrison, Palestine Archaeological Museum, dome of tower hall, 1928–35	71
2.8	Austen St Barbe Harrison, Palestine Archaeological Museum, reading room/library	71
2.9	Austen St Barbe Harrison, Palestine Archeological Museum, west gallery during construction, 1928–35	72
2.10	Austen St Barbe Harrison, Palestine Archeological Museum, roofs during construction, 1928–35	72
2.11	Austen St Barbe Harrison, Palestine Archaeological Museum, central court facing pavilion	73
2.12	Austen St Barbe Harrison, Palestine Archaeological Museum, interior of central court pavilion	73
2.13a	Austen St Barbe Harrison, Palestine Archaeological Museum, interior of tiled pavilion	76
2.13b	Detail of tiles from Alhambra Palace, Granada, Spain, fourteenth century	76
2.14	Cenacle (Chamber of the Last Supper), Jerusalem, twelfth–thirteenth centuries	77
2.15	Austen St Barbe Harrison, model for the Palestine Archaeological Museum, 1929	78
2.16	Austen St Barbe Harrison, Palestine Archaeological Museum	80
2.17	Welles Bosworth, Floor plan of the Egyptian Museum, 1925	82
2.18a	Austen St Barbe Harrison, Plan for the Palestine Archaeological Museum, 25 March 1924	83
2.18b	Austen St Barbe Harrison, Plan for the Palestine Archaeological Museum, November 1927	83
2.19	Mayers, Murray and Phillip, Chicago House, Luxor, Egypt, 1930	84

2.20	Ivory reliefs from Samaria and Eric Gill's 'Philistia' relief	89
2.21a–j	Eric Gill, reliefs in the central court of the Palestine Archaeological Museum, c. 1934–5	90
2.22	Eric Gill, Asia and Africa reliefs in the tympanum at the main entrance to the Palestine Archaeological Museum, c. 1934–5	93
2.23	Eric Gill, Palestine Archaeological Museum, south gallery signage, c. 1934–5	94
3.1	Arthur Loomis Harmon, Jerusalem YMCA Building, Jerusalem, 1926–33	102
3.2	Charles Robert Ashbee, Plan for a Jerusalem YMCA Building, 1920	107
3.3	Arthur Loomis Harmon, Jerusalem YMCA Building, ground floor plan, main building and wings with key functions as allocated in 1933	115
3.4	Arthur Loomis Harmon, Jerusalem YMCA Building, south 'kiosk' of the arcade, 1926–33	115
3.5	Jerusalem YMCA Building, west façade	116
3.6	Carrère and Hastings, Hotel Ponce de León (Flaggler College), St Augustine, Florida, 1888	117
3.7	Abbé Brisacier and Abbé Etienne Boubet, Notre Dame de France, Jerusalem, 1884–1904	119
3.8	Robert Leibnitz, Auguste Victoria Endowment (Auguste Victoria Stiftung), Jerusalem, 1907–10/14	119
3.9	Jerusalem YMCA Building, gymnasium wing	121
3.10	Jerusalem YMCA Building, auditorium wing	121
3.11	Holy Sepulchre, Jerusalem, 1149	122
3.12	Al Jazzar Pasha Mosque, Acre, 1781–2	122
3.13	Hurva Synagogue, Jerusalem, completed 1864, demolished 1948	123
3.14	Tiferet Yisrael Synagogue, Jerusalem, 1862–72	123
3.15	Jerusalem YMCA Building, interior of auditorium wing	125
3.16	Jerusalem YMCA Building, tower	126
3.17	Arthur Loomis Harmon, Jerusalem YMCA Building, apostle sculpture on observation balcony of the tower	127
3.18	Arthur Loomis Harmon, Jerusalem YMCA Building, sculptures for the evangelist symbols at the belfry level (St John), 1926–33	128
3.19	Jerusalem YMCA Building, seraph relief on the tower	129
3.20	Minaret of the White Mosque, Ramla, 1318	131
3.21	Bertram Grosvenor Goodhue, Tower of the Nebraska State Capitol, Lincoln, Nebraska, 1922–32	131
3.22	Bertram Grosvenor Goodhue, Nebraska State Capitol, competition entry, 1920	132
3.23a	Jerusalem YMCA Building, arcade capital: doves and grapevines	135
3.23b	Alfred Waterhouse and [Auguste?] Dujardin, bird capitals at the Natural History Museum, London, 1871–81	135

FIGURES   ix

3.23c	Jerusalem YMCA Building, arcade capital: wheat/barley	135
3.23d	Jerusalem YMCA Building, arcade capital: doves	135
3.23e	Jerusalem YMCA Building, arcade capital: shepherdesses and shepherds	135
3.23f	Jerusalem YMCA Building, arcade capital: shepherdesses and shepherds	135
3.24	Jerusalem YMCA Building, portal	136
3.25a	Jerusalem YMCA Building, façade inscription in Hebrew	137
3.25b	Jerusalem YMCA Building, façade inscription in Arabic	137
3.26	Jerusalem YMCA Building, multifaith chapel	138
3.27	Jerusalem YMCA Building, Ottoman-style fireplace in the lobby (present-day restaurant)	141
3.28	First soccer match at the Jerusalem YMCA, 1 April 1933	143
3.29	United Nations Special Committee on Palestine (UNSCOP) meeting at the Jerusalem YMCA Building auditorium, 1947	144
4.1	Mehmet Nihat Nigisberk, Palace Hotel, Jerusalem, 1928–9	146
4.2	Mehmet Nihat Nigisberk, Palace Hotel, ground plan of first floor, 1928–9	157
4.3	Mehmet Nihat Nigisberk, Palace Hotel, typical floor plan, storeys 2–4, 1928–9	157
4.4	Mehmet Nihat Nigisberk, Palace Hotel, lobby, 1928–9	158
4.5	Mehmet Nihat Nigisberk, Palace Hotel, lobby following conservation	159
4.6	Palace Hotel, skylight following conservation	159
4.7	Mehmet Nihat Nigisberk, Palace Hotel, restaurant, 1928–9	160
4.8	Palace Hotel, north façade	160
4.9	Mehmet Nihat Nigisberk, First Vakif Han, Istanbul, 1909–14	162
4.10	Mehmet Nihat Nigisberk, Palace Hotel, north elevation, 1928–9	164
4.11	Ahmet Kemalettin Bey and Vedat Bey, Ankara Palas Hotel, Ankara, 1924–7	165
4.12a	Palace Hotel, detail of main entry capitals	166
4.12b	Palace Hotel, north façade balcony	166
4.13a	Palace Hotel, pilaster detail	166
4.13b	Al Aqsa Mosque, detail of carved wooden beam	166
4.14a	Palace Hotel, octagonal rosette on pilaster	167
4.14b	Al Aqsa Mosque, Salah al-Din Minbar, detail of wood carving on the right panel, Jerusalem, 1168–74	167
4.15	Palace Hotel, dedication plaque	169
4.16	Palace Hotel, detail of ceiling stucco decoration	171
4.17	Haim Weizmann testifying before the Peel Commission in the Palace Hotel restaurant, 1936	177
4.18	The Grand Mufti, Haj Amin eff. el-Husseini, with attendants, leaving the offices of the Palestine Royal Commission [at the Palace Hotel] after testifying, 1937	178

4.19	Hussni Kattawi, Jaljulia Mosque, Jaljulia, completed 2014	179
5.1	Yohanan Ratner, Zionist Executive Building, Jerusalem, 1929–38	182
5.2	Yohanan Ratner, model for the Zionist Executive Building and Yeshurun Synagogue, c. 1927, Jerusalem, 1929–38	186
5.3	Yohanan Ratner and JNF director Menachem Ussishkin, 1930s	189
5.4	Yohanan Ratner, Zionist Executive Building, isometric drawing, c. 1930	190
5.5	Yohanan Ratner, Zionist Executive Building, plan showing division into wings (with proposed additions), 25 April 1937	191
5.6	Yohanan Ratner and Michael Ratner, Zionist Executive Building, final plan, after 1948	192
5.7	Yohanan Ratner, Zionist Executive Building, elevation for new addition, 1929–38, Jerusalem	193
5.8	Yohanan Ratner, Zionist Executive Building, plan including entrance court, Jerusalem, c. 1935	194
5.9	Yohanan Ratner, Zionist Executive Building, entrance court	194
5.10	Yohanan Ratner, Zionist Executive Building, entrance to Keren Ha'Yesod wing	195
5.11	Yohanan Ratner, Zionist Executive Building, entrance to JNF wing	196
5.12	Zionist Executive Building, balcony above the main entrance, 1934	197
5.13	Dr Weizmann at a Jewish Agency meeting in the main board room of the Zionist Executive Building, 1945	198
5.14	Zionist Executive Building, Herzl Room in the JNF wing, n.d.	198
5.15	Zionist Executive Building, Golden Books Room in the JNF wing	199
5.16	Yohanan Ratner, Zionist Executive Building, main entrance elevation, 22 July 1932	201
5.17	Zionist Executive Building, JNF wing	201
5.18	Zionist Executive Building, kindergarten children at a Shavuot holiday ceremony in the entrance court, 1935	213

Abbreviations

Archives/collections frequently cited have been identified by the following abbreviations:

CHIR	Center for Heritage and Islamic Research, Abu Dis, Palestinian Territories
CZA	Central Zionist Archives, Jerusalem
KFYA	Jerusalem YMCA Records, Kautz Family YMCA Archives, University of Minnesota Libraries
NAGB	National Archives Great Britain
PEF	Palestine Exploration Fund Archive, London
YA1918–27	'Palestine 1889, 1905–1927' (General Correspondence), Jerusalem YMCA Records, Kautz Family YMCA Archives, University of Minnesota Libraries
YA1929–30n	Negotiations with Jerusalem Board of Directors, 1929–1930, Jerusalem YMCA Records, Kautz Family YMCA Archives, University of Minnesota Libraries
YAAd	Architectural details files, Jerusalem YMCA Records, Kautz Family YMCA Archives, University of Minnesota Libraries

Digital Archives

Arabic Newspaper Archive of Ottoman and Mandatory Palestine, National Library of Israel, http://web.nli.org.il/sites/nlis/he/jrayed

British Newspaper Archive, https://www.britishnewspaperarchive.co.uk/

Historical Jewish Press, National Library of Israel/Tel Aviv University, http://web.nli.org.il/sites/JPress/Hebrew/Pages/default.aspx

The Times Digital Archive 1785–2012, http://find.galegroup.com/ttda/start.do?prodId=TTDA&userGroupName=leipzig&finalAuth=true

Acknowledgements

I wrote the greater part of this book while I was on a sabbatical leave from Sapir College in Leipzig, Germany. It was an inspiring experience to be far from home in a northern European city, watching the seasons change from the reds of autumn into snow, followed by the blossoms of spring and the calm of summer. There I was, writing in a place that was home to two of my grandparents before they escaped Nazi Germany in 1933. They probably walked the same sidewalks, passing along the same buildings and parks as I did during that year.

So, my first thanks go to the Leibniz Institut für jüdische Geschichte and Kultur–Simon Dubnow, which hosted my visit. Its staff and researchers opened their doors to me and were most gracious in sharing their knowledge. Special thanks go to my hosts, Yfaat Weiss, Jörg Deventer and Nicolas Berg, and to Jeannette Van Laak, Arndt Engelhardt, and all my friends and colleagues at the institute.

The research for this book and its publication was funded by generous grants from the Israel Science Foundation (#503/18 and #33/20). I am most grateful for that support, which helped me to make this project the best it could possibly be. I would like to thank my friends and colleagues at Sapir Academic College. I am also indebted to this wonderful workplace for its ongoing financial support.

Many colleagues provided expert advice and invaluable input. Special thanks go to Nirit Ben-Aryeh Debbie, Ruth Iskin, Sarah Offenberg and Daniel Unger at Ben-Gurion University of the Negev; Eli Osheroff and Walid Ganem at the Dubnow Institute, and Yael Allweil, Shlomo Egoz, Ron Fuchs, Reuven Gafni, Muhammad Gharipour, Anat Geva, David Kroyanker, Arie Lev Kapitaikin, Sharona Zilberstein and Hana Taragan. I thank Mark Johnson from the American YMCA, and Dorothy Harman and Rana Masoud from the Jerusalem YMCA; Haim Gitler, Fawzi Ibrahim and Noam Gal at the Israel Museum in Jerusalem; Micha Ratner and Natan Roi with regard to the Zionist Executive Buildings and Shlomit Shani at the Waldorf Astoria Jerusalem for sharing what they know about the buildings under discussion. As always – a special note of appreciation to my lifelong mentor and friend, Edina Meyer-Maril.

I would also like to thank my language editor, Evelyn Grossberg, for her excellent work, and the editors and other staff at Edinburgh University Press

– Nicola Ramsey, Kirsty Woods and Eddie Clark for making publication such a pleasure.

My photographer, Diego Rosman, accompanied me on very chilly winter days in Jerusalem to produce many of the photos included in this book. I am grateful for his open and inquisitive eyes and his love of architecture, which comes across in every image.

Research for Chapter Four of this book was done in collaboration with Elvan Altan and Cem Dedekargınoğlu from the Middle East Technical University, Ankara, and their contribution was invaluable. Our cross-border collaboration gives me hope for a better future in the Middle East.

Four research assistants helped in this project, forming a wonderful, dedicated and intelligent team: Shira Gottlieb, Adi Hammer-Yacobi, Bar Leshem and Waed Mansur – all graduate students at Ben-Gurion University of the Negev. My deepest gratitude goes to them, and I look forward to seeing each of them becoming an independent academic.

Finally, I would like to express my appreciation to my family: my parents, Naomi and Jiftah Ben-Asher, and my parents-in-law, Becky and Carlos Gitler; and most of all to my partner, Daniel Gitler, and our three children, Daphna, Erran and Noam, for many hours of patience, cooking, laughing and togetherness throughout.

*This book is dedicated in loving memory to my grandparents:
Menachem Dorman, Tamar Bester Dorman, Hannah Mingelgrün Ben-Asher,
and Haim Ben-Asher: Haluzim who made Eretz-Israel/Palestine their home
during the tumultuous years of the British Mandate.*

Figure I.1 *Work at the building site of the Palestine Archeological Museum, 1930s. ABHC.*

Introduction

IT IS ALMOST midday on the site where the Palestine Archaeological Museum is being built, as seen in a photograph from the early 1930s (Figure I.1). Men – mostly Arabs wearing *kaffiyahs*, which shield them from the already scorching sun – climb a pair of ladders that rise from the museum's unfinished Octagon Hall, carrying buckets of concrete to pour on the building's reinforced ceiling. To the right of the ladders, two men, possibly Jews judging by their dress, are also part of the construction team. A short distance away, visible from the new roof, we see the Dome of the Rock and the Al Aqsa Mosque – the monuments that mark the holiest place in Jerusalem for both Muslims and Jews.

As is often the case with photographs, this one does much more than document construction. It evidences the integration of ancient building techniques – stone cladding and traditional arches – with modern technology, in this case poured reinforced concrete. Further, it reveals that Jews and Arabs worked together on this British-American project, and even reflects their ratio. Lastly, this photograph reminds us that no site or building project in Jerusalem is neutral and that architecture always relates to culture and religion, as well as to buildings or sites that connote ancient histories and beliefs.

The three aspects that this photograph reveals are the subjects of the present book. I discuss the exportation of modernism to Jerusalem and its meeting with tradition; I investigate the ways in which architecture was impacted by, and responded to, intercommunal and intracommunal relations in the city; and I analyse how architects and their communities engaged Jerusalem's multilayered and complex built environment to create a novel architectural culture during the period of the British Mandate.

Jerusalem, a city holy to three monotheistic religions – Judaism, Christianity and Islam – has one of the longest and most contested histories known to mankind. Following World War I, the city, along with all of Palestine, changed hands from Ottoman to British rule. The three decades that ensued, during which the British ruled the country (1917–48), marked a watershed in the shaping of Middle East politics and geographies and, more specifically, in the history of Palestine and Jerusalem. During this period, Jerusalem, as the British seat of government, experienced radical urban transformations and became home to several of the most prominent and influential architectural projects constructed in Palestine at the time. British Mandatory visions for urban and architectural development of the city were manifested in projects initiated and carried out by the British themselves and by the city's diverse local communities, as well as by benefactors, architects and entrepreneurs from abroad. The charged political atmosphere in Jerusalem often acted as a catalyst, encouraging communities and political entities to inscribe their physical presence on the city.

In the pages that follow, I look at the architectural production of this period. I analyse the ways in which cross-cultural relations under the British Mandatory regime impacted and were affected by some of the major buildings designed and constructed during this period. By exploring these interrelationships and architectural histories, I reveal the role architecture played as a mediator of religious, cultural and political identities during a period rife with discord and conflict.

The remarkable development of Jerusalem's built environment coincided with major changes in global architecture during the interwar period. That being the case, I contextualise Jerusalem's architectural culture and production within these global transformations, critically examining the adaptation of modern architecture to the Middle East. Within this framework, I investigate the way architects negotiated historicist and vernacular architecture while adopting modern designs and technologies.

Four buildings and the communities that built them stand out as exceptional examples of the local and international phenomena described herein: the Palestine Archaeological Museum (better known as the Rockefeller Museum), the Zionist Executive Building (ZEB), the Palace Hotel and the Jerusalem YMCA Building. All public or civic secular structures, they were among Jerusalem's most distinguished new edifices and served as the spatial and visual manifestations of their communities. To this day, they remain among the most prominent urban landmarks in the city (Figure I.2).

The Palestine Archaeological Museum was built by the British with American funding and involvement and was intended to serve all of Palestine's communities; the Zionist Executive Building was erected by the Zionist Movement and sought to represent Palestine's Jewish community in its entirety; the Palace Hotel was built by Muslim Palestinians; and the Jerusalem YMCA was constructed by the Young Men's Christian Association of the United States to serve all of the city's groups, as well as to give Jerusalemites a taste of American culture. All four buildings were designed and built through cooperation among the city's diverse communities, sects and subsects. Owing to this cooperation and the prominence of the buildings, these edifices acquired a special significance for the city's general public.

These four buildings, which are at the core of the present volume, evolved within the unique sociohistorical circumstances that characterised the Mandate period in Palestine. The relationship between architecture and cross-cultural

Figure I.2 Henry Kendall, *The 1944 Scheme: Zoning Plan. H. Kendall, Jerusalem: The City Plan. Preservation and Development during the British Mandate 1918–1948* (London: His Majesty's Stationery Office, 1948), map facing p. 26. *Location of buildings added by the author.*

phenomena that is evident in the accounts of their constructions represents a characteristic, but little-known, aspect of this important epoch in the history of Jerusalem and Palestine. This quadri-graphy is designed to reveal the important role that secular architecture designed to accommodate modern functions had in Jerusalem's mixed, multi-ethnic and multireligious contested space. Moreover, all four of these buildings were seen by the communities that built them as their most representative spatial manifestation in the city and, to some extent, in all of Palestine. This respective communal acknowledgement was the primary reason that I singled them out for this study, but their secularity and modernism also played a role in my choice. I contend that researching the architecture and construction of these buildings, as well as the discourses surrounding them, can offer new insights on significant historical processes during the Mandate period. Such a study can also provide answers to such pertinent questions as: what was architecture's role in the struggle to define communal or national identity and authority? How did cooperation among Jerusalem's communities affect the architectural product, and to what extent did intercommunal and intracommunal relations help to shape these buildings?

The buildings were erected between 1926 and 1938. As much of the architecture in Palestine, they reflected new approaches to planning, design and diverse adaptations of modern architecture, which, after World War I, differed significantly from those of the first two decades of the twentieth century. In both Europe and the United States, functionalism became paramount and ornamentation was rejected; new approaches to form, plan, materials and building technologies, as well as new typologies, were developed.[1] Recent scholarship has underscored that these new approaches to design should not be viewed merely as styles, but rather as expressions of cultural, political and social processes.[2] Clearly, modernism took on different guises and developed from diverse ideologies and social circumstances in its places of origin.[3] However, modernism's iterations become even more complex when discussing its exportation beyond the borders of Europe and the United States. In studying the spread of modernism, Mark Crinson makes a case for using the contemporary, early twentieth-century terms *international* or *internationalism* to describe it. He argues that internationalism was not merely a consequence of improved communication and travel, which supported the flow of ideas, capital and material. He notes that it was also 'a willed principle of modernist architecture, it made a claim on ethics, on something higher than localize politics, wider than custom and tradition and more ambitious than the quotidian matters of

---

[1] Sarah Williams Goldhagen, 'Coda: Reconceptualizing the Modern', in *Anxious Modernisms: Experimentation in Postwar Architectural Culture*, eds Sarah Williams Goldhagen and Réjean Legault (Montreal: Canadian Centre for Architecture, and Cambridge, MA: MIT Press, 2000), 301–23.
[2] Ibid. 302–7.
[3] Ibid. 302–3.

building'.[4] Viewing the spread of modernism in such terms calls not only for a re-examination of its absorption or adaptation in various locales. It demands, as Crinson observes, overthrowing biases that have clung to the concept of international modernism as a result of its association with colonialism and neocolonialism, as well as its framing within discourses of twenty-first century globalisation.[5] That is not to say, of course, that these connections are irrelevant. Rather, considering the frameworks of colonialism, neocolonialism and globalisation points to the importance of opening the discussion to include additional perspectives and processes that took place in the first half of the twentieth century. As I show in this book, the buildings studied here provide a window onto such processes. They are buildings that challenge accepted definitions of what we call 'modern' and their construction processes add insight as to how architecture and the ideas at its root were circulated, reconsidered and adapted.

The spread of international modernism to the Middle East has recently been studied by several scholars, who examined architectural constructions in various locales across the region in its wider geographical definition.[6] Architectural historians repudiated accepted dichotomies that presented modernism as a clear-cut break with architectural traditions. They proposed a more nuanced perception of East versus West and rejected the premise that interactions between the metropole and its periphery comprise a one-directional transfer of ideas.[7] Moreover, researchers have demonstrated a reciprocity wherein vernacular traditions, historicism and international modernism were negotiated and often intertwined. Architecture in British Mandate Palestine fully reflects these phenomena, and it was during this period that Jerusalem experienced a surge in major construction. Additional factors that should be considered are the profound changes that the city experienced owing to the transfer from Ottoman to British rule. Moreover, the Mandatory regime itself effected political and sociohistoric transformations.[8]

---

[4] Mark Crinson, *Rebuilding Babel: Modern Architecture and Internationalism* (London and New York: I. B. Tauris, 2017), 10.

[5] Ibid. 10–11.

[6] See, e.g., Aziza Chaouni, 'Depoliticizing Group GAMMA: Contesting Modernism in Morocco', 57–84, and Elâ Kaçel, 'This is not an American House: Good Sense Modernism in 1950s Turkey', 165–86, both in *Third World Modernism: Architecture, Development, and Identity*, ed. Duanfang Lu (Abingdon and New York: Routledge, 2011); Sandy Isenstadt and Kishwar Rizvi, *Modernism and the Middle East: Architecture and Politics in the Twentieth Century* (Seattle and London: University of Washington Press, 2008); Zeynep Çelik, *Urban Forms and Colonial Confrontations: Algiers under French Rule* (Berkeley: University of California Press, 1997).

[7] Nezar AlSayyad, ed., *The End of Tradition?* (London: Routledge, 2003), 8–12; Elvan Altan Ergut and Belgin Turan Özkaya, 'Editors' Introduction: Culture, Diplomacy, Representation: "Ambivalent Architectures" from the Ottoman Empire to the Turkish Republic', *New Perspectives on Turkey* 50 (2014): 5–8.

[8] See, e.g., Rory Miller, ed., *Britain, Palestine and Empire: The Mandate Years* (Farnham: Ashgate, 2016); Ruth Kark and Michal Oren-Nordheim, *Jerusalem and its Environs: Quarters, Neighborhoods, Villages, 1800–1948* (Jerusalem: Magnes Press of the Hebrew University, and Detroit: Wayne State University Press, 2001); Yehoshua Ben-Arieh and Moshe Davis, *Jerusalem in the Mind of the Western World, 1800–1948* (Westport: Praeger, 1997).

All of these circumstances fostered the erection of buildings that are prime examples of the exportation and negotiation of European and American architectural modernism to the region. In the present volume, I demonstrate that alongside new designs, functions and technologies, the implementation of modernism engaged diverse local architectural traditions, spatially and temporally embedded in the built environment. I show that new buildings provided sites for experimentation with new theories and practices, which were tested against local design requirements. Relating to tradition and negotiating site-specificity were not unique to modern architecture's exportation; its masters – Le Corbusier, Frank Lloyd Wright, Alvar Aalto, Eileen Gray, and others –confronted these issues during the same period.[9] However, architects faced with such confrontations and discourses with the past in a non-Western setting devised new, unexpected, and at times boldly experimental solutions.

Was the architecture created in Jerusalem indeed experimental? Did it pose a challenge to both modernism and tradition? Criticism of construction outside the Old City walls suggests that it was certainly perceived as such by contemporary professionals. For example, the engineer William H. McLean, author of the first British plan for Jerusalem, found fault with the city's 1920s and 1930s architecture: 'It is the recent unsatisfactory architecture in the Modern City, beyond the outer protective belt, which Professor Bentwich doubtless refers to ... It is difficult to provide a remedy by regulation, but improvement may often be made by persuasion and special arrangement.'[10]

McLean wrote the above to the London *Times* in 1937 in response to an article by Norman Bentwich in the same newspaper. McLean's call for remedying the modern city's architecture indicates the difficulty involved in accepting new structures in this holy and ancient town. Upon arriving in Jerusalem in 1918, McLean himself had prescribed an architecture that would be 'in harmony and in scale with the Old City'.[11]

Adapting and experimenting with modernism was a process that took place especially in connection with designs for buildings of a secular and civic character, such as the ones I have chosen to discuss. Jerusalem's rapid development during the Mandate years included religious edifices, as well as buildings with traditional public functions such as schools and hospitals. The city had already experienced significant growth in the heyday of the Ottoman rule, as Jerusalem expanded beyond its ancient walls. This expansion has been researched in the context of communities, and studies illustrate how Christian and Jewish groups, assisted by foreign funding, were permitted to build as a result of the Ottoman reforms (*Tanzimat*).[12] These studies further show that Muslim

---

[9] Goldhagen, 'Coda: Reconceptualizing the Modern', 303–7.
[10] William H. McLean to the editor of the *Times* (London), 'Spoiling the Holy City', 2, no. 4, March 1937, *Holy Places* file *NAGB* CO 733/339/3.
[11] Ibid. 1.
[12] Kark and Oren-Nordheim, *Jerusalem and its Environs*, 74–136; Vincent Lemire, *Jerusalem*

INTRODUCTION

Palestinians built mostly new housing and schools and relatively few public buildings.[13]

From the onset of British military rule in 1918, which was superseded by the Mandate regime in 1922, the development of the city outside the walls proceeded with renewed impetus. The British introduced new, far-reaching plans, which I discuss in Chapter One. During the thirty years of the Mandate, Jerusalem more than doubled in size, maintaining a steady ratio of 55–60 per cent Jews, 21 per cent Muslims, and some 20 per cent Christians.[14] Forty-six new neighbourhoods were established, and a large number of religious, civic and commercial buildings were constructed. Outstanding examples are buildings commissioned by the various sects, such as the St Andrew's Church of Scotland, the Catholic Terra Santa College, the Jewish Zionist Hebrew University of Jerusalem and the new building of the Jewish-Orthodox Diskin Orphanage.[15] Numerous commercial buildings were constructed by different communities, such as Christian- and Muslim-Palestinian dual-use apartment/office buildings; new edifices were erected to house foreign banks, among them the Anglo-Palestine Bank and the Ottoman Bank; and hotels and cinemas were built (in most cases by Zionist Jews).[16] Some of these facilities implemented partial use of new technologies and – in certain aspects – new design approaches. However, in the four buildings I focus on here, I identify, first, a clear selection of relatively new typologies – the hotel, museum, office building and community centre – intentionally chosen by four of the city's communities as their most representative expression of presence in Jerusalem; second, these typologies were exploited for exhibiting the use of modern technologies and design concepts intended, in turn, to mediate values of advancement, social development and – perhaps most importantly – political presence.

The publics that commissioned these buildings – British, American, Jewish and Muslim – played very different roles in Jerusalem and in Palestine in general. The British, as the rulers, had an immense impact on plotting the country's political and economic course. There is ample research concerning Britain's mandate in Palestine, and I discuss the most relevant texts. The Palestine Archaeological Museum was arguably the most important cultural institution that the British founded and built in Palestine, comparable in a sense with commercial ventures such as the Haifa port, roadway development and the establishment of towns and industries across Palestine.[17]

1900: The Holy City in the Age of Possibilities, trans and eds Catherine Tihanyi and Lys Ann Weiss (Chicago: University of Chicago Press, 2017), 77–85; Roberto Mazza, *Jerusalem: From the Ottomans to the British* (New York: Tauris Academic Studies, 2014), 16–30.

[13] Kark and Oren-Nordheim, *Jerusalem and its Environs*, 116–22.

[14] Ruth Kark and Michal Oren-Nordheim, *Yerushalayim ve'Svivoteyiha: Reva'im, Shechunot ve'Kfarim, 1800–1948* (Jerusalem: Akademon, 1995), 176.

[15] The best survey on these buildings is David Kroyanker, *Adrichalut Bi'Yerushalayim: HaBni'ya BiTkufat HaMandat HaBriti* (Jerusalem: Keter, 1989).

[16] Ibid. 305, 314–17.

[17] Much has been written on this subject. See, e.g., Gilbert Herbert and Silvina Sosnovsky, *Bauhaus*

The Americans were a relatively new community. A small yet influential group, their presence began with the American Colony in Jerusalem.[18] Interestingly, the Jerusalem YMCA building project was not initiated by the American Colony; rather, it was a social and religious manifestation of growing American involvement in the post-war Middle East. It is thus of great interest as a major urban project that was a product of global transformations, rather than a result of local change. For Muslim Palestinians – the largest group in the country – building a hotel was intended to present the Jerusalem Waqf (discussed in more detail in the third section of this Introduction) as a modern institution that developed the city. Construction took place in tandem with the evolving traditional typologies noted above, which were seen in schools, mosques, hospitals and the expansion of Jerusalem's Muslim neighbourhoods. As the hotel's style reflected historicist tendencies, although it cannot be called modernist in the stylistic sense of the word, I show that functionally it was conceived as an advanced, up-to-date facility. The Zionist Jews established new neighbourhoods, synagogues, schools, the Hebrew University and medical institutions in Jerusalem. Secular modernist architecture was generally a hallmark of Zionism in Palestine since, as a movement based on the modern idea of the nation, its institutions, dwellings and business ventures were largely conceived as a part of this ideology. The ZEB should therefore be seen as an integral part of Zionist development in Palestine. Its singular importance, however, lies in the fact that it housed the key institutions of the Zionist Movement in Palestine and was thus the locus of the de-facto government of the Jewish Yishuv (settlement).

Hence, the four buildings that are at the core of the present book were part of a modernising process that Jerusalem experienced from the later years of the nineteenth century and during the first half of the twentieth. However, as large-scale representative urban projects, study of these edifices, more than that of others, can significantly add to our characterisation of modern architecture and to an understanding of the transfer of architectural knowledge during the interwar years. Contemporary reception of this architecture provides an additional aspect to critically assessing modernism, and it is of no less consequence that Jerusalem's new architecture was perceived as modern by both its makers and the city's communities.

---

on the Carmel and the Crossroads of Empire: Architecture and Planning in Haifa during the British Mandate (Jerusalem: Yad Izhak Ben-Zvi, 1993); Haim Yacobi, 'The Architecture of Ethnic Logic: Exploring the Meaning of the Built Environment in the "mixed" city of Lod–Israel', Geografiska Annaler: Series B, Human Geography 84, no. 3–4 (2002): 171–87; Benjamin Hyman, 'British Planners in Palestine, 1918–1936' (PhD diss., London School of Economics and Political Science, 1994).

[18] Avner Amiri and Annabel Wharton, 'Home in Jerusalem: The American Colony and Palestinian Suburban Architecture', Post-Medieval Archaeology 45, no. 2 (2011): 237–65; Heleen Murre-van den Berg, '"Our Jerusalem": Bertha Spafford Vester and Christianity in Palestine during the British Mandate', in Britain, Palestine, and Empire: The Mandate Years, ed. Rory Miller (Farnham: Ashgate, 2010), 67–84.

The present book is among the first comparative studies of Jerusalem's architectural history, as research to date has tended to explore the city's buildings only in terms of the groups that commissioned them.[19] I approach Jerusalem's architectural history using relational history – a methodology that examines the inter- and intracommunal relationships of individuals and groups during a specific era and in a given social space.[20] Several scholars have recently dealt with its application to the social, political and economic histories of Palestine and Jerusalem. These studies have afforded new perspectives on the history of the Israeli–Palestinian conflict by engaging microhistories demonstrating that conflict, strife and competition for political and economic assets existed alongside routine interactions and cooperation. Relational history was utilised in this way, for example, in the works by Zachary Lockman, Abigail Jacobson and Moshe Naor, who investigated the periods of Ottoman and British regimes in Palestine.[21] Other scholars have adopted this approach as well, albeit not identifying their work as 'relational history'. Such is the case in Vincent Lemire's illuminating study of Jerusalem at the turn of the twentieth century[22] and the important comparative work on Zionist and Palestinian identities by Baruch Kimmerling and Taysir Nashif, which were done as early as 1980.[23]

In the field of architectural history, this approach was recently implemented by Yael Allweil, whose research of dwellings in Palestine/Israel not only relates to chronological development, but also deals with intercommunal politics and compares Zionist and Arab dwelling formations.[24] Other studies include Daniel

---

[19] See, e.g., Kroyanker, *Adrichalut Bi'Yerushalayim*; Marina Epstein-Pliouchtch and Michael Levin, eds, *Richard Kaufmann VeHapro'yekt HaZioni* (Tel Aviv: Hakibbutz HaMeuchad, 2016); Adnan Abdelrazek, *The Arab Architectural Renaissance in the Western Part of Occupied Jerusalem* (Limassol: Rimal Books, 2017).

[20] Akin Sefer, 'New Approaches to the History of Palestine: Relational History and the Ottoman Past', *New Perspectives on Turkey* 48 (2013): 129–40.

[21] Zachary Lockman, *Contending Visions of the Middle East: The History and Politics of Orientalism* (Cambridge: Cambridge University Press, 2004); Zachary Lockman, 'Land, Labor and the Logic of Zionism: A Critical Engagement with Gershon Shafir', *Settler Colonial Studies* 2, no. 1 (2012): 9–38; Zachary Lockman, *Comrades and Enemies: Arab and Jewish Workers in Palestine, 1906–1948* (Berkeley: University of California Press, 1996); Zachary Lockman, 'Railway Workers and Relational History: Arabs and Jews in British-Ruled Palestine', *Comparative Studies in Society and History* 35, no. 3 (1993): 601–27; Abigail Jacobson and Moshe Naor, *Oriental Neighbors: Middle Eastern Jews and Arabs in Mandatory Palestine* (Waltham: Brandeis University Press, 2016); Abigail Jacobson, *From Empire to Empire: Jerusalem between Ottoman and British Rule* (Syracuse: Syracuse University Press, 2011); Abigail Jacobson, 'A City Living through Crisis: Jerusalem during World War I', *British Journal of Middle Eastern Studies* 36, no. 1 (2009): 73–92.

[22] Lemire, *Jerusalem 1900*.

[23] Baruch Kimmerling, *Clash of Identities: Explorations in Israeli and Palestinian Societies* (New York: Columbia University Press, 2012); Baruch Kimmerling, 'A Model for Analysis of Reciprocal Relations between the Jewish and Arab Communities in Mandatory Palestine', *Plural Societies* 14 (1983): 45–68; Baruch Kimmerling, 'The Formation of Palestinian Collective Identities: The Ottoman and Mandatory Periods', *Middle Eastern Studies* 36, no. 2 (2000): 48–81; Taysir Nashif, 'Palestinian Arab and Jewish Leadership in the Mandate Period', *Journal of Palestine Studies* 6, no. 4 (1977): 113–21.

[24] Yael Allweil, *Homeland: Zionism as Housing Regime, 1860–2011* (Abingdon and New York: Routledge, 2017).

Monk's book, *An Aesthetic Occupation*, in which he demonstrates the important role of Jerusalem's ancient sacred architecture in the political discourses produced by the British, the Palestinians and the Zionists in Mandatory Palestine.[25] Thus, applying relational history to the study of Jerusalem's architecture can offer new perspectives on the shaping of the built environment in Israel/Palestine and can delineate a differentiated image of intercommunal and intracommunal relations.

About Terminology

I begin by enumerating concepts and terminologies as common grounds for discussion. First, the term 'cross-cultural' might leave anthropologists, historians and cultural studies' scholars uneasy with its epistemic implications. The term, which is indeed evasive, is often used as a catchword, without regard for the difficulty in positioning it against 'culture', 'multiculturalism' and related words. Although a discussion of the many theoretical and social interpretations of the term are beyond the scope of this book, briefly clarifying my use of 'cross-cultural' is essential for this study. First, I rely on the intrinsic relationship between culture and identity,[26] as the former is a central component in the construction of all forms of identity – individual as well as communal and national – and their interfaces.[27] Second, recent criticism of the concept of culture has proposed scrutinising its components and viewing it as comprising multifaceted processes linked with politics, economics and various social as well as biological and environmental realms.[28] This specific interpretation resists a hermeneutic positioning of culture that runs the risk of ignoring such connections and the similarities and the ties among the cultures.[29] Drawing on these premises, the term cross-cultural in this book denotes the intersection of cultures and the crossing of cultural boundaries.[30] Further, this approach is based on the assumption that cultural boundaries do exist, which was the case in British Mandate-era Jerusalem, where religion, ethnicity and politics created separate cultures for diverse groups.

Within this framework, Jerusalem's architecture is understood as both product and producer of meeting points, interactions, discourses and conflicts among the city's cultures. Cultural boundaries were crossed in both practical and aesthetic aspects, and communities interacted on various levels in regard to construction in

---

[25] Daniel Bertrand Monk, *An Aesthetic Occupation: The Immediacy of Architecture and the Palestine Conflict* (Durham, NC: Duke University Press, 2002).

[26] Richard Handler, 'Culture', in *The Social Science Encyclopedia*, eds Adam Kuper and Jessica Kuper, vol. 1, 201. http://www.questia.com/read/109437237/the-social-science-encyclopedia.

[27] Akhil Gupta and James Ferguson, 'Beyond "Culture": Space, Identity, and the Politics of Difference', *Cultural Anthropology* 7, no. 1 (1992): 6–23.

[28] Adam Kuper, *Culture: The Anthropologists' Account* (Cambridge, MA: Harvard University Press, 2000), 246.

[29] Ibid. 246.

[30] Margaret Kumar, 'Postcolonial Theory and Cross-culturalism: Collaborative "Signposts" of Discursive Practices', *The Journal of Educational Enquiry* 1, no. 2 (2000): 82–92.

the city. These premises also require briefly addressing the concept of 'architectural culture', which titles the book and runs through the course of my study. I use this term when discussing the broader dimensions of Jerusalem society's engagement with architecture. Accordingly, architectural culture during the Mandate period encompassed, in addition to design, practice and professional discourses, communal interactions in connection with architecture, mass communication responses to architectural practices and buildings, and architecture's role in urban spatial planning.[31] These components enable an understanding of Jerusalem's architecture in broad local and international contexts and help to explicate its immense impact on the city and its various communities.

Another point that needs clarification is what the term 'community' signifies in this context. My use of this term relies on sociological theories that view the concept of community as dependent on longstanding ties based on ethnicity, race or religion, but I also understand it as a pragmatic construct.[32] Consequently, practical concerns, local governance and a shared geographical space all have a part in forming communities.[33] This emphasis is useful especially when approaching the British and the Americans residing in Jerusalem as an 'Anglo' community, as they did not have the historical continuity and familial ties that characterised the Jews, the Muslims and the local Christians. Moreover, I use the prefixes 'inter' and 'intra' to describe the interactions among different kinds of groups. Those between clearly defined communities such as Jewish, Christian and Muslim are termed *intercommunal* relations, whereas the term *intracommunal* describes the internal relationships within a community, such as a subcommunity based on family ties, one that is grounded in a shared geographical origin, and so on. I use these classifications below to describe the communities I discuss in this book and the changes they experienced with the advent of the British Mandate.

Jerusalem's Communities

For the British Empire, whose armies conquered Palestine during the final stages of World War I, control of Jerusalem was part of a 'package deal' involving the postwar segmentation of the Ottoman Empire among the Western powers.[34] The British wanted to hold onto Palestine for strategic considerations and coveted

---

[31] For a discussion of this approach in architectural history methodology, see Eve Blau, 'Plenary Address, Society of Architectural Historians Annual Meeting, Richmond, Virginia, April 18, 2002; Eve Blau, "A Question of Discipline"', *Journal of the Society of Architectural Historians* 62, no. 1 (2003): 125–9; Andrew Leach, *What is Architectural History?* (Cambridge: Polity Press, 2010), 76–96.

[32] Vered Amit, 'Community', in *The Social Science Encyclopedia*, eds Kuper and Kuper, vol. 1, 139. http://www.questia.com/read/109437237/the-social-science-encyclopedia.

[33] Ibid. 139

[34] Roger Adelson, *London and the Invention of the Middle East: Money, Power and War, 1902–1922* (New Haven: Yale, 1995), 169–89; Yehoshua Porath and Yaacov Shavit, eds, *HaHistoryia shel Eretz Israel: HaMandat VeHabayit HaLe'umi, 1917–1947* (Jerusalem: Keter and Yad Itzhak Ben Zvi, 1998), 12–14.

Jerusalem for its religious significance.[35] General Edmund Allenby entered the city on 11 December 1917 and immediately invoked military rule.[36] In 1922, Britain formally received the Mandate for Palestine. (Civilian rule was initiated and a high commissioner was nominated in 1920, albeit in the face of Ottoman/Turkish opposition to formally and publicly relinquishing sovereignty.)[37] Reception of the Mandate meant that the British Empire would serve as a trustee for the land, accountable to the League of Nations.[38] However, the terms of the Mandate contained a basic contradiction between a commitment to establish a 'National Home' for the Jews in Palestine and a pledge to protect Arab land rights there.[39] This soon proved to be a predicament that engendered a fundamental conflict between Jews and Arabs and contributed significantly to intracommunal tensions.[40] It also posed serious and detrimental political, diplomatic and military challenges for the British.

Several studies have shown that religious, ethnic and national identities in Jerusalem, as in all of Palestine, were often fluid, precluding clear-cut definitions.[41] Thus, intercommunal and intracommunal relationships were complex. This reality was spatially expressed in a delicate urban fabric, which the British regime controlled and tried to develop in cooperation with the local communities, which were divided into various sects and denominations. These included Muslim Palestinians, whose sectional division usually accorded with family and clan ties; further sectarian ties within the Muslim community were based on places of origin, such as the Maghribi community, which comprised Muslims from North Africa.[42] The main Christian Palestinian sects were Greek Orthodox, Armenian Orthodox and Catholics; there were also numerous smaller sects and

---

[35] For a general discussion of the British religious and spiritual ties to the Holy Land, see Barbara Tuchman, *Bible and Sword: England and Palestine from the Bronze Age to Balfour* (New York: New York University Press, 1956).

[36] Eitan Bar-Yosef, 'The Last Crusade? British Propaganda and the Palestine Campaign, 1917–18', *Journal of Contemporary History* 36, no. 1 (2001): 87.

[37] Porath and Shavit, eds, *HaHistoryia shel Eretz Israel*, 183–4; Martin Gilbert, *Jerusalem in the Twentieth Century* (New York: John Wiley & Sons, 1996), 85.

[38] Gilbert, *Jerusalem in the Twentieth Century*, 85.

[39] Ibid. 200–5; Porath and Shavit, eds, *HaHistoryia shel Eretz Israel*, 11–14, 20–33. The history of this clash of interests, especially as reflected in the Balfour Declaration, is discussed in Tuchman, *Bible and Sword*, 198–203; Adelson, *London and the Invention of the Middle East*, 149–54. For a discussion of the unique terms of the Palestine Mandate in the framework of the mandate system as a whole, see *The Mandate System: Origins – Principles – Application* (Geneva: League of Nations, 1945), 24–32.

[40] Charles D. Smith, *Palestine and the Arab-Israeli Conflict: A History with Documents*, 5th ed. (Boston, MA: Bedford/St Martins, 2004), 71–85.

[41] Jacobson and Naor, *Oriental Neighbors*, 3–4, 196–9; Rashid Khalidi, *Palestinian Identity: The Construction of Modern National Consciousness* (New York: Columbia University Press, 2009), 146, 150–4; Daphne Tsimhoni, 'The Status of the Arab Christians under the British Mandate in Palestine', *Middle Eastern Studies* 20, no. 4 (1984): 167.

[42] Yehoshua Ben-Arieh, 'The Growth of Jerusalem in the Nineteenth Century', *Annals of the Association of American Geographers* 65, no. 2 (1975): 252–4.

monastic orders.[43] Jews were also divided on several levels – Zionists and non-Zionists, Sephardi and Ashkenazi Jews, Orthodox and ultra-Orthodox Jews, and more.[44]

Jerusalem's many communities had evolved over millennia. With the advent of nineteenth-century imperialism and the new possibilities afforded by the Ottoman reforms mentioned above, European, British and American newcomers also created groups in the city. After World War I, the British reasserted their presence, as they were now the city's rulers, and growing American political and economic interests in the Middle East intensified the latter's participation in Jerusalem's politics and culture.[45] In view of the importance of British and American architectural production in Jerusalem, it is most important to frame their communities at the outset. The British and Americans arrived in Palestine with well-established national identities, which set them apart from the Arab Palestinians and Zionists. Nevertheless, both the British and the Americans formed distinct communities in Jerusalem from the mid-nineteenth century on.[46] Spatially they concentrated in the American Colony, mentioned above, and in the German Colony, established by German Templars in the 1870s.[47] Both groups were made up primarily of Protestant sects, which had fostered American and British activity in the region prior to World War I, as reflected in the establishment of numerous educational, philanthropic, medical and missionary institutions throughout the Middle East.[48] During the Mandate, the British and American publics remained small yet made up the ruling elite, and were thus very influential.[49]

[43] Ibid.; Tsimhoni, 'The Status of the Arab Christians', 167.
[44] Jacobson, 'A City Living through Crisis', 80, n. 30; Gideon Biger, 'HaHitparsut HaMerchavit shel Uchlusi'yat Yerushalayim BaMachatsit HaRishona shel Tkufat HaMandat', *Cathedra: For the History of Eretz Israel and its Yishuv* 39 (1986): 138; Ben-Arieh, 'The Growth of Jerusalem in the Nineteenth Century', 268.
[45] David Fromkin, *A Peace to End all Peace: The Fall of the Ottoman Empire and the Creation of the Modern Middle East* (New York: Avon Books, 1990), 253. For American activity in the Middle East, see John A. DeNovo, *American Interests and Policies in the Middle East, 1900–1939* (Minneapolis: University of Minnesota Press, 1963); David H. Finnie, *Pioneers East: The Early American Experience in the Middle East* (Cambridge, MA: Harvard University Press, 1967).
[46] Ruth Kark, *American Consuls in the Holy Land, 1832–1914* (Jerusalem: Magnes Press of the Hebrew University, and Detroit: Wayne State University Press, 1994), 24–38; Alexander Scholch, 'Britain in Palestine, 1838–1882: The Roots of the Balfour Policy', *Journal of Palestine Studies* 22, no. 1 (1992): 41–2.
[47] For the Templar settlement in Palestine and in Jerusalem, see Yossi Ben-Artzi, *MiGermania Le'Eretz HaKodesh: Hityashvut HaTemplerim Be'Eretz Israel* (Jerusalem: Yad Yizhak Ben-Zvi, 1996).
[48] Yaakov Ariel and Ruth Kark, 'Messianism, Holiness, Charisma, and Community: The American-Swedish Colony in Jerusalem, 1881–1933', *Church History* 65, no. 4 (1996): 641–57; William R. Hutchison, *Errand to the World: American Protestant Thought and Foreign Missions* (Chicago: University of Chicago Press, 1987); Rafiq A. Farah, *In Troubled Waters: A History of the Anglican Church in Jerusalem 1841–1998* (Leicester: Christians Aware, 2002); Mark Crinson, *Empire Building: Orientalism and Victorian Architecture* (London and New York: Routledge, 1996).
[49] Amiri and Wharton, 'Home in Jerusalem', 237–65; Tom Segev and Haim Watzman, *One Palestine, Complete: Jews and Arabs under the British Mandate*, trans. Haim Watzman (New York: Metropolitan Books, 2000), 82–4.

An important aspect of Jerusalem's sociocultural makeup was the division of the Arab Palestinian community into Christians and Muslims. As noted, the British commitment to develop a 'national home for the Jews', in accord with the Mandate's fourth article, created new and crucial political challenges for Palestinian Arabs. Thus, historians consider the Mandate period a turning point in the shaping of Palestinian identity and an incentive in its crystallisation as independent and separate from other Arab national configurations.[50] This was true for both Christians and Muslims, yet the balance of power between these two communities changed dramatically under British rule. The Muslims, who were the reigning political and religious elite during the Ottoman regime, became one among three communities under Christian (British) hegemony.[51] Despite this virtual demotion, Arab Palestinian national identity remained inclusive of Christians and Muslims.[52] But British policies created interreligious tensions, which seriously impacted the coming-into-being of defined and more clearly separated Christian and Muslim identities within the Arab Palestinian community.[53] Religious differentiation is thus important in any discussion of modern architectural production in the region. However, additional factors must also be considered since, as Rashid Khalidi observes, these separate Christian and Muslim identities imbricated and coincided with identities derived from geographical origin, social strata, and so on.[54]

The Muslim Palestinian community in Jerusalem has been extensively researched with relation to Palestinian identity.[55] Scholars have shown that during the early days of the Mandate period, this community was aligned by affiliation with Jerusalem's two leading rival Muslim families – the Hussaynis and the Nashashibis.[56] The changing role of the Muslim Pious Endowments Directorate – the Waqf – was also significant when rising Palestinian nationalism emerged during the later Mandate years as a powerful force in shaping the public.[57] Moreover, owing to British interventions, which attempted to solidify

[50] This process is discussed in detail by Kimmerling, 'The Formation of Palestinian Collective Identities', 48–81; Khalidi, *Palestinian Identity*, 145–78.
[51] Kimmerling, 'The Formation of Palestinian Collective Identities', 48–81.
[52] Khalidi, *Palestinian Identity*, 169; Kimmerling, 'The Formation of Palestinian Collective Identities', 66.
[53] Jacobson, *From Empire to Empire*, 153, 158–9; Laura Robson, *Colonialism and Christianity in Mandate Palestine* (Austin: University of Texas Press, 2011), 44–5.
[54] Khalidi, *Palestinian Identity*, 146, 150–4.
[55] See, e.g., Taysir Nashif, 'Social Background Characteristics as Determinants of Political Behavior of the Arab Political Leadership of Palestine under the British Mandate', *Journal of Third World Studies* 26, no. 2 (2009): 161–73; Weldon Matthews, *Confronting an Empire, Constructing a Nation: Arab Nationalists and Popular Politics in Mandate Palestine* (London: I. B. Tauris, 2006).
[56] Nicholas E. Roberts, 'Rethinking the Status Quo: The British and Islam in Palestine, 1917–1929' (PhD diss., New York University, 2010), 201.
[57] Yitzhak Reiter, 'Waqf BiNsibot Mishtanot', in *Kalkala VeChevra Bi'Ymei HaMandat, 1918–1948*, eds Avi Bra'eli and Nahum Kralinski (Be'er Sheba: Ben-Gurion University of the Negev, 2003), 349–66; Philip Mattar, 'The Mufti of Jerusalem and the Politics of Palestine', *Middle East Journal* 42, no. 2 (1988): 227–40.

a representative Muslim leadership in Palestine, the leading Muslim families of Jerusalem gained immense influence throughout the country.[58]

The Christians, who belonged historically to the bourgeois elite among Arab Palestinians, were arguably the most heterogeneous and internally sectarian among Jerusalem's communities.[59] They were often implicated in the sectarian interventions of European powers, which, as I noted above, increased significantly from the nineteenth century on.[60] As has been demonstrated by several scholars, the British imposition of a political system delineated by religious sects engendered dramatic contradictions in the construction of Christian-Palestinian identity.[61] In addition to the already noted solidarity between Muslim and Christian Palestinians, owing to their mutual opposition to Zionism,[62] Christian intracommunal sectarianism and strife rendered this community more and more dependent on the Muslim Palestinian political majority.[63] Consequently, the Christian community's architectural production during the Mandate years was sectarian, limited to mission and sect-related churches, schools and hospitals. Although these buildings often served others apart from the sects for whom they were intended, none of them represented the Christian-Palestinian community conceptually in its broader sense, which is the reason that I did not select one of their buildings for discussion in this book. However, I should mention one sectarian building again – the Italian Catholic Terra Santa College, which served in a somewhat similar way to the Jerusalem YMCA. Planned between 1924 and 1927 by the Italian architect Antonio Barluzzi (1884–1960), it was originally intended as a Catholic cultural centre for Catholic youth. However, unable to compete with the services offered by the interdenominational and intercommunal Jerusalem YMCA, Terra Santa was soon converted into a Franciscan high school and ceased functioning as a secular cultural centre.[64]

As already noted, the third group – Jews – accounted for the majority of Jerusalem's inhabitants during the Mandate period.[65] They, too, included several subcommunities with imbricated identities with varying associations in regard to Zionism, ethnic origin and religiosity. Jewish Zionist immigration to Palestine/Eretz Israel

---

[58] Uri Stendell, 'Mishpachot HaNichbadim BeKerev Aravi'yei Yerusahlayim', in *Sefer Ze'ev Vilnai*, ed. Eli Schiller, vol. 2 (Jerusalem: Ariel, 1984), 69.

[59] Avraham Sela, 'Chevra VeMosdot BeKerev Arvi'yei Palestine BiTkufat HaMandat: Tmura, He'ader Ni'ut VeKrisa', in *Kalkala VeChevra Bi'Ymei HaMandat*, eds Bra'eli and Kralinski, 308–10; Tsimhoni, 'The Status of the Arab Christians', 166–92; Daphne Tsimhoni, 'The Armenians and the Syrians: Ethno-religious Communities in Jerusalem', *Middle Eastern Studies* 20, no. 3 (1984): 352–69.

[60] Seth J. Frantzman and Ruth Kark, 'The Catholic Church in Palestine/Israel: Real Estate in Terra Sancta', *Middle Eastern Studies* 50, no. 3 (2014): 370–96.

[61] Robson, *Colonialism and Christianity in Mandate Palestine*, 44.

[62] Jacobson, *From Empire to Empire*, 158–9, 176.

[63] Tsimhoni, 'The Status of the Arab Christians', 186–7.

[64] Kroyanker, *Adrichalut Bi'Yerushalayim: HaBni'ya BiTkufat HaMandat HaBriti*, 110–11.

[65] Kark and Oren-Nordheim, *Jerusalem and its Environs*, 146–7.

increased significantly during the interwar years,⁶⁶ and during the Mandate period, Zionist Jews, of all ethnic origins and with varying religious practices, constituted the primary force in the Jewish development of Jerusalem. They initially enjoyed Great Britain's diplomatic and political support⁶⁷ and the perception, shared by both the British and the Zionists, that the region required modernisation was an important factor in the British endorsement of Zionist ideas. The Zionist project in Palestine/Eretz Israel, which has been the subject of vast scholarship and contentious debate,⁶⁸ caused not only intercommunal conflict, but also engendered intracommunal tensions within the Jewish Yishuv: for example, Orthodox Jews perceived Zionists, with their secular European culture, as a threat to their way of life and traditional beliefs.⁶⁹ This tension was especially marked in Jerusalem, whose large ultra-Orthodox and Zionist communities were often in conflict with one another in political, cultural and economic spheres.

Architecture as a Cross-cultural Project

Jerusalem's urban space underwent remarkable changes during the Mandate period, which included British schemes for preservation of the Old City's character, as well as modernisation of its extramural space.⁷⁰ In addition to the neighbourhoods built outside the ancient walls during the nineteenth century, new ones were also constructed mostly northwest and southwest of the Old City, areas generally termed 'West Jerusalem'.⁷¹ The northeastern and eastern parts of the city developed as well, and were commonly known as 'East Jerusalem'. The new neighbourhoods largely replicated the communal and sectarian spatial divisions that characterised the Old City and the older extramural neighbourhoods. Similarly, there was some heterogeneity in the social makeup of these new neighborhoods as well.⁷²

---

⁶⁶ Gilbert, *Jerusalem in the Twentieth Century*, 67–72; Michael Shalev, *Labour and the Political Economy in Israel* (Oxford: Oxford University Press, 1992), 338, http://www.questia.com/read/48984458/labour-and-the-political-economy-in-israel; Jacob Metzer, 'Jewish Immigration to Palestine in the Long 1920s: An Exploratory Examination', *Journal of Israeli History* 27, no. 2 (2008): 221–51.

⁶⁷ Smith, *Palestine and the Arab-Israeli Conflict*, 67–87.

⁶⁸ The Zionist settlement of Palestine/Eretz Israel has been placed in the context of either settler-immigrant projects, colonising missions, or both. Noteworthy for the present study are Lockman, *Comrades and Enemies*; Lockman, 'Land, Labor and the Logic of Zionism'; Gershon Shafir, *Land, Labor, and the Origins of the Israeli-Palestinian Conflict, 1882–1914* (Berkeley: University of California Press, 1996).

⁶⁹ For discussion of specific examples, see Jacobson and Naor, *Oriental Neighbors*, 23–8; Amos Israel-Vleeschhouwer, 'The Mandate System as a Messianic Alternative in the Ultra-Religious Jurisprudence of Rabbi Dr Isaac Breuer', *Israel Law Review* 49, no. 3 (2016): 339–63.

⁷⁰ Inbal Ben-Asher Gitler, '"Marrying Modern Progress with Treasured Antiquity": Jerusalem City Plans during the British Mandate, 1917–1948', *Traditional Dwellings and Settlements Review* 15, no.1 (2003): 39–58; Ruth Kark and Michal Oren-Nordheim, 'Colonial Cities in Palestine?' *Israel Affairs* 3, no. 2 (1996): 50–94.

⁷¹ Biger, 'HaHitparsut HaMerchavit shel Uchlusi'yat Yerushalayim', 128–9.

⁷² Ibid. 125–40.

Figure I.3 *Panorama of Jerusalem facing Mamilla Cemetery and southeast Jerusalem. Photograph c. 1940–6. ACM, https://www.loc.gov/pictures/item/2019694836/, retrieved 11 February 2020.*

Figure I.4 *American School of Oriental Research and Olivet from St George's Cathedral Tower, Jerusalem, detail, c. 1940–6. (Shown in the background: Mount Scopus, northern slopes of the Mount of Olives [Olivet], with Augusta Viktoria Endowment and the Church of Ascension.) ACM, https://www.loc.gov/pictures/item/2019704791/, retrieved 11 February 2020.*

Three of the buildings discussed in this book were erected in West Jerusalem: the Jerusalem YMCA, the Zionist Executive Buildings and the Palace Hotel. Figure I.3 is a photograph of that section of the city taken near the Zionist Executive Building, looking toward the Mamilla Cemetery, with the Palace Hotel and the YMCA Building in the background. Thus, it offers an excellent image of the area where these edifices were constructed. The Palestine Archaeological Museum was built in East Jerusalem, adjacent to the Old City wall, and can be seen in Figure I.4, behind new residential buildings in northeast Jerusalem, set against the Mount of Olives.

Land designation and distribution underwent significant changes during the Mandate, initiated by the British in line with their new schemes, by the Muslim Endowments, and by considerable land purchases made by Jews. One important factor that facilitated major developments in West Jerusalem was the selling of large tracts of land by the Greek Orthodox Patriarchate. These sales, which both Muslim and Christian Palestinians strongly opposed but were not able to prevent, caused significant intercommunal tensions, as the Jews greatly benefited from these transactions.[73]

In Chapter One, entitled 'A Holy City for the Twentieth Century', which elaborates on these urban transformations, I discuss British urban schemes in light of the Mandate system and its interpretations. I argue that the case of Jerusalem – with its multicultural public and contested spaces – unsettled accepted premises that regarded Palestine as a newly established 'British Colony'. I go on to demonstrate that notion by exploring plans for the development of the city and by discussing British intentions, interventions, and the Mandatory discourses that supported these.

In Chapter Two, 'Appropriating Multi-histories', I look at the Palestine Archeological Museum, analysing its architecture as a British and American articulation of Palestine's past. I describe how British architect Austen St Barbe Harrison, with the aid of American archaeologist Henry Breasted and with the approval of the patron, John D. Rockefeller, implemented new concepts of museum planning and architecture for archaeological research in designing the building. The outcome was a sophisticated blend of modernism, historicism and vernacular architecture. It included a didactic sculptural programme and, taken together, all of these features expressed a vision of thriving coexistence under British and American custodianship.

Chapter Three, 'Americans Imagining Jerusalem', deals with the Jerusalem YMCA Building, designed by the American architect Arthur Loomis Harmon. Built by a Christian organisation, it was assigned an important role within the Christian-Palestinian community, but also provided a venue for modern cultural activities for all of the city's inhabitants. I show that the YMCA's explicit multicultural and interreligious design, as well as its sculptural programme, expressed a veiled message of Christian hegemony, a message that asserted American cultural authority, which, in fact, extended beyond the building's modern functions.

In Chapter Four, entitled 'Constructing Palestinian Identity', I examine the

[73] Itamar Katz and Ruth Kark, 'The Greek Orthodox Patriarchate of Jerusalem and its Congregation: Dissent over Real Estate', *International Journal of Middle East Studies* 37, no. 4 (2005): 519; Kroyanker, *Adrichalut Bi'Yerushalayim: HaBni'ya BiTkufat HaMandat HaBriti*, 162–3.

construction of the Palace Hotel as a reflection of emerging Muslim-Palestinian identity. With his patron, Hajj Amin al Husayni, Turkish architect Mehmet Nihat Nigisberk forged this identity by singling out the sacred monuments of the Haram al-Sharif as Muslim-Palestinian national icons, integrating them into the hotel's design through implementation of Ottoman and Turkish architectural theory and practice. I further show that political tensions, religiosity and relations with the Arab world all impacted the Palace Hotel's construction and design.

In Chapter Five, 'Constructing Zionist Identity', I discuss the Zionist Executive Building (ZEB), designed by Zionist architect Yohanan Ratner. The extent to which Jerusalem was important for the Zionist project has long been subject to debate,[74] and I offer additional perspectives on this issue as I explore the political and symbolic role of the building's architecture. Similar to the Palace Hotel's significance for the Muslim-Palestinian community, in the ZEB I identify a key formative process of enlisting modernism as the Jewish national style in Palestine. I further demonstrate the intercommunal and intracommunal challenges engendered by this project, which decidedly reflected broader dilemmas and controversies in Palestine.

In my Conclusion, I propose that these four buildings reflect differing approaches to modernism, historicism and vernacular architecture. I argue that their designs provide new perspectives with regard to the spread of modernism and its engagement with global and local traditions and trends. Furthermore, I contend that the contradicting and conflicting ideologies revealed in Jerusalem's Mandate-era architectural culture foregrounded, initiated and anticipated current spatial dilemmas. I suggest that exploring its ramifications, which involved communal cooperation, competition and controversy, can contribute significantly to our understanding of architecture's important role not only in Jerusalem, but in mixed cities and contested spaces elsewhere in the world.

---

[74] Motti Golani, 'Hanhagat Ha'Yishuv VeShe'elat Jerusalem BeMilchemet Ha'Atzma'ut (December 1947–May 1948)', *Cathedra: For the History of Eretz Israel and Its Yishuv* 54 (1989): 156–72; Tamar Mayer, 'Jerusalem in and out of Focus: The City in Zionist Ideology', in *Jerusalem: Idea and Reality*, eds Tamar Mayer and Suleiman A. Mourad (London and New York: Routledge, 2008), 224–44.

CHAPTER ONE

A Holy City for the Twentieth Century: Urban Planning during the British Mandate

Palestine for most of us was an emotion rather than a reality.
– Charles Robert Ashbee, 1923[1]

UPON CONQUERING JERUSALEM in 1917, the British immediately began a process of long-term urban planning. They had two distinct goals: to preserve the walled Holy City's historic sites, which hold immense religious significance for Judaism, Christianity and Islam, and to transform Jerusalem into a modern city.

In this chapter, I explore the British approach to urban planning in Jerusalem as reflected in official Mandatory publications. I analyse the meaning of urban schemes and their relationship to the cultural and political complexities during the period of British rule in Palestine. British urban plans set the stage for the construction of the individual projects discussed in the ensuing chapters. Investigating the background and implementation of these ventures will enhance understanding of the significance of architecture for Jerusalem's various communities, for assessing the buildings' spatial relationship to the Old City, and for new areas developed beyond the ancient walls.

Several urban schemes were devised during the thirty years that the British held the Mandate. William Hannah McLean (1877–1967) drafted the first plan in 1918; the second was conceived by Sir Patrick Geddes (1854–1932) in 1919. These were followed by plans made during the next three decades, devised by Charles Robert Ashbee (1863–1942), Albert Clifford Holliday (1897–1960) and Henry Kendall (1903–1983). In this chapter I focus on the 1922 plan formulated by Ashbee and the 1944 plan by Kendall, and briefly analyse the plans by McLean, Geddes and Holliday. Ashbee's and Kendall's plans were included in three official British publications dealing with town planning in Jerusalem, and thus provide the most complete documentation of this aspect of British Mandatory rule. Ashbee's books were titled *Jerusalem 1918–1920: Being the Records of the Pro-Jerusalem Council during the Period of the British Military Administration*, published in 1921, and

---

[1] Charles Robert Ashbee, *A Palestine Notebook: 1918–1923* (Garden City: Doubleday, Page & Co., 1923), 276.

Jerusalem 1920–1922: Being the Records of the Pro-Jerusalem Council during the First Two Years of the Civil Administration, published in 1924. Kendall's book was titled *Jerusalem: The City Plan. Preservation and Development during the British Mandate 1918–1948*, published in 1948.[2] In addition to describing his own town plan, Kendall's book summarises his predecessors' schemes, so is useful for a broad scope understanding of British Mandatory urban planning in Jerusalem.

The three extensive, lavishly illustrated English-language publications produced by Ashbee and Kendall are among the most important manifestations of the profound reverence the British held for Jerusalem. British plans in Jerusalem and Palestine were an important aspect of Mandatory rule and have been explored by several scholars.[3] Studies of the urban and architectural histories of Jerusalem initially approached the British enterprise there as a colonial project,[4] but others avoided using this paradigm in connection with British planning in Jerusalem.[5] More recently, however, researchers including Rosa El-Eini, Abigail Jacobson and myself have proposed a reassessment of British interventions in the city, highlighting important differences between the mandatory and the colonial conditions.[6] As noted by Benjamin Hyman, a thorough methodological comparison between Jerusalem and cities in British colonies – or even colonies of other European powers such as France – would be required to fully understand the distinction.[7] I do not attempt such a detailed comparison. Rather, I present a more conceptual analysis of official British plans for Jerusalem in relation to current research on colonial urbanism and, more specifically, on British colonial town planning. In this respect, I identify the Mandate system as a hybrid form of foreign rule, historically parallel to processes of decolonisation.

---

[2] Charles Robert Ashbee, ed., *Jerusalem 1918–1920: Being the Records of the Pro-Jerusalem Council during the Period of the British Military Administration* (London: John Murray, 1921); Charles Robert Ashbee, ed., *Jerusalem 1920–1922: Being the Records of the Pro-Jerusalem Council during the First Two Years of the Civil Administration* (London: John Murray, 1924); Henry Kendall, *Jerusalem: The City Plan. Preservation and Development during the British Mandate 1918–1948* (London: His Majesty's Stationery Office, 1948).

[3] Haim Yacobi, 'The Language of Modernity: Urban Design in Mandatory Lydda', *The Jerusalem Quarterly* 42 (2010): 80–93; Gilbert Herbert and Silvina Sosnovsky, *Urban Developments in Down-Town Haifa during the British Mandate* (Haifa: Technion–Israel Institute of Technology, Faculty of Architecture and Town Planning, Documentation Unit of Architecture, 1984); Gilbert Herbert, 'Crossroads: Imperial Priorities and Regional Perspectives in the Planning of Haifa, 1918–1939', *Planning Perspectives* 4, no. 3 (1989): 313–31.

[4] See, e.g., Ron Fuchs and Gilbert Herbert, 'A Colonial Portrait of Jerusalem: British Architecture in Mandate-Era Palestine', in *Hybrid Urbanism: On the Identity Discourse and the Built Environment*, ed. Nezar AlSayyad (Westport: Praeger, 2001), 83–109.

[5] Benjamin Hyman, 'British Planners in Palestine, 1918–1936' (PhD diss., London School of Economics and Political Science, 1994), 26–30.

[6] Roza El-Eini, *Mandated Landscape: British Imperial Rule in Palestine 1929–1948* (London: Routledge, 2004), 448–54; Jacobson, *From Empire to Empire*, 130–8; Ben-Asher Gitler, 'Marrying Modern Progress with Treasured Antiquity', 39–58.

[7] Hyman, 'British Planners in Palestine', 26.

Early Twentieth-century Jerusalem

Jerusalem is situated on a plateau in the midst of a mountain region, about 800 metres (2600 ft) above sea level, its topography characterised by rocky hills. In the heyday of Ottoman rule, from the mid-1800s, the city experienced a rapid growth in population,[8] which triggered urban development beyond the ancient city walls. The layout of Jerusalem's walled Old City resembles the casbahs of other Middle Eastern cities, with densely built neighbourhoods and narrow streets. Its crowded urban fabric and Middle Eastern architecture that features stone-clad buildings, domes and minarets can be seen, for example, in Figures 3.11, 3.13 and 3.14. But at the end of the nineteenth century and the beginning of the twentieth, new residential neighbourhoods and commercial areas were constructed outside the Old City walls. These developments were comparable to contemporary transformations of Damascus, Cairo and Baghdad,[9] but unlike these other cities, Jerusalem had a unique sociocultural makeup, a result of its place as the centre for the three monotheistic religions. This reality led to a historic division of the Old City into four quarters: Jewish, Christian, Armenian Christian and Muslim. Three prominent historical holy sites dictated the quarters' locations: the Muslim quarter was adjacent to the holy sanctuary of the Haram al-Sharif (the Noble Sanctuary), which included the Dome of the Rock (Qubbat al-Sakhrah) and the Al-Aqsa Mosque (Al-Masjid al-Aqsa). The Christian and Armenian quarters developed around the Church of the Holy Sepulchre and the Jewish quarter lay near the Wailing Wall. As I noted in the Introduction, within this overall religious division of the city, there was a further sectionalising of urban space according to sects. Thus, new neighbourhoods outside Jerusalem's walls developed, for the most part, in a manner similar to the sectional structure of the Old City and maintained existing patterns of religious and ethnic affiliations. The multicultural and multireligious character of the city at the beginning of the Mandate Period was in large measure responsible for its urban layout and architecture.[10]

At the outset of the present analysis, I should consider two particularly important factors that influenced the cityscape of Jerusalem prior to the British conquest. First, the final decades of Ottoman rule were characterised by accelerated development in the city, both within and outside the Old City walls. By regulating urban planning, the Ottoman regime was able to improve building supervision, which fostered the growth and development of the city's neighbourhoods, infrastructure and public construction.[11] Second, European presence in the city grew, manifested in grand architectural projects for churches, hospitals, missions and

---

[8] Yehoshua Ben-Arieh, *Yir BeRe'yi Tkufa: Yerushalayim BaMe'a HaTesha-Esre* (Jerusalem: Yad Izhak Ben-Zvi, 1977), 155–9, 316–18.
[9] Stefano Bianca, *Urban Form in the Arab World* (London: Thames and Hudson, 2000), 169–71.
[10] Ben-Arieh, *Yir BeRe'yi Tkufa*. This entire book provides an excellent source of information on the subject. See, e.g., 616–27. See also Gilbert, *Jerusalem in the Twentieth Century*, 9–10.
[11] Kark and Oren-Nordheim, *Jerusalem and its Environs*, 34–6.

consulates. The European powers perceived their activity in Jerusalem as involving more than just a religious mission, and their efforts to establish a political presence in the Ottoman controlled city led to competition for the best plots of land and ever more ostentatious displays of architecture.[12] Thus, when the British entered Jerusalem, they had to contend with the diverse forces that were shaping the city, while addressing its inhabitants' needs, their religious and secular spatial practices, as well as Jerusalem's important holy sites.

British Approach to Urban Preservation and Development

One of the clearest indications of the deep ties that the British manifested toward Jerusalem was their sense of urgency in gaining control of its physical space. Shortly after they gained control, Ronald Storrs (1881–1955), the city's new military governor, issued an edict intended to prevent alteration or destruction of monuments within the walls of the Old City and closely adjacent areas:

> No person shall demolish, erect, alter or repair the structure of any building in the city of Jerusalem or its environs within a radius of 2,500 meters from the Damascus gate ... until he has obtained a written permit from the Military Governor.[13]

This imperative eventually formed the basis for a more complete system of building regulation for the Holy City. Writing in 1948, Henry Kendall attempted to convey the urgency of this preservation mission at the time:

> The enemy was still on the Nablus-Jordan valley line astride the centre of Palestine when Allenby asked the then City Engineer, Alexandria [Mr William McLean], to come to Jerusalem and report and advise upon what measures should be taken to institute the necessary control of building operations and town development, keeping in view the architectural traditions of Jerusalem and the importance of preserving its historic monuments.[14]

To the British, the Old City was above all a place of religious practice and historical significance, which had to be singled out for preservation. The British administration thus set out to design a new town plan that would enhance

---

[12] A historical account of these developments is given in Ben-Arieh, *Yir BeRe'yi Tkufa*, 178–203; Kark and Oren-Nordheim, *Jerusalem and its Environs*, 112–13. Specific building projects are discussed in Crinson, *Empire Building*, 198–226; David Kroyanker, *Adrichalut Bi'Yerushalayim: HaBni'ya Ha'Eropit-Notsrit MiChutz LaChomot, 1855–1918* (Jerusalem: Keter, 1991); Edina Meyer, 'Die Dormition auf dem Berge Zion in Jerusalem, eine Denkmalskirche Kaiser Wilhelms II. im Heiligen Land', *Architectura* 14, no. 2 (1984): 149–70; Edina Meyer-Maril, 'Binyan Augusta-Victoria al Har-Hazeytim', *Ariel*, no. 122–3 (1997): 51–62.
[13] Ashbee, ed., *Jerusalem 1918–1920*, v.
[14] Kendall, *Jerusalem: The City Plan*, 4.

conservation within the Old City walls and promote the development of a modern city beyond them. However, since Jerusalem was still under military authority and Britain's hold on Palestine was as yet unrecognised, an interim administration was required in order to execute these urban plans. Thus, in 1918 Storrs established an advisory society, or council, for matters of urban development.[15] Named the Pro-Jerusalem Society, it was to have a say in decisions pertaining to city planning and, to some extent, assist with their implementation and funding. The Society's declared goal was the 'preservation and advancement of the interests of Jerusalem, its district and inhabitants ...'.[16] Among other things, this meant preserving antiquities, developing modern urban cultural facilities such as museums, libraries, theatres, and so on, and fostering the education and welfare of the city's inhabitants.[17]

The society comprised representatives of most of the religious sects and national groups in the city, as well as archaeologists, historians and architects. In his memoirs, an optimistic Storrs supplied a long list of its members:

> I was able to assemble together round one table the Mayor of Jerusalem, the British Director of Antiquities, the Mufti, the Chief Rabbis, the Presidents of the Italian Franciscans and the French Dominicans, the Orthodox, the Armenian and the Latin Patriarchs, the Presidents of the Jewish Community, the Anglican Bishop, the Chairman of the Zionist Commission, the Dominican Fathers Abel and Vincent, Capitano Paribene (with the Distaccamento and afterwards Italian Minister of Fine Arts), with other leading members of the British, Arab, Jewish and American communities.[18]

The multicultural character of the city prompted the British to seek the cooperation of this diverse assemblage of clerics and national representatives of countries and ethnic groups – some of whom had been Britain's allies during World War I, and could not be ignored.[19] But the establishment of the Pro-Jerusalem Society also prefigured an important characteristic of British Mandate-era rule: a commitment to creating a democratic, unifying body with the active participation of the local population. However, although the Pro-Jerusalem Society declared its commitment to including the local population in its activities, its members still regarded Jerusalem's inhabitants as having 'much to learn yet in the elementary duties of citizenship', as Ashbee put it.[20] Moreover the publications discussed here

---

[15] A detailed account of the founding of the Pro-Jerusalem Society, its aims and actions, is given in Ronald Storrs, *Orientations* (London: Ivor Nicholson & Watson Limited, 1937), 363–70.

[16] Ashbee, ed., *Jerusalem 1918–1920*, vii.

[17] A detailed analysis of Storrs' activity and philosophy is provided in Annabel Wharton, *Selling Jerusalem: Relics, Replicas, Theme Parks* (Chicago: University of Chicago Press, 2006), 206–19.

[18] Ronald Storrs, *The Memoirs of Ronald Storrs* (New York: G. Putnam's Sons, 1937), 327.

[19] For a comprehensive account of Britain's alliances during and after World War I, see Fromkin, *A Peace to End All Peace*, especially parts 6–9.

[20] Ashbee, ed., *Jerusalem 1918–1920*, 4–5.

indicate that it was primarily the British development ideas and town plans that were implemented.

The Pro-Jerusalem Society was active until 1926, although its influence and activism diminished after the British Mandate over Palestine went into effect in 1922. The group published two out of the three books noted above: *Jerusalem 1918–1920* and *Jerusalem 1920–1922*, both edited by Ashbee. These constituted the records of the society's activities, which included plans for archaeological and architectural preservation and Ashbee's town planning schemes.

To a great extent, it was Storrs and the Pro-Jerusalem Society that delineated the British approach to preservation and conservation. Their decisions in this regard also had distinct political purposes, the first of which was to delegitimise the recent years of Ottoman rule. British officials combed the region's history, preserving first and foremost their own romanticised notion of Jerusalem. This process of preservation was similar to their engagement in India where, as the subcontinent's colonisers, they sought to 'order [India's] past into a coherent narrative that extended up to the present'.[21] Similarly, in Jerusalem, ancient Israelite, Roman, Muslim and Crusader archaeological remains and monuments were treasured, as were Ottoman monuments from the age of Sultan Süleyman the Magnificent. The archaeologists and historians who collaborated in the production of Ashbee's volumes marvelled at sites attributed to these epochs, and their preservation was discussed in detail. Henry Kendall also repeatedly expressed admiration for the archaeological evidence and the buildings that remained from these eras.[22]

In sharp contrast, more recent projects of the Ottoman period were systematically devalued. Erasure of physical evidence from this later stage of Ottoman rule was justified by a continuing debasement of the Turks.[23] Thus, an article in the London *Times* from 5 February 1919, hailing the new British schemes for Jerusalem, apparently written by Ashbee, included the following:[24]

> It is difficult to imagine a sharper contrast between the Jerusalem of man's imagination, whether he thinks of it in terms of Mahomed's vision and ascent to Heaven, of Solomon's grandeur, or of Christ's Sermon on the Mount, and the actual Jerusalem left us by the Turk. This latter concrete Jerusalem is a picturesque but filthy medieval town, with sprawling suburbs; ill timbered, unwatered, with roads inconvenient and leading nowhere.[25]

---

[21] Thomas R. Metcalf, *Ideologies of the Raj* (Cambridge: Cambridge University Press, 1994), 148.
[22] Kendall, *Jerusalem: The City Plan*, see, e.g., pages 12, 14.
[23] A useful definition of architectural erasure is given in Annabel Wharton, 'Erasure: Eliminating the Space of Late Ancient Judaism', in *From Dura to Sepphoris: Studies in Jewish Art and Society in Late Antiquity*, eds Lee Israel Levine and Ze'ev Weiss (Portsmouth, RI: Journal of Roman Archaeology, 2000), 195–214.
[24] The article as it appears in the London *Times* is not signed, only the words '(from a correspondent)' appear under the title 'Reconstruction in Jerusalem'. In *A Palestine Notebook*, Ashbee includes this article, citing the same date, as written by himself. See Ashbee, *A Palestine Notebook*, 78–80.
[25] *Times* (London), 5 February 1919.

Indeed, the British faced serious problems upon their arrival. The *Times* article emphasised these difficulties, while intentionally ignoring more recent Ottoman improvements, using the city's sites of disrepair to strengthen the British claim on the city.

Both of Ashbee's books and Kendall's *Jerusalem: The City Plan* include numerous comments similar to those in the *Times* article. A recurring theme was hygiene, or rather the lack of it. Claims of inferior hygiene and sanitation in colonised lands were routinely used as justification for their possession by European powers. In the case of Palestine, both Ashbee and Kendall used this theme to delegitimise the land's former rulers.[26] Generally, in the colonial setting, the 'native city' was seen as a site of 'picturesque' architecture, erratic traffic flow, and filth.[27] However, instead of using this discourse of debasement to establish the superiority of the 'European City', Ashbee and Kendall used it to deplore their predecessors' negligence. Both discussed the need to clean up the refuse left by the Turks.[28] Moreover, McLean, Ashbee and Kendall all emphasised what they perceived to be the Turks' lack of regard for the archaeological significance of the Old City walls, which the latter encroached upon and damaged.[29] At one point, Kendall reported that 'prior to the arrival of the British the condition of the buildings generally in the Old City was appalling'.[30]

Perhaps the most symbolic act of erasure concerning the period of Ottoman rule was the demolition of the ornate City Clock Tower and its adjacent *sebil*, which Kendall referred to as 'unsightly' and Ashbee called 'hideous' (Figure 1.1).[31] These structures, which were erected in 1901 near the Jaffa Gate to commemorate the twenty-fifth anniversary of the rule of Sultan ʿAbd al-Hamid II,[32] were dismantled in 1924, despite public protest.[33] Kendall also wrote about 'clearing of the unsightly shops in the vicinity of the Damascus Gate',[34] and in this case he related the process by which such a demolition might legitimately occur:

> With the collaboration of the local authority notices were served on the owners of these properties giving them ample time to find alternative accommodation.

---

[26] See, e.g., the case of India, described in Metcalf, *Ideologies of the Raj*, 171–6.
[27] Anthony D. King, *Colonial Urban Development: Culture, Social Power, and Environment* (London: Routledge & Kegan Paul, 1976), 88.
[28] Ashbee, ed., *Jerusalem 1918–1920*, 2.
[29] Ashbee, ed., *Jerusalem 1918–1920*, 22; William H. McLean to the editor of the *Times* (London), 'Spoiling the Holy City', 1, 4 March 1937; McLean to Boyd, 16 June 1937. Holy Places file *NAGB* CO 733/339/3.
[30] Kendall, *Jerusalem: The City Plan*, 37.
[31] Ibid. 6; Ashbee, *A Palestine Notebook*, 182.
[32] For a discussion of the events related to the demolition of the clock tower, see Fuchs and Herbert, 'A Colonial Portrait of Jerusalem', 89–91.
[33] Kark and Oren-Nordheim, *Jerusalem and its Environs*, 35.
[34] Kendall, *Jerusalem: The City Plan*, 17. For photographs and correspondence concerning this project, see Holy Places file *NAGB* CO 733/339/3.

Figure 1.1 *Jaffa Gate with the Ottoman Clock Tower (erected 1901, demolished 1924), c. 1898–1914. ACM, https://www.loc.gov/pictures/item/2019704791/, retrieved 11 February 2020.*

Expropriation proceedings were commenced and after a period of some months the buildings were demolished and owners compensated.[35]

In a section of his book dealing with urban traffic flow, Kendall provided the following description of the western entrance to Jerusalem: 'the Jaffa road straggles through a partly built-up locality and provides frontage to some buildings which fall within a reconstruction area and which are *ripe for demolition* [my emphasis]'.[36] Here, too, he noted: 'It is hoped that the local authorities will achieve in collaboration with competent persons a more satisfactory type of architectural expression for buildings.'[37]

Although Kendall's opinions can be perceived today as colonial in their attitude, he did stress the advantages of collaborating with 'local authorities'. Although the identity of those 'authorities' was not revealed, he was most likely referring to Jerusalem's semiautonomous municipal administration.[38] This again reflected the terms of the Mandate, which required that Britain foster a new tradition of autonomy and self-governance among the local population.[39] Yet, whereas the local authorities were to be consulted, Kendall showed no interest in the views of the local inhabitants. Ashbee also wrote, in a manner consistent with colonial discourses, about how the local population could be enlisted to clean up the 'Turkish' debris and implement archaeological conservation. Content with the prospect of enforced cooperation, he observed that 'Work with the hands ... keeps men from empty political speculation.'[40]

In general, the British approached the conservation and development of Jerusalem in a manner similar to their earlier interventions in India and comparable also to that of French colonial authorities in the cities of the Maghreb. In Delhi, for example, the British preserved the large medieval urban complex of Qutb, which accorded with their selective 'scientific' assessment of India's past.[41] In North Africa, the French singled out the Medina of Rabat and the Casbah of Algiers for preservation because of their picturesque Oriental fabric.[42] In all these colonies, as in Jerusalem, preservation carried a clear political agenda of domination and was

[35] Kendall, *Jerusalem: The City Plan*, 17.
[36] Ibid. 20.
[37] Ibid. 20.
[38] The history of the municipality during the Mandate period is discussed in P. A. Alsberg, 'HaMa'avak al Rashut Iriyat Yerushalayim BiTkufat HaMandat', in *Prakim Betoldot Yerushalayim Bazman Hachadash*, ed. Eli Shealtiel (Jerusalem: Yad Ben-Zvi and Israel Ministry of Defense, 1981), 302–54.
[39] *The Palestine Mandate* 1, no. 3, June 1930 (Geneva: League of Nations Association of the US), 23.
[40] Ashbee, ed., *Jerusalem 1918–1920*, 34.
[41] Mrinalini Rajagopalan, 'A Medieval Monument and its Modern Myths of Iconoclasm: The Enduring Contestations Over the Qutb Complex in Delhi, India', in *Reuse Value: Spolia and Appropriation in Art and Architecture from Constantine to Sherrie Levine*, eds Richard Brilliant and Dale Kinney (Abingdon and New York: Routledge, 2016), 199–222.
[42] This aspect is discussed in relation to Rabat in Gwendolyn Wright, *The Politics of Design in French Colonial Urbanism* (Chicago: University of Chicago Press, 1991), 85–90. Algiers is discussed in Çelik, *Urban Forms and Colonial Confrontation*, 25–6.

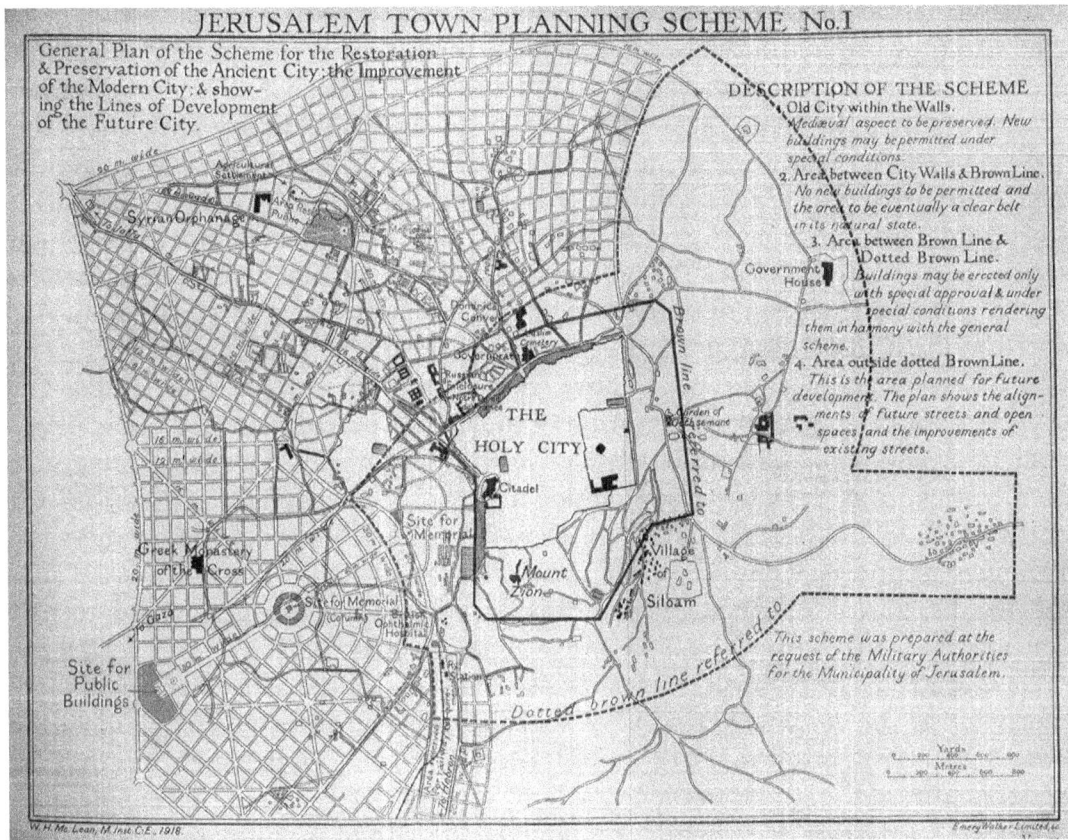

Figure 1.2 *William McLean, Jerusalem Town Planning Scheme No. I, 1918.* © National Archives, Great Britain, CO1047/773.

characterised by similar verbal modes of justification in colonial texts.⁴³ Despite this similarity, the objective of protecting Jerusalem's multireligious facilities prescribed that segregation of the population was not to be imposed, thus setting it apart from many British and French colonial cities.⁴⁴

Early Initiatives: The Plans of William McLean and Patrick Geddes

Jerusalem 1918–1920 presented the first two comprehensive plans for developing the city, which were commissioned consecutively from William Hannah McLean and Patrick Geddes, which informed the basis for subsequent schemes. McLean, who was an engineer, formulated the first British plan for Jerusalem in 1918 (Figure 1.2). His impact on the early stages of the plans for Jerusalem was

---

⁴³ See Wright, *The Politics of Design in French Colonial Urbanism*, 89–90, 117–18; Çelik, *Urban Forms and Colonial Confrontations*, 40–2.
⁴⁴ Anthony J. Christopher, 'Urban Segregation Levels in the British Overseas Empire and its Successors in the Twentieth Century', *Transactions of the Institute of British Geographers* (1992): 95–107.

acknowledged nearly two decades later when, in 1937, he was asked to submit a report to the high commissioner in Palestine, Sir Arthur Wauchope. In this report, McLean addressed the city's actual development in relation to the plans that had been devised for it.[45] McLean's 1918 plan encircled the Old City with two belts: one (indicated by a brown line in Figure 1.2) designated an area, where, in accordance with Storr's regulations, 'no new buildings [were] to be permitted'. In the legend, McLean specified that this area was to be left 'in its natural state'.[46] The second belt, located between the brown line and a dotted one, indicated an area for special planning, where building would be allowed with special permission. As I noted in the Introduction, in his 1937 report McLean explained that buildings for which special permission was granted should harmonise with those in the Old City. Among other things, the location of the belts dictated that new urban development would take place primarily to the west and north of the Old City. Such development was envisioned to include a British Governorate complex (to the north of the Old City, near the Notre Dame de France Hospice) and, to the west, a grand axis, linking what is referred to on the map as 'public buildings' with sites for two memorials. A grid street plan was devised for the area designated for new development and, in effect, was imposed upon the city.

Having arrived from Egypt, McLean was familiar with the urban development of Cairo during the colonial period.[47] He had also planned an extension of an earlier British plan for Khartoum, the capital of Sudan, in 1912.[48] Hyman believes that the grid structure of the streets in the Jerusalem plan was derived from McLean's earlier plan for Khartoum.[49] Meanwhile, the new grand axis of monuments planned for Jerusalem may have been inspired by plans for New Delhi, the new capital of the British Raj in India.[50] The 1913 plan for that city, devised by George S. C. Swinton, John A. Brodie and Edwin L. Luytens (Figure 1.3), featured a similar central axis with Government House at one end, a plaza with a commemorative column, and other buildings and memorials along a central axis.[51] The similarities in the urban schemes for New Delhi and Jerusalem indicate that McLean's approach toward the planning of the latter was a colonial one, in that it regarded the city as a future

[45] Arthur Wauchope to McLean, 19 April 1937; Arthur Charles C. Parkinson, assistant secretary at the Colonial Office to Wauchope, 4 May 1937, *Holy Places* file *NAGB* CO 733/339/3.

[46] The edict appears as item 2 on the map's legend. See map CO 1047/773, National Archives, Great Britain.

[47] Urban transformations that took place in Cairo during the colonial era are discussed in Mohamed Sharabi, 'Stadt- und Stadtarchitektur im Nahen Osten zur Kolonialzeit: Das Beispiel Kairo', *Architectura* 15, no. 1 (1985): 47–68; Janet Abu-Lughod, *Cairo: 1001 Years of the City Victorious* (Princeton, NJ: Princeton University Press, 1971), 99–143.

[48] Hyman, 'British Planners in Palestine', 45–7.

[49] Ibid. 41–2.

[50] Hyman also noted this affinity. He also compares the grand monument axis to the one in Washington, DC. See Hyman, 'British Planners in Palestine', 82. This comparison is noteworthy as the plans for Washington, DC, apparently influenced those of New Delhi. See Robert Irving, *Indian Summer: Luytens, Baker and Imperial Delhi* (New Haven: Yale University Press, 1981), 82–4.

[51] Irving, *Indian Summer*, 73–5.

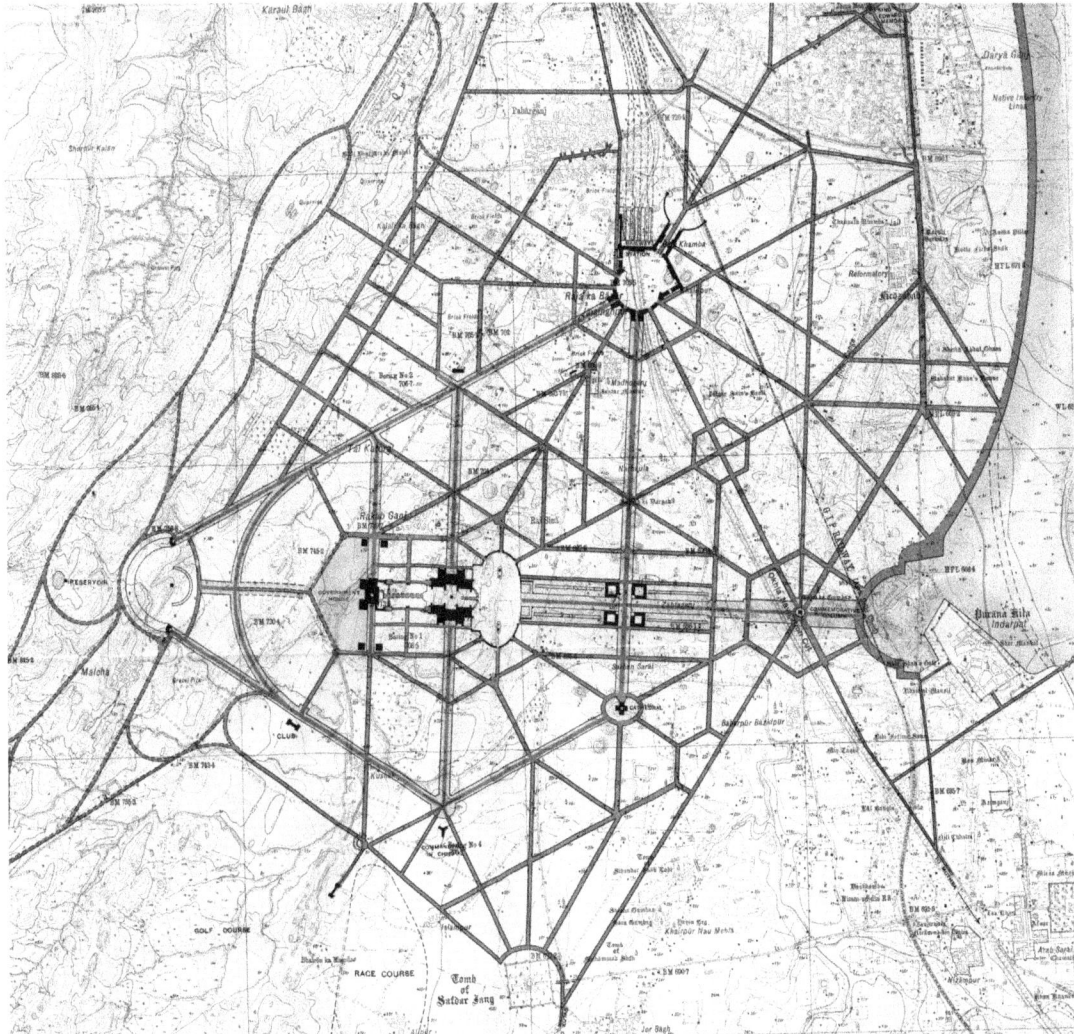

Figure 1.3 *George S. C. Swinton, John A. Brodie and Edwin L. Luytens, Urban Plan of New Delhi. Layout titled 'Accompaniment to the Final Report of the Delhi Town Planning Committee on the Town Planning of the New Imperial Capital', 20 March 1913. © British Library Board, OP-fCd.5979.*

capital in the British Empire.[52] McLean's scheme indicated both to the local population and to competing European powers that the British Empire was capable not only of plotting the course of Jerusalem's future development, but also of negotiating a new physical space for colonial architecture in the city. It would be simplistic to define British policy in the Middle East during this period as colonial, but it is important to stress that whereas World War I presented Britain with new realities in the international arena, retaining control of Palestine was one of its top

---

[52] For an analysis of the principles and layout of colonial cities using New Delhi as a case study, see King, *Colonial Urban Development*, especially chap. 10.

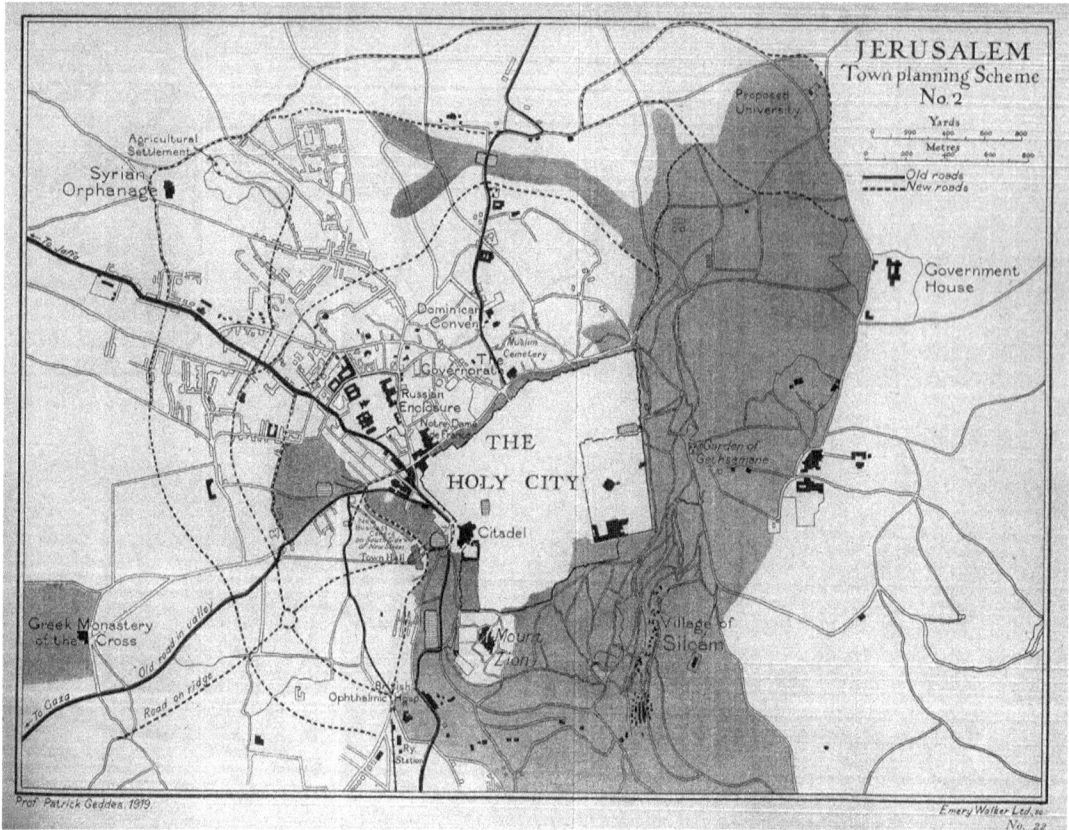

Figure 1.4 *Patrick Geddes, Jerusalem Town Planning Scheme No. 2, 1919. C. R. Ashbee, ed., Jerusalem 1918–1920: Being the Records of the Pro-Jerusalem Council during the Period of the British Military Administration (London: John Murray, 1921), no. 22.*

strategic goals.[53] McLean's far-reaching and comprehensive street plan, calling out the location of new monuments and government institutions, was certainly the reification of a policy of long-term domination.

One year after McLean presented his proposal, Sir Patrick Geddes offered another plan for the city (Figure 1.4). The famous Scottish sociologist and town planner had travelled to Palestine in 1919 to design a future Hebrew University on behalf of the Zionist Commission.[54] But Storrs also asked Geddes to comment on McLean's

[53] Britain's strategic interest lay in protecting the Suez Canal. Having control over Palestine would create a buffer between Britain's most important artery to its dominions in the east and any threat from the north. The terms of this control were delineated in post-World War I negotiations primarily between Britain and its allies, and involved Britain's top diplomats, including Prime Minister David Lloyd George, Foreign Secretary Arthur Balfour, and others. See Tuchman, *Bible and Sword*, 210–14; Adelson, *London and the Invention of the Middle East*, 136–54; Gilbert, *Jerusalem in the Twentieth Century*, 42–3.

[54] The plans for the Hebrew University conceived by Geddes in collaboration with his son-in-law, the architect Frank Mears, are discussed in Helen Meller, *Patrick Geddes: Social Evolutionist and City Planner* (London: Routledge, 1990), 263–84; Diana Dolev, 'Architectural Orientalism in the Hebrew University – the Patrick Geddes and Frank Mears Master-Plan', *Assaph* 3 (1998): 217–34;

plan, which had been exhibited in 1919 at the Royal Academy in London and had been criticised as inappropriate to the region's hilly topography.[55] Geddes had acquired experience in colonial town planning during his sojourn in India and used this experience to emphasise preservation of the Old City and preventing its overcrowding.[56] His approach to preservation also accorded with his own philosophy of 'conservative surgery' – the attempt to widen the scope of conservation from individual buildings to the entire historical city.[57] In India, this notion had led Geddes to advocate greater respect for local culture as an alternative to the typical colonial practice of planning new city quarters based on grids of streets.[58] Accordingly, whereas McLean's plan combined preservation of the Old City with a grid plan outside the walls, Geddes's design was more fluid and included a clearly defined park or greenbelt encircling the Old City, an enhancement of McLean's 'natural state' zone.[59] This greenbelt was narrow toward the west, where there was major new urban development outside the walls, but was wider in the northeast and southeast areas. Geddes's plan also emphasised the role of future beltways. These would connect new suburbs with the Old City, substituting for the rigid grid of streets favoured by McLean. In sum, what Geddes presented for the city was a modern urban scheme based on up-to-date Western town-planning ideas, but it abandoned the idea of a grand axis of monuments, so its representation of British power was understated in comparison to McLean's plan.

A City of the Mind: Charles Robert Ashbee

Charles Robert Ashbee served as Civic Adviser between 1918 and 1922, that is, during the years of the British military administration and shortly after the beginning of the Mandate. His plan for Jerusalem was presented in 1922 (Figure 1.5). Ashbee, a central figure in Britain's second-generation Arts and Crafts Movement, was summoned to Jerusalem by Storrs in the spring of 1918 and commissioned to survey the extant crafts in Jerusalem and advise on town planning.[60] To fulfil these

---

Fuchs and Herbert, 'A Colonial Portrait of Jerusalem', 98–102; Volker Welter, *Biopolis: Patrick Geddes and the City of Life* (Cambridge, MA: MIT Press, 2002), 229–39.

[55] Meller, *Patrick Geddes*, 276. This criticism is also mention by Ashbee in *Jerusalem 1918–1920*, 12, and by Kendall in *Jerusalem City Plan*, 4.

[56] Meller, *Patrick Geddes*, 276–7.

[57] Geddes's concept of conservative surgery is discussed in Pierre Clavel, 'Ebenezer Howard and Patrick Geddes: Two Approaches to City Development', in *From Garden City to Green City: The Legacy of Ebenezer Howard*, eds Kermit C. Parsons and David Schuyler (Baltimore: Johns Hopkins University Press, 2002), 53–5; Welter, *Biopolis*, 109.

[58] Welter, *Biopolis*, 116–20.

[59] The idea of the greenbelt came from Ebenezer Howard's concepts and was promoted by leading British planner-architect Raymond Unwin, who had collaborated with Geddes on a plan for a suburb of Dublin in 1914. See Robert Freestone, 'Greenbelts in City and Regional Planning' and Mervyn Miller, 'The Origins of the Garden City Neighborhood', both in *From Garden City to Green City*, 73–4, 120.

[60] For a biography of Ashbee, see Alan Crawford's landmark work, *C. R. Ashbee: Architect, Designer and Romantic Socialist* (New Haven: Yale University Press, 1985).

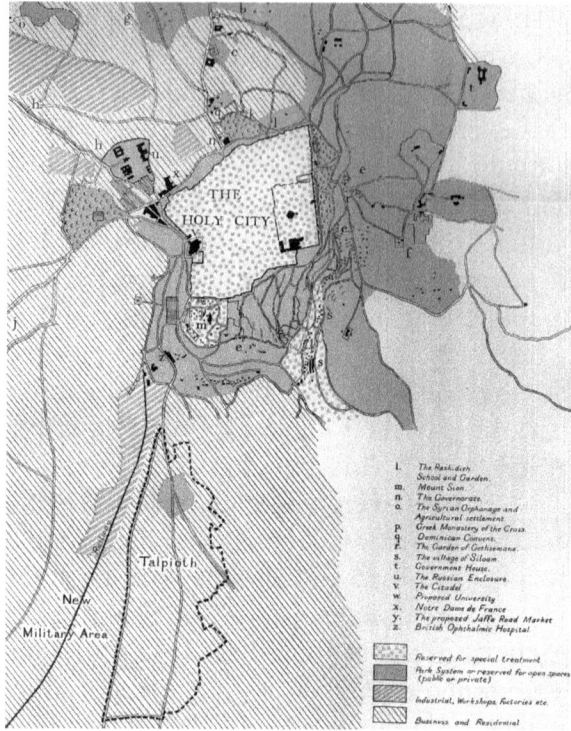

Figure 1.5 *Charles Robert Ashbee, Jerusalem: zoning plan, 1922.* C. R. Ashbee, ed., Jerusalem 1920–1922: Being the Records of the Pro-Jerusalem Council during the First Two Years of the Civil Administration (London: John Murray, 1924), no. 35. Excerpt from legend: a) dotted area: 'Reserved for special treatment'. b) grey: 'Park System or … open spaces'. c): thick slanted lines: 'Industrial, workshops, factories'. d) thin slanted lines: 'Business and residential'.

duties, he held the post of Civic Adviser of Jerusalem until 1922, serving as well as the secretary and chief coordinator of the Pro-Jerusalem Society.

Ashbee regarded Jerusalem as a 'city of the mind', by which he meant a spiritual place, a place dedicated to culture and religion. Initially, Ashbee shared the optimism of many of his fellow countrymen that Palestine could become a binational Jewish–Arab entity under British guidance. However, as many other British administrators, he later became disillusioned as the Arab–Zionist conflict escalated.

Although Ashbee ardently carried out his mission, he also had a rare gift of sensitivity and was able to see how the indigenous population perceived the British presence. For example, writing about the transition from Ottoman to British rule, he observed, 'They did not risk their lives to change masters.'[61] Ashbee was also anti-imperialist, and in *A Palestine Notebook*, he advocated the notion of commonwealth over empire.[62] Thus, unlike Storrs and Kendall, Ashbee questioned the basic assumptions of the Mandate and was fully aware of the complicated political situation and the national aspirations of both Jews and Palestinian Arabs. In his memoir, he also commented on the weakness of the British administration in Palestine, noting that this weakness was a result of the unjust nature of the British presence and its support for Jewish colonisation, a policy he opposed:

---

[61] Ashbee, *A Palestine Notebook*, 205.
[62] This is evident, e.g., when he discusses the Egyptian Nationalist Manifesto of 1919 as a model for Palestine. See Ashbee, *A Palestine Notebook*, 182–3.

> The Administration is in one of its recurrent states of nervous collapse. That is to say, being an essentially timid Administration, with an uneasy Protestant conscience, it is arming itself cap-a-pie and shaking as to its knees: route marches, demonstrations in the streets, displays of Indian soldiery, armoured cars, and all for the sake of the Mandate and this unhappy 'Wa'd Balfour' which we should be so much better without ... You cannot govern well or wisely except by consent.[63]

Ashbee's criticism of the British presence in Palestine was not unique. Ambivalence about the necessity of the Mandate ran through British thinking of the period. Written in 1938, *The Colonial Problem*, for example, referred to 'the common assumption that the mandates were veiled protectorates destined to indefinite duration'.[64] Historical research has often reinforced this 'common assumption', and the mandate system itself has often been seen as a refinement of imperialistic doctrine to meet the needs of the time.[65] However, the mandate system, subject to oversight by the League of Nations and emphasising the eventual institution of self-government in the 'entrusted' territories, introduced new expectations, created different perceptions of foreign policy, and produced entities that diverged from colonial practices.[66] During the mandate system's formative years, British foreign policy also underwent rapid yet profound changes. In the post-World War I years, growing nationalism and assertion of the right to self-determination by indigenous populations in many colonised or occupied territories brought about a re-examination of issues pertaining to the whole of Britain's overseas empire. In the case of Palestine, which was indeed conceived of as a 'veiled protectorate', these changes led to criticism of the burdensome temporary rule almost as soon as it had begun.[67] Prime Minister David Lloyd George, for example, was most interested in keeping Palestine in British hands, but there were others, such as Maurice Hankey, who favoured an American trusteeship.[68] Winston Churchill was also critical. In 1920 he wrote: 'Palestine is costing us 6 million a year to hold. The Zionist movement will cause continued friction with the Arabs ... The Palestine venture ... will never yield any profit of a material kind.'[69] The cost of an enduring British presence in the Middle East did much to sway public opinion in Britain.[70] Ashbee's opposition to the Mandate in *A Palestine Notebook* shows how these dilemmas filtered through all echelons of

---

[63] Ashbee, *A Palestine Notebook*, 206. Written 11 July 1922.
[64] *The Colonial Problem* (London: British Royal Institute of International Affairs, 1938), 249.
[65] Raymond F. Betts, *Uncertain Dimensions: Western Overseas Empires in the Twentieth Century* (Minneapolis: University of Minnesota Press, 1985), 48–9.
[66] F. S. Northedge, '1917–1919: The Implications for Britain', *Journal of Contemporary History* 3, no. 4 (October 1968): 202–3.
[67] Fromkin, *A Peace to End All Peace*, 361–3.
[68] Ibid. 374.
[69] Ibid. 448.
[70] Ibid. 499–501, 556. See also Gilbert, *Jerusalem in the Twentieth Century*, 94–5.

the British administration. Nevertheless, he did not allow his personal opinions or political ideals to enter into the books he edited for the Pro-Jerusalem Society. Rather, he emphasised the need for Western guidance in the specific field of town planning, seeing it as his mission to advise and direct the local population. However, he did this in an often condescending manner, in contrast to the more egalitarian tone of his memoir.

Like his friend Geddes, Ashbee regarded town planning as an art that embraced all aspects of the physical and cultural space of living. He formulated this conception in his book, *Where the Great City Stands*, published 1917,[71] which included a theory of modern town planning based on the ideals of the Arts and Crafts, the Garden City, and the City Beautiful movements, along with other examples of modern town planning that he had seen in the United States.[72]

Ashbee was enthusiastic about the prospect of implementing those ideals in Jerusalem and, as I noted above, these were included in his Jerusalem volumes. His meticulously developed plan for the city appeared in the second volume, entitled *Jerusalem 1920–1922*, where he presented schemes for the development of the entire city as well as programmes for individual neighbourhoods or sections.[73] Ashbee introduced the novel aspect of a 'zoning system', which had been absent from his predecessors' plans (Figure 1.5). Most likely based on the 1916 zoning scheme for New York City,[74] which he discussed in *Where the Great City Stands*, Jerusalem was to be divided into functional areas of residence, industry and business.[75]

Ashbee proposed several zones in the Jerusalem plan. A dotted area in Figure 1.5, referred to in the legend as 'reserved for special treatment', marks the Old City and the Valley of Siloam to the south. A red area to the east of the Old City and surrounding it marks 'the Jerusalem Park System'. Industrial zones are indicated by slanted lines on a red background, whereas business and residential zones appear as thin slanted lines on a white background. A space to the south is marked as a 'new military area'.

Like the two plans that preceded it, Ashbee's proposal called for future development of the city to take place toward the west and north of the Old City, but he also envisioned expansion toward the south. In general, his scheme also suggested an ambitious project for modernising Jerusalem, which included new roads, new

---

[71] Charles Robert Ashbee, *Where the Great City Stands: A Study in New Civics* (London: Essex House Press, 1917).

[72] For a detailed discussion, see Noah Hysler-Rubin, 'Arts & Crafts and the Great City', *Planning Perspectives* 21, no. 4 (2006): 350–3.

[73] The photographs form an intriguing record of Jerusalem at the beginning of the twentieth century. Most of the photos serve to document sites designated for architectural conservation or renovation. They are coupled with sketches that Ashbee made suggesting how to implement these projects.

[74] Ashbee, *Jerusalem 1920–1922*, 61–3. For the development of the New York City zoning scheme, see Anthony Sutcliffe, *Towards the Planned City: Germany, Britain, the United States and France 1780–1914* (New York: St Martin's Press, 1981), 116–21.

[75] Ashbee discusses his zoning principles in *Where the Great City Stands*, 59–67.

water and energy supply systems, museums, galleries, centres for performing arts, schools, and more.

However, Ashbee's plan for the modern city was most remarkable for what was missing: the historical division of the Old City and existing areas outside its walls into quarters or neighbourhoods representing the three major religions and their many subcultures. Ashbee's zones created the illusion (or perhaps the optimistic prediction) that these quarters would eventually blend into a homogeneous residential fabric. Thus, in effect, his plan was an embodiment of political policies during the Mandate's early years, which attempted to merge the different sections of the city.[76] This ideology proscribed segregation according to religion in urban planning and encouraged spatial flexibility. The shift from Ottoman to British regulations in connection with land ownership further complicated the planning process.[77] The changeover proved to have extremely complex ramifications, which were exacerbated by the fact that land ownership was a frequent cause of conflict between Jews and Palestinians.[78] In view of these complications, confirming the presence of religious or sectarian boundaries on the maps would reify them, and thus might impede British attempts to resolve them.

As already noted, one of the salient characteristics of colonial cities – often seen, for example, in British colonial India and French colonial North Africa – was the physical separation of the indigenous population from the ruling colonial elite.[79] Among other factors, this segregation led to the creation of 'dual cities', which were divided into 'native' and 'European' quarters.[80] Ashbee's 1922 plan is notable in its divergence from colonial planning in this regard. The presence of a foreign regime is indicated by the military zone in the southern part of the new city, but Ashbee did not refer to it in the text accompanying the map (the presence of military force was conspicuously absent from the earlier plans by McLean, Geddes, and by Ashbee himself). More importantly, the map does not designate a British or European quarter. Rather, the British presence is understated, intentionally

---

[76] For this policy, see Porath and Shavit, eds, *HaHistoryia shel Eretz Israel*, 28–9; Storrs, *Orientations*, 364–5.

[77] British land ownership policies in Palestine are discussed by Kark and Oren-Nordheim, *Jerusalem and its Environs*, 167, 178, 259–76, 299–300; Martin Bunton, '"Progressive Civilizations and Deep-Rooted Traditions": Land Laws, Development, and British Rule in Palestine in the 1920s', in *Colonialism and the Modern World: Selected Studies*, eds Gregory Blue, Martin Bunton and Ralph Croizier (Armonk and London: M. E. Sharpe, 2002), 145–63.

[78] Rashid Khalidi, *Palestinian Identity: The Construction of Modern National Consciousness* (New York: Columbia University Press, 1997), 114–17; Porath and Shavit, eds, *HaHistoryia shel Eretz Israel*, 103–6; Shafir, *Land, Labor, and the Origins of the Israeli-Palestinian Conflict*, 18–21, 41–4.

[79] Anthony D. King, 'Colonial Cities: Global Pivots of Change', in *Colonial Cities*, eds Robert Ross and Gerard J. Telkamp (Dordrecht: Martinus Nijhoff, 1985), 22–3; Anthony D. King, 'Exporting Planning: The Colonial and Neo-colonial Experience', in *Shaping an Urban World*, ed. Gordon E. Cherry (London: Mansell, 1980), 212–13. For case-specific discussions, see Janet Abu-Lughod, *Rabat: Urban Apartheid in Morocco* (Princeton, NJ: Princeton University Press, 1980), especially chapters 7–8; Çclik, *Urban Forms and Colonial Confrontations*, 26–7, 35–9; Irving, *Indian Summer*, 75–6; Wright, *The Politics of Design in French Colonial Urbanism*, 145–9.

[80] King, 'Colonial Cities', 25–6.

diffused within the urban fabric – although, in reality, the British did tend to concentrate in the German Colony, which, as I noted in the Introduction, was established in the nineteenth century by German Templars.[81] Ashbee's 'industrial zone' does not refer to the development of modern industry, but to the revival of traditional crafts practised in Jerusalem.[82] In accordance with Western town planning methods, Ashbee wished to transfer most of these from the Old City and its environs to this new industrial zone.

There were other differences between Ashbee's plan and typical colonial precedents. The greenbelt, or park system, surrounding the Old City of Jerusalem was not intended to serve as a *cordon sanitaire* or esplanade, which in colonial cities augmented the separation between the 'European' and 'native' quarters.[83] In India, cities such as Allahabad and New Delhi incorporated these greenbelts into their segregating schemes for reasons of hygiene and security.[84] In Morocco, plans that projected greenbelts around old cities in the major urban centres were justified not only by reasons of hygiene and security, but to 'preserve' indigenous culture.[85] In Ashbee's scheme, the park system was intended to provide Jerusalem's new modern spaces with open areas, or 'lungs'. But as originally suggested by Geddes, a park system would also frame the Old City and preserve it from the damaging effects of new development.

The park system's largest area was set out east of the Old City in a way that integrated and thus preserved ancient Jewish and Muslim cemeteries in the foothills of the Mount of Olives. In general, Ashbee designated the area around the walls as a public space where one could enjoy the city's 'romantic beauty and grandeur'.[86] He planned the park system down to its smallest details in order to arouse emotional and religious sentiment.[87] With the park encircling it, the Old City was symbolically set in the centre of future modern Jerusalem. Modernisation of the Old City was thus all but prohibited so as to preserve the past and cultivate a picturesque mosaic of religious places of worship, Middle Eastern architecture, and ancient archaeological sites.[88]

In this sense, the park system conformed to the colonial idea of assisting

---

[81] Kark and Oren-Nordheim, *Jerusalem and its Environs*, 167, 212. Ashbee, e.g., chose to live in the Arab village of Wadi Joz, to the north of the Old City. See Ashbee, *A Palestine Notebook*, 208.

[82] Ashbee, ed., *Jerusalem 1918–1920*, 30–4. Ashbee's concepts regarding industry in Jerusalem are discussed in Inbal Ben-Asher Gitler, 'C. R. Ashbee's Jerusalem Years: Arts & Crafts, Orientalism and British Regionalism', *Assaph* 5 (2000): 29–36; Fuchs and Herbert, 'A Colonial Portrait of Jerusalem', 88. A similar approach to 'industrial' development was shared by the French in colonial Morocco. See Wright, *The Politics of Design in French Colonial Urbanism*, 112–13.

[83] The use of the greenbelt as a means of segregation in the colonial city is discussed in King, 'Colonial Cities', 24–6; King, *Colonial Urban Development*, 39–40.

[84] Metcalf, *Ideologies of the Raj*, 180–1; King, *Colonial Urban Development*, 88, 271.

[85] Abu-Lughod, *Rabat: Urban Apartheid in Morocco*, 142–7.

[86] Ashbee, ed., *Jerusalem 1918–1920*, 21.

[87] Ben-Asher Gitler, 'C. R. Ashbee's Jerusalem Years', 36–41.

[88] The long-term adverse effects that halting urban development had on the Old City are discussed in Eli Schiller, 'Ha'Yir Ha'Atika KaYom', *Ariel* 57–8 (1988): 70–92 (special issue titled *Yerushalayim: Ha'Yir Ha'Atika*, eds Eli Schiller and Gideon Biger).

preservation – although in this case the need for preservation was defined more in historical and religious terms. That is not to say that Ashbee did not take an interest in conserving social and cultural forms, as can be seen in his concern for traditional crafts.[89] But that aspect was minimised in annotations to his urban schemes. Moreover, he was fully aware of Jerusalem's cultural diversity. Indeed, his views in this regard might best be compared to those of Geddes, who approached the subject of cultural preservation in India based on an awareness of the complexities of the indigenous cultures themselves.[90] Nevertheless, this awareness did not surface in Ashbee's spatial schemes for Jerusalem. This obfuscation of diversity becomes even more evident when one observes the differences between Ashbee's plan and a typical example of colonial city planning, as in a British proposal for Kampala, Uganda, dated 1919 (Figure 1.6).[91] The zoning plan for the capital of Uganda, which became a British protectorate in 1888, is discussed in Henry Kendall's book *Town Planning in Uganda*.[92] Kampala had initially developed as a dual city, Kampala-Mengo, with Europeans and Indians residing in Kampala and Africans in Mengo.[93] However, a major feature of the 1919 plan was the creation of a central greenbelt that would augment the separation of the European residential areas from the rest of the city. As seen in Figure 1.6, the projected European quarter is a large, diagonally shaded area in the upper part of the town, which includes the neighbourhoods of Kololo and Nakasero. Its southern boundary dictates the shape of the greenbelt (which would feature foliage and a golf course for the health and amusement of the European inhabitants of the city).[94]

In contrast, Ashbee's zoning plan for Jerusalem does not recognise any existing sociocultural divisions. Residential, commercial and industrial zones are all shown as homogeneous urban spaces, undifferentiated by cultural or ethnic characteristics, but the situation in Jerusalem rendered the imposition of such a clear separation difficult. First, the new neighbourhoods outside the ancient walls had already formed in ways that replicated the diverse cultural mosaic of the Old City. Second, centuries of multidenominational religious practices deriving from

[89] For a discussion of this aspect of Ashbee's work, see Hysler-Rubin, 'Arts & Crafts and the Great City', 347–68; Ben-Asher Gitler, 'C. R. Ashbee's Jerusalem Years', 29–52.
[90] Welter, *Biopolis*, 116–20.
[91] Interestingly enough, in 1903 the British offered Uganda to the Zionist leader Theodore Herzl as a land where a national home for the Jewish people could be established. This offer, unacceptable to the majority of members of the World Zionist Congress, who envisioned a return to the land of the Bible, died with Herzl in 1904. See Fromkin, *A Peace to End All Peace*, 272–4.
[92] Henry Kendall, *Town Planning in Uganda: A Brief Description of the Efforts Made by Government to Control Development of Urban Areas from 1915 to 1955* (London: The Crown Agents, 1955), facing 21. Kendall became director of town planning for Uganda sometime after his Palestine commission terminated with the end of the British Mandate in 1948.
[93] For a detailed discussion, see Ben-Asher Gitler, 'Marrying Modern Progress with Treasured Antiquity', 46; Fredrick Omolo-Okalebo *et al.*, 'Planning of Kampala City, 1906–1962: The Planning Ideas, Values, and Their Physical Expression', *Journal of Planning History* 9, no. 3 (2010): 151–69.
[94] Kendall, *Town Planning in Uganda*, 21.

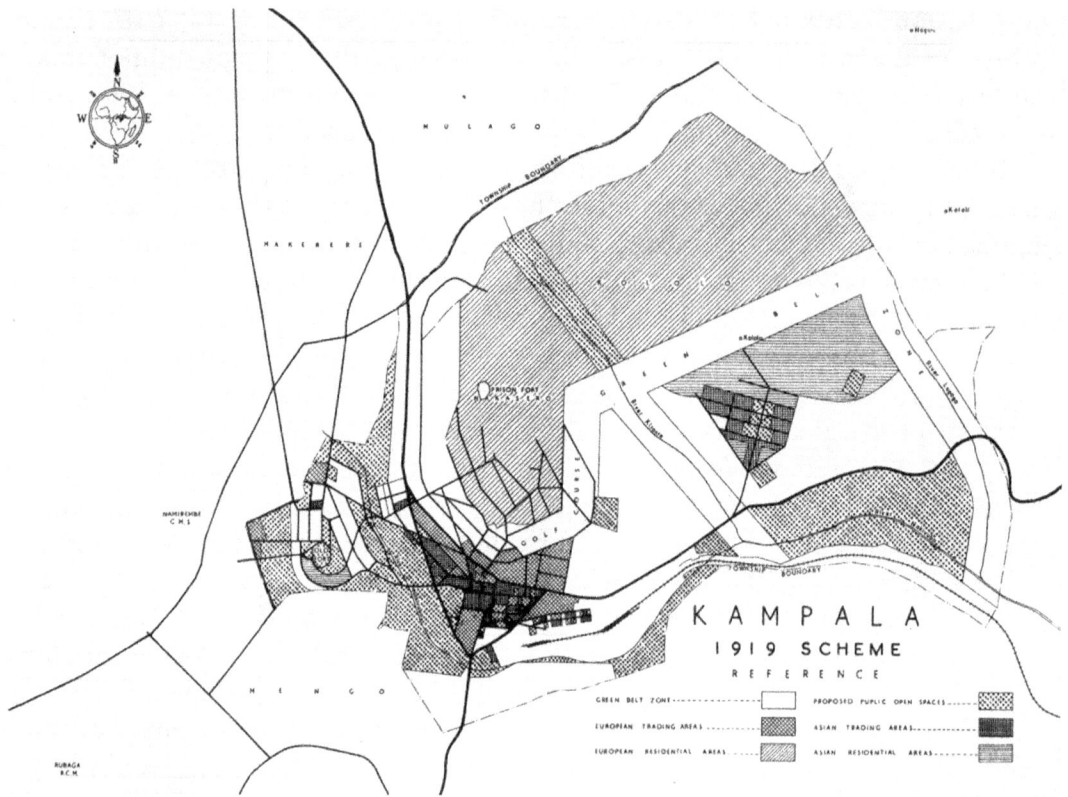

Figure 1.6 *Kampala 1919 Scheme.* H. Kendall, Town Planning in Uganda: A Brief Description of the Efforts Made by Government to Control the Development of Urban Areas from 1915 to 1955 (London: The Crown Agents, 1955), facing p. 21.

different places of origin, including Europe, had created a population that largely defied the definitions of 'indigenous' or 'nonindigenous'/'European'.

Among other things, this meant that any greenbelt or park system around the Old City would have to be a porous rather than a segregated strip. It should be noted here that Jerusalem was not unique in having pre-existing patterns of ethnic and religious separations. Various colonial cities in Asia and Africa evinced forms of cultural and social segregation prior to the arrival of Europeans. In each case, the colonial powers simply imposed a new level of separation on top of the one that already existed.[95] But the situation in Mandate-era Jerusalem differed from these cities in two respects. First, urban tensions and confrontations between Arabs and Jews resulted in spatial dilemmas, which the planners chose to ignore. Second, the planners decided not to impose a colonial dual city form of segregation on the existing arrangement of spaces.

In *Jerusalem 1920–1922*, Ashbee featured only one plan for a residential neighbourhood – a proposal for a modern Jewish 'garden suburb' designed by

---

[95] King, 'Colonial Cities', 22.

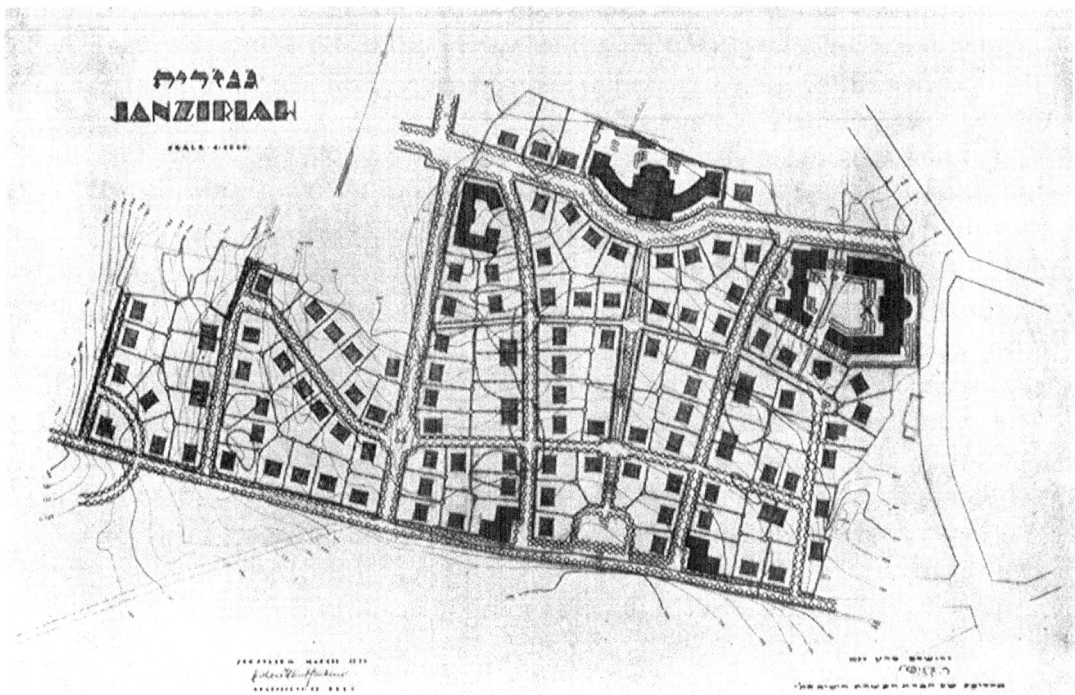

Janjirieh Garden City. Block plan. No. 65.

Figure 1.7 Richard Kaufmann, Plan for Janjirieh Garden City [Rehavia]. C. R. Ashbee, ed., Jerusalem 1920–1922: Being the Records of the Pro-Jerusalem Council during the First Two Years of the Civil Administration *(London: John Murray, 1924), no. 65.*

Zionist architect and town planner Richard Kauffmann (Figure 1.7).[96] The neighbourhood, laid out according to Garden City principles, which was later given the Hebrew name Rehavia and was selected as the site of the Zionist Executive Buildings, is discussed in detail in Chapter Five.[97] Curiously, Ashbee chose not to refer to it as a Jewish neighbourhood and only mentioned it by its traditional Arabic name, Janjirieh Garden City (spelled Janziriah on the plan itself), thus refraining once again from reference to sectarian divisions. Like other Garden City neighbourhoods of the time, it had houses surrounded by gardens whose proximity to the street varied so as to avoid the appearance of excessive symmetry. Streets were generally laid out in relation to a main boulevard that traversed the

[96] Richard Kauffmann planned most of the first modern Jewish garden suburbs in Jerusalem, such as Talpioth, Be'it-HaKerem, and Ba'yit VaGan. He was influenced primarily by the modern urban planning of his native Germany but was also well aware of the British Garden City Movement. See Epstein-Pliouchtch and Levin, eds, *Richard Kaufmann*, 96–8; Kroyanker, *Adrichalut Bi'Yerushalayim: HaBeny'ia BeTkufat HaMandat HaBriti*, 248–84; Kark and Oren-Nordheim, *Jerusalem and its Environs*, 169; Richard Kauffmann, 'Talpioth, Erlaeuterungsbericht zum Bebauungsplan', CZA, Jerusalem, L18/78/4,1, n.d.

[97] The principles of the Garden City Neighborhood are discussed in Miller, 'The Origins of the Garden City Neighborhood', 99–130.

neighbourhood, but a strict grid was avoided, and a separate system of footpaths was provided to facilitate pedestrian movement.

It is further noteworthy that Ashbee never referred on his maps or in his book to the relationship between neighbourhood planning and local housing traditions. During the nineteenth and early twentieth centuries, traditional residential structures in Jerusalem were largely of the Palestinian Arab *hosh*, or courtyard-type house and its Jewish counterpart, the *chatzer* (court) – both based on similar principles.[98] But Ashbee never referred to the close-knit urban fabric that was created by these apartments, nor to the family nuclei around which these houses evolved. Nor did he mention extant early twentieth-century neighbourhoods in which dwellings had evolved beyond the traditional types. Nor did he elaborate on which Jewish, Christian or Muslim sects would reside in the proposed new Garden-City neighbourhoods. Nevertheless, by incorporating Janjirieh Garden City into his book, Ashbee probably intended to show how a Jerusalem neighbourhood could be representative of modern town planning. Further, as an advocate for Garden City ideas, he was probably also advocating such a model for the many neighbourhoods of private dwellings constructed during the first decade of the British Mandate by Jews, Christian and Muslim Palestinians.[99]

Clifford Holliday's Statutory Plan

Albert Clifford Holliday served as Town Planning Adviser to the city of Jerusalem between 1922 and 1928/1929 and was Adviser to the Central Town Planning Commission from 1927 until 1935. He was also a practising architect in Palestine; his notable extant buildings in Jerusalem include a wing of the St John's Ophthalmic Hospital (1922–30), St Andrew's Church (1927–30), the Bible Society Building (1926–8), and the Mandate-era Jerusalem City Hall (1930–4); the latter two were built in association with Zionist architect Zoltán Shimshon Harmat.[100] Holliday devised plans for Haifa as well as other cities in Palestine. Although little has survived of his town plan for Jerusalem (Figure 1.8), it was important because, as the first statutory plan, it was the model for all subsequent Mandate-era parcellation and building plans. Furthermore, it was implemented during years when building in Jerusalem peeked, roughly between 1925 and 1935.[101]

[98] For the Jewish residential building types, see Kark and Oren-Nordheim, *Jerusalem and its Environs*, 137–40; Ben-Arieh, *Yir BeRe'yi Tkufa*, 248–53, 257, 273–8; for the Palestinian type, see Ron Fuchs, 'The Palestinian Arab House and the Islamic Primitive Hut', *Muqarnas* 15 (1998): 157–77; Ruth Kark and Shimon Landman, 'HaYetsi'a HaMuslemit MiChutz LaChomot BeShalhey HaTkufa Ha'Ottomanit', in *Prakim Betoldot Yerushalayim Bazman Hachadash*, ed. Eli Shealtiel (Jerusalem: Yad Ben-Zvi and Israel Ministry of Defense, 1981), 194–207.

[99] The various approaches to planning of the different sections' neighbourhoods are discussed in Kark and Oren-Nordheim, *Jerusalem and its Environs*, 138–88.

[100] David Kroyanker, *Adrichal Z. S. Harmat: Shishim Shnot Yetsira* (Jerusalem: HaMoreshet HaBnuya, Center for Social Policies in Israel, 1990), 10–12; Kroyanker, *Adrichalut Bi'Yerushalayim: HaBni'ya BiTkufat HaMandat HaBriti*, 123, 168.

[101] Hyman, 'British Planners in Palestine', 460.

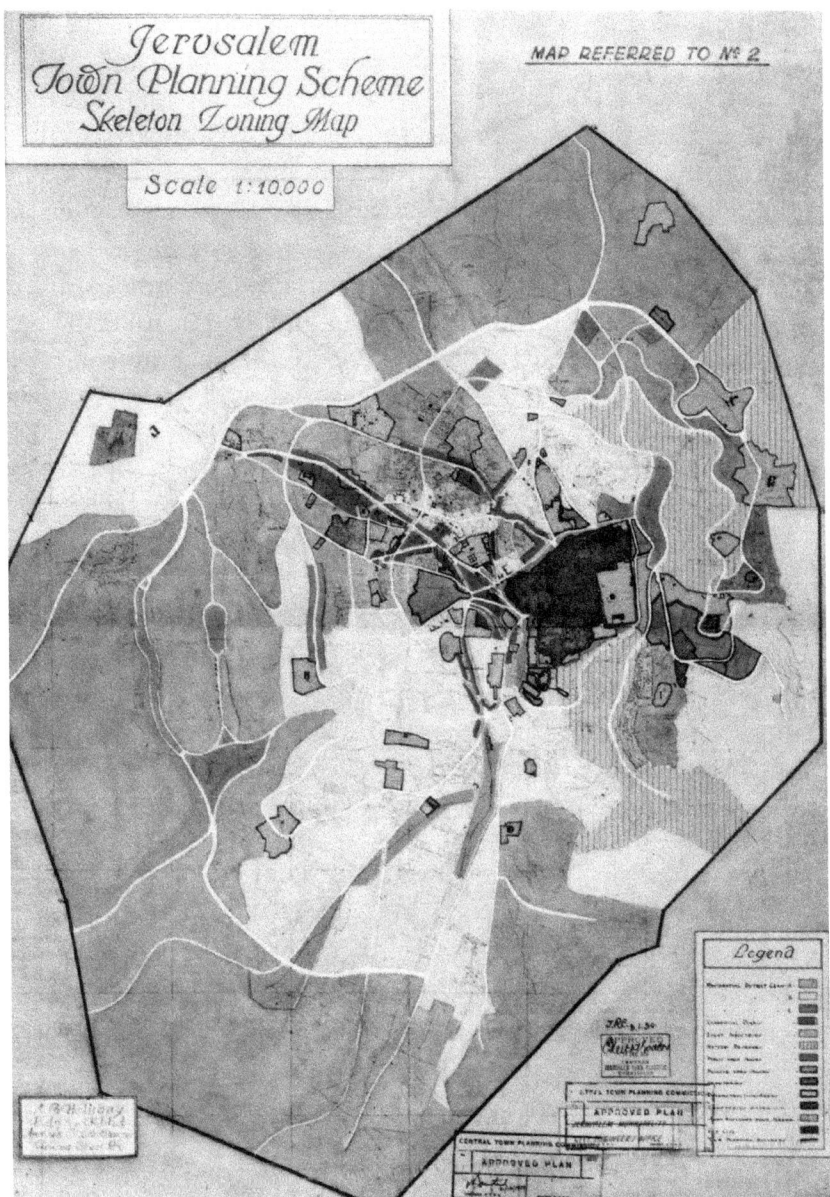

Figure 1.8 *Clifford Holiday, Jerusalem Town Planning Scheme, 1930. Wiki Commons, https://commons.wikimedia.org/wiki/File:Clifford_Holliday_plan_for_Jerusalem_1930.jpg, retrieved 1 January 2020.*

Holliday set out to improve upon his predecessors' plans, and unlike McLean, Geddes and Ashbee, his professional method included conducting a large-scale civic survey, which included collecting and analysing facts regarding the extant physical environment. Holliday only submitted his scheme in 1926, four years after his arrival.[102] Another way that Holliday's design differed from earlier ones

[102] Ibid. 437–8.

was that it included a firmer demand to demolish what he perceived as slums or unfit dwellings. He, too, adopted a condescending approach toward many of Jerusalem's existing neighbourhoods. Hyman notes as an example that Holliday was vehemently opposed to the Jewish neighbourhoods constructed outside the Old City walls during the nineteenth century (an opinion also voiced by Geddes): 'No city of the future will tolerate such filthy and unsanitary homes for a greater part of its population,' wrote Holliday.[103]

Although Holliday criticised his predecessors, there were more similarities than differences between his plan and those of Geddes and Ashbee. In the scheme shown here (Figure 1.8), published in 1930, which differed in several aspects as a result of his expansion of the city's area, Holliday proposed the following zones: roads, housing, industrial, commercial, open spaces, nature reserves, and public building sites. He allocated housing primarily west and north of the Old City as in previous plans; he developed a road system that included beltways, as had Geddes, and retained the industrial zone to the south, as Ashbee had done. Although he agreed that Jerusalem should have mostly light industry, he nonetheless mentioned that the inclusion of some heavy industries should be allowed.[104] Furthermore, he continued to place emphasis upon the city's park system. Although, as noted above, only parts of these plans have survived, textual material suggests that his scheme for urban green zones overall was more detailed. The key feature of Holliday's park system was to surround the Old City with a greenbelt, thus clearly following previous proposals. Acknowledging, as did his predecessors, the immense significance of historic and religious sites, Holliday provided a more precise definition of archaeological zones within the greenbelt and the park system, so as to give more authority and control to the Department of Antiquities, whose major role in Palestine's archaeological research is discussed in Chapter Two.[105]

As with previous schemes, consideration of the sociocultural makeup of the city was glaringly absent from Holliday's plan, which is perhaps even more surprising than Ashbee's ignorance of this aspect, taking into account Holliday's commitment to conducting a civic survey. As Ashbee before him, Holliday refrained from attributing any sectarian identity to his housing zones, and they differed from each other only in the size of their dwellings. Holliday's plan for Jerusalem thus exhibited an approach similar especially to Ashbee's, which delineated modern development combined with profound historical and religious awareness. Just as the plans drawn up by McLean, Geddes and Ashbee largely dismissed the cultural urban fabric of Jerusalem, Holliday's schemes also ignored the sectionalisation that determined much of the city's development.

---

[103] Ibid. 451.
[104] Ibid. 452. This zoning map was reproduced in ibid. 442, fig. 5.3.
[105] Ibid. 456–8, 462–6.

Commemoration: Henry Kendall

Henry Kendall was named the Government Town Planner for Palestine in 1935 and served in that office until 1948. I discuss his urban schemes here as they appeared in his book *Jerusalem: The City Plan. Preservation and Development during the British Mandate 1918–1948*. As previously noted, in addition to his own contribution, Kendall's book also includes a summary of Jerusalem's urban development during the thirty years of the British Mandate in Palestine. Further, a large and lavishly illustrated section is devoted to describing the Old City, its history, and British preservation and restoration projects. Finally, the book includes photographs of the official British buildings constructed in Jerusalem during the Mandate.[106] Clearly, the purpose of publishing this volume on the eve of British withdrawal from Palestine was to bequeath an official record of Britain's central role in preserving and developing Jerusalem to posterity. Indeed, the last High Commissioner for Palestine, Sir Alan Gordon Cunningham, presented this volume as a commemoration 'of the efforts made to conserve the old while adding the new in keeping with it, of the process of marrying modern progress with treasured antiquity'.[107]

The last ten years of the British Mandate were very violent times in Palestine. Both Zionist and Arab nationalism became more defined and extreme, leading to frequent and serious clashes. The British attempted to use force to restrain this violence, while also seeking diplomatic solutions to its underlying sources.[108] The progress of World War II further complicated British policies in the Middle East and in Palestine in particular. Moreover, misgivings regarding the Mandate were underscored by disputes within the British Government itself and, as time went on, it became clear that the Mandate would not become a permanent arrangement.[109]

During those years, several proposals were posited for the partition of Palestine into Jewish and Palestinian states, all of which were rejected by one or both sides. Interestingly enough, none of these partition proposals relinquished Jerusalem to either party. Even though by the end of World War II this particular 'A-type' mandate occupied more than a fair share of the energies of an exhausted empire, a third and final British proposal in 1946 still left Jerusalem in British hands.[110] This may indicate that whereas independence was intended for Palestine, the British

---

[106] The most prominent of these were built by the British architect Austen St Barb Harrison. They are discussed in Ron Fuchs, 'Austen St. Barbe Harrison – Architect Briti Be'Eretz HaKodesh' (PhD diss., Technion Haifa, 1992); Fuchs and Herbert, 'A Colonial Portrait of Jerusalem', 91–8.

[107] Kendall, *Jerusalem: The City Plan*, v.

[108] A historical account of these events is given in Nicholas Bethell, *The Palestine Triangle: The Struggle between the British, the Jews and the Arabs 1935–48* (London: Andre Deutch, 1979); Ronald W. Zweig, *Britain and Palestine during the Second World War* (Martlesham: Boydell Press, 1986).

[109] Michael Cohen, *Palestine: Retreat from the Mandate: The Making of British Policy, 1936–45* (New York: Holmes & Meier, 1978), 160–85.

[110] Porath and Shavit, eds, *HaHistoryia shel Eretz Israel*, 77–9; Bethell, *The Palestine Triangle*, 257, 269–70.

were still hoping to keep Jerusalem. The fourth partition proposal, submitted by the United Nations in 1947, proposed that Jerusalem should remain an international enclave.[111]

Although the plans and ordinances included in Kendall's book outlined a course of development for many years to come and the official British architecture it featured was anything but temporary – an example of which we shall see in the Archaeological Museum, discussed in Chapter Two – Kendall had a cautious attitude regarding the city's future:

> This publication is . . . more of an expression of the various plans and schemes that have been prepared and are in force, rather than a civic survey with recommendations for the development of a master plan. Too much has been heard in recent times of ambitious plans that have been abandoned almost as soon as they have been launched. The development of the modern town of Jerusalem is bound up with its political future, and that is a matter for the attention of the United Nations.[112]

Kendall's new city plan for Jerusalem, devised in 1944, included several schemes, some of which documented Jerusalem's layout at that time and some of which, as noted above, contained plans for future development. But Kendall's development schemes were characterised by numerous ambiguities. Among other things, they were disassociated from each other and lacked elaboration and clarification in the text. Delineated in 1944, they above all reflected the tumultuous period during which they were devised. As in Ashbee's earlier plan, this uncertainty about Jerusalem's future was embodied in Kendall's lack of method for coping with urban realities.

During the period of the British Mandate (and with the encouragement of British officials), the area outside the Old City walls had undergone a process of accelerated growth and modernisation, including massive infrastructure development. Kendall's 1944 zoning plan (Figure 1.9) shows that the greater part of the city had generally developed according to earlier directives: residences and business had been built toward the west, north and south, and the park system, which Kendall termed a 'nature reserve', had developed toward the east, although the city's rapid growth entailed a significant reduction in the dimensions of its green spaces. Similarly, as Ashbee had intended, the park system had been used to frame the Old City and protect it from new development (but not to segregate its residents from the rest of the city). Similar to Geddes's 1918 scheme (Figure 1.4), the 1944 plan also included a modern road system, with a beltway surrounding the modern city. The plan also allocated a much larger area for industry, although, like Ashbee,

---

[111] Porath and Shavit, eds, *HaHistoryia shel Eretz Israel*, 46–54, 79–84; Bethell, *The Palestine Triangle*, 30–8, 194–202, 294–7.
[112] Kendall, *Jerusalem: The City Plan*, xi.

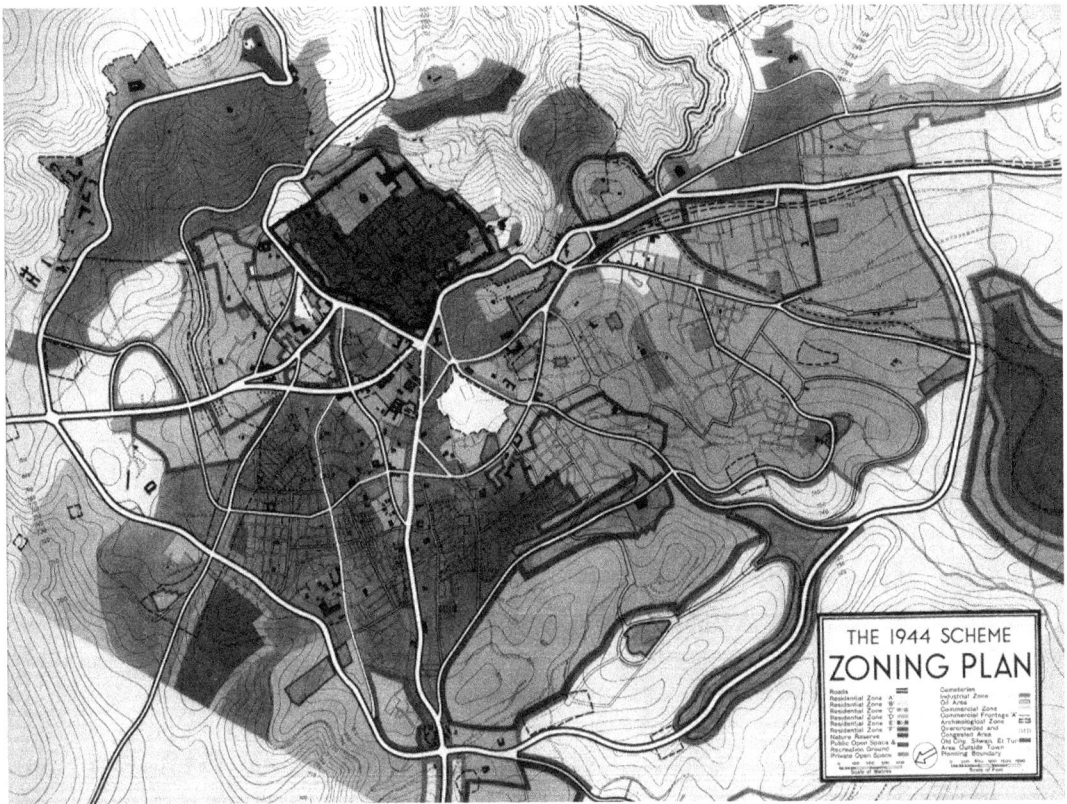

Figure 1.9 Henry Kendall, The 1944 Scheme: zoning Plan. H. Kendall, Jerusalem: The City Plan. Preservation and Development during the British Mandate 1918–1948 (London: His Majesty's Stationery Office, 1948), map facing p. 26.

Kendall commented that 'Jerusalem is unsuited for heavy industries … such a development would conflict seriously with its more important cultural and religious aspects.'[113] Despite the fact that more than twenty years had gone by since Ashbee's plan and although Holliday's proposal made some allowance for heavy industry, Kendall still stressed the city's spiritual assets, rather than its potential for commercial and industrial development.

Preservation areas, identified in the legend as 'Archaeological Zones', also appear on the 1944 zoning map (Figure 1.9). However, they are only indicated as dashed black frames, so their location is often illegible. Most of these zones are also layered over residential areas, so that it is unclear how they would be excavated or how neighbourhoods would continue to exist if excavations were to be carried out.[114]

When attempting to analyse the allocation of residential zones, the obscurities

---

[113] Ibid. 3.
[114] The existence of ancient archaeological sites within areas of urban development was a recurring phenomenon owing to Jerusalem's long history, and these sites pose a substantial challenge to urban planners and architects until the present day.

in Kendall's 1944 zoning plan are even more perplexing. The legend divides residential zones into areas A–F, a classification based on the size of individual dwellings in each zone.[115] Two ideas may be instructive here. First, as did Ashbee, Kendall proposed garden suburbs for outlying areas, although these would include modern apartment blocks and not just private villas.[116] Second, his plan, like those of Ashbee and Holliday, evidenced considerable insensitivity toward indigenous housing patterns.[117] Kendall justified severe limitations on house size owing to an account that noted that 'a house of 150 to 180 square meters in area is ample for the normal requirements of most families in Jerusalem'.[118] He dismissed the possibility of larger homes for the wealthy and ignored the fact that traditional or orthodox Arabs and Jews often had very large families. In the end, Kendall integrated such housing regulations into a town plan ordinance, which was viewed as restrictive even by Holliday who, in his 1948 review of Kendall's book, blamed him for adopting an outdated plan with 'regulatory and restrictive control of development'.[119]

In a critique of Le Corbusier's *Plan Obus* for Algiers, created during the 1930s and early 1940s, Michele Lamprakos discussed how that plan's modern housing dismissed the relationship of traditional Muslim dwellings to such suprafamilial institutions as the extended family and clan.[120] She argued that in the colonial city, planners often viewed such traditional patterns as a hindrance to the development of a capitalist economy.[121] Kendall's emphasis on modern housing, coupled with his use of dwelling size as a criterion for zoning subdivisions, was consistent with the use of income level and financial capability as the variables dictating urban planning. Indeed, his zoning plan may have been indicative of a desire to introduce modern criteria, based on the modern structures of a capitalist economy, to Jerusalem. In this sense, Kendall's plan for Jerusalem follows contemporary colonial patterns, which, by imposing a zoning system based on economics, once more ignored the city neighbourhoods' intrinsic sociocultural distribution.

This dismissal was further accentuated by the use of a confusing colour scheme. In most sections of the 1944 zoning map, it is impossible to connect the colours in the legend, which in some cases are framed or striped, and the colours of the map

---

[115] Kendall, *Jerusalem: The City Plan*, 25.
[116] Ibid. facing 44 and 50.
[117] It is noteworthy that in *Town Planning in Uganda*, Kendall does take into account certain cultural aspects of local indigenous dwellings. His zoning plan for Kampala, drawn in 1951 and apparently exhibiting a preliminary expression of decolonisation, is an intriguing comparison to the Jerusalem 1944 scheme, but is beyond the scope of this book. See Kendall, *Town Planning in Uganda*, 24 and map facing 25.
[118] Kendall, *Jerusalem: The City Plan*, 19.
[119] Clifford Holliday, 'Jerusalem City Plan by Henry Kendall (1948)', *RIBA Journal* (August 1948): 469.
[120] Michele Lamprakos, 'Le Corbusier and Algiers: The Plan Obus as Colonial Urbanism', in *Forms of Dominance*, ed. Nezar AlSayyad (Aldershot: Avebury, 1992), 198–9. Another example that can be cited is Michele Ecochard's failed attempt to provide adequately sized dwellings for Morrocans in Casablanca in 1946. See Rabinow (in same volume), 'Colonialism, Modernity', 180–1.
[121] Lamprakos, 'Le Corbusier and Algiers', 198–9.

itself. Thus, it is unclear which neighbourhoods and roads were then extant and which were being proposed for future development. Moreover, several of the residential areas appear to overlap the open-space zones. Holliday sharply criticised this graphic ambiguity in his above-cited review. It may have been, as Holliday put it, that this was the result of 'faulty reproduction',[122] but I suggest that the incoherence of the map was at least partially intentional. In the 1944 plan no 'Residential Zone' is mentioned by name, so that its division into religious and sectarian neighbourhoods was invisible. The legend does mention 'Old City', 'Silwan' and 'Et Tur', which appear next to a bluish square, but no reason is given for singling them out. Quite simply, no zoning plan that ignored the basic divisions in a city such as Jerusalem into neighbourhoods could ever convey the reality of its existing urban fabric, let alone project its future. Further, as Palestinian Arabs and Jews contested many areas of the city, Kendall may also have been attempting to avoid any political statement that could be construed as allocating territory for future development by one group or another. Another key feature of Kendall's plan was that it did not identify a 'British' or 'European' neighbourhood. The reality here was that during the last years of the Mandate – even more than in Ashbee's time – such an explicit declaration of foreign presence would only have hindered British attempts to resolve the conflict between Arabs and Jews and undercut Britain's image as a mediator not just in the eyes of the local population, but in the eyes of the world as well. The omission of the British presence from the maps also accentuated the fact that Kendall's publication was conceived as a commemoration of Britain's trusteeship, rather than a statement of continuing ownership of the city.

Despite his decision not to mark ethnic and religious divisions on the main zoning map, Kendall's book includes another map entitled 'Distribution of the Population' (Figure 1.10), which describes areas populated by Jews, Christians and Muslims, blue indicating areas of Jewish population, green for Muslim, and purple for Christian. Yet even that map does not address subdivisions by sect, nor does it indicate areas co-populated by two or more groups. Furthermore, the map's fluid blocks of colour are rendered even less legible by such additional designations as 'overcrowded areas', and 'commercial' and 'industrial' zones. Moreover, Kendall made no attempt to connect the information on the general zoning scheme (Figure 1.9) to this second map, so there is no correlation between his proposed patterns of development and the city's already extant religious spatial divisions.

Another of Kendall's maps, which describes 'Grouping of Neighbourhood Units' (Figure 1.11), was also entirely divorced from Jerusalem's reality. Clearly, this was an application of contemporary British neighbourhood planning theories, according to which cellular neighbourhoods, each containing a primary school and shops, were joined together by zoning hierarchies and roads to form a town.[123] On

---

[122] Holliday, 'Jerusalem City Plan by Henry Kendall (1948)', 469.
[123] W. Houghton-Evans, 'Schemata in British New Town Planning', in *Shaping an Urban World*, ed. Gordon E. Cherry (London: Mansell, 1980), 109–10.

Figure 1.10 *Henry Kendall, 1944 Survey: Distribution of the Population.* H. Kendall, Jerusalem: The City Plan. Preservation and Development during the British Mandate 1918–1948 *(London: His Majesty's Stationery Office, 1948), map facing p. 34.*

Kendall's map, however, biomorphic shapes in dark brown and beige representing neighbourhoods float freely among the main roads of the city. The dark brown forms indicate 'existing quarters', beige frames or halos surrounding them are their extensions, and earth brown forms suggest future neighbourhoods. True to the theoretical British model, the nucleus of each Jerusalem neighbourhood contains a school (indicated by a red dot) and shops (indicated by blue dots). However, they are devoid of such basic Middle Eastern facilities as places of worship (be they mosques, synagogues or churches) or the typical public baths – the *hamaam* and the *mikveh*. By omitting these cultural and religious signifiers, Kendall again avoided committing his neighbourhoods to one group or the other. Thus, the map in Figure 1.11 also ignores the sectarian urban neighbourhoods and creates the illusion of a unified urban space. Set among the many photographs and illustrations that filled the rest of his book, Kendall's urban plans, which were actually never realised, represent an attempt to erase the fundamental ethnic, religious and cultural characteristics of the city, in order to portray a seemingly unencumbered urban development.

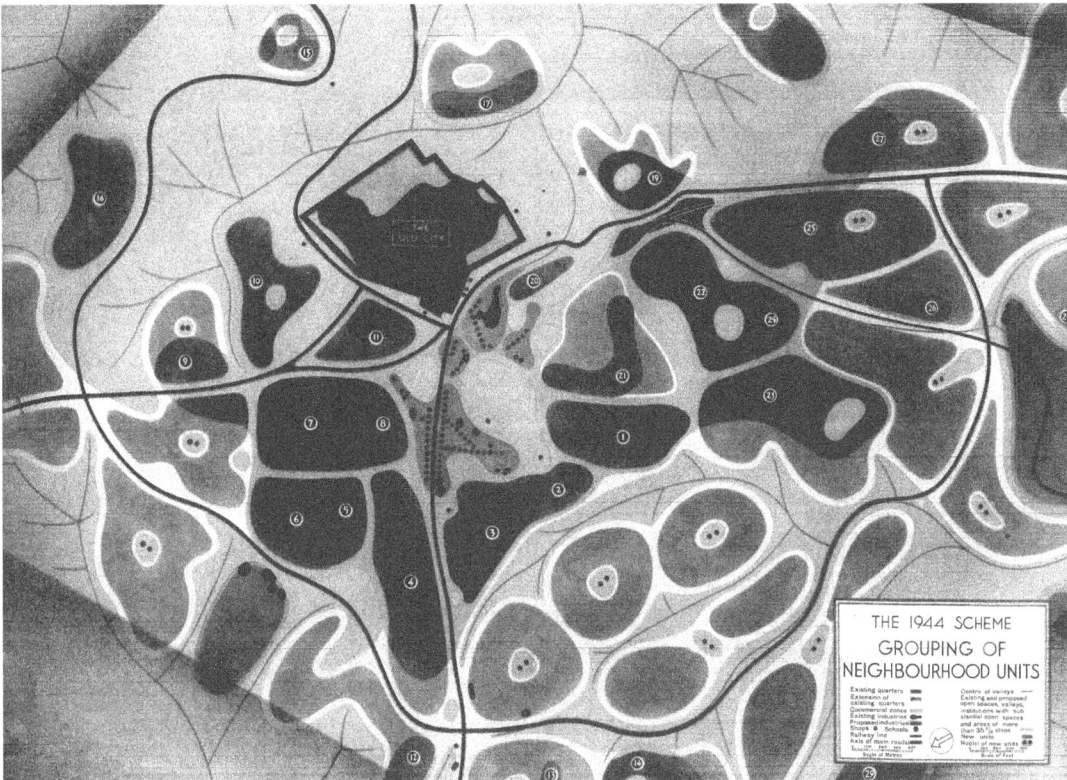

Figure 1.11 *Henry Kendall, The 1944 Scheme: Grouping of Neighbourhood Units. H. Kendall, Jerusalem: The City Plan. Preservation and Development during the British Mandate 1918–1948 (London: His Majesty's Stationery Office, 1948), map facing p. 40.*

The Image of Coexistence

The British urban plans analysed in this chapter informed Jerusalem's physical layout during the Mandate. Although many aspects of these plans only remained on paper, their impact upon ensuing developments was immense and can still be seen today. The greenbelt around the walls of the Old City still exists and has been further accentuated by landscape design and excavated archaeological sites. The city's main arteries have developed in a way similar to British plans and predictions, and sections of the zoning plan that were implemented during the Mandate have remained intact. However, the significance of these plans goes beyond delineating Jerusalem's city plan. They are important not only for the elements that they devised that were implemented, but also provide a powerful visual testimony of the policies of mandatory rule and reflect British perceptions of Jerusalem, its population, and the United Kingdom's role as a foreign power.

As Jerusalem never became the capital of a British colony, one cannot speak of an expression of colonialism or a process of decolonisation in its urban plans. However, certain characteristics of these processes can be noted, and these constituted a renegotiation of the urban space. First, colonialist attitudes dehistoricised and petrified the Old City, while attempting to erase marks of the Ottoman regime and introduce new urban policies. Indeed, preservation of the Old City was propagandised to justify British rule. One can almost hear the slogan 'nobody does it better' echoing through British Mandate-era writing. Second, it is clear that neighbourhood planning did not take local cultural practices and traditional dwellings into account. Third, planning policies for Jerusalem exhibited certain aspects of a decolonisation process inasmuch as they reflected a city that seemed to belong to its native inhabitants, who were to fulfil certain administrative functions and were encouraged to collaborate with the British authorities.

Yet, despite these similarities to colonial cities, the planning of Jerusalem differed markedly from the colonial model. We have seen that the purpose of its greenbelt was not to segregate, but to create a 'spiritual' zone; the neighbourhood divisions according to sects was ignored in all the plans; and the presence of the British as a ruling power was virtually absent, despite accompanying texts that revealed rhetorical devices common to discourses of colonial alterity.[124]

In recent postcolonial studies, colonial cities have been termed 'hybrid spaces'. Although many researchers have questioned the appropriateness of the term 'hybridity' for describing cultures or spaces,[125] Nezar AlSayyad, as well as scholars of global phenomena in the arts, have demonstrated that – despite its fluidity – the term 'hybridity' can accurately relate spatial and cultural experiences in places that are characterised by multiculturalism and where identities intersect.[126] I use the term here in keeping with AlSayyad's use of Homi Bhabha's concept of hybridity to the study of urbanism. AlSayyad argues that in mixed cities, hybridity is 'a condition of fundamental interaction among parties with concretely differing positions of power, who must nevertheless cohabit'.[127] Jerusalem had always been a hybrid space, and British interventions during the first half of the twentieth century can indeed be described as such. British 'absence' from the plans, as well as the functions allocated to the Old City and the greenbelt, certainly fit Bhabha's notion of hybridity, which he describes as an 'articulation of the ambivalent space where the rite of power is enacted on the site of desire, making its objects at once disciplinary and disseminatory – or ... a negative transparency'.[128]

Both Bhabha and AlSayyad refer largely to colonial dominions and cities, most of which had precolonial and colonial histories that engendered hybridity in differing guises. It would therefore be an oversimplification to attempt to explain the differences between Jerusalem and other colonial cities solely on the basis of

[124] For a discussion of these devices, see Ania Loomba, *Colonialism/Postcolonialism* (London: Routledge, 1998), 43–57.
[125] Katharyne Mitchell, 'Different Diasporas and the Hype of Hybridity', *Environment and Planning D: Society and Space* 15, no. 5 (1997): 533–53; James Elkins, Zhivka Valiavicharska and Alice Kim, *Art and Globalization* (University Park: Pennsylvania State University Press, 2010), 51–2.
[126] Elkins, Valiavicharska and Kim, *Art and Globalization*, 51–62.
[127] Nezar AlSayyad, ed., *Hybrid Urbanism: On the Identity Discourse and the Built Environment* (Westport: Praeger, 2001), 8.
[128] Homi K. Bhabha, *The Location of Culture* (London and New York: Routledge, 2004), 112.

the former's unique hybridity. It is instead necessary to examine the mandatory situation, which was different from the colonial one. Considering this context, one can see that the urban plans discussed here reflect an ambivalence owing to the uncertainty of the British trusteeship and a resultant vagueness regarding the future of the city. Indeed, the blurring of Jerusalem's sociocultural realities in all the plans discussed here is evidence of a persisting atmosphere of temporality and political instability, which was sometimes voiced by British officials regarding the Mandate period. In particular, the British schemes conveyed the necessity of manifesting control while at the same time acknowledging the growing right of Jews and Palestinians to assert their respective national identities. Thus, on an urban level, the schemes were shaped by the need to camouflage an emerging conflict, which evolved from the aspirations of cultures and subcultures to define their urban spaces in the same geographical zone. In an effort to maintain the image of successful urban custodianship, the planners' rhetoric avoided discussing conflicts within the city, since discussions of this nature would have adversely reflected on the Mandate's success. Rather, the texts reiterate Jerusalem's importance to the British and their willingness to maintain its guardianship. British dedication to the city was further commemorated by the emphasis given in Ashbee's and Kendall's books to those sections of the city plans that materialised during the Mandate years, such as government building projects and conservation efforts in the Old City.

Although the British presence was consistently muted in these maps, the act of prescribing new town plans was in itself a reification of political and cultural authority. By shaping the urban space for its inhabitants, British administrators created a 'cartography of hegemony'.[129] In other words, they conveyed the Mandate's supremacy through a graphic enunciation of Jerusalem's urban space. In this process, the cartography that delineated Mandate-era plans for Jerusalem constructed an illusionary space of coexistence and created the image of Britain as a neutral mediator striving for a peaceful city and a unified urban plan. The Old City was at the centre of this cartography, its historical narratives serving not as a reminder of the complexities of its multicultural space, but, rather, as a symbol of a coveted peaceful coexistence, the 'site of desire'.[130] The modern Western town plan that was imposed on the city, with its parks, highways and garden neighbourhoods, did not merely convey the message that modernity can cross social and cultural barriers, but also disguised those barriers. The modern schemes also emphasised the need for the presence of a guiding Western entity capable of their implementation. In the absence of direct colonial rule, the imperative of modernisation provided justification for the presence of the mandatory power.[131]

[129] The term 'cartography of hegemony' is used in the context of colonial space–power relations by Ananya Roy in '"The Reverse Side of the World": Identity, Space and Power', in *Hybrid Urbanism*, ed. Nezar AlSayyad (Westport: Praeger, 2001), 241.
[130] Bhabha, *The Location of Culture*, 112.
[131] The role of modernisation is discussed by David Spurr in *The Rhetoric of Empire: Colonial*

The ambiguities in the maps are thus better understood in the context of the broader historical conditions, exposing the diverse sentiments of British administrators, planners and politicians. These distinct voices reflected a renegotiation of the different cultural and political realities that existed in the British Empire and its dominions during the interwar period, which in turn affected the way the schemes deviated from more typical colonial urban planning. It is because of these distinctions that I suggest that these be viewed as mandatory, and not colonial, urban schemes.

A report of the League of Nations Research Committee regarding the Palestine Mandate, dated June 1930, ends its review with the conclusion that 'The Palestine Mandate represents one of the great political and social experiments of history.'[132] In many ways, this is also true for the urban development schemes for Jerusalem, which can be seen as urban experiments characterised by an ambiguity that reflected neither the city's cultural realities nor the Jewish–Arab conflict and Britain's role in it. Rather than reiterating Jerusalem's tormented existence during the Mandate era, these plans represented both a perception of its past and a hope for a peaceful future on the Holy City's hilly topography.

Discourse in Journalism, Travel Writing and Imperial Administration (Durham, NC: Duke University Press, 1993), 70.

[132] *The Palestine Mandate* 1, no. 3, June 1930 (Geneva: League of Nations Association of the US), 16.

CHAPTER TWO

Appropriating Multi-histories: The Palestine Archaeological Museum

Jerusalem [will become] a centre of Archeological activities in the near east . . . for the horizon North, South and East is all historical; and I believe the future will bring historical revelations, not only locally but far afield, that will no doubt surprise and delight future generations.

– John Garstang, 1927[1]

DURING THE THIRTY years of the Mandate, the British carried out extensive construction of civic facilities in all of Palestine, including administration buildings, military and police bases, schools, clinics, banks, and more. Among these, one building stands out as the most prominent cultural institution that took new physical form – the Palestine Archeological Museum, also known as the Rockefeller Museum (Figure 2.1).

Before addressing the history of its establishment, it is important to place the museum within the contemporary archaeological scientific discourse and activities that were taking place in the aftermath of World War I. With the changes in power structures and alliances in the Middle East, both American and European research institutions seized the opportunity to undertake more excavations and supplying their countries with new and important artefacts.[2] Moreover, archaeological expeditions to the Middle East involved cultural-political interests, which intensified after the war. Concurrently, emerging national identities in the region brought about greater awareness of the importance of curating artefacts in local national museums, such as those established in Egypt, Iraq, and elsewhere.[3]

There was an inherent contradiction between encouraging digs by Western institutions – intended for enriching the collections of the governments funding

---

[1] John Garstang to Sir John Shuckburgh, 24 November 1927, *Museum for Palestine* file, *NAGB* CO 733/142/5.
[2] Geoff Emberling, ed., *Pioneers to the Past: American Archaeologists in the Middle East, 1919–1920 [in Conjunction with the Exhibition Pioneers to the Past: 1919–1920, Presented at the Oriental Institute Museum, 12 January to 29 August 2010]* (Chicago: Oriental Institute of the University of Chicago, 2010).
[3] Ibid. 85–9, 97–8.

Figure 2.1 Austen St Barbe Harrison, Palestine Archaeological Museum, Jerusalem, 1928–35. ACM, https://www.loc.gov/pictures/item/2019696674/, retrieved 11 February 2020.

them – and the attempts to institutionalise cultural heritage locally. The British attempted to reconcile the two, and one of the major ventures in this process of localising heritage in Palestine was the establishment of an archaeological museum. The first phase was the founding of the British School of Archaeology, quickly set up in 1919 under the Military Administration. The school was established in Jerusalem with a declared commitment to cooperate with the American School of Oriental Research, and the two functioned for several years under the aegis of the Allied School, which was one of the clearest American cultural interventions in the post-World War I Middle East.[4] British-American cooperation was significant, so in order to mollify the fears of other powers – especially France – that the archaeological 'scene' would be dominated by Anglo-Saxons, the British created a joint Archeological Advisory Board comprising representatives from all the relevant local and foreign institutions.[5] Ensuring international access to the Holy Land's archaeological sites was further reinforced in 1922, in Article 21 of the Palestine Mandate of the League of Nations, which stated that any member of the League may conduct digs and research there.[6]

The Palestine Archaeological Museum was also part of a larger plan for museum culture in Palestine. During the Mandate years, the British posited several plans for museums: in 1927 preliminary plans were drawn up to transform part of the ancient Acre arsenal into a 'Northern District Museum';[7] in 1939 there was a proposal for a Palestine Folk Museum in Jerusalem, intended for ethnography and for documenting Palestine's more recent past.[8] The plan to establish a museum for archaeology in Jerusalem was conceptualised in a new Antiquities Ordinance, formulated in 1920 by the renown British archaeologist John Garstang, who headed both the British School of Archaeology and the new Mandatory Department of Antiquities.[9] Prior to this, a joint archeological museum had been planned for the Allied School.[10] The idea for a museum was thus the product of British and American cooperation from the beginning, well before an American donation for construction and operation was secured.

An investigation of the museum's objectives and potential audiences requires revisiting the Mandatory Antiquities Ordinance. Although partially relying on its predecessor, the Ottoman Antiquities Law of 1906, the British ordinance introduced two new clauses: first, it stated that all antiquities discovered are the

---

[4] For a discussion of American archeological activity in Palestine following World War I, see Rachel Hallote, 'Before Albright: Charles Torrey, James Montgomery, and American Biblical Archaeology 1907–1922', *Near Eastern Archaeology* 74, no. 3 (2011): 156–69.
[5] Shimon Gibson, 'British Archaeological Institutions in Mandatory Palestine, 1917–1948', *Palestine Exploration Quarterly* 131, no. 2 (1999): 115–43.
[6] Emberling, *Pioneers to the Past*, 89.
[7] See *Acre Museum* file, *NAGB* CO 733/138/3.
[8] See *Folk Museum* file, *NAGB* CO 733/413/15.
[9] Gibson, 'British Archaeological Institutions in Mandatory Palestine', 115–17.
[10] Hallote, 'Before Albright', 165; Frederic G. Kenyon to Ashbee, 21 February 1919, 1, *PEF* BASJ Minute Book 1918–1961.

property of the Civil Government of Palestine, meaning that they belong to the inhabitants of the country, not to the British or, as had been true during Ottoman reign, to the ruling empire.[11] Second, the Department of Antiquities would allocate artefacts first to the 'Palestine Museum' for its 'scientific completeness', and the remainder would be divided between the museum and the expedition responsible for unearthing the artefacts.[12] The Antiquities Ordinance was primarily the result of legislative precedents in the British Empire.[13] As argued by Paul Basu and Vinita Damodaran, this 'legislative migration'[14] demonstrates the changing views and the amendments to such laws, and provides insight with regard to 'the significance of a region's heritage and whose interests should be prioritized in the measures proposed'.[15] The nineteenth century witnessed continuous plundering and hoarding of the cultural heritages of colonised people and of regions under some form of Western influence.[16] But by the beginning of the twentieth century there was a growing acknowledgment of the rights of indigenous peoples to their own excavated material culture and that it should no longer be intended solely for European acquisition in distant places.[17] This awareness was reflected in these legislative changes. In the case of Palestine, the Mandatory Antiquities Ordinance appears to have been similarly reformulated, for although it still permitted dealing in artefacts and exporting them to museums abroad, priority was given to a local, civil museum rather than to the great institutions of Europe, Britain and America. This edict was probably an outcome of the new mandate system, which decreed that no imperial ruler or imposing power could enrich its own collections exclusively, and it was especially important in the case of the land of the Bible, which findings were coveted by every Western nation. The ordinance (and the League of Nations' article that followed) was formulated in an unbiased way that effectively limited the dispersal of artefacts. Although enacted by a Western entity, the importance of the Palestine ordinance lay in its reiteration that archaeological finds were first and foremost the cultural property of the inhabitants of the lands where they were found. It implied not only a reconsideration of the status of the West vis-à-vis this 'cradle of civilisation', but also a significant change in the relationship of local Middle Eastern publics to their cultural heritage.

Alongside these approaches, similarities can also be found between British curatorial practices implemented in Palestine and the preceding Ottoman approaches

---

[11] Gibson, 'British Archaeological Institutions in Mandatory Palestine', 137.
[12] Ibid. 137; for a discussion of the 1928 ordinance, see Nadia Abu El-Haj, 'Producing (Arti)Facts: Archaeology and Power during the British Mandate of Palestine', *Israel Studies* 7, no. 2 (2002): 40–2.
[13] Gibson, 'British Archaeological Institutions in Mandatory Palestine', 137.
[14] Paul Basu and Vinita Damodaran, 'Colonial Histories of Heritage: Legislative Migrations and the Politics of Preservation', *Past & Present* 226, no. 10 (2015): 245.
[15] Ibid. 245.
[16] Christopher Whitehead, 'National Art Museums in Britain', in *National Museums: New Studies from Around the World*, eds Simon Knell, Peter Aronsson and Arne Bugge (Abingdon and New York: Routledge, 2014), 109.
[17] Ibid. 105–12.

to archaeology, both in Palestine and across the Ottoman Empire. Aware of the importance of antiquities for the West, during the nineteenth and twentieth centuries, the Ottomans crafted three antiquities laws, the latest of which was the one issued in 1906.[18] As noted by Wendy Shaw, these laws reflected 'a struggle between archaeological sites scattered across Ottoman territories and foreign archaeologists interested in enhancing European museum collections'.[19] Thus, the laws were first and foremost designed to retain finds in the Ottoman Empire and prevent their exportation. Seen in a broader context, they formed part of an Ottoman agenda geared toward defining the empire's cultural identity. Coupled with the designation of archaeology as a science and the creation of collections, antiquities' legislation was part of the search for a national image that balanced modernity and heritage.[20] As we shall see in Chapter Four, this balance was also reflected in the work of Turkish architects on Jerusalem's Muslim heritage sites and the new Jerusalem Palace Hotel.

Whereas during the nineteenth century Ottoman policies dictated that most artefacts found their way to Istanbul, in the early twentieth century local and regional museums were established in several cities recognised as central to archaeological excavations. Jerusalem was included, and a small 'Turkish Archaeological Museum' was created there.[21] Little is known of this museum,[22] but it is documented that the Tower of David, called 'the Citadel' by the British, was to be fitted out as its permanent home.[23] The Ottoman renovations on the Haram-a-Sharif, which I discuss in Chapter Four, suggest that Ottoman engagement with Jerusalem's Muslim heritage was highlighted in the museum's collections, alongside other ancient cultures and civilisations.[24] Hence, the display of Jerusalem and Palestine's past, as well as the policies and curatorship that guided it, actually began prior to the British initiatives.

In the context of the British plans for an archaeology museum in Jerusalem, it is further instructive to consider them from the perspective of contemporary museological practices in the West, especially in Great Britain. In the nineteenth century, large national collections were heterogeneous in nature and included exhibits in the fields of art, archaeology, anthropology, geology, zoology, and more. Toward the turn of the century collections became more specific, with the establishment of specialised museums for archaeology, natural history, anthropology, and so

---

[18] Wendy M. K. Shaw, *Possessors and Possessed: Museums, Archaeology, and the Visualization of History in the Late Ottoman Empire* (Berkeley: University of California Press, 2003), 70.
[19] Ibid. 169.
[20] Zeynep Çelik, 'Defining Empire's Patrimony: Late Ottoman Perceptions of Antiquity', in *Scramble for the Past: A Story of Archaeology in the Ottoman Empire, 1753–1914*, eds Zainab Bahrani, Zeynep Çelik and Edhem Eldem, trans. Willard Wood, Leyla Tonguc Basmac and Doolie Sloman (Istanbul: SALT, 2011), 446.
[21] Shaw, *Possessors and Possessed*, 169.
[22] Ibid. 169–70.
[23] Ibid. 170–1.
[24] For a discussion of Ottoman curatorship of the numerous civilisations that existed in the empire, see Shaw, *Possessors and Possessed*, 126–9.

on.²⁵ The creation of archaeology museums in British-controlled regions abroad was an exportation of these new concepts. In the land of the Bible and its ensuing pagan, Christian and Muslim histories, establishing such a museum was decidedly important. In what follows, I explore the way these multi-histories were negotiated in the development of the museum and its architecture.

Before the Building: Architecture for Archaeology

The planning of the archaeological museum in Jerusalem reflected not only new museum practices, but also specialised architecture built for housing members of the archaeological expeditions. With the new post-World War I possibilities available to archaeologists from Europe and America who were conducting digs in the Middle East, the need arose for architectural facilities to serve the archaeological schools and their missions. These would provide administration, laboratory and publishing facilities, and meeting spaces; to some extent, findings would also be displayed in these specialised buildings. At the beginning of 1919, Sir Fredric Kenyon, director of the British Museum, approached Charles Ashbee with an outline for designing a building for the Allied School.²⁶ The building was to 'be erected on the Citadel site ... which [would] comprise (a) accommodations for the British School, (b) accommodations for the American School, (c) accommodation to be used jointly by the two schools, such as a hall, a library, and large lecture room.'²⁷ Kenyon noted additional functions for caring for the finds and researching them but did not include exhibition spaces. His programme called for construction to be financed jointly by the Americans and the British.

However, Kenyon's plan was never realised. Bute House, a small rented space, which included offices, lecture halls and a library, served as the temporary building of the Allied School in Jerusalem in the early 1920s.²⁸ A building for the American School of Oriental Research, which had similar functions but was also intended to serve as a museum,²⁹ was completed in Jerusalem in 1925.³⁰ The Allied School and the Antiquities Department installed an exhibition space in 'Way House' in Jerusalem, a modest building, similar to those of the American School and Bute House.³¹ Named the Palestine Antiquities Museum,³² it served

---

[25] Whitehead, 'National Art Museums in Britain', 109; Tony Bennett, *Pasts beyond Memory: Evolution, Museums, Colonialism* (London: Routledge, 2004), 34–5, 65–82.
[26] Frederic G. Kenyon to Ashbee, 21 February 1919, 1, PEF BASJ Minute Book 1918–1961.
[27] Ibid.
[28] A plan of Bute House is featured in Hallote, 'Before Albright', fig. 11.
[29] Hallote, 'Before Albright', 165.
[30] Dating based on an account by James A. Montgomery, President of the Schools from 1918–33. See James A. Montgomery, 'The Story of the School in Jerusalem', *The Annual of the American Schools of Oriental Research* (1924): 4–5.
[31] Fuchs, 'Austen St. Barbe Harrison', 105–8; Gibson, 'British Archaeological Institutions in Mandatory Palestine', 131–2; Ronny Reich and Ayala Sussman, 'LeToldot Muse'on Rockefeller BiYerushalayim', in *Sefer Ze'ev Vilnai*, ed. Eli Schiller, vol. 2 (Jerusalem: Ariel, 1984), 83–91.
[32] The museum's formal name appears on the *Guide Book to the Palestine Museum of Antiquities*

Figure 2.2 *The Archaeological Museum at 'Way House', Jerusalem, 1921–35, photograph c. 1940–6.* ACM, https://www.loc.gov/pictures/item/2019701346/, retrieved 11 February 2020.

as such from 1921 until 1935, at which time the new building for the Palestine Archaeological Museum was completed, with the former's contents providing the core of the new museum's collection.[33] Defining Way House's makeshift exhibition as a 'museum' seems rather pretentious. However, its collection was open to the public, and artefacts were presented with labels in Arabic, English and Hebrew (Figure 2.2). Historic photos show a trilingual 'Do Not Touch the Exhibits' sign and opening hours advertised at the gate, although apparently there was no official 'Palestine Archaeological Museum' sign. Display cases were crowded into the small space and set against its walls, and ancient sarcophagi and sculptures – in excellent condition and artistically outstanding – were placed in the small

(Jerusalem: Department of Antiquities, 1924). *PEF*, W. J. Pythian Adams file.
[33] Gibson, 'British Archaeological Institutions in Mandatory Palestine', 131–2.

entrance court exposed to the elements. This exhibition space demonstrates the importance that the British and the Americans (as well as the other foreign archaeological missions) assigned to the museum's establishment, and the aspirations for its development.

Comparable facilities for archaeologists were built in Egypt. American Egyptologist James Henry Breasted, one of the leading figures of the American archaeological mission to Egypt, was among those who established the chief American facility, Chicago House, located in Luxor.[34] Breasted also played a central role in the establishment of the Palestine Archaeological Museum and, as I demonstrate further on, his involvement in both projects facilitated a transfer of planning ideas from Luxor to Jerusalem.

All these accommodations indicate that by the time the Palestine Archaeological Museum began to take physical form in 1927, architecture for archaeology was already known in the region and could provide precedents for a museum intended to house, in addition to exhibition spaces, facilities for excavations and for the various studies and processes regarding their finds.

Ron Fuchs and Shimon Gibson have both termed the new Palestine Archaeological Museum 'national'. However, as this terminology does not surface in contemporary discourse, official or otherwise, I propose that the British deliberately refrained from attaching the prefix 'national' to the museum's name. They had used this concept in the Balfour Declaration in declaring a 'national home' for the Jews, thus connecting the modern notion of nationality with Jewish presence, which exacerbated the tension between the emerging Zionist and Palestinian identities.[35] As noted by Eitan Bar-Yosef with regard to the British conquest of Jerusalem, which took place only a few weeks after the Balfour Declaration, British actions appear to have been formulated to counterbalance the declaration's overwhelmingly pro-Zionist objectives.[36] In this vein, calling the museum 'national' would have immediately raised the question: whose nationality? Which publics are being represented and who are the intended audiences? Conversely, the name 'Palestine Archaeological Museum' suggested neutrality, implied British nonpartisanship, and defined curatorial content by a disciplinary characterisation unconnected to a specific cultural heritage.

Rockefeller's Bequest

Severe shortage of display and storage space at Way House led to requests for an adequate building as early as 1924.[37] Breasted, who was involved in excavations across the Middle East, persuaded his most important patron, John D. Rockefeller Jr, to

---

[34] Emberling, *Pioneers to the Past*, 50–2.
[35] Jacobson, *From Empire to Empire*, 143–7; Segev and Watzman, *One Palestine, Complete*, 91–2, 102–9.
[36] Eitan Bar-Yosef, 'The Last Crusade?', 98.
[37] Reich and Sussman, 'LeToldot Muse'on Rockefeller', 83.

donate the sum of $2,000,000 toward the construction of a new museum building and an endowment for its maintenance.[38] Rockefeller was renowned for his generosity toward international missions, such as the Palestine Museum and the Jerusalem YMCA. These gifts accorded with his philanthropic principles, both within the United States and abroad, and represented a kind of cultural hegemony.[39] His philanthropy in Palestine in the 1920s was facilitated by the new conditions afforded by the British Mandate. This situation stood in contrast to the state of affairs in Egypt, where Breasted failed to establish an archaeological museum in Cairo with Rockefeller's funding, a failure that was due in part to the waning of British control in Egypt following World War I and to rising Egyptian nationalism. In his analysis of the abortive attempt to establish the Egyptian museum, James Goode underscores the significance of Breasted's negotiations not only with the Egyptians but also with the British administration.[40] Thus, by the time he had secured Rockefeller's donation for the museum in Jerusalem, Breasted had already gained a great deal of experience in negotiating with British officials. He had successfully enlisted their support for most of his archaeological expeditions in territories under their control and had received British endorsement for purchases of artefacts on behalf of the Chicago University Oriental Institute and the Art Institute of Chicago.[41] Breasted's connections, of which Rockefeller was well aware, encouraged the latter to reallocate his donation to Jerusalem in 1927, where the British had full control of Mandatory projects such as the projected museum. On 9 June 1927, Breasted personally informed the High Commissioner of Palestine, Lord Herbert Charles O. Plumer, that he had secured this dramatic and generous donation toward 'education and science in Palestine'.[42] He later also underscored the museum's importance for 'cordial Anglo-American cooperation in the field of archaeology'.[43]

The terms of the gift, formulated in a letter from Rockefeller to Plumer and publicised by the British administration in the official *Palestine Gazette* on 16 November 1927, provide important insight into the museum's intended location, goals and management.[44] The British called the site allocated for the museum, which is adjacent to the northern Old City wall, Karm-el Sheikh or Abraham's

---

[38] Breasted to the High Commissioner of Palestine, Lord Herbert Charles O. Plumer, 9 June 1927, 1, *Museum for Palestine* file, *NAGB* CO 733/142/5.
[39] Donald Fisher, 'The Role of Philanthropic Foundations in the Reproduction and Production of Hegemony: Rockefeller Foundations and the Social Sciences', *Sociology* 17, no. 2 (1983): 206–33; Lily E. Kay, 'Rethinking Institutions: Philanthropy as an Historiographic Problem of Knowledge and Power', *Minerva* 35, no. 3 (1997): 283–93; Inderjeet Parmar, '"To Relate Knowledge and Action": The Impact of the Rockefeller Foundation on Foreign Policy Thinking during America's Rise to Globalism 1939–1945', *Minerva* 40, no. 3 (2002): 235–63. The scholars cited here differ in their interpretation of the concept of cultural hegemony; this application to American philanthropy is most clearly contested by Karl and Katz, whose work is cited below (see n. 49).
[40] James F. Goode, *Negotiating for the Past: Archaeology, Nationalism, and Diplomacy in the Middle East, 1919–1941* (Austin: University of Texas Press, 2007), 102–115.
[41] Emberling, *Pioneers to the Past*, 31–6, 39–41, 52–83.
[42] Breasted to Plumer, 9 June 1927, 2, *Museum for Palestine* file, *NAGB* CO 733/142/5.
[43] Breasted to Plumer, 18 June 1927, 2, *Museum for Palestine* file, *NAGB* CO 733/142/5.
[44] Rockefeller to Plumer, 13 October 1929, *Museum for Palestine* file, *NAGB* CO 733/142/5.

Vineyard. Rockefeller ensured that it would be included in Jerusalem's Town Planning Scheme, so as to preclude possible attempts to separate the museum from the holy and symbolic Old City – demonstrating his awareness of the fragility of territorial claims to the Holy City. This site afforded a scenic view of the Old City wall, and as the new building's plan developed, a tower was included to enhance the magnificent views of the Holy City and – to the east – the Mount of Olives, Mount Scopus, and their surroundings (see Figure I.4), thus connecting the museum with Jerusalem's historic past.[45] Rockefeller further asserted that 'the adjoining municipal incineration plant will be permanently removed from the immediate vicinity'.[46] This secured the museum's location in a suitable cultural or civic centre, and not in a utility zone, and was in keeping with Mandatory plans, discussed in Chapter One, for a large governorate complex immediately north of the Old City. The museum's curatorial practices, likely defined in consultation with Breasted, reflected the contemporary emphasis on specialisation, which I noted above:

> [T]he collections in the new Museum will include all material throwing light on the past of man in Palestine; that natural resources and materials pertaining to natural science would therefore be included only in so far as they concern the human career in the past; In short that the Museum is to be an archaeological Institution, not a museum of natural science.[47]

Choosing archaeology as the core of the museum's content reflects Palestine's importance as the site where major human histories and religions were forged. The country's flora and fauna were of no concern except when clearly connected to archaeology. This emphasis on archaeology suggests more than professional interests: it demonstrates the British Christian approach to the custodianship of the land, and – no less important – Rockefeller's and Breasted's religiosity. Breasted viewed archaeology as a source for understanding Judeo-Christian religious and moral codes.[48] An idealist raised as a Baptist, Rockefeller was an avid supporter of Western religious and educational initiatives in the Near East. Several scholars have demonstrated that religious beliefs were important incentives for the Rockefellers's (John Sr and John Jr) charities.[49] Barry Karl and Stanley Katz

---

[45] Report by surveyor Murry Rosenberg sent to Colonel Symes, Governor of Jerusalem, 27 November 1927, 1–2, *Museum for Palestine* file, NAGB CO 733/142/5.
[46] Official Gazette of the Government of Palestine, 16 November 1927, 802. http://sesame.library.yale.edu/fedoragsearch/ameelreader?pid=agaz:22894&size=1.7, accessed 25 November 2017.
[47] *Palestine Official Gazette*, 16 November 1927, 802; Rockefeller to Plumer, 13 October 1929, *Museum for Palestine* file, NAGB CO 733/142/5.
[48] Jeffrey Abt, 'Toward a Historian's Laboratory: The Breasted-Rockefeller Museum Projects in Egypt, Palestine, and America', *Journal of the American Research Center in Egypt* 33 (1996): 180.
[49] Barry D. Karl and Stanley N. Katz, 'Foundations and Ruling Class Elites', *Daedalus* 116, no. 1 (1987): 1–40; W. Ross Winterowd, 'Capitalism and Culture: John and John and Scripture; Andy and Adam, Herb, Matt, and Waldo', *JAC* 27, no. 3 (2007): 539–62.

argue that charity is an obligation firmly grounded in the Judeo-Christian tradition, yet its expression in modern philanthropy, as in the Rockefellers's cases, developed with the advance of industry and science, and thus 'rests on a recognition of progress and choice [and] calls for an educational system and an educable public, together with a body of knowledge available to all'.[50] Thus, the idea of exhibiting Palestine's history integrated modern museological concepts and the science of archaeology with a desire to educate the publics of a land considered underdeveloped, which indeed had no such institution. To complement these interests, Palestine had the significant advantage of being the site of the origin of the donor's faith.

Rockefeller's pledge further refers to the museum being controlled by the Palestine Government, meaning that although the artefacts belong to the public, as stated in the Antiquities Ordinance, the museum itself would be under British Control.[51] An international advisory board would secure American involvement in decisions pertaining to the museum and allow for some participation of other foreign archaeological missions. It appears that this clause resulted from the unrealised Egyptian museum project, where Breasted and Rockefeller failed to retain 'Western' control of Egypt's antiquities.[52] Thus, in addition to the clear advantage of British control envisaged by Breasted and Rockefeller, international involvement would ensure that 'Western' archaeological activity in Palestine would continue uninterrupted. The pledge thus formulated three crucial features of the future museum: its location near the Old City wall and within the civic centre projected for the town; archeological finds representing the region's history would be exhibited, providing Jerusalem and Palestine's publics access to their pasts; and the museum would be managed, developed and mediated to the public by the British, together with an international committee. By 1929 a British, rather than an international, committee was set up, whose members included Palestine administrators and representatives of the Department. They determined that the museum would store and showcase archaeology, house the Department of Antiquities and 'be an educational centre of which the library, the Museum and the Lecture Theatre will be the means whereby archaeological knowledge will be made accessible to, or will be distributed to, the general public and to students'.[53] Thus, what began as a progressive approach, which sanctioned artefacts to their country of origin in the Antiquities Ordinance, ended up – at least in the case of the museum – with largely British decision-making with regard to the museum's functions and exhibits. The new building's architecture was also the product of British planning with enthusiastic American involvement.

[50] Karl and Katz, 'Foundations and Ruling Class Elites', 5–6.
[51] *Palestine Official Gazette*, 16 November 1927, 802; Rockefeller to Palestine High Commissioner Herbert Plumer, 13 October 1929, *Museum for Palestine* file, *NAGB* CO 733/142/5.
[52] Abt, 'Toward a Historian's Laboratory', 186; Goode, *Negotiating for the Past*, 102–15.
[53] 'Outline of proposed organization of the Department of Antiquities', 1929, *Antiquities Department: Rearrangement of Cadre of Senior Officers* File, *NAGB* CO 733/172/4.

The Architecture of the New Museum Building

Planning for the museum progressed in several stages. Its final design reveals a remarkable integration of historicism and modernism, which I analyse here as deriving from both British and American approaches. Plans for the new museum building began taking shape in 1927, immediately following the publication of Rockefeller's pledge. On 9 December 1927, William Ormsby-Gore, Undersecretary of State for the Colonies, informed Rockefeller that High Commissioner Plumer had hired Austin St Barbe Harrison (1891–1976) as the architect for the new museum.[54] Harrison, Chief Architect of the Palestine Public Works Department, spent fifteen years in Palestine, between 1922 and 1937, during which time he designed most of the government buildings.[55] After serving in World War I, which interrupted his training as an architect, he completed his degree. His career included extensive work in the Middle East, Greece, Malta and Africa, and he rarely returned to England after becoming a practising architect. He was a very private man, who kept to himself and had no family of his own. Completely dedicated to his craft, he nonetheless did not write much, and his legacy remains in his buildings and in some drawings.[56] According to Plumer, Harrison gained Breasted's trust and the latter asked that the Chief Architect design the new museum.[57] Breasted approved the plans for the museum on behalf of Rockefeller, and the high commissioner's office wrote to London that 'the Government Architect deserves high praise for his excellent design'.[58]

The museum was planned as a series of adjoining galleries and administrative spaces with seven enclosed courts (the seventh was not built) (Figure 2.3). It is set on a plot that slopes rather steeply toward the road encircling the Old City wall, rendering the museum very visible from the wall's lower, northwestern façade, but far less so from its southeastern side. The museum's most prominent feature is its octagonal tower, located in the centre of the building's symmetrical entrance façade, above a spacious entrance hall, which opens onto two wings at forty-five-degree angles. In front of the tower is a vestibule with an arched entrance, topped by a small dome. There are similarities in the arrangement of the ground plans of these wings, most noticeable in the North and South Octagons, where each wing begins, and in the North and South Courts, around which they are built. These wings house most of the museum's administrative

---

[54] Ormsby-Gore to Rockefeller, 9 December 1929, 2, *Museum for Palestine* file, *NAGB* CO 733/142/5.

[55] Ron Fuchs and Gilbert Herbert, 'Representing Mandatory Palestine: Austen St. Barbe Harrison and the Representational Buildings of the British Mandate in Palestine, 1922–37', *Architectural History* 43 (2000): 287–8; Fuchs and Herbert, 'A Colonial Portrait of Jerusalem', 91–2.

[56] Fuchs, 'Austen St. Barbe Harrison', 66–9, 76–8.

[57] Plumer to Secretary of the Colonies Leo Amery, 18 November 1927, 2, *Museum for Palestine* file, *NAGB* CO 733/142/5.

[58] Official on behalf of the High Commissioner to Amery, 4 December 1928, *Museum for Palestine* file, *NAGB* CO 733/146/5.

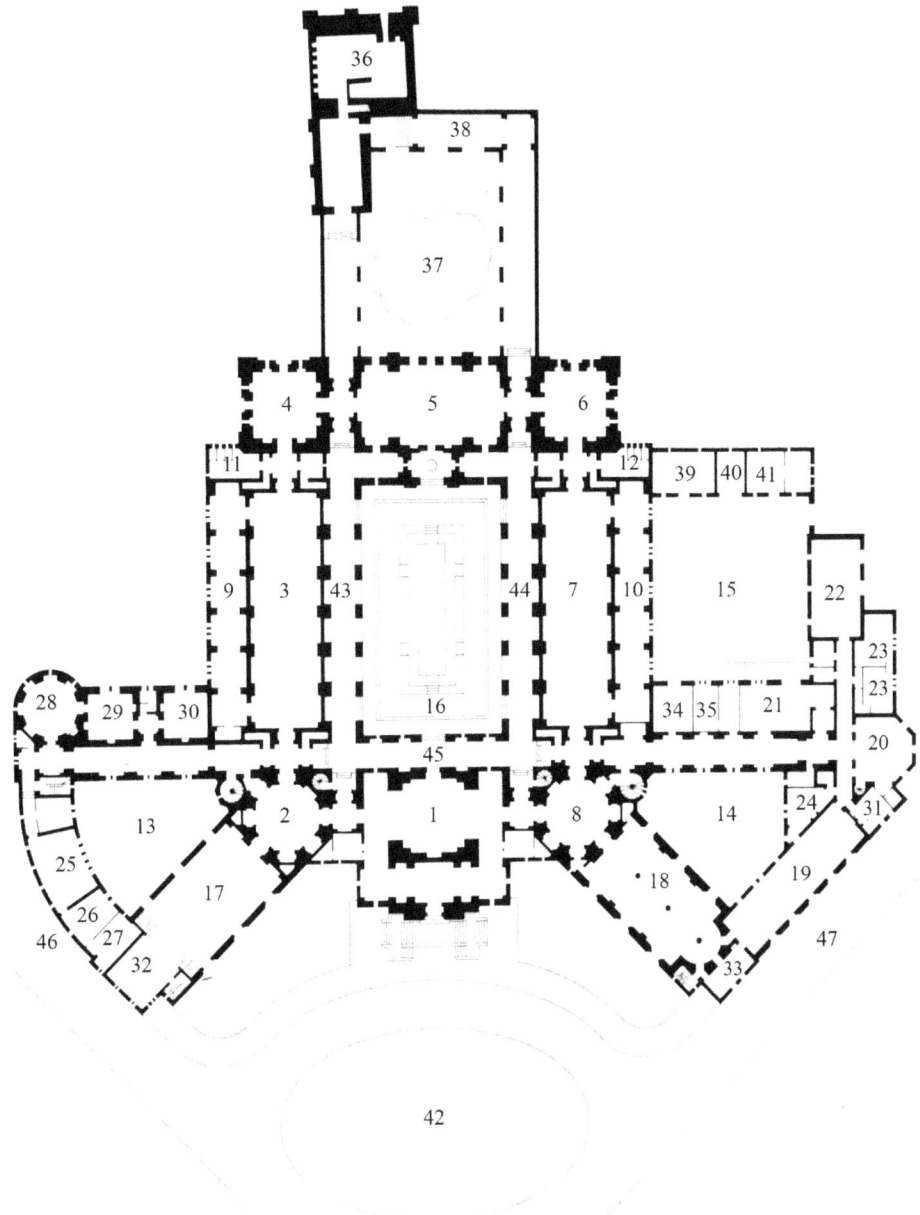

Figure 2.3 *Austen St Barbe Harrison, Palestine Archaeological Museum, ground plan, 1928–1935.*
© *IAA.*

Legend. 1. Entrance/Tower Hall. 2. South Octagon. 3. South Gallery. 4. South Room. 5. West Gallery. 6. North Room. 7. North Gallery. 8. North Octagon. 9. South Students' Room. 10. North Students' Room. 11. Men's Public Lavatory. 12. Women's Public Lavatory. 13. South Court. 14. North Court. 15. Service Court. 16. Central Court. 17. Lecture Theatre. 18. Reading Room. 19. Record Room. 20. Arranging Room. 21. Reception Room. 22. Studio. 23. Dark Room. 24. Librarian. 25. Registry. 26. Typists. 27. Files. 28. Archeological Advisory Board Room. 29. Director of Antiquities. 30. Chief Inspector. 31. Curator. 32. Optical Lantern Room. 33. Catalogue Clerk (of Library). 34. Assistant Curator. 35. Museum Catalogue Room. 36. Existing Ancient House. 37. Tree. 38. Cloister not yet built. 39. Store. 40. Garage. 41. Store. 42. Forecourt. 43. South Cloister. 44. North Cloister. 45. East Cloister. 46. South Approach. 47. North Approach.

Figure 2.4 *Austen St Barbe Harrison, Palestine Archaeological Museum, south gallery. Photographed by Diego Rosman.*

and research facilities. Although angled, the symmetry of the vestibule and wings appears to conceal a traditional Beaux-Arts plan, but it has several features that significantly break with this tradition: the southern court is flanked by an arched wall, whereas the north court has a straight one. Thus, the ground plan of one court forms a forty-five-degree angle enclosed by a semicircular wall, whereas the other creates a pentagon. Overall, Harrison achieved a sophisticated interplay between formal elements of the plan that highlight symmetry and order, and areas that were designed differently to accommodate their functions. The museum's central exhibition spaces (Figure 2.4) are an example of the former: planned as elongated galleries – the 'North Gallery' and the 'South Gallery' – they delineate the museum's Central Court (Figure 2.5). At the perimeter of each gallery is a hall

Figure 2.5 Austen St Barbe Harrison, Palestine Archaeological Museum, central court facing tower. Photographed by Diego Rosman.

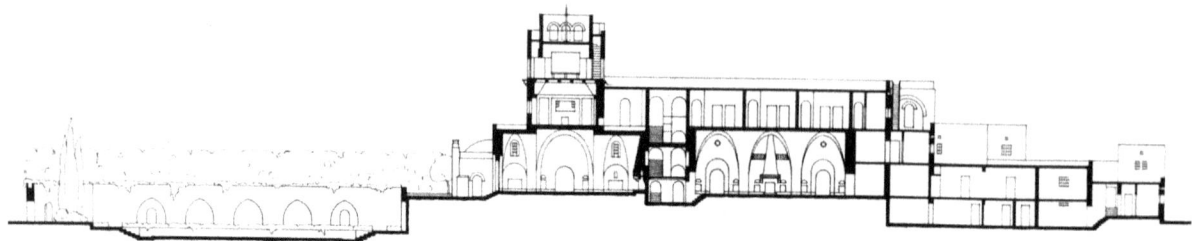

Figure 2.6 *Austen St Barbe Harrison, Palestine Archaeological Museum, section, 1928–35. © IAA.*

originally designated as a student room. Each gallery leads to an additional square exhibition hall connected across the Central Court by a rectangular 'West Hall', which completes visitor circulation around the entire court in a progression from one exhibition space to another.

The main galleries, as well as the square and octagonal rooms that form their connecting corners, have the same overall height, whereas the entrance wings that surround the North and South Courts are lower, as are the exterior rooms flanking the North and South Galleries (Figure 2.6). This difference in height creates two-level clerestories, which admit light into the galleries. The lower clerestory has a row of triple windows and the higher, a row of small rectangular ones. The higher clerestory is pitched, so that the galleries' coffered ceilings are narrower than their floor. Similarly, the octagonal and square halls have high windows admitting light, as do several other connecting spaces and rooms. The windows vary in size and include some that are deep-set and arched, rectangular fenestration, and blind arcades that frame square windows in the tower.

In addition to the vestibule dome, Harrison designed domes for the square exhibition halls and one side of the South Court. Vaults top several of the connecting halls, and the two octagons flanking the tower are roofed by octagonal pyramids. As with the pitched gallery ceilings, these various roofing elements take on different forms in the building's interior. They are usually shaped as tall domes resting on squinches, as can be seen in the entrance hall (Figure 2.7); the reading room has vaulted ceilings on heavy columns (Figure 2.8). Photographs, such as the one shown here of the West Gallery during construction (Figure 2.9), indicate that traditional techniques were used for the domes and arches, and the building's local-stone facing gives it a traditional ambience. Nevertheless, modern technology was used for most of the work with the use of both poured and reinforced concrete, as can be seen in photographs documenting the roofs during construction (Figure 2.10).[59]

The building's floor plan has many passages, and to an uninformed visitor can appear to be quite labyrinthine. Surrounded by a vaulted pointed-arch arcade and having a long central decorative pool, the Central Court is probably the structure's

---

[59] Ibid. 320; Fuchs, 'Austen St. Barbe Harrison', 123.

Figure 2.7 *Austen St Barbe Harrison, Palestine Archaeological Museum, dome of tower hall, 1928–1935. © IAA.*

Figure 2.8 *Austen St Barbe Harrison, Palestine Archaeological Museum, reading room/library. Photographed by Diego Rosman.*

Figure 2.9 *Austen St Barbe Harrison, Palestine Archeological Museum, west gallery during construction, 1928–1935. ABHC, Austen St Barbe Harrison Collection.*

Figure 2.10 *Austen St Barbe Harrison, Palestine Archeological Museum, roofs during construction, 1928–1935. ABHC, Austen St Barbe Harrison Collection.*

Figure 2.11 *Austen St Barbe Harrison, Palestine Archaeological Museum, central court facing pavilion. Photographed by Diego Rosman.*

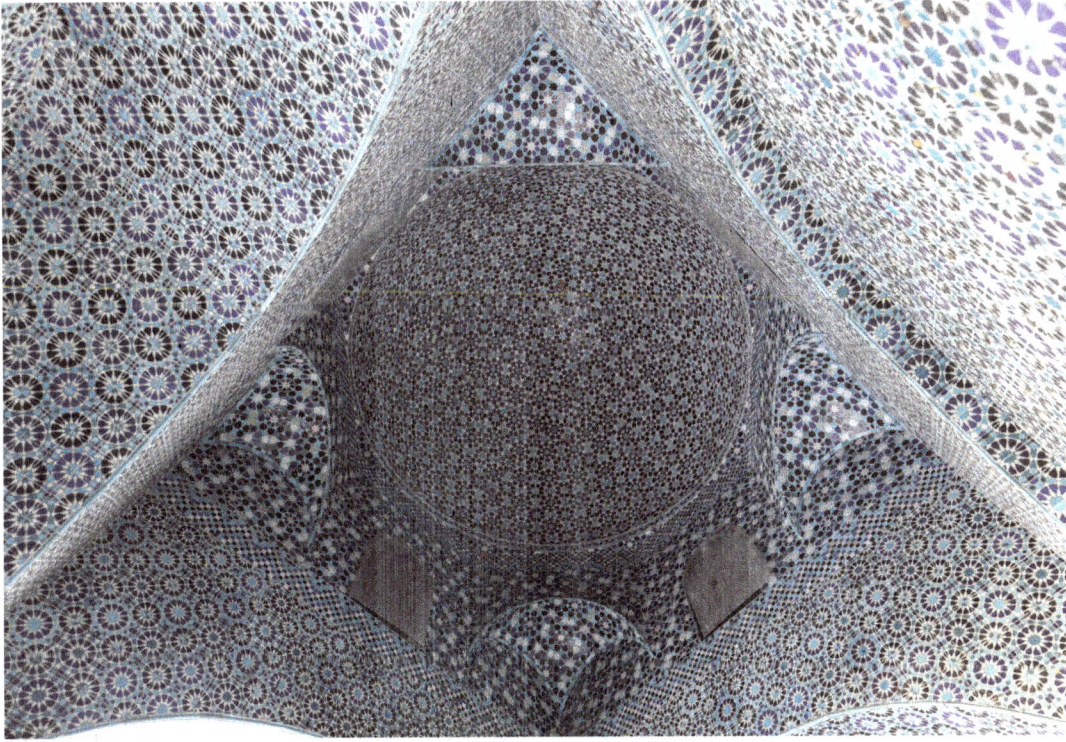

Figure 2.12 *Austen St Barbe Harrison, Palestine Archaeological Museum, interior of central court pavilion. Photographed by Diego Rosman.*

most impressive enclosed space (Figure 2.11). The interior of a small domed pavilion on the court's northern side, which originally had a fountain and is now faced with ceramic tiles (Figure 2.12), serves as a serene counterpoint to the tower across the court.

The museum's complex forms and spaces have been interpreted by Fuchs and Gilbert Herbert as having a 'Beaux-Arts inspired rationality', that integrates 'a brilliant ensemble of prisms'.[60] These researchers' rich description of the museum addresses its spatial effects and its architect's approach to the relationship between building and site, as well as the magnificent detailing of structural and decorative elements.[61]

What I focus on here is the question of the architectural precedents that may have inspired Harrison – a question intrinsically tied to the transfer of knowledge and cultural exchange. The museum's architecture problematises the temporal and geographical migration of ideas. As Fuchs and Herbert note, it is difficult to ascertain Harrison's sources.[62] Fuchs ascribes this difficulty primarily to Harrison's personality. A man of few words, who travelled extensively, his possible sources of inspiration were numerous and uncorroborated; furthermore, most of his sketchbooks have been lost.[63] Although indeed hindering the historian's task, this multiplicity of sources reflects broader issues of changing attitudes toward historicism in architecture and the way architects bound by a largely traditional set of concepts engaged modernism.

In the museum, Harrison apparently appropriated local precedents of both domestic and public architecture: the low domes that top the entrance vestibule and the central court pavilion certainly reflect Palestinian dwellings, as does the use of local stone. Scholars have also proposed architecture seen by Harrison during his trips in Palestine and Egypt, such as the Mamluk khanqah and mausoleum of Sultan Faraj Ibn Barquq in Cairo (1400–11); the thirteenth-century Mamluk Maqam Nabi Musa on the outskirts of Jerusalem, which was restored by the Ottomans in the early nineteenth century;[64] and courtyards in Jerusalem's Armenian Quarter.[65] The museum's central court was clearly inspired by the Court of the Myrtles at the famed Alhambra Castle in Granada, Spain, constructed in the fourteenth century.[66] This is apparent in its general proportions and its pool, in the court's receding façades, and in the remarkable 'Alhambresque' ceramic

---

[60] Fuchs and Herbert, 'Representing Mandatory Palestine', 320, 325, fig. 25.
[61] Ibid. 281–333.
[62] Ibid. 318.
[63] Fuchs, 'Austen St. Barbe Harrison', 72–6.
[64] For a discussion of the Nabi Musa complex, see Hana Taragan, 'Historical Reference in Medieval Islamic Architecture: Baybars's Buildings in Palestine', *Bulletin of the Israeli Academic Center in Cairo* 25 (2002): 31–4; Shmuel Tamari, 'Maqam Nebi Musa SheLeyad Jericho', *Cathedra for the History of Eretz Israel and Its Yishuv* 11 (1979): 153–80.
[65] Fuchs and Herbert, 'A Colonial Portrait of Jerusalem', 93; Ada Karmi-Melamed and Dan Price, *Architecture in Palestine during the British Mandate, 1917–1948* (Jerusalem: The Israel Museum, 2014), 36–43.
[66] Fuchs and Herbert, 'A Colonial Portrait of Jerusalem', 138.

tile pattern used for the court's pavilion. The tiles' resemblance to those at the Alhambra can be seen in the concentric pattern of cobalt, turquoise and white (Figures 2.12 and 2.13A), which is comparable to a pattern from the Nasrid castle (Figure 2.13B). I emphasise this point as I later elaborate on its significance for analysing the wider implications of Harrison's use of architectural sources. In trying to point to additional possible precursors, the Archaeological Museum's reading room (Figure 2.8) and the cross-vaults in the central court are reminiscent of the Cenacle, in the ancient Mount Zion complex bordering Jerusalem's Old City (Figure 2.14). This Crusader-era architecture, believed by Christians to be the site of the Last Supper and sanctified by Jews and Muslims as King David's tomb, was always coveted and disputed by the city's religious communities, and was a source of contention throughout the Mandate period.[67] These possible precedents are all Christian or Muslim, dating from medieval times or earlier, which raises a question as to whether Harrison appropriated anything of a Jewish character for the building. In posing this question, it is important to note that scarcely any distinctly Jewish medieval architecture has survived in Jerusalem, so it is difficult to determine whether Harrison deliberately avoided the implementation of any supposed visual Jewish identity.

These multiple sources of inspiration exemplify Harrison's deep appreciation of the architecture of the region, but of no less significance is his novel approach to this transfer of knowledge and cultural appropriation. As I demonstrate in the following passages, his approach deviated from conventional historicist adoption, evident in his abstraction of architectural elements. Moreover, I argue that functional rather than representational considerations were central to his plan. It is significant that no new large-scale museums were being built in Britain when Harrison devised the plans for the museum, so no new British models were available for emulation or consideration. The years during which the Archaeological Museum was planned in Jerusalem were a period of deep social and financial crises in Great Britain, with drastic unemployment and inflation in 1926, followed by the Great Depression of 1929–31, so few large-scale cultural investments were undertaken.[68] Nevertheless, in December 1927, when Rockefeller announced his endowment, Harrison travelled to London to consult specialists in museum architecture and to familiarise himself with the leading museums and the lessons learned from their planning.[69] Thus, in studying museums he would have had

---

[67] Sergio I. Minerbi, 'Pe'Yilut Memshelet Italia LeHasagat HaBe'alut al 'Cheder HaSe'uda Ha'Achrona' BeHar Zion', *Cathedra: For the History of Eretz Israel and Its Yishuv* 25 (1982): 37–64.

[68] Susan Kingsley Kent, *Aftershocks: Politics and Trauma in Britain, 1918–1931* (Basingstoke and New York: Palgrave Macmillan, 2009), 122–5, 180–6. Among the few major projects that were completed was the new Science Museum, designed by Richard Allison and opened in 1928. It was neo-classical in style and planned according to Beaux-Arts principles. See 'The New Science Museum, South Kensington, designed by Sir Richard Allison', *Architectural Review* 64 (1928): 23–5.

[69] Plumer to Amery, 18 November 1927, 2, *Museum for Palestine* file, NAGB CO 733/142/5; 'Journalists' interview with the Civic Secretary [Col. George Stewart Symes]', *Doar Hayom*, 22 December 1927, 1.

Figure 2.13a *Austen St Barbe Harrison, Palestine Archaeological Museum, interior of tiled pavilion. Photographed by Diego Rosman.*

Figure 2.13b *Detail of tiles from Alhambra Palace, Granada, Spain, fourteenth century. Photographed by Liza Barky-Harrington.*

Figure 2.14 *Cenacle (Chamber of the Last Supper), Jerusalem, twelfth–thirteenth centuries, c. 1898–1914. ACM, https://www.loc.gov/item/2019698390/, retrieved 11 February 2020.*

to rely largely upon nineteenth-century precedents which, when conceived and constructed, constituted a relatively new building typology.[70] Breasted, for his part, consulted 'an experienced museum authority ... in America',[71] but it is not known whom, or whether any American museums were consequently recommended to Harrison as sources of inspiration.

The style of the British museums seen by Harrison was historicism, which, while eclectic, usually related a very clear cultural message, evoking either 'Renaissance' or 'Baroque', 'Gothic' or 'Classical', and so on. Not every building had a totalising style; rather, even in eclectic structures, specific spaces were designated as clear stylistic sources for evoking cultural meaning. This was especially true in the case of museums designed in accordance with Beaux-Arts principles, which adopted various revival styles reflecting different countries' national histories or cultures.[72] However, the commitment to an all-encompassing style in

---

[70] Nikolaus Pevsner, *A History of Building Types* (London: Thames and Hudson, 1976), 111–38.
[71] Breasted to Plumer, 18 June 1927, 1, *Museum for Palestine* file, *NAGB* CO 733/142/5.
[72] Andrew McClellan, *The Art Museum from Boullée to Bilbao* (Berkeley and London: University of California Press), 67.

Figure 2.15 *Austen St Barbe Harrison, model for the Palestine Archaeological Museum, 1929. © IAA.*

architecture generally diminished significantly at the beginning of the twentieth century. Harrison was surely aware of these changes and was exposed to them during his 1927 visit.

In the Archaeological Museum, Harrison's divergence from tradition and historicism is apparent in his abstracted treatment of elements such as windows, ceilings and details of the façades and interiors. This can be clearly seen in the design of the tower: the change from its square base to the octagon is treated with abstracted squinches constructed of a chamfered corner and three-quarters of a pyramid. The tower's balustrade is adorned with a simple geometric frieze consisting of a circle-diamond-halfcircle pattern. It evokes stalactites, as well as other decorative elements familiar from Jerusalem's minarets which, when abstracted, suggest other types of traditional stonework. Harrison abandoned a plan to top the tower with a low dome, seen in a model from 1929 (Figure 2.15). A dome would have given the tower a more clearly defined 'Oriental' identity. In a letter to a Lloyd at the Colonial Office, Harrison mentioned arguments between himself and the planning committee in London with regard to the tower, so it might have been the committee that rejected the dome.[73] As executed, the tower's shape contributes to the vagueness of Harrison's sources and their cultural antecedents.

Abstraction can also be observed in the flat double rows of voussoirs in many of the arches, in the faux voussoirs that echo the structural arches, and in the thin connecting bevelling of various arches, which streamlines the walls. The smooth,

[73] Harrison to Lloyd, 7 February 1917, 1–2, *Museum for Palestine* file, *NAGB* CO 733/146/5.

frameless continuation from windows, vaults or domes to wall or ceiling surfaces further creates an undulating sense of space. Built-in benches in the courtyard, as well as the cascading stonework of the stairs leading to the vestibule all have a simple, abstract geometry that lends itself to a sophisticated articulation of layered and visually interconnected geometrical forms.

As I have already noted, Harrison relied on diverse Muslim and Crusader-era architectural precedents. There were several instances where this reliance was direct, such as in the shapes of domes and the use of Alhambresque tiles. These clear sources of inspiration served as a 'point of departure', almost a counterpoint, to most of the elements, all of which were significantly abstracted.

Fuchs and Herbert associate Harrison's abstraction with an exportation of Beaux-Arts principles to the colonial context. They argue that he continued Beaux-Arts planning principles but relinquished classical decorative schemes. They contend that architects planning for the colonies, in places such as India and Palestine, combined this strategy with the appropriation of local elements, which they abstracted and thus made relevant for both colonisers and colonised.[74] The researchers interpret this process as distinctly different from 'the modernism of the then emerging Modern Movement',[75] which addressed the problems of modern society and proposed architectural solutions to twentieth-century requirements. Whereas this might have been true of India, Harrison's departure from Beaux-Arts planning locates his work within modernism, albeit in a method that differs from how it was applied in exemplars of the so-called International Style, which was considered the modern movement's epitome. I elaborate on this further in the ensuing paragraphs. At this point I argue that the fact that the Archaeological Museum was interpreted as 'modern' in contemporary media coverage is significant: the *Illustrated London News* termed it 'A fine example of the modern Jerusalem architecture' and, interestingly, showed a photograph of the museum's southern façade, which is streamlined and asymmetrical and features the building's most 'modern' elevation (Figure 2.16).[76]

The development of Art Deco in Britain should also be considered in this connection. The presence of Art Deco elements does not preclude the idea that Harrison was influenced by British architecture in India, as suggested by Fuchs, or even that he took inspiration from neoclassical and other nineteenth-century British examples.[77] However, Harrison's treatment of volumes and façades – as independent features that protrude, recede and create a sense of sculptural cascading – is akin to outstanding British examples that reflect Art Deco influence, such as Charles Holden's post-World War I buildings.[78]

---

[74] Fuchs and Herbert, 'Representing Mandatory Palestine', 282–3, 320.
[75] Ibid. 282.
[76] 'From the World's Scrapbook, News of Topical Interest', *Illustrated London News*, 28 September, 1935, 516.
[77] Fuchs and Herbert, 'Representing Mandatory Palestine', 282–3.
[78] Prominent examples are: (a) Holden's London University (1931–7). During the first building phase

Figure 2.16 *Austen St Barbe Harrison, Palestine Archaeological Museum.* Illustrated London News, *28 September 1935, 516 ('From the World's Scrapbook, News of Topical Interest').*

Harrison's novel approach was apparent not only in his abstractions, but also in his rigorous engagement with the functional requirements of a modern archaeological museum. In order to demonstrate this, the museum's objectives should be examined in more detail. As I noted above, its two wings differed from each other: the South Wing was to accommodate the Department of Antiquities and the North Wing was to house the museum's administrative offices.[79] In effect, the design merged the functions outlined earlier by Kenyon for the Allied School with those of an archaeological museum. The Department of Antiquities' wing housed offices, a board room located in the circular space at the wing's southwest corner, and a spacious lecture hall with its adjacent projection room. The North Wing included up-to-date facilities for researching artefacts and preparing their display. These included a receiving and arranging room, a dark room, a records room, and more. This wing also had a service court for receiving artefacts and a large reading room/library. A basement spanned both wings and was used for storage and addi-

---

only the Senate House and library were completed, owing to the above-mentioned financial crisis. See Eitan Karol, 'Naked and Unashamed: Holden in Bloomsbury', *Past and Future* 4 (2008): 6–7; Darcy Braddell, 'Academy Architecture, 1936, a Brief Review', *Architectural Review* 79 (1936): 273. (b) Head offices of the underground railway, designed by Adams, Holden and Pierce, completed in 1929. Eric Gill, who sculpted the Archaeological Museum's reliefs, discussed below, designed some of this building's reliefs as well. See Walter Bayes, 'Sense and Sensibility. The New Head Offices of the Underground Railway, Westminster, London. Adams, Holden and Pierce', *Architectural Review* 66 (1929): 225–41.

[79] Gibson, 'British Archaeological Institutions in Mandatory Palestine', 122–3.

APPROPRIATING MULTI-HISTORIES   81

tional facilities. The plans for this part of the building were clearly explicitly devised to accommodate these various functions.

Fuchs suggests that the difference in the sizes and shapes of the two wings was due to the site's limitations and the need to move large objects.[80] These limitations, however, do not provide a full explanation for such a significant divergence from the commitment to Beaux-Arts symmetry. The different treatments of courtyards, fenestration, the stairwells that access the mezzanine, and more, all suggest additional or alternative concepts. This also surfaces when considering Breasted and Rockefeller's influence: Breasted was intimately involved in developing the plans for the Palestine Archaeological Museum. He and Harrison prepared preliminary designs in 1927 and these were to be approved by Rockefeller himself.[81] Thus, their concepts for the project had a significant impact. Rockefeller and Breasted both had previous experience with similar projects, and it appears that their approach toward museum design underwent a profound transformation following the failure of their grand plan for an archaeological museum in Cairo. A comparison between the unexecuted Cairo plans, devised by the American architect William Welles Bosworth (1869–1966), and the Palestine Archaeological Museum is instructive in this respect. Bosworth, who received his education at the École des Beaux-Arts in Paris, created a plan that was approved by both Rockefeller and Breasted (Figure 2.17).[82] It was strictly symmetrical, orthogonal and completely in accord with Beaux-Arts concepts of museum design: it had a series of inner courts connected by long galleries, with smaller (court-centred) square pavilions at their corners. Furthermore, the Cairo museum design had the grandeur of spacious galleries separated internally by colossal colonnades (with Luxor-inspired capitals), and a classical portico façade. In examining the differences in plans, other factors should also be considered: the Palestine Archaeological Museum was to receive one-fifth of the budget that had been allocated for the museum in Egypt ($2 million and $10 million, respectively), and their sites and projected sizes were very different. However, there were other initial differences in monetary and physical conditions that influenced both patrons' and architect's move away from the rigidity of the Beaux-Arts plan when engaging in the project in Jerusalem.

This shift can be clearly seen when tracing Harrison's development of his designs. An early plan, made in 1924, prior to the selection of the site and Rockefeller's donation, is entirely symmetrical (Figure 2.18A), as is one he devised following the endowment, dated 1927 (Figure 2.18B). The 1924 plan is completely orthogonal, whereas the 1927 version exhibits diagonally adjacent wings, which are already distant from Beaux-Arts precedents and the designs of earlier museums. Both the 1924 and the 1927 plans have square corner rooms adjacent to each of the long galleries, possibly derived from the earlier plan for the Egyptian museum.

[80] Fuchs, 'Austen St. Barbe Harrison', 111–12.
[81] Plumer to Leo Amery, Secretary of the Colonies, 18 November 1927, 2, *Museum for Palestine* file, *NAGB* CO 733/142/5; 'Col. Symes' speech at the press briefing', *Davar*, 21 December 1927, 2.
[82] Abt, 'Toward a Historian's Laboratory', 175.

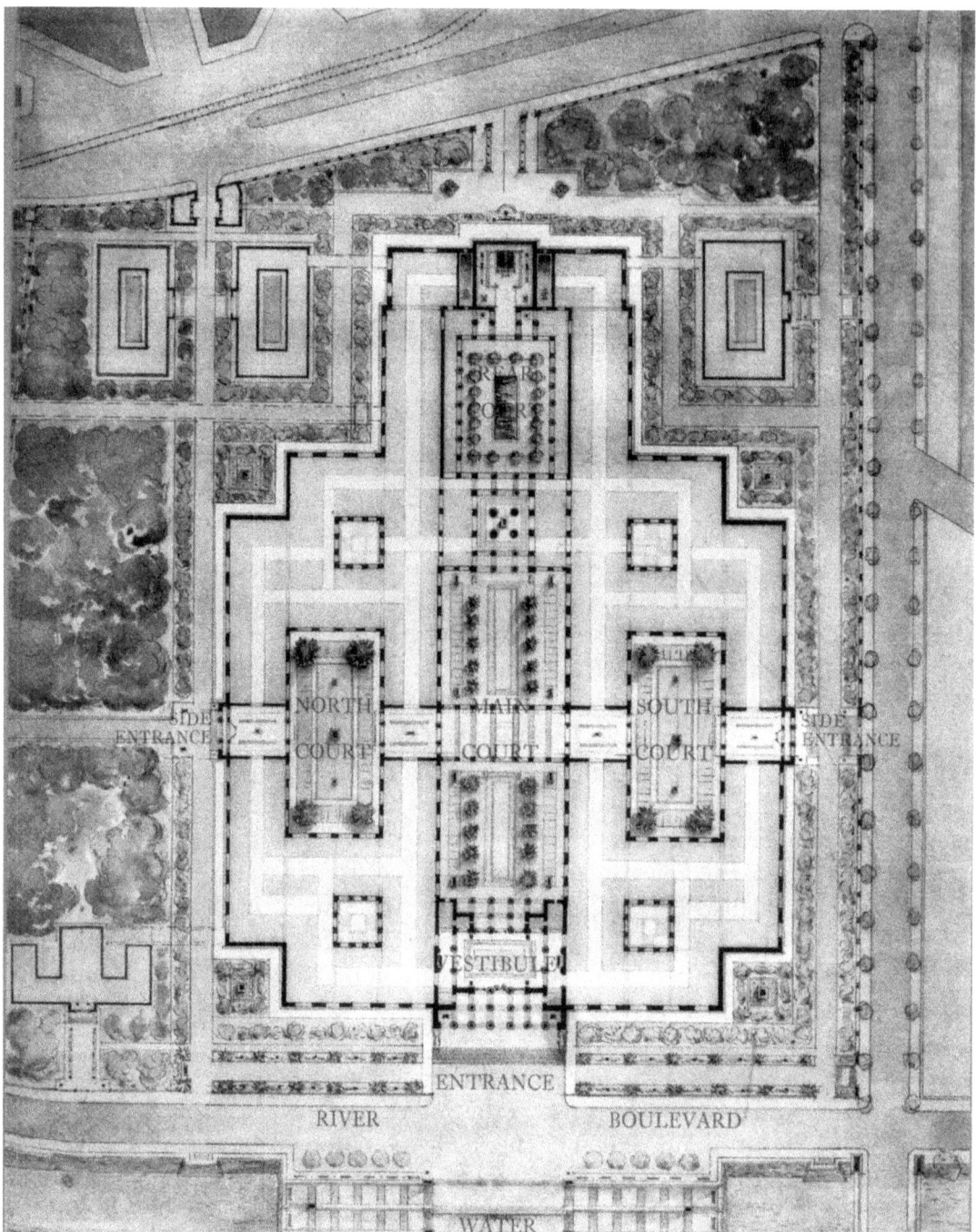

Figure 2.17 *Welles Bosworth, Floor Plan of the Egyptian Museum, 1925. Photo originally published in James Henry Breasted,* The New Egyptian Museum and Research Institute at Cairo, *New York: privately printed, 1925. © Oriental Institute, University of Chicago.*

Figure 2.18a *Austen St Barbe Harrison, Plan for the Palestine Archaeological Museum, 25 March 1924. ABHC.*

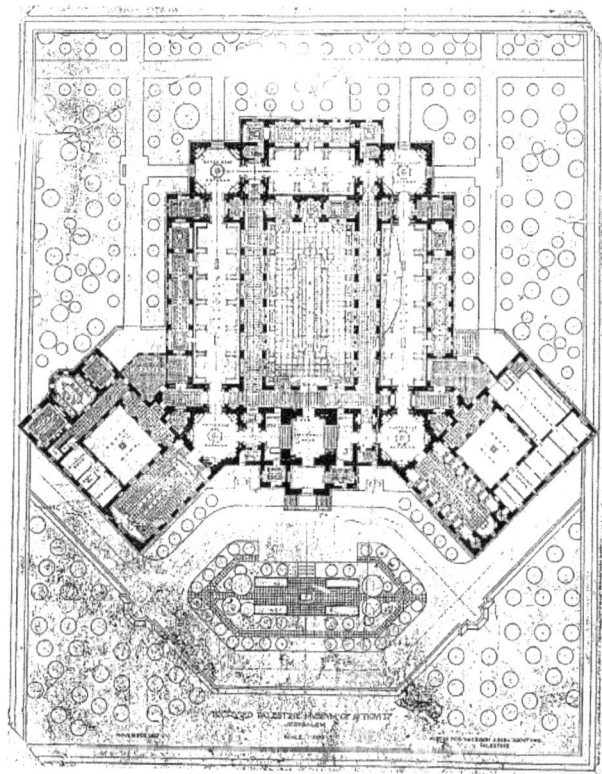

Figure 2.18b *Austen St Barbe Harrison, Plan for the Palestine Archaeological Museum, November 1927. Austen St Barbe Harrison Collection – whereabouts unknown. Source: Fuchs, 'Austen St. Barbe Harrison', fig. B.7.6.*

Figure 2.19 *Mayers, Murray and Phillip, Chicago House, Luxor, Egypt, 1930. © Oriental Institute, University of Chicago.*

Other possible models that Breasted and Harrison may have jointly considered were the archaeological facilities in Luxor, Egypt, mentioned earlier. The Chicago University Oriental Institute's Chicago House was built there in the 1920s, and then rebuilt, more lavishly and spaciously, during the early 1930s by the American architectural firm of Mayers, Murray & Phillip (Figure 2.19).[83] Both had work spaces, a library, and accommodations for the archeological excavation teams and their servants. The first house had a dome and arched openings. The second, larger house had two separate wings, an inner arcaded courtyard with a tiled fountain, a combination of arched and rectangular fenestration, and high, vaulted ceilings.[84] Thus, Harrison's plan for the Jerusalem museum was comparable to the two Chicago houses in its integration of functionalism with a simple, almost unadorned Orientalism. Harrison's 1924 plan included the service facilities for personnel and director's dwelling within the museum complex, a fact that makes it all the more probable that the Chicago houses were models even before Breasted's involvement, and certainly afterward.

Harrison's final plan appears to have been influenced by these facilities for

[83] Emberling, *Pioneers to the Past*, 111–12; for photos of the first house, see 51, fig. 4.22.
[84] Ibid. 50–2.

archaeology and, in effect, merges them with the representative, magisterial qualities of Beaux-Arts museum planning. Had Harrison wanted to adhere to a symmetrical plan, he could have managed it within the allocated site and budget, just as numerous architects had done before him when planning according to Beaux-Arts principles.

Harrison's approach can be further understood by exploring how Rockefeller and Breasted's impact was informed by the style of their architectural projects in the United States. There, the Rockefellers steered projects they endorsed toward architectural firms that espoused the integration of Beaux-Arts and modernism. These firms include the above-mentioned Mayers, Murray & Phillip, which, in addition to Chicago House, built the Chicago Oriental Institute in Chicago, also funded by Rockefeller through Breasted's solicitation. Their predecessors in planning the Oriental Institute – first Bertram Grosvenor Goodhue and then William Lescaze and George Howe – also integrated the two approaches. I discuss Goodhue's engagement with these methods in more detail in Chapter Three; Lescaze and Howe worked with Nelson Rockefeller (John D. Rockefeller's son) on related projects, presenting him with (unrealised) plans for New York's Museum of Modern Art in 1935.[85] In his discussion of Howe's work from the late 1920s and early 1930s, Robert Stern characterises it as a 'rational expressionism' that integrated Beaux-Arts principles with modernist functionalism.[86] The fact that the Rockefellers espoused this architecture supports a reading of the Palestine museum as a building that was the outcome of a similar conscious integration of these two approaches, encouraged by the patrons, which entailed an abstraction of architectural elements representing the region's histories merged with a functional plan.

Moreover, Harrison's appropriation of vernacular architecture, expressed in features such as the low domes and cubic forms of the vestibule and fountain, demonstrates modernist tendencies. As shown in recent studies, the Mediterranean vernacular constituted an important source for the development of the modern movement. Thus, using the borrowed Mediterranean vernacular was in itself a modernist gesture that relied on functionalism, climate consideration and site specificity as a basis for innovation.[87] Hence, just as the Mediterranean scene proved influential for renown architects such as Eric Mendelsohn and Le Corbusier, who as early as in the 1920s reflected it in their writing and architecture,[88] Harrison's

---

[85] William B. Scott and Peter M. Rutkoff, *New York Modern: The Arts and the City* (Baltimore: Johns Hopkins University Press, 2001), 178.

[86] Robert A. M. Stern, 'PSFS: Beaux-Arts Theory and Rational Expressionism', *Journal of the Society of Architectural Historians* 21, no. 2 (1962): 94.

[87] Jean-François Lejeune and Michelangelo Sabatino, eds, *Modern Architecture and the Mediterranean: Vernacular Dialogues and Contested Identities* (Abingdon and New York: Routledge, 2009).

[88] Benedetto Gravagnuolo, 'From Schinkel to Le Corbusier: The Myth of the Mediterranean in Modern Architecture', in *Modern Architecture and the Mediterranean*, eds Jean-Francois Lejeune and Michelangelo Sabatino, 29–35; Ita Heinze-Greenberg, 'An Artistic European Utopia at the Abyss of Time: The Mediterranean Academy Project, 1931–34', *Architectural History* 45 (2002), 441–82.

use of these sources indicates both his awareness of their work and his own appreciation of these factors. Harrison was surely inspired by Mendelsohn, who practised in Palestine between 1935 and 1941 and was already considered one of the leading figures of twentieth-century modernism.[89] The force of this inspiration is remarkably prominent in other buildings that Harrison planned in Jerusalem, such as the General Post Office (1934–8; now the Israeli Central Post Office) and the Government Printer (1937).

Thus, the Archaeological Museum reveals a type of modernism that embraces the past in both its formal and decorative schemes. This is not a latent, undeveloped modernism, nor a lingering historicism. Rather, this architectural approach merits a historicity that unravels its own complexity and explains it as a set of consciously selected concepts that interpret modernism not as a histrionic break with tradition, but as a path that assimilates traditional elements – in plan, volume or ornamentation. Moreover, Harrison's work on the museum at a time when no similar institutions were being constructed in the British Isles turned Palestine – the periphery – into the actual testing ground for new ideas that were produced in the centre but not realised there. This relates to developments in the field of museology, in Harrison's negotiation of architectural modernism, and in his formulation of locality. In order to convey meaning and a connection to place, Harrison's modernism embraced local architecture in a twofold way: regionally in its absorption of indigenous forms and temporally in its appropriation of features derived from past epochs. These epochs received an additional, didactic enunciation in the museum's reliefs and inscriptions, which represent yet another meeting point between modernism and the past.

Eric Gill: Reliefs and Inscriptions

The ten square reliefs that decorate the exterior walls of the Central Court's arcade (see Figure 2.21a–j), carved by British sculptor Eric Gill (1882–1940), feature various historic cultures from Jerusalem's and Palestine's past. Gill also created a relief for the tympanum above the building's entrance door (see Figure 2.22) and designed the museum's signage (see Figure 2.23). When Gill came to Jerusalem in the spring of 1934, he was already a famous sculptor, engraver and typographer, and he is acknowledged today as one of the foremost British artists and typographers of the twentieth century.[90] His work in the museum, which references ancient styles of the Near East in both image and text, reflects his Art Deco tendencies and his innovative fonts.

The circumstances of Gill's commission for the Archaeological Museum are

---

[89] For Mendelsohn's influence on Harrison, see Fuchs, 'Austen St. Barbe Harrison', 170, 302, n. 199.
[90] Monographs discussing Gill include Walter Shewring, *Letters of Eric Gill* (London: Cape, 1947); Malcolm Yorke, *Eric Gill: Man of Flesh and Spirit* (London: Constable, 1990); Fiona MacCarthy, *Eric Gill* (London: Faber & Faber, 2011); Robert Speaight, *The Life of Eric Gill* (London: Methuen, 1966).

not entirely clear. His biographer, Fiona MacCarthy, writes that Eric Mendelsohn facilitated it.[91] This is entirely possible as less than a year earlier, in the summer of 1933, Mendelsohn and his future business partner, Serge Chermayeff (1900–96), recruited Gill for their planned European Mediterranean Academy.[92] Although this project was not realised, Gill's involvement evidences his interest in an all-encompassing Mediterranean artistic heritage. There was also another party that may have facilitated Gill's work in Jerusalem. In a letter to his American friend Graham Carey during his second trip to the city, dated 7 July 1937, Gill wrote:

> Well, well, this is all absurdly inadequate to convey to you (a) my overwhelming love for Jerusalem & for Palestine – oh my dear Graham you can't believe how lovely they are, and (b) my very deep and inexpressible gratitude to you for your part in our privilege.[93]

Graham Carey, an art critic connected with the Fogg Art Museum in Boston, had also commissioned work from Gill.[94] It is possible that Gill, mentioning Carey's part in his coming to Jerusalem, referred to the museum commission, as well as to later projects that the former carried out in the city.[95] In the same letter, Gill described his friendship with Harrison: he and his wife stayed with Harrison during their 1937 visit to Jerusalem, and sculptor and architect travelled to Egypt together.[96] Gill often expressed a strong emotional tie toward Jerusalem and Palestine, and MacCarthy describes his first trip as remarkably formative, 'so much that Gill's life can almost be divided into pre- and post-Jerusalem phases'.[97] Gill was deeply interested in the political situation in Palestine, as evidenced by two letters he wrote in 1936 to *The Tablet*, the weekly London-based Catholic review. He opposed, although not vehemently, the industrialisation 'fostered by the Jews and their financial backers, with the result that Palestine is becoming an industrial country on English lines, and the Mohammedan and Arab culture is being destroyed'.[98] This approach reflects the romantic and Orientalist perception of Palestine as an unchanging land with a primitive society and economy. A perception that, as we have seen, was shared by several other British artists and architects working in the country.

Gill described the museum commission in a letter from 1933: Harrison gave him a 'list of ancient nations for the Jerusalem Museum carvings: Canaan, Israel,

---

[91] MacCarthy, *Eric Gill*, 263.
[92] Heinze-Greenberg, 'An Artistic European Utopia at the Abyss of Time', 450–2.
[93] Shewring, *Letters of Eric Gill*, 389.
[94] Carey's *Eric Gill in Yorkshire* was published in 1998 by the Henry Moore Sculpture Trust in Leeds. For the commission from Gill, see Speaight, *The Life of Eric Gill*, plate 16.
[95] Gill executed a few commissioned inscriptions, developed an Arabic type for the Government Printer and a Hebrew type for a new Hebrew press; see Shewring, *Letters of Eric Gill*, 387.
[96] Ibid. 386–9.
[97] MacCarthy, *Eric Gill*, 263.
[98] Shewring, *Letters of Eric Gill*, 360.

Philistia, Assyria–Babylonia, Egypt, Persia, Greece–Macedonia, Rome, Byzantium – Crusades, Islam'.[99] The reliefs are arranged in chronological order: the most ancient civilisations are depicted on the southern wall and the later cultures on the northern one. Each of these ten reliefs is positioned between the arcade's gently pointed arches and is framed by a triple stone border cut into the wall's cladding. As both the cladding and the low reliefs are cut from the same stone, the latter are unobtrusive. The reliefs are consistent with Gill's 1930s style as can be seen, for example, in his work for the British Broadcasting Corporation (BBC) House in London (1932). His figures are abstracted and have large limbs and heads. A few low-relief geometricised lines delineate such details as eyes, nose, hair and muscles; drapery, hair and wings are stylised. As the reliefs were to be viewed from a distance from below, gestures are clear and varied – such as bending, kneeling, raised arms, and so on. The incisions and protrusions used for details are repetitive, which clearly identifies them as Art Deco.[100] Archaeology was a major source of inspiration for this style, especially the exciting new artefacts that Breasted and his colleagues unearthed during the 1920s in the Near East.[101] Near Eastern reliefs from ancient Egypt and Mesopotamia were admired for their streamlining of human or animal bodies and their abstraction by patterning. A large spread in the *Illustrated London News*, published when the Palestine Archeological Museum finally opened to the public in 1938, laid out Gill's relief, *Philistia*, flanked by two photographs of ivory reliefs from Samaria, Palestine, counted among the prized artefacts in the museum's collection (Figure 2.20):[102] one ivory depicted a winged sphinx exhibiting Assyrian influence, and a second had seated figures in an Egyptian style. Thus, it is safe to assume that Gill was encouraged to use these treasures as sources for his reliefs, which can be clearly seen in the outcome. Using these archaeological sources reflected Art Deco tendencies, which Gill expressed in the ancient art form of relief. Coupled with the turn to abstraction in European sculpture, in which he participated, the merging of these influences engendered figurative reliefs that had a modern, graphic appearance.

The first relief on the south side, *Canaan* (Figure 2.21a), which was probably intended to portray Canaan as a land with a strong agricultural basis, depicts a bent over wheat harvester, his sheaf creating a sharp diagonal of repetitive stems across the composition. The second relief, *Egypt* (Figure 2.21b), portrays a typically skirt-clad Egyptian male leaning forward, his right hand raised, and his left holding a long cane that frames a kneeling figure below him. What is probably a chariot wheel is shown to the right. This image is reminiscent of the Bible

---

[99] Ibid. 280.
[100] For the characteristics of the Art Deco style and select architectural sculpting, see Don Vlack, *Art Deco Architecture in New York, 1920–1940* (New York: Harper & Row, 1974), 5–6, 57–60, 89–94 and figures.
[101] Archaeology's impact on Art Deco is discussed in Bridget Elliott, 'Art Deco Worlds in a Tomb: Reanimating Egypt in Modern(ist) Visual Culture', *South Central Review* 25, no. 1 (2008): 114–35.
[102] 'A New Temple of Archaeology in Jerusalem: Antiquities Shrined', *Illustrated London News*, 22 January 1938, 137.

A NEW TEMPLE OF ARCHÆOLOGY IN JERUSALEM: ANTIQUITIES SHRINED.

Figure 2.20 *Ivory reliefs from Samaria and Eric Gill's 'Philistia' Relief.* Illustrated London News, 22 January 1938, 137 ('A New Temple of Archaeology in Jerusalem: Antiquities Shrined').

story of Moses and the Hebrew slave, but it is likely a generalised description of authority and of the Egyptian Pharaonic period. The third relief, *Philistia* (Figure 2.21c), depicts three men rowing a boat, afloat on stylised waves. Ronny Reich and Ayala Sussman identify this relief as *Phoenicia*,[103] but there is no reason to doubt its initial identification by Gill as *Philistia*, whose people were also sea-goers. This association was important, as it commemorated the descendants of modern Palestinians. It may also have been related to Garstang's excavations concerned with Philistia in Ashkelon and Gaza in the mid-1920s.[104] The fourth relief is entitled *Assyria–Babylonia* (Figure 2.21d), but Reich and Sussman contend that Persia is also represented.[105] This is possible, as Gill eventually separated Byzantium from Crusades, and thus had to merge three cultures. The resulting relief, termed by Reich and Sussman *Fertile Crescent*, depicts a double-horned winged horse (somewhat like a chimera), reminiscent of the ivory of the sphinx from Samaria in its large limbs, hoofs and stylised wings. The fifth relief, *Israel*, portrays Moses holding the stone tablets, incised with the first letter of each commandment (Figure 2.21e). The stylised drapery of Moses's robe and beard is accentuated by rays of light, which represent his radiance after he received the commandments.[106] As a convert to Catholicism and a devout believer, Gill was well-versed in these biblical events and their significance.

[103] Reich and Sussman, 'LeToldot Muse'on Rockefeller BiYerushalayim', 86.
[104] These excavations are discussed in Gibson, 'British Archaeological Institutions in Mandatory Palestine', 183, n. 10.
[105] Reich and Sussman, 'LeToldot Muse'on Rockefeller BiYerushalayim', 86.
[106] The Bible, Exodus 34: 29–35.

Figure 2.21a–j *Eric Gill, reliefs in the central court of the Palestine Archaeological Museum, c. 1934–5:* **a** *Canaan;* **b** *Egypt;* **c** *Philistia;* **d** *Assyria/Babylonia;* **e** *Israel;* **f** *Greece/Macedonia;* **g** *Rome;* **h** *Byzantium;* **i** *Islam;* **j** *Crusades. All photographed by Diego Rosman except j photographed by the author.*

On the north wall, the first relief, *Greece–Macedonia*, portrays a crouching nude male figure. His head is turned back, and his left arm is bent over his shoulder, fist closed. The word 'Greece', spelled out in Greek letters, is written vertically to his left (Figure 2.21f). This relief probably represents the Greek creation myth of Deucalion and his wife, Pyrrha. The couple, having survived the Deluge, re-inhabited the world by throwing stones behind them, which became men and women when they landed on the ground.[107] The choice of this myth, which

---

[107] Richard Y. Hathorn, *Greek Mythology* (Beirut: American University of Beirut, 1977), 17–18.

APPROPRIATING MULTI-HISTORIES

articulates the dawn of mankind, relates to the museum's mandate to curate and display artefacts that relate to the history and origins of cultures.

The Roman culture is depicted by Romulus, Remus and the she-wolf (Figure 2.21g). Two unchildlike males look up to the wolf's teats, as she bends her neck so that an arch is formed above them. The letters RO–MA are inscribed in the upper corners, and one can discern the initials SPQR – which stand for *Senatus Populusque Romanus*, the ancient Roman republican government – at the bottom, behind the twins' legs. The next relief, *Byzantium* (Figure 2.21h), portrays St Helen and Emperor Constantine, crowned and holding sceptres, facing one another, with the cross found by Helen outlined in the background. The image is based on ancient Byzantine depictions of the legend of the True Cross,[108] which was central to Jerusalem's sanctity for Christianity and, accordingly, the Latin sentence *O Crux Ave* ('Hail the Cross') is inscribed between the two figures.[109]

Gill's next image, *Islam*, portrays Muhammad's ascension from the Temple Mount (the *Mi'raj*; Figure 2.21I). This event, which sanctified Jerusalem for Muslims, is figured by showing Buraq, the prophet's horse, the veiled head of Muhammad and his leg. Muhammad appears to be holding a scroll – the Quran. This representation is derived from sixteenth-century, mostly Persian, Muslim illustrated manuscripts, which depict Buraq as a winged horse with a human, crowned, female head.[110] In Muslim art, this representation figured in manuscripts and other small mediums, but never on buildings. Thus, while constituting a choice that was very apt for establishing Muslim ties to Jerusalem, the depiction of the *Mi'raj* on the wall of a secular, British civic building most likely did not sit well with the Muslim community.

The last relief, *Crusades*, depicts a Crusader knight kneeling in front of a Crusader cross, the symbol of the Kingdom of Jerusalem (Figure 2.21J). A relic believed to be of the True Cross was the most important object of veneration in the kingdom.[111] By separating *Byzantium* from *Crusades*, Gill allotted these cultures prominent places. Both depict a cross and can thus be interpreted as an assertion of Christian claims for the city and a manifestation of Christianity as the truest among the three monotheistic creeds. Chronologically, the Crusades relief closes the series and connects past Christian hegemony with the present British rule.

As I noted earlier, Gill also carved a relief on the museum entrance tympanum (Figure 2.22). It portrays male personifications of Asia and Africa kneeling on either side of a tree, which might represent the Tree of Knowledge in the Cartesian sense of the concept: in depictions on maps, the tree traditionally signified Europe as the

[108] Barbara Baert, 'New Observations on the Genesis of Girona (1050–1100). The Iconography of the Legend of the True Cross', *Gesta* 38, no. 2 (1999): 115–27.
[109] I wish to thank Sarah Offenberg for her assistance in identifying this scene and its meaning.
[110] Christiane Gruber, 'The Prophet Muhammad's Ascension (*Mi'Raj*) in Islamic Painting and Literature: Evidence from Cairo Collections', *Bulletin of the American Research Center in Egypt* 185 (Summer 2004): 24–31.
[111] Adrian J. Boas, *Jerusalem in the Time of the Crusades: Society, Landscape and Art in the Holy City under Frankish Rule* (London: Routledge, 2001), 33.

Figure 2.22 *Eric Gill, Asia and Africa reliefs in the tympanum at the main entrance to the Palestine Archaeological Museum, c. 1934–5. Photographed by Diego Rosman.*

source of knowledge.[112] To the left of the tree, Asia appears robed, holding a sword, whereas Africa – wearing only a skirt, his torso left bare, and holding a spear – is kneeling on its right. The figures' garb and attributes reflect the distinct and traditional European perception of the Oriental and African Other, which surfaced especially from the fifteenth century on.[113] Within this perception, hierarchies of nations and peoples were developed to evaluate foreign cultures. In this case, the speared and loosely clad figure interprets Africa as habitat to the most primitive of cultures. Moreover, the meeting of Africa and Asia under the supposed Tree of Knowledge informs visitors that Palestine is a bridge – both physical and cultural – between the two continents. Knowledge of these continents is created by the Western disciplines of geography, archaeology and history, which convey European ideas. The relief thus signifies that through the museum, the West – in this case Britain and America – brings the knowledge of archaeology to the developing Palestine. As such, the relief reiterates established representations of European domination over conquered and colonised lands. However, the fact that males, rather than females, are imaged may be significant, in that this visualisation, which requires further

[112] Michael Wintle, 'Renaissance Maps and the Construction of the Idea of Europe', *Journal of Historical Geography* 25, no. 2 (1999): 156.
[113] Ibid. 149–50.

Figure 2.23 *Eric Gill, Palestine Archaeological Museum, south gallery signage, c. 1934–5. Photographed by Diego Rosman.*

analysis, might well reflect the difference between the mandatory and the colonial contexts, as it negates the traditional sexual aspects of colonial tropes.[114]

In Great Britain, Gill was considered an expert in carving serif fonts on stone.[115] The museum commission constituted his first attempt to introduce Arabic and Hebrew fonts in his craft. The museum's signage appeared in the two principal local languages: Arabic and Hebrew, as well as in English, reflecting a desire for intercommunal participation in the museum. Stone signage enhanced other ancient elements in the building's architecture, such as the domes and the vaulting, indicating that the museum was expected to function for posterity and that its exhibits were permanent.

The inscriptions were painted in red on the natural stone and indicated, for example, facilities such as 'library' and 'drinking water' and names of cultures and civilisations in exhibition spaces (Figure 2.23). In all three languages, the fonts are rather traditional in concept – serif lettering for English and Hebrew signs and Naskhi for Arabic. Whereas Gill contended that san-serif fonts are most suited for architecture, he also believed that fonts had to be appropriate to 'place and occasion'.[116] Apparently, he considered the more traditional serif fonts more suitable for a museum displaying antiquities. Accordingly, the English inscriptions are similar to other stone carvings Gill executed in the 1930s and, compared to his typographic fonts, they resemble the Aries typeface. Reich and Sussman, who analysed the museum's Hebrew inscriptions, contend that Gill was inspired

---

[114] In European art, the continents were usually represented by female personifications and, as such, reflected discourses of dominance – male over female, white ethnicity over black or Asian. See ibid. 153–6, 159.
[115] Nigel Holmes, 'Eric Gill: Cut in Stone', *Visual Communication Quarterly* 15, no. 1–2 (2008): 47.
[116] Eric Gill, 'What is Lettering?' *Architectural Review* 73 (1933): 28.

by an important first-century Hebrew-letter inscription (in Aramaic) preserved in the Russian Patriarchy of Jerusalem, as well as by other ancient inscriptions in the museum's collection.[117] For the Hebrew letters in the relief depicting Moses and the Ten Commandments, Gill used a serif font similar to the Frank Rühl font circa 1911.[118] The Zionist newspaper *Doar Hayom* reported that the Hebrew lettering was prepared by Zionist archaeologist Eliezer Sukenik according to an inscription on an ancient sarcophagus, with the assistance of the artist Ze'ev Raban, and Dr Marcus Reiner, a Jewish engineer in the Public Works Department and a close friend of Harrison's.[119] It is indeed likely that Gill had assistance with these designs, and *Doar Hayom*, along with the *Illustrated London News*, indicated that Gill referred to archaeological findings not only for designing the reliefs, but for the inscriptions as well, as he had done in developing other new fonts.[120] Enlisting ancient inscriptions was for Gill a means for perfecting new, modern fonts, and a method for tackling the subtleties of the letters' apertures, modulations and serif shapes. In the museum, although the grammar in the languages foreign to Gill is antiquated and even erroneous (which is curious, considering the help he had), the signage represents one of the first attempts to adapt new fonts to modern, multilingual museum signage, which gives this project an importance beyond its specific function.

Communal Participation in the Building Process

The Palestine Archaeological Museum was constructed during years that witnessed a serious deterioration in the relations between Arabs and Jews, and in both these communities' relations with the British. Whereas the project had the potential to alleviate strife at least in some small measure, the following discussion shows that it was actually yet another catalyst for tensions, and that the museum itself failed to create an intercommunal sense of belonging to the region's local heritage.

Hiring Harrison for planning the museum was not without its political implications: it was a commission handed to the British chief architect without competition, although there were already practising Zionist and Palestinian architects in the country.[121] Harrison complained in private correspondence that the Zionist architects had already protested in the press against the Mandatory Government not employing them for the work on Government House, which construction was completed according to Harrison's plans in 1931. In the case of the museum, the

---

[117] Ronny Reich and Ayala Sussman, 'Al Otiot Ivriot She'Yitsev Erik Gill', *Cathedra: For the History of Eretz Israel and Its Yishuv* 95 (2000): 173–6.
[118] Raphael Frank, *Al Otiyot Dfus VeGofanim*, intro. Jacques Adler, trans. Moshe Yarden (Berlin: Berthold, 1926).
[119] 'Be'in Ovdey 'Bezalel', *Doar Hayom*, 18 November 1935, 7.
[120] Holmes, 'Eric Gill: Cut in Stone', 47.
[121] Fuchs, 'Austen St. Barbe Harrison', 108.

Royal Institute of British Architects (RIBA) also protested against the fact that no competition was held, writing to the Undersecretary of State of the Colonial Office that 'the design of a building of such universal importance and magnitude should be the subject of an international competition amongst architects'.[122] By December 1927, Harrison had hired three British architects: Paul Victor Edison Mauger (1896–1982), T. A. L. Concannon (n.d.), and W. Price (n.d.) as assistants for the project.[123] This, Harrison wrote, also brought about public protest in the press.[124] No newspaper articles support this contention, but the Hebrew press did publish numerous general complaints with regard to the fact that Jewish construction workers were not being hired by the Mandate authorities for various projects.[125] Hiring Jews and Arabs for British Mandate projects in Palestine was more than an economic issue. It was intrinsically connected to the formation of Zionist and Palestinian identities and to these communities' competing for cultural and political dominance.[126] In the existing split labour market, the British administration's attempts to create an image of a fair employer of both Jews and Arabs were implemented by hiring Jewish professionals and Arab nonprofessional builders.[127] This policy was impacted by the fact that Jewish labourers, such as construction workers, were unionised and demanded higher wages, which led to complaints from Arabs over unequal salaries, potentially increasing each project's budget. Thus, the British avoided hiring Jewish labourers as much as was politically possible.[128] Moreover, although, as I explained above, Jewish professionals were hired, the most important professional assignment in this project – the architect – was not given to a Jew. These practices reflected the British desire to maintain the appearance of neutrality in their governance in light of heightened tensions in the city. Professional tasks of lesser importance were indeed given to Jews. Artists Ze'ev Raban and Meir Gur-Arieh, from the Workshop for Industrial Arts in Jerusalem, were hired to execute some of Gill's inscriptions, in addition to the preliminary planning in which Raban participated.[129] The artists probably received this commission in light of the reputation they acquired for their acclaimed work

---

[122] RIBA Secretary to Ormsby-Gore, 8 March 1928, *Museum for Palestine* file, *NAGB* CO 733/146/5.
[123] 'Archaeological Museum, Jerusalem; Architects: A. St. B. Harrison, Paul Mauger, W. Price', *American Architect & Architecture*, October 1936, 54; documented date of hire refers to three (unnamed) architects. See *Museum for Palestine* file, *NAGB* CO 733/142/5.
[124] Fuchs, 'Austen St. Barbe Harrison', 108.
[125] See, e.g., a report concerning Government House: Arieh(?), 'Al Avoda Achat', *Davar*, 30 March 1931, 3, or the report 'Poaley Yerushalayim Tovim Zechutam Le'Avoda', *Davar*, 7 July 1932, 1. This latter article discusses work at the Rockefeller Museum and other government projects in Jerusalem.
[126] Deborah Bernstein, '"Ka'Asher Avoda Ivrit Eynena Omedet Al HaPerek": Histadrut Ha'Ovdim LeNochach HaMigzar HaMemshalti HaMandatory', in *Calcala Ve'Chevra BiYemey HaMandat, 1918–1948*, eds Avi Bareli and Nachum Karlinsky (Be'er Sheva: Ben-Gurion Institute, 2003), 80.
[127] Ibid. 87–8.
[128] Ibid. 87–8.
[129] 'Be'in Ovdey 'Bezalel', *Doar Hayom*, 18 November 1935, 7. For a general discussion of Raban's work, see Bat-Sheva Ida Goldman, *Ze'ev Raban: Symbolist Ivri*, Exhibition Catalogue (Tel Aviv: Tel Aviv Museum of Art, and Jerusalem: Yad Yizhak Ben-Zvi, 2001).

on the YMCA Building sculptures, which I discuss in Chapter Three. The first stages of construction were managed by Shimon Diskin, a Jew who had formerly worked on the British governor's house in Amman, Jordan.[130] Another specialised task was designing the ceramic tiling for the pavilion in the Central Court. These were executed by the Ohanessian ceramic workshop in Jerusalem, established by Ashbee, who, as I noted Chapter One, ardently promoted the 'revival' or 'conservation' of local arts and crafts in the city. David Ohanessian, the workshop's master craftsman, was an Armenian Christian from Kutahia, Turkey, and was initially invited to take part in the restoration work on the Dome of the Rock.[131] The installation of such tiles in the museum reflects Harrison's grounding in British arts-and-crafts traditions.[132] Unlike the Alhambra, where tiles were used only on walls, Harrison decided to tile the entire interior of the pavilion, even its squinches and dome (Figure 2.13). This choice represents an important aspect of Jerusalem and Palestine's Mandatory architectural culture, where tiles became a hallmark for all ethnic and religious groups and were used for public and private buildings, as well as for streets signs.[133] The use of tiles was thus an important aspect of communal participation. It signified the inclusion of the Armenian community in the work on the museum and created a discourse concerned with other buildings that employed this technique, such as the Jerusalem YMCA, as well as with other workshops – such as that of Raban and Gur-Arieh, who designed many of the tiles in Tel Aviv's architecture during the period.

Work on the museum's foundations began in 1929. The contract was awarded to the Christian-Arab-Jewish firm of ʿAwaḍ, Dunie & Katinka, who built the Jerusalem Palace Hotel and the YMCA Building; I discuss details about the firm in Chapters Three and Four.[134] Commissioning ʿAwaḍ, Dunie & Katinka was an additional endorsement of Jewish expertise and political encouragement for the unusual partnership of Arab and Jewish contractors. However, their involvement in the museum project was limited: in 1931 the major part of the construction was handed over to an Egyptian-based Italian firm, De Farro & Co., already working in Jerusalem, despite the fact that both Jewish and Arab contractors proposed bids.[135]

[130] 'The Archaeological Museum', *The Palestine Bulletin*, 14 February 1929, 3.
[131] Hysler-Rubin, 'Arts & Crafts and the Great City', 356; Ben-Asher Gitler, 'C. R. Ashbee's Jerusalem Years', 29–52. See also the discussion in Chapter Four of the present book.
[132] Fuchs, 'Austen St. Barbe Harrison', 114.
[133] Nirit Shalev-Khalifa and Yair Wallach, 'Ke'Even Kechel al Rekah Nof Ha'Even HaTzehavhav', *Et-Mol* (2011): 36–8; Maoz Azaryahu, 'Hebrew, Arabic, English: The Politics of Multilingual Street Signs in Israeli Cities', *Social & Cultural Geography* 13, no. 5 (2012): 466–8; Batia Carmiel, Edina Meyer-Maril and Alec Mishori, *Arichim Me'atrim Yir: Keramika Bezalel BeBatey Tel Aviv 1923–1929* (Tel Aviv: Eretz Israel Museum, 1996), 461–79; Nurith Kenaan Kedar, *HaKeramika Ha'Armanit shel Yerushalayim, Shlosha Dorot 1919–2000* (Tel Aviv: Eretz Israel Museum, 2002).
[134] 'Azhara m M.P. [Moctzet Poaley] YM [Yerushalayim]', *Davar*, 6 November 1929, 1.
[135] *Report by His Majesty's Government in the United Kingdom of Great Britain and Northern Ireland to the Council of the League of Nations on the Administration of Palestine and Trans-Jordan for the Year 1931* (London: His Majesty's Stationary Office), 161, *NAGB* CO 1071/308; 'Museum Rockefeller – LeKablan Italki', *Davar*, 1 April 1931, 1; 'Binyan Be'it HaMuse'on

By not contracting local Jews or Arabs for this major stage, the British continued their attempts to reflect an impartial image with regard to work on the museum. However, tension regarding hiring Jewish builders, as well as Jewish pressure on the British administration and the contractor to increase their numbers, continued throughout the construction process.[136] Zionist and Jewish newspapers claimed that during 1931–2 Jewish builders were boycotted by the construction company, with behind-the-scenes support from the British. This despite the fact that Jews were the concrete experts in Palestine and dominated other areas of professional construction.[137] Reports in 1929 noted that 26 Arabs and 6 Jews were employed; in 1931 there were only 10 Jews out of a total of 160 workers, whereas a 1932 report lists 15 Jews out of 300 builders working on site.[138] According to the Chicago-based Jewish newspaper, *The Sentinel*, Rockefeller denied knowledge of this virtual exclusion of Jews and waived responsibility for the issue contending that 'the gift is being administered by the British Government'.[139] A series of confidential reports sent from High Commissioner Wauchope to Secretary of the Colonies in London Sir Philip Cunliff-Lister in 1933 confirm that the British indeed viewed equal job distribution in British public works as problematic, since it did not reflect the relative size of the Jewish and Arab populations, nor the greater financial hardships that the Arabs were experiencing.[140] Accordingly, their policy was to adjust employment according to the sizes of the populations and economic status, which in effect mandated limiting Jewish employment rather than increasing it.[141]

Concurrently, Hebrew newspapers commented that the Arab builders were working at the museum under inhumane conditions and were being exploited by the contractor.[142] In an attempt to create some proletarian solidarity between Arab and Jewish workers,[143] Hebrew and Jewish newspapers reported strikes that

Ha'Archaeology', *Doar Hayom*, 6 May 1931, 4; 'Be'it HaNchot Le'Atikot a's Rockefeller', *Doar Hayom*, 21 February 1929, 1. De Farro's Jerusalem office is mentioned in A. Q. Adamson, 'Constructors Submitting Tenders for Jerusalem YMCA Building Work', 2 December 1929, YAAd.

[136] See, e.g., H. Frumkin, 'Kalkalatenu She'Amda BaMivchan', *Davar*, 13 December 1929; 'LeMatzav Ha'Avoda Ba'Aretz', *Davar*, 2 June 1931, 1; Arieh Livschütz, 'Le'Matzav Ha'Avoda Ve'Hairgun BiYerushalayim', *Davar*, 20 November 1931, 3; 'Poaley Yerushalayim Tovim Zechtam Le'Avoda', *Davar*, 7 July 1932, 1.

[137] 'Binyan Rockefeller al Taharat HaCherem', *Davar*, 26 October 1932, 1; 'Few Jews Employed on Building of Palestine Rockefeller Museum', *The Sentinel*, 28 August 1931, 29.

[138] 'Huchal Beninyan Muse'on Rockefeller', *Davar*, 2 April 1929, 1; 'Few Jews Employed', *The Sentinel*, 28 August 1931, 29; H. Frumkin, 'Ksut Eynayim', *Davar*, 20 June 1932, 2.

[139] 'Rockefeller Unaware of Prejudice', *The Sentinel*, 13 November 1931, 19.

[140] Arthur Wauchope to Philip Cunliff-Lister, 18 February 1933; 10 August 1933, NAGB CO 733/238/3.

[141] Ibid.

[142] Arieh Livschütz, 'LeMatzav Ha'Avoda Ve'Hairgun BiYerushalayim', *Davar*, 20 November 1931, 3; 'Hnitzul BeBinyan Muse'on Rockefeller', *Davar*, 22 June 1932.

[143] 'Hafsakat Avoda BeBinyan Muse'on Rockefeller', *Davar*, 2 May 1929; 'DeFaro Mitnakem BaPoalim', *Davar*, 1 August 1932, 1; 'Riv be'in Poalim Be'Museon Rockefeller', *Doar Hayom*, 1 August 1932, 2; 'Works on Rockefeller Museum Declare Strike', *The Sentinel*, 17 May 1929, 36.

took place during construction, expressing support for the labourers.[144] These reports reflect the politics of employment that Jews and Arabs demanded from the Mandate government, wherein Jews protested the conditions of Arab labourers in order to promote higher wages for both communities, notwithstanding Arab objections to the government hiring Jews.[145] As these conflicts arose regarding connection with work on the museum's construction as well, the project, originally conceived as an opportunity to bridge the gap between Jews and Arabs, in effect created strife and even increased hostility between the city's construction companies and labourers, which extended to other projects. When the Palestine Archaeological Museum finally opened in the winter of 1938, one of the years that saw the Arab Revolt, these hostilities painfully revealed that the cultural act of establishing a museum could not resolve the situation. British archaeologist J. L. Starkey was murdered by Arabs on his way to the museum's official opening ceremony.[146] Owing to the violence in Palestine at the time, the ceremony, modest to begin with, was cancelled after the murder. The accolades that the building received were tainted with the tragic consequences of intercommunal tensions.

Increasing the 'Knowledge of the Past of Men in the Holy Land'

The fact that articles in local newspapers concerning the Palestine Archaeological Museum – both describing the building and addressing its construction – were often on the front pages clearly indicates that it was perceived as a major architectural and cultural undertaking in Jerusalem. Its opening received significant coverage in the United Kingdom as well. The *Belfast News Letter* reported that:

> A Museum collection which has taken three years to classify and arrange is now open to the public in Jerusalem ... It has been financed by John D. Rockefeller, Jr. with the object of 'helping to encourage interest in and increase knowledge of the past of men in the Holy Land'.[147]

Although this description carries a reminder of the colonial 'civilizing mission', the absence of a benevolent empire and a targeted 'primitive culture' locates it within the more nuanced discourses of Mandatory iteration. The museum was

---

[144] For other attempts at creating such solidarity, see Lockman, 'Railway Workers and Relational History', 601–27.

[145] Bernstein, '"Ka'Asher Avoda Ivrit Eynena Omedet Al Haperek"', 89–90. The gap between wages paid to Jews and Arabs is reported and discussed in the *Report by His Majesty's Government in the United Kingdom of Great Britain and Northern Ireland to the Council of the League of Nations on the Administration of Palestine and Trans-Jordan for the Year 1933* (London: His Majesty's Stationary Office), 98–100, 108. *NAGB* CO 1071/309. The report notes that in 1933 two-thirds of the museum building was complete. See ibid. 224.

[146] 'Be'it HaNechot Ha'Archaeology Niftach', *Davar*, 13 January 1938, 1; 'A New Temple of Archaeology in Jerusalem: Antiquities Shrined', *Illustrated London News*, 22 January 1938, 137.

[147] 'Holy Land's History: Rockefeller Museum in Jerusalem', *Belfast News Letter*, 31 January 1938, 5.

perceived as having a cultural role in a loosely defined geographical region and hence was hailed as a 'modern institution of its kind that has the means of definitely stamping the Holy City as the recognized center for archaeological study in the Middle East'.[148]

In discussing museums in Britain, Christopher Whitehead argues that at the turn of the twentieth century, British museums favoured exhibiting remote histories from across the empire, so as to avoid exhibits that were 'too close to home', that is, could be associated by visitors with the social and economic rifts in Britain itself. The Palestine Archaeological Museum adopted a similar, broad historical approach, wherein the cultures and histories of the Middle East succeed one another in a seemingly uninterrupted temporal and cultural flow. Such an alignment poignantly presents an image of peaceful cultural exchange across space and time, neither suggesting specific national aspirations nor delineating borders. As Whitehead argues, 'knowledge and cultures of the "nation" [were] fitted into the ostensibly neutral territories of disciplinary taxonomy rather than into overtly ideological expressions of identity'.[149] Archaeology, in this case, provided the appropriate discipline for a neutral negotiation of the region's histories.

As is always the case with architecture in Jerusalem, no building, function or content can be unequivocally described as neutral. Hence, although Zionists and Palestinians frequented the museum, they perceived it as a British entity and did not consider it their own. British aspirations to create intercommunal shared histories and a sense of belonging through these neutral displays and declaring archeological finds as the cultural property of Palestine's inhabitants met with little or no success. Hebrew newspapers criticised the museum, writing that there was no mention of ancient Israelite culture in its official explanatory texts;[150] the Supreme Muslim Council opened its own archaeological museum in the area of the Haram-a-Sharif in 1934;[151] the Hebrew Society for the Excavation of Palestine and Its Antiquities established a small museum; and the Hebrew University planned a museum dedicated to Jewish antiquities.[152] These intracommunal ventures all indicate that in the eyes of both the Zionists and the Palestinians, the new Palestine Museum of Archaeology could not fulfil their desire to forge their own national visual cultures. As I argued at the outset of this discussion, the form and content of British custodianship, as reflected in the museum, elicited ambiguous and even contentious responses from Jerusalem's local inhabitants. The museum's architecture, which sought to express the region's multi-histories, thus became an additional feature of British and American cultural authority.

---

[148] 'Jerusalem's New Treasure House', *The Sphere*, 2 April 1938, 48.
[149] Whitehead, 'National Art Museums in Britain', 120.
[150] 'Be'it HaNechot Ha'Archaeology Niftach', *Davar*, 13 January 1938, 1.
[151] 'Be'it Nechot Muslami Be'Har HaBayit', *Davar*, 21 November 1934, 1.
[152] 'Ha'Asepha HaShnatit shel HaKirat Eretz Israel Va'Atikoteyha', *Doar Hayom*, 6 April 1932, 3; Z. Schocken, 'Al Inyaney Ha'Universita', *Davar*, 23 January 1936, 1.

CHAPTER THREE

Americans Imagining Jerusalem: The Jerusalem YMCA Building

One late afternoon I watched the setting sun pick out the domes and columns with splashes of vivid gold and this soft Palestine twilight throw a mellow diffused glow into the cloisters and arches. I realized then that without one single exception this is the most beautiful YMCA building in the world.
– Marion Dimmock, 1932[1]

FOR MARION DIMMOCK, assistant architect for the Jerusalem YMCA Building, who came from New York to supervise the final stages of construction, the golden late afternoon sun bathing the nearly completed YMCA was more than that. For him, it evoked an imagined Jerusalem revered by Americans, reminiscent, for example, of Mark Twain's pilgrimage sixty-four years earlier, when he saw Jerusalem 'perched on its eternal hills, white and domed and solid ... the venerable city gleam[ing] in the sun'.[2] These descriptions reveal their writers' profound appreciation of Jerusalem's history and Christian past and the city's central place in American Protestantism.[3] In many respects, the building erected in the city by the Young Men's Christian Association, better known by its acronym, YMCA, was a consummation of these religious sentiments (Figure 3.1).

In this chapter, I discuss the creation of this building, which was planned by American architect Arthur Loomis Harmon (1878–1958). Conceived as a hostel and community centre, the YMCA was designed to assert American presence and re-establish Christian prominence in Jerusalem. It was also intended to promote interfaith relations by welcoming Christians, Jews and Muslims. In the following pages, I analyse the building's architecture as a key component in extending this invitation to all the various sects of the three monotheistic religions.

Founded in England in 1844, the YMCA undertook to improve the religious and

---

[1] Dimmock to Frank W. Ramsey, General Secretary of the YMCA of the United States, 4 September 1932, 3, Jerusalem General Correspondence, 1931–1932, *KFYA*.
[2] Mark Twain, *The Innocents Abroad, or The New Pilgrims' Progress*, vol. 2 (New York: P. F. Collier & Son, 1911), 295.
[3] John Davis, *The Landscape of Belief* (Princeton, NJ: Princeton University Press, 1996), 13–15; Moshe Davis, *America and the Holy Land* (Westport: Praeger, 1995), 11–15.

Figure 3.1 Arthur Loomis Harmon, Jerusalem YMCA Building, Jerusalem, 1926–33. © KFYA. https://umedia.lib.umn.edu/item/p16022coll224:27772/p16022coll224:27727?child_index=6@query=6@sidebar_page=3, retrieved 16 February 2020.

cultural well-being of young men travelling far from home and family to work in cities that were expanding rapidly owing to the industrial revolution.[4] This was to be achieved by nurturing mind, body and spirit by offering activities in three realms of education: secular, physical and religious. The association viewed religion as a cultural product, wherein faith undergoes a process that sociologist Jurgen Habermas terms the profaning of religion's sacramental character, transposing it from the ecclesiastical sphere to the public one.[5] This approach, which YMCA historian Charles Howard Hopkins calls 'cultural evangelization', was the focus of YMCA activity.[6] YMCAs also generally offered reasonably priced modest lodgings for working men, as well as a cafeteria or dining hall.[7]

In accordance with its cultural ideology, the YMCA aligned itself with liberal and ecumenical Christian foreign missions to non-Western countries, including those in the Middle East.[8] These missions reflected new ideologies pertaining to global Christian missionary work and its discourse with other religions. Their missionaries believed that cultural education, rather than Christian teachings, were the means of salvation.[9] The YMCA embraced this ideology, offering modern Western community services in numerous locations around the globe: physical activities such as swimming, tennis and soccer, and game rooms and vocational courses, as well as history, language and Bible classes.[10] When exported from Europe or America, these activities provided many in Asia, Africa and South America with their first direct experience of the Western lifestyle and secularisation.

The Jerusalem YMCA: An American Mission

The British YMCA founded a small branch in Jerusalem in 1890.[11] Owing to the city's interreligious significance, it was considered a special foreign mission. Viewed as a means for promoting British and American involvement in the region, the Jerusalem YMCA's importance increased significantly after World War I.

---

[4] The history of the YMCA has been described in numerous publications. See, e.g., Charles Howard Hopkins, *History of the Y.M.C.A. in North America* (New York: Association Press, 1951).

[5] Jürgen Habermas, *The Structural Transformation of the Public Sphere* (Cambridge, MA: MIT Press, 1989), 36–7.

[6] Charles Howard Hopkins, *John R. Mott, 1865–1955: A Biography* (Geneva: World Council of Churches, 1979), 455.

[7] Paula Lupkin, 'YMCA Architecture: Evangelical Equipment for the American City, 1867–1920' (PhD diss., University of Pennsylvania, 1996), 10–22.

[8] Kenneth S. Latourette, *World Service: A History of the Foreign Work and World Service of the Young Men's Christian Associations of the United States and Canada* (New York: Association Press, 1957), 33–45.

[9] Hutchison, *Errand to the World*, 104–7; Eleanor S. Tejirian and Reeva Spector Simon, eds, *Altruism and Imperialism: Western Cultural and Religious Missions in the Middle East* (New York: Middle East Institute, Columbia University Press, 2002).

[10] See, e.g., Jon Thares Davidann, *A World of Crisis and Progress: The American YMCA in Japan, 1890–1930* (Cranbury: Associated University Press, 1998).

[11] There were earlier unsuccessful attempts to establish a Jerusalem YMCA in 1876 or 1878. See Latourette, *World Service*, 352.

In order to fully understand the motives for establishing an American YMCA in Jerusalem after the war, it is important to note the activism of John R. Mott, the general secretary of the American YMCA.[12] A pious Methodist, Mott was deeply involved in the development of the Jerusalem YMCA. Closely acquainted with President Woodrow Wilson, Mott was eager to promote new missionary activity in areas that had formerly belonged to the Ottoman Empire. President Wilson, for his part, insisted on securing an Open Door economic policy and American rights to missionary, archaeological, commercial and maritime activities, as well as oil exploration rights in the Middle East.[13] It was within this framework that Mott initiated and endorsed the founding of an American YMCA in Jerusalem in cooperation with the British branch of the organisation. In 1919, with the approval of the chief British YMCA secretary, Sir Arthur Yapp, Mott appointed an American, Dr Archibald Clinton Harte, as the local Jerusalem YMCA secretary.[14]

It was Harte, a Methodist minister and an experienced YMCA secretary, who turned the Jerusalem branch into a significant entity of the city's cultural landscape. The construction of an association building on an ambitious scale was central to his goals, and with Mott's support he was able to turn that dream into a reality.[15] The correspondence among Harte, Mott and other functionaries involved in the project reveals a sense of urgency in promoting American, rather than British, interests in Jerusalem.[16] Now that their British allies were in control of Palestine, a space for Christian-American culture could be constructed with the endorsement of the Mandate authorities, as was the case with American archaeological missions, which I discussed in Chapter Two.[17] Maintaining an open channel of communication with British authorities was important to Harte. He also nurtured relationships with the Anglo-Saxon community,[18] which paved the way for the YMCA's activity among the wider population.

Between New York and Jerusalem: Preliminary Steps

Beginnings were slow and problematic for this large-scale American overseas project. The purchase of a site, the selection of an architect and a construction

---

[12] The main source for Mott's career is Hopkins, *John R. Mott 1865–1955*.
[13] Fromkin, *A Peace to End All Peace*, 533–6; Adelson, *London and the Invention of the Middle East*, 134–7.
[14] Edward C. Jenkins, 'Memorandum on the Relationships of A. C. Harte', 6 October 1919, *YA1918-27*.
[15] Harte resigned from the building project in 1930, owing to irreconcilable differences with the YMCA planners and directors. See Inbal Ben-Asher Gitler, 'The Architecture of the Jerusalem YMCA Building (1919–1933): Constructing Multiculturalism' (PhD Diss., Tel Aviv University, 2006), 107–10. He spent the last years of his life in Peniel, the YMCA branch that he established near Tiberias. See Y. M. Deen, 'Amidst a Grove of Olive Trees', paper presented at Chicago Literary Club, 2003, 19.
[16] Harte to Mott, 28 November 1919, *YA1918-27*.
[17] Harte to Mott, 31 March 1919, 1, *YA1918-27*.
[18] See, e.g., Mott to Harte, 14 June 1921, *YA1918-27*.

supervisor, and the preliminary planning lasted ten years – from Harte's arrival in Palestine in 1919 until 1929. As the main stages in this process are important for understanding the building in context, I review them briefly here.

Wealthy, devout Protestant Americans endorsed the construction of the Jerusalem YMCA Building. In 1924, Harte and Mott solicited the generous donation of James Newbegin Jarvie, a millionaire from Montclair, New Jersey, who funded roughly 90 per cent of the project, which cost more than $1.2 million.[19] Jarvie was a Presbyterian renowned for his Christian philanthropy. He served on the National Board of Missions of the Presbyterian Church, to which he bequeathed millions.[20] John D. Rockefeller Junior, also made a significant contribution of $200,000.[21] An adamant supporter of Mott's foreign missions' activities, Rockefeller perceived them as a unifying force for Christianity and, ultimately, the world.[22] As such, this donation constituted an additional aspect of Rockefeller's charitable work, which I discussed in Chapter Two, and it, too, was grounded in his Christian beliefs. When soliciting the support of these donors, Mott declared his vision of a peaceful Jerusalem, as can be seen in a letter written to Rockefeller in 1925:

> Dr. Harte and his colleagues have built up a remarkable Association. It unites ... all the Eastern Churches, ... the various Protestant denominations ... and also, what is more remarkable, over one hundred of the ablest Jewish young men and about as many more fraternal Moslems. Thus, in the city where there is most need of it because of the startling and shameful exhibition of division and strife among the adherents of different religions, including different branches of Christianity, the Association is demonstrating in a most attractive way the possibility of realizing its guiding principles of international and interracial brotherhood and of fraternal cooperation among all Christians ...[23]

Harte and Mott shared this vision of the Jerusalem YMCA as a promoter of cross-cultural relations. They prescribed three major goals to be implemented in the building's plan to realise their vision. First was the creation of an international study centre, where missionaries and YMCA activists would attend

---

[19] Mott to Harte, 14 June 1921, 2; Mott to John E. Manley, 22 June 1922, 1; Hibbard to Jarvie, 25 February 1924; 'Contract between the Central Union Trust Company and New York', 19–21 January 1925, 1–10; 'History of the Jerusalem YMCA', 4 (all *YA1918-27*); Ramsey to Amelia Jarvie, 1 April 1932, Carillon file, 1932–1933, Jerusalem YMCA Records, *KFYA*; Letter attributed to McMillan, written to Ramsey, 17 January 1929, 6; 'Contract between Central Hanover Bank and Trust Company (the new name given to Central Union Bank) and the International Committee of the YMCA', 7 June 1929, 1–9 (both *YA1929-30n*); 'Jarvie, James Newbegin', in *The National Encyclopedia of American Biography* (New York: James T. White & Co., 1932), 421.

[20] 'J. N. Jarvie Left Millions to Church', *New York Times*, 11 July 1929, 14.

[21] Rockefeller's contribution was part of a $1,250,000 donation he made to the YMCA Building programme that was established after World War I. See Mott to Rockefeller, 30 March 1925, 1–2, *YA1918-27*.

[22] Charles E. Harvey, 'Speer versus Rockefeller and Mott, 1910–1935', *Journal of Presbyterian History* 60, no. 4 (1982): 283–99.

[23] Mott to Rockefeller, 30 March 1925, *YA1918-27*.

workshops, conferences, and so on, which Harte described as 'a world spiritual and cultural center'.[24] Second, in the face of the city's numerous Christian sects, the association sought to promote its own ecumenical image, so as to further Christian interdenominational cooperation. Third was the offering of cultural services to non-Christians while fostering a familiarity with Christianity, as was the case in other YMCA foreign missions. In Jerusalem these services were focused on promoting coexistence through the association's cultural curriculum.

As with all new buildings in Jerusalem, the question of where to build was important. The building was originally intended to be erected on a site near Jaffa Gate,[25] which would have placed it close to the Old City walls, as was the case with the Palestine Archeological Museum. Unlike the museum, however, which was located on the northeast side of the wall, the YMCA was to be near the city's business centre in the west.[26] A better opportunity soon presented itself in an area known as Nikophoriah, located along Julian's Way (present-day King David Street), where the Palace Hotel would also be built. The Nikophoriah site became available in the wake of the post-World War I bankruptcy of Jerusalem's Greek Orthodox Patriarchy, which, in 1921, began to sell the vast stretches of land it owned in the city in order to cover its debts.[27] There were many advantages to the Nikophoriah site. It was relatively close to Jerusalem's commercial centre and there were plans for many governorates, consulates and hotels there.[28] On 27 September 1923, a site of 28,761.50 square metres was purchased by the YMCA for $85,000.[29]

The first plans for the building were drawn by Charles Robert Ashbee as early as 1920, two years into his tenure as the British civic adviser.[30] Harte specified a building divided into three wings: a main building, a hostel and a physical facilities department,[31] and his detailed description referred to all the intended cultural, religious and hospitality functions. Several of Ashbee's drawings have survived (Figure 3.2),[32] and these reflect Harte's three-wing conception as a U-shaped building open toward the street. Ashbee created a series of domes,

---

[24] 'Excerpt from a letter from Harte to Mott', 23 August 1922, 1, *YA1918-27*.
[25] Harte to Ned(?), 22 January 1920, 1–2, *YA1918-27*.
[26] Document attributed to Harte, 'Concerning the Jerusalem YMCA Building and Site', 17 February 1920, 1, *YA1918-27*.
[27] Kark and Oren-Nordheim, *Jerusalem and its Environs*, 180–3; Katz and Kark, 'The Greek Orthodox Patriarchate of Jerusalem and its Congregation', 509–34. Harte mentioned the economic troubles of the Greek Orthodox Church in several letters: Harte, memoranda of 16 November 1920; Harte to Paul F. Vaka, 14 February 1921; both documents, *YA1918-27*.
[28] Kark and Oren-Nordheim, *Jerusalem and its Environs*, 180–3.
[29] 'Information about property in countries outside of the United States and Canada toward the cost of which funds have been contributed or pledged through the International Committee', 1 August 1924, *YA1918-27*.
[30] Harte to Ashbee, 8 January 1920, *YA1918-27*.
[31] Ibid.
[32] Ibid.

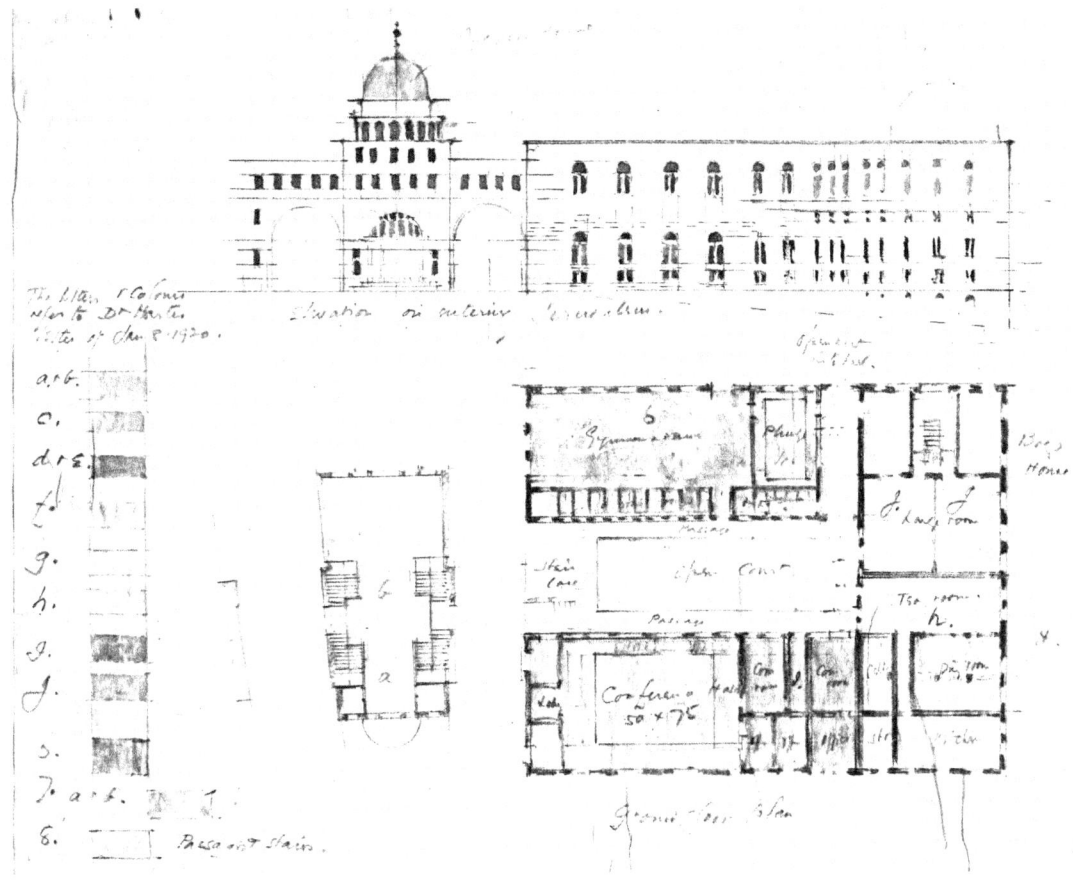

Figure 3.2 *Charles Robert Ashbee, Plan for a Jerusalem YMCA Building, 1920. Jerusalem City Archive – Jerusalem Municipality, Box 361 (C. R. Ashbee).*

reflecting his Orientalist conceptions for preserving Jerusalem's 'Middle Eastern' character.[33]

The idea of entrusting planning to a British designer was unacceptable to architect Neil McMillan Junior, director of the Building Bureau of the American YMCA. McMillan had invested significant effort in centralising the YMCA's building policies and project management, so he was determined to export the examples and experience of American YMCA planning to Jerusalem.[34] As argued by Jeffery Cody, successful exporters of American architecture (of both material and knowledge) familiarised themselves with building practices of the target country and accommodated their product and process to it.[35] This was precisely what McMillan

---

[33] For a discussion of Ashbee's approach, see Ben-Asher Gitler, 'Marrying Modern Progress with Treasured Antiquity', 50–3.

[34] For a detailed analysis of the Building Bureau's operations in the United States and abroad, see Paula Lupkin, *Manhood Factories: YMCA Architecture and the Making of Modern Urban Culture* (Minneapolis: University of Minnesota Press, 2010), 159–65.

[35] Jeffrey W. Cody, *Exporting American Architecture, 1870–2000* (London: Routledge, 2003), 51–2.

wanted, and his policy was to send American architects to 'missionary territories' – architects capable of adapting the modern devices of association building to local conditions. Accordingly, in 1925 Arthur Loomis Harmon was hired to design the building that was to house the Jerusalem YMCA.[36]

Although responsible for major commissions in New York City, New York State and elsewhere in the United States, Harmon remains a rather obscure figure in American architectural historiography. Among his important works are the addition to the Metropolitan Museum of Art, which he designed while practising at McKim, Mead & White;[37] the Shelton Hotel (presently the Marriott East Side Hotel); and the Allerton Houses, all in New York City.[38] For many years he was a partner at Shreve, Lamb & Harmon. Their most famous creation is the Empire State Building (1931),[39] but Harmon is specifically credited with projects such as an addition to the Julliard School of Music (1931–3), the Seamen's YMCA (1932)[40] and the Bankers Trust Company Building – also all in New York City.[41] Harmon's architecture integrated historicism and modernism. He worked in a range of styles, applying neo-Renaissance elements to modern tall buildings or creating Art Deco masterpieces such as the Empire State Building.

Harmon held firm views regarding architecture's role in society, which he expressed in articles on design, housing and urban planning in newspapers and professional journals.[42] He received many awards for the Shelton Hotel, the Empire State Building, and more.[43] He was active in architectural education and in professional societies, such as the Bund Deutscher Architekten, the Beaux-Arts Institute of Design and the National Academy of Design.[44] He headed the New

[36] McMillan to Mott, 13 November 1925, 2, YA1918-27.
[37] 'Harmon, Arthur Loomis', in *Who Was Who in America* (Chicago: Marquis, 1960), 371.
[38] 'The Shelton: Arthur Loomis Harmon, Architect', *Architecture* 49 (April 1924): 101–12; C. Bragdon, 'The Shelton Hotel, New York: Arthur Loomis Harmon, Architect', *Architectural Record* 58 (July 1925): 1–18; Arthur Loomis Harmon, 'The Allerton Houses', *Architecture* 47, no. 1 (1923): 41–4.
[39] For the history of the Empire State Building, see John Tauranac, *The Empire State Building: The Making of a Landmark* (New York: Scribner, 1995); Carol Willis, *Form Follows Finance: Skyscrapers and Skylines in New York and Chicago* (New York: Princeton Architectural Press, 1995), 90–101.
[40] 'Seamen's House, YMCA, NYC by Shreve, Lamb & Harmon', *Architectural Record* 71 (1932): 321–4; 'Seamen's House, YMCA, NYC by Shreve, Lamb & Harmon', *Architecture and Building* 64 (1932): 16–17.
[41] *Photographs of the Work of Shreve, Lamb & Harmon*, 2, 193, Avery Rare Books Collection, Avery Library, Columbia University, New York.
[42] Among Harmon's publications are: 'Contemporary Industrial Art', *Metropolitan Museum Bulletin* 29 (1934): 203–4; 'Politics and Architecture', *New York Times*, 6 January 1935, 4: 7; 'Contemporary American Industrial Art at the Museum', *Bulletin of the Metropolitan Museum of Art* 35 (1940): 132–3; 'Thoughts on War Memorials', *AIA Journal* 2, no. 5 (November 1944): 222–3; 'Architecture – Business, Profession and Art: Part I', *AIA Journal* 20, no. 2 (August 1953): 93–6; 'Architecture – Business, Profession and Art: Part II', *AIA Journal* 20, no. 2 (September 1953): 144–8; 'Styles in Architecture', *New York Times*, 6 March 1955, 10: 7.
[43] 'Honor Architects for Empire State', *New York Times*, 27 January 1932, 23: 3; 'Arthur L. Harmon Dies; Headed Architect Groups', *New York Herald Tribune*, 18 October 1958, 6.
[44] 'Arthur Harmon, Architect, Dead', *New York Times*, 18 October 1958, 21; 'Panorama', *Architectural Forum* 62 (1935): 44.

York Architectural League in 1933–5 and was president of the New York Chapter of the American Institute of Architects (AIA) 1937–9.[45]

It is surprising that Harmon never visited the YMCA Building while it was being constructed. He had travelled to Jerusalem when he was commissioned in 1926, but did not even come to the inauguration. This fact is significant, as it reveals a pioneering architectural process that implemented historical strides in communication for architectural production. The Jerusalem YMCA Building was arguably among the first large-scale projects in the world where the architect remained in his headquarters at a great distance from the construction site. Management and administration were almost completely dependent on the new, turn-of-the-century technologies of telegraph and telephone, as well as photography and the utilisation of fast and safe trans-Atlantic ocean liners. Harmon and the YMCA headquarters in the United States were in constant contact with the project's Jerusalem team. Ideas pertaining to art and ideology, consultations and deliberations, as well as disagreements and crises, were all handled with the aid of modern communication technologies.

With Harmon on board, the Building Bureau appointed a construction executive in Jerusalem, the architect Arthur Quincy Adamson.[46] Adamson was for years the director of the YMCA Building Bureau in China and was thus experienced in managing architectural projects overseas. By the time he arrived in Jerusalem in 1929, excavations for the building were complete. The cornerstone had been laid on 16 July 1928, in conjunction with the World Conference of the International Missionary Convention.[47] From 1929 until the building's dedication in 1933, the project progressed apace.

The Project and its Communities: Constructing Multiculturalism

Intercommunal cooperation was fully manifested in the YMCA Building project. In this section, I discuss the importance attached to this cooperation by the project's executives and describe the professionals and labourers from the local communities who were employed in the building project.

Extant correspondence regarding the building process provides a telling example of Jerusalem's architectural culture in the making. Both Harte and Adamson placed importance on consulting with local architects,[48] among whom were British

---

[45] 'Architects Pick Harmon', *New York Times*, 3 March 1933, 15: 2; 'Named by Architects: Arthur Loomis Harmon', *New York Times*, 23 June 1937, 9: 2; 'Architect's Institute Elects', *New York Times*, 3 June 1938, 19: 3; 'Arthur Harmon, Architect, Dead', *New York Times*, 18 October 1958, 21.

[46] Document signed by Ramsey and Harte, 4 May 1929, Jerusalem Agreements/Legal Documents 1923–9, KFYA.

[47] Invitation to the cornerstone laying ceremony, 16 July 1928, Jerusalem General Correspondence, September–December 1928, KFYA.

[48] Slack to McMillan quoting from an 18 July 1925 letter by Harte to Mott, 20 August 1925, YA1918-27; Adamson to McMillan, 30 March 1925, 2, YA1929-30n; Hyman, 'British Planners in Palestine', 430–577.

architects Austen Harrison (1891–1976), Ernst Richmond (1874–1955) and Clifford Holliday (1897–1960), and the Zionist architect Benjamin Chaikin (1885–1950).[49] The latter two were proposed by Harte as possible 'local experts' who could participate in the YMCA project.[50] Turkish architects Ahmet Kemalettin Bey (1870–1927) and Mehmet Nihat Nigisberk (1880–1945) were apparently also consulted.[51] These interactions demonstrate that there was an ongoing exchange of ideas among the planners of major projects in Jerusalem: Harrison was busy with the governor's house and the Archeological Museum; Holliday was planning St Andrew's Scottish Church; Chaikin was continuing his work both on the Hebrew University and as one of the designers of the King David Hotel;[52] Nigisberk was working on the Palace Hotel, and during the preliminary planning phase of the YMCA Building collaborated with Kemalettin on restorations for the Dome of the Rock, which I describe in Chapter Four.

The contractors for the YMCA formed an intercommunal partnership, which included Baruch Katinka and Tuvia Dunie, Zionist Jews, and Stello Elyās ʿAwaḍ, a Christian Palestinian.[53] As I noted in Chapter Two, the firm also undertook the preliminary construction work on the Palestine Archaeological Museum. Katinka was one of the leading contractor-engineers in the country. Raised in Eastern Europe, he received his engineering diploma from the Mittweida Technical University (*Hochschule*) in Saxony, Germany, and by the time he took on building the Jerusalem YCMA, he had already had twenty years of experience in Palestine.[54] Dunie, who also came from Eastern Europe and studied in Germany, was an experienced engineer.[55] There is no record of ʿAwaḍ beyond his mention as a partner in the firm of ʿAwaḍ, Dunie & Katinka in various sources, including those pertaining to the Palace Hotel, which the firm built as well. As I note in Chapter Four, the three established their firm in 1928, in order to compete for the Palace Hotel construction tender. They received the YMCA contract in May 1930, bidding against eight other construction companies, including De Farro & Co., who suc-

---

[49] Harte to Jarvie, 21 September 1928, Jerusalem General Correspondence, September–December 1928, *KFYA*; Adamson to McMillan, 25 March 1930, 2; cable from Adamson to McMillan, 14 July 1930, 2, both *YA1929-30n*.

[50] Harte to Jarvie, 21 September 1928, Jerusalem General Correspondence, September–December 1928, *KFYA*.

[51] In 1925, Harte wrote that he intends to consult 'the architect of the Moslem supreme council who is planning and supervising the changes on the mosque of Al Aksa and the repairs on the Mosque of Omar'. This statement could refer to Richmond, Kemalettin (see Chapter Four) or Nigisberk. See Slack to McMillan quoting from an 18 July 1925 letter from Harte to Mott, 20 August 1925, *YA1918-27*.

[52] Chaikin's work is discussed in Dolev, 'Architectural Orientalism in the Hebrew University', 220–34; Kroyanker, *Adrichalut Bi'Yerushalayim: HaBni'ya BiTkufat HaMandat HaBriti*, 238–42.

[53] ʿAwaḍ's full name is cited in the contract for the construction of the Palace Hotel, discussed in the following chapter. See Contract with ʿAwaḍ, 1928, file 20/44/,6/28/13, *CHIR*.

[54] Baruch Katinka, *Me'az Ve'Ad Hena* (Jerusalem: Kiryat Sefer, 1961), 257.

[55] David Tidhar, *Entsiklopedyah LeChalutsey Ha'Yishuv UBonav*, vol. 4, 1920. Retrieved from http://www.tidhar.tourolib.org/tidhar/view/4/1920.

ceeded them in building the Palestine Archaeological Museum.⁵⁶ The political significance of hiring an intercommunal firm was obvious, as noted by Adamson:

> Mr. Awad is a Christian Arab and Messrs. Dounie & Katinke are Hebrew engineers. This combination in the contracting firm is excellent for YMCA interests. It automatically solves all problems so far as we are concerned, involving the question of Jewish and Arab labor. Had the contract fallen to an entirely Arab firm or an entirely Jewish firm we would have been beset with criticism from both factions in the country from start to finish.⁵⁷

The above passage reflects the building project's executives' heightened political awareness of the volatile situation in Palestine.⁵⁸ Hence, in addition to the contractors, they knew that it was equally important to hire workers from all three communities. More than 400 Christian and Muslim Palestinians, as well as many Jews, participated in the project.⁵⁹ Political tensions occasionally impacted construction: for example, Harmon wrote to Harte following the violence between Arabs and Jews that erupted in the summer of 1929:⁶⁰ 'It is too bad about the troubles between the Jews and the Moslems. I hope that it does not affect you, although I am afraid it must affect the work at the Y.M.C.A.'⁶¹

The passionate debate over the building's furniture and interior design is also a clear indication of the importance that the planners ascribed to the idea of intercommunal participation. The YMCA required functional furniture and also was determined to give the local communities a sense of pride and ownership by using goods manufactured in Palestine.⁶² No less a personage than Palestine's high commissioner asked that the furniture be made locally, attesting to the importance of this matter.⁶³ However, this approach was not in line with McMillan's modern concepts of practical modularity and mass design, and many stencils, patterns and fixtures were imported from the United States. As to the furniture itself, although

---

⁵⁶ Adamson to McMillan, 7 May 1930, 2–4, *YA1929-30n*; Adamson to Ramsey, 13 May 1930, 1, *YA1929-30n*; A. Q. Adamson, 'Contractors Submitting Tenders for Jerusalem YMCA Building Work', 2 December 1929, *YAAd*.
⁵⁷ Adamson, *YMCA Building Project: Jerusalem, Palestine*, 12 July 1930, 3, *YAAd*.
⁵⁸ This was also communicated in a letter from Harte to William D. Murray (vice-chairman of the YMCA International Committee), 18 June 1920, 1, *YA1918-27*.
⁵⁹ Katinka, *Me'az Ve'Ad Hena*, 266.
⁶⁰ These events are discussed in Ilan Pappe, 'Haj Amin and the Buraq Revolt', *Jerusalem Quarterly File* 18, no. 18 (2003): 6–16; Segev and Watzman, *One Palestine, Complete*, 307–27.
⁶¹ Harmon to Harte, 27 August 1929, *YAAd*. Other correspondence reflecting the 1929 riots includes: Harmon to Adamson, 5 September 1929; McMillan to Adamson, 17 September 1929, 1, both *YA1929-30n*; A. C. Harte, 'Report of the General Secretary', 23 September 1929, 1, Jerusalem Annual Reports, Oversized/General, *KFYA*.
⁶² See, e.g., Adamson to McMillan, 28 March 1931; McMillan to Adamson, 2 April 1931; Smith to Ramsey, 12 June 1931; Adamson to McMillan, 18 June 1931. All documents, *YAAd*.
⁶³ Senior YMCA Secretary for Egypt and Palestine Wilbert Smith to Frank Ramsey, 12 June 1931, 1, *YAAd*.

drawings for some of the pieces survive, it is not clear where they were eventually manufactured.[64]

There are no records regarding the ratio of Muslims, Christians and Jews participating in the project, but it appears that, similar to the case of the Archaeological Museum, masonry and general construction were delegated to Arabs, whereas Jews were assigned welding, cement work and, in this case, artistic sculpting and interior painting. It is also clear that contracts with Jewish specialists included a clause securing the employment of Arabs as well.[65] In 1930, *Davar* protested that at the YMCA site 'Awaḍ, Dunie & Katinka were deliberately diverting cement work from Jews – similar to this newspaper's protests with regard to the Archaeological Museum;[66] in 1931 the newspaper went on to criticise Jewish plastering specialists for doing nothing to stop the practice of paying Jewish labourers higher wages than their Arab counterparts at the YMCA site.[67] Two of the Palestine labour market's chief predicaments were thus revealed in the YMCA project, just as they surfaced with regard to the other buildings under discussion here. The YMCA planners and supervisors were well aware of these complexities and of the improved conditions of the unionised Jews.[68] Although this awareness of employment challenges in Palestine was apparently not translated into improving on-site egalitarianism, the YMCA did make plans for a 'small training school for native workers', intended for 'industrial and commercial education for employed men',[69] demonstrating its intention to integrate Arab Palestinians in specialised vocations.[70] A building to house the trade school was erected on the premises (No. 12 on the plan in Figure 3.3), but was then utilised for storage and the plans for the school never materialised. However, these plans provide further evidence of the YMCA's awareness that politics were always implicated in vocational issues in the country.

The most important specialised work in the building was the execution of its sculptural programme, done according to drawings and, in specific cases, models sent from New York. In his search for sculptors, Adamson also considered hiring Eric Gill, who later came to work on the Archaeological Museum reliefs.[71] Eventually he hired Zionist artists Ze'ev Raban (1890–1970) and Meir Gur-Arieh (1891–1951), who headed the Workshop for Industrial Arts in Jerusalem.[72] Adamson described

---

[64] *Jerusalem International YMCA, Pictorial Record: Construction of Y.M.C.A. Bldgs Jerusalem*, Jerusalem International YMCA, n.d.
[65] 'Mi Be'in Catley Habinyan BiYerushalayim', *Davar*, 2 December 1931.
[66] 'Yerushalayim: Hodot Lekablanin Yehudim', *Davar*, 4 July 1930, 1.
[67] 'Mi Be'in Catley Habinyan Biyerushalayim', *Davar*, 2 December 1931.
[68] Tucker to Harmon, 16 January 1928, 2, *YAAd*.
[69] Harte to William Murray, 18 June 1920, 1, *YA1918-27*.
[70] Harte to Mott, 9 April 1925, 1–2; A. C. Harte, 'Memoranda Concerning the Jerusalem and Palestine YMCAs', written to J. R. Mott and other YMCA functionaries in the United States, 16 November 1920, 2. Both documents *YA1918-27*.
[71] A. C. Harte, 'Memoranda Concerning the Jerusalem and Palestine YMCAs', 1; Adamson to Harmon, 15 August 1929, 1, *YAAd*.
[72] For a discussion of these artists, see Nurit Shiloh-Cohen, ed., *Bezalel shel Schatz, 1906–1929*, Exhibition Catalogue (Jerusalem: Israel Museum, 1983), 364, 366; Goldman, *Ze'ev Raban*; Ruth

them as having 'real imagination and ability . . . [and] who could work just as well in Jerusalem as though [they] were in New York'.[73] The workshop team included alumni from the Bezalel School of Art[74] – Yehoshuah Yashpan (1903–81) and Abraham Giat (1891–1979).[75] Batia Lishansky (1900–92), famous for her portrait busts and commemorative sculpture, also carved the YMCA sculptures.[76] Zionist newspapers reported the procuring of this commission with much excitement, a clear indication that the Jewish community regarded it as an acknowledgement of its achievements in the fields of art and design.[77]

The YMCA's planners' and administrators' inclusiveness and their concern about Jerusalem's politics demonstrate the association's conception of its own role as an intercommunal mediator. These aspects of the project's management, while clearly not always free of prejudices and inequalities in considering labourers, wages and expertise, nonetheless created an enterprise that fostered and, in effect constructed, multiculturalism.

The Building's Functions, Plan and Construction Technology

The three major goals that the YMCA was to fulfil in Jerusalem, discussed earlier, were expressed in the building's architecture, ornamentation and iconographic programme. The first goal – creating an international Christian centre – would be met by including a large pilgrim hostel for both men and women visiting the Holy Land in the footsteps of Christ. Unlike a workingmen's dormitory in a YMCA in the United States, it would require facilities for tourists and for hosting international conferences. The second objective – promoting Christian ecumenism – would be realised by building cultural facilities such as an auditorium and multipurpose activity rooms. Sports facilities were also important, and would include an athletic/soccer field, tennis courts and a gymnasium. Most of these functions were similar to those in a modern American community centre – a concept that was still evolving during this period.[78] The third, and perhaps most important goal in Jerusalem – that of fostering religious coexistence – was to be achieved by the above-mentioned functions and by others, such as a divinity library[79] and a multifaith chapel.

Debel, *Meir Gur-Arie: Ta'arucha, 22.9.8–17.10.81*, Exhibition Pamphlet (Jerusalem: Debel Gallery, 1981); The Gabriel Sherover Information Center for Israeli Art at the Israel Museum (Meir Gur Arieh file).
[73] Adamson to Harmon, 15 August 1929, 1, *YAAd*.
[74] Bezalel, the Jewish School of Arts and Crafts, was founded in 1906 by Boris Schatz (1866–1932). For the early history of the school, see Shiloh-Cohen, ed., *Bezalel shel Schatz*.
[75] Goldman, *Ze'ev Raban*, 146, 201, n. 4. A photo album of Giat's work is preserved at the Jerusalem YMCA.
[76] Katinka, *Me'az Ve'Ad Hena*, 265; 'Yerushalayim: Ba'avoda', *Davar*, 16 September 1930.
[77] 'Yerushalayim: Avodat Situt Amanutit – Le Yehudim', *Davar*, 22 March 1928; 'Yerushalayim: Ba'avoda', *Davar*, 16 September 1930; 'Chevley Haba'ah', *Davar*, 11 November 1930.
[78] Lupkin, 'YMCA Architecture', 2, 53–4.
[79] Harte to Mott, 31 March 1919, 1, *YA1918-27*.

The Jerusalem YMCA has a flat-roofed, rectangular main building with four storeys and a basement (Figure 3.3) with two sections that project forward, visually dividing the main façade into five parts and two rectangular wings that create a U-shaped complex facing the street and framing a garden. In this respect, Harmon's plan echoed Ashbee's earlier proposal.

In Harmon's design, which was the one that eventually materialised, the main building houses the hostel, the cafeteria, the chapel, and rooms for various social and educational activities. The south wing has a gymnasium on its main floor and a swimming pool in its basement.[80] Jerusalem's first indoor heated swimming pool, it highlighted the novelty of the YMCA's sports facilities in their surroundings. The north wing includes the auditorium, which is used for concerts, films and theatre. The wings are not identical, as they have different functional requirements, but both are topped by domes, so that their exterior gives a balanced façade to the entire structure. The building's most prominent feature is a tower that rises from the centre of the central section. Measuring 46 metres (151 feet) tall and projecting forward from the building's centre, it creates a portal at ground level. The tower's corners resemble clasping buttresses. An *in antis* arcaded terrace, or loggia, stretches across the façade, connecting the main building and its wings. Two projecting terraces extend from the arcade into the garden. Altogether, the overall design creates a rhythm of monumental units pulled together by the main building.

The central building's storeys comprise four tiers of windows and openings; the arcade has stilted arches faced with bi-chrome voussoirs (Figure 3.4). The first and second floors have rectangular windows, some with pointed blind arches; the third floor has an open arcaded terrace and arched windows in its projecting sections. The tower's windows complement those on the three storeys, and there are arched balconies on two of its levels. The west facade (Figure 3.5; see also Figure 3.28 later) has a tripartite arrangement. Only the southern gymnasium wing forms a visual part of it, as the auditorium extends toward the street and can hardly be seen. Fenestration is varied and exhibits abundant use of bi-chrome voussoirs; there are several cantilevered balconies, the most prominent one being on the third floor of the west façade (Figure 3.5).

The building's materials and technology included reinforced concrete, which was used also for vaults, domes and openings.[81] Reinforcement against earthquake shock was added to the tower's construction specifications after a strong earthquake caused heavy damage in Jerusalem in 1927.[82] The building's exterior is completely faced with stone, entirely concealing its modern construction methods. Internally, however, many concrete beams are visible, and one can see devices such as heating equipment and an elevator.

---

[80] The pool is currently not in use. It has been replaced by a new one in the residential development that is adjacent to the building. The plan is to renovate it and use it as a water therapy centre.

[81] Harmon to Harte, 2 November 1927, 2; Harmon to Harte, 11 February 1927, 2. Both documents, *YAAd*.

[82] Harmon to Ramsey, 6 February 1930, *YA1929-30n*.

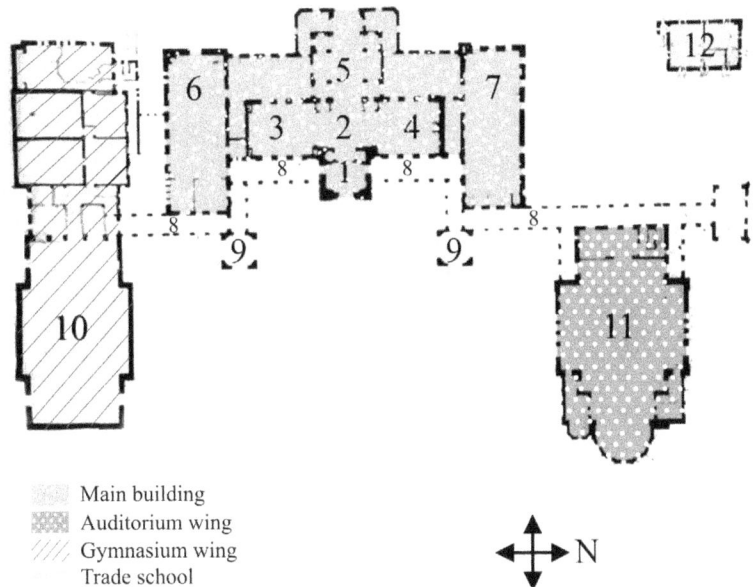

Figure 3.3 *Arthur Loomis Harmon, Jerusalem YMCA Building, ground floor plan, main building and wings with key functions as allocated in 1933. © Jerusalem YMCA. Plan edited using Adobe®. 1. Vestibule. 2. Threshold. 3. South lounge. 4. North lounge. 5. Social hall. 6. Boy's department. 7. Cafeteria. 8. Arcade. 9. Kiosks. 10. Gymnasium. 11. Auditorium. 12. Trade school.*

Figure 3.4 *Arthur Loomis Harmon, Jerusalem YMCA Building, south 'kiosk' of the arcade, 1926–33. © KFYA.*

Figure 3.5 *Jerusalem YMCA Building, west façade. Photographed by Diego Rosman.*

Figure 3.6 *Carrère and Hastings, Hotel Ponce de León (Flaggler College), St Augustine, Florida, 1888. Photographed by William Henry Jackson. Library of Congress, Prints and Photographs Division, Washington, DC. Detroit Publishing Company Photograph Collection, https://www.loc.gov/resource/det.4a26939, retrieved 16 February 2020.*

Sources of Inspiration

The Jerusalem YMCA Building embodies a merging of American, European and Middle Eastern architecture. In this section, I show how the building's design integrated these diverse sources of inspiration and discuss the discourses surrounding them.

As it had an American architect and was built by an American association, the Jerusalem YMCA evinces significant American characteristics. Harte nonchalantly dismissed local critics that called the building 'American', adding that this 'means that [the critics] know nothing whatever about architecture . . .'[83] Contrary to Harte's statement, the building's conception and function were indeed derivative of modern American typologies, no less than of local traditional ones. The first of these typologies was hotel architecture, and the YMCA's U-shape was conceived with this in mind. Harmon was an experienced and highly praised hotel architect, and his designs for this typology were considered the most advanced of their time.[84] However, the Jerusalem YMCA's plan may have been inspired by examples that preceded Harmon's early twentieth-century hotels, such as the Hotel

---

[83] Harte to Harmon, 1 September 1926, 1, *YAAd*.
[84] 'Editorial and Other Comment', *Architecture* 49, no. 4 (1924), 111.

Ponce de León in St Augustine, Florida, built in 1886–8 by Carrère and Hastings (Figure 3.6).⁸⁵ Considered very advanced when first erected, it was designed in a neo-Iberian style, reflecting Florida's Spanish colonial heritage. Similar to the YMCA, the Ponce de León had an open U-plan. Its garden was separated from the street by an arcade, and its façade was fronted by a raised arcaded terrace. This use of an open portico in resort hotels had already been well-established, and Harmon adopted it as he likely identified Florida's mild climate and the Ponce de León's Mediterranean sources as suitable for Jerusalem as well. The towers that were included in the design of both buildings are also significant. Intended to provide visitors with a view, they represented a relatively recent addition to American resort hotel architecture, and in relation to Jerusalem they acquired additional import.

Other facilities that served as precursors to the YMCA Building were Jerusalem's turn-of-the-century pilgrim hospices.⁸⁶ Two of these come to mind: the French-built pilgrim hospice, Notre Dame de France (1884–1904; Figure 3.7), and the German-built Auguste Victoria Endowment (1907–10/14; Figure 3.8). The French hospice was planned by Catholic ministers Brisacier (1831–1923) and Etienne Boubet (1865–1934),⁸⁷ and the German one by Robert Leibnitz (1863–1921).⁸⁸ The Notre Dame de France is a U-shaped complex featuring an arcade that connects the main building with its wings. The Auguste Victoria Endowment has an arcade on the ground floor of its northeast façade. Its massive square, helm-roofed bell tower was for years the highest in the city and thus served as a precedent for the inclusion of a prominent tower within a religious pilgrim complex.

Both compounds were inspired by civic and religious architecture and included a chapel or a church. They served as socio-religious centres and catered to the spiritual and physical needs of pilgrims in the Holy Land.⁸⁹ In serving these functions, the Notre Dame de France and the Auguste Victoria Endowment were similar to the YMCA. Perceived as representing their countries of origin – in these cases France and Germany – they were built in associated historicist styles, and thus attained political significance.⁹⁰ In planning the Jerusalem YMCA, Harmon could thus relate to these precedents of local travel and pilgrimage architecture, relying on their manifested hybrid typology of hotel and site of religious spirituality.

---

⁸⁵ The hotel is described in George Everard Kidder Smith, *Source Book of American Architecture: 500 Notable Buildings from the 10th Century to the Present* (New York: Princeton Architectural Press, 1996), 278–9. Today the building serves as Flaggler College, named after Henry Flaggler, the entrepreneur who built the Ponce de León.

⁸⁶ These buildings are surveyed in Kroyanker, *Adrichalut Bi'Yerushalyim: HaBni'ya HaEropit-Notsrit MiChutz LaChomot, 1855–1918*; David Kroyanker, *Adrichalut Bi'Yerushalyim: HaBni'ya Ba'Yir Ha'Atika* (Jerusalem: Keter, 1993).

⁸⁷ Kroyanker, *Adrichalut Bi'Yerushalyim: HaBni'ya HaEropit-Notsrit*, 287–93.

⁸⁸ Ibid. 241–52; Meyer-Maril, 'Binyan Auguste Victoria al Har HaZeitim', 51–62.

⁸⁹ Today, the Auguste Victoria Endowment serves as a Palestinian hospital, and the Notre Dame de France is a hospice for the terminally ill.

⁹⁰ Kroyanker, Adrichalut Bi'Yerushalyim: *HaBni'ya HaEropit-Notsrit*, 241–52; 287–93.

Figure 3.7 *Abbé Brisacier and Abbé Etienne Boubet, Notre Dame de France, Jerusalem, 1884–1904.* © IGPO, digital ID D220-023.

Figure 3.8 *Robert Leibnitz, Auguste Victoria Endowment (Auguste Victoria Stiftung), Jerusalem 1907–10/14.* Wiki Commons, https://commons.wikimedia.org/wiki/File:Augbrit.jpg, retrieved 16 February 2020.

Local Middle Eastern inspiration is also apparent in the building's design, with the gymnasium and auditorium wings being its clearest manifestations (Figures 3.9 and 3.10). Each wing forms a rectangle topped by a tunnel vault along its longer axis, traversed by a shallow vaulted space. The auditorium (Figure 3.10) has an additional trapezoid bay resembling an apse on its eastern façade. The wings' domes are hemispherical; pierced by twelve barrel-vaulted windows, they rest on low octagonal drums supported by four pendentives or squinches.

For the wings, Harmon appropriated the hemispheric dome, which was common in Jerusalem and used by all its communities for their sacred spaces. The Crusader-built Church of the Holy Sepulchre (Figure 3.11), consecrated in 1149 and among the Old City's most prominent landmarks, was a likely Christian source of inspiration. Both its domes are hemispheric and have proportions similar to the domes of the YMCA, as well as arched windows. The Crusader Church of the Ascension on the Mount of Olives (1102–6/7) may have also been a model.[91] Deriving inspiration from sites of such holiness might have been perceived as ambitious, even presumptuous, and indeed drew criticism that the YMCA's domes are too church-like.[92] This resemblance to churches was especially evident in the auditorium wing with its cross-shaped plan and apse. Nevertheless, the domes were important to Harmon precisely because they evoked religious architecture and represented the YMCA's spiritual and religious educational agenda; as the architect wrote: 'nearly everything which takes place in this building will have, if not a directly religious motive, an association with religious movements centered in Jerusalem'.[93]

'Religious movements' included Judaism and Islam, and the prominence of domes in the sacred architecture of these religions and their use for the YMCA was deemed to be particularly appropriate. Jewish and Muslim precedents could have included, for example, the Al Jazzâr Pasha Mosque in Acre (1781–2; Figure 3.12). There is no evidence that Harmon visited Acre during his 1926 tour, yet he might well have been familiar with this building. Considered by scholars as 'the best example of a mosque in the classical Ottoman style in Palestine',[94] it often appeared in publications about the Holy Land.[95] Prominent nineteenth-century Jewish models were the Hurva and the Tiferet Yisrael synagogues – the hallmark of Jewish sacred architecture in Jerusalem (Figures 3.13 and 3.14).[96] The Al

---

[91] This church is discussed in Bianca Kühnel, 'Ti'aruch Knesi'yat Ha'Ali'ya Be'Har Haze'itim', in *Prakim BeToldon Yerushalayim Bi'Ymei HaBeinayim*, ed. Benyamin Ze'ev Kedar (Jerusalem: Yad Izhak Ben-Zvi, 1979), 327–37.

[92] Harte to Harmon, 1 July 1926, YAAd.

[93] Harmon to Harte, 24 September 1926, 2, YAAd; see Letter attributed to Harte written to Harmon, 15 September 1926, 4, YAAd.

[94] Andrew Petersen, *A Gazetteer of Buildings in Muslim Palestine (Part 1)* (Oxford: Oxford University Press, 2001), 76.

[95] See, e.g., W. H. Bartlett, *Footsteps by Our Lord and His Apostles* (London: H. G. Bohn, 1851) and John Wilson, *The Lands of the Bible*, 2 vols (Edinburgh: William Whyte, 1847), reproduced in Nathan Schur, *Toldot Ako* (Tel Aviv: Dvir, 1990), 239, 247.

[96] Kroyanker, *Adrichalut Bi'Yerushalayim: HaBni'ya Ba'Yir Ha'Atika*, 188–91; Edina Meyer-Maril, 'Synagogenbau in Palästina zwischen Tradition und Moderne. Vom jüdischen Viertel in der

Figure 3.9 *Jerusalem YMCA Building, gymnasium wing. Photographed by Diego Rosman.*

Figure 3.10 *Jerusalem YMCA Building, auditorium wing. Photographed by Diego Rosman.*

Figure 3.11 *Holy Sepulchre, Jerusalem, 1149. Photograph by Félix Bonfils. Palestine, Jerusalem Album, fig. 107 titled 'Jérusalem. Vue générale des coupoles du Saint Sépulcre', c. 1870, albumen print, 28.5 × 22.2 cm. © Israel Museum, Jerusalem.*

Figure 3.12 *Al Jazzar Pasha Mosque, Acre, 1781–2. © IGPO, digital ID D234-029.*

Figure 3.13 *Hurva Synagogue, Jerusalem, completed 1864, demolished 1948. Photograph by John Cramb,* Jerusalem in 1860: A Series of Photographic Views Album, *photo titled '[The] Jews Quarter and New Synagogue, 1860', albumen print, 21.7 × 16.8 cm. © Israel Museum, Jerusalem.*

Figure 3.14 *Tiferet Yisrael Synagogue, Jerusalem, 1862–72. Wiki Commons, https://en.wikipedia.org/wiki/Tiferet_Yisrael_Synagogue#/media/File:Tiferet_Yisrael_Synagogue.jpg, retrieved 16 February 2020.*

Jazzâr Pasha Mosque and the two synagogues appropriated the forms of Ottoman mosques in their basic shape of a hemispherical dome poised on a cube, the sides of which are constructed of piers connected by a wide arch. Structurally, these types of domes are supported by wide interior squinches. Harmon adapted these elements in a simplified manner by lowering the drum, unifying the windows with the dome, and raising the supporting wall arches above their cubical planes. Harmon's use of accentuated corners and tall arcaded fenestration emphasised streamlined height, rather than the cubic massing characteristic of the Ottoman-style precedents. His adaptation thus represented an articulation of regional architecture integrated with an Art Deco emphasis on height.

The similarity of the YMCA Building's wings to Byzantine sources of inspiration was also discussed by the building's planners, who were well aware of the architectural 'lineage' linking Ottoman mosques to the famous Hagia Sophia Church in Istanbul (532–7), planned by Anthemius of Tralles and Isidorus of Miletus. The inspiration provided by Ottoman mosques is no less apparent in the auditorium's interior design (Figure 3.15), which exhibits beautifully detailed wall stenciling. This lavish decoration features large rosettes on the dome's squinches – a decoration common to those mosques; it further displays a frieze that enhances the lower part of the dome, which has an Islamic-inspired geometrical design that intentionally integrates Byzantine-style crosses, and more. Harmon's approach thus reveals a heightened awareness of the mutual influence of Muslim and early medieval Christian architecture, which he and Harte regarded as 'one of the chief characteristics of Jerusalem'.[97]

As I showed earlier in relation to Harrison's design for the Palestine Archaeological Museum, domes were often utilised as an expression of vernacular architecture. Harmon similarly used the hemispherical dome not only as a religious precursor, but also as an appropriation of the vernacular, so as to integrate the building with its surroundings.

The building's dome-topped tower, which serves as both a belfry and an observation tower, also has very interesting formal sources (Figure 3.16). Harte wanted it to be higher than any of the church steeples in Jerusalem and visible from everywhere. This wish to compete with other denominations demonstrates Harte's ambivalent approach to Jerusalem's Christian sects. As I noted earlier, the YMCA's ideology was ecumenical and fostered interdenominational cooperation. Yet, Harte's determination to establish the prominence of the American YMCA led to his constant striving for magnificent architecture that would overshadow neighbouring Christian institutions. Indeed, the tower was for years the highest vantage point in the city. Harte envisioned how 'from the top of the building we would look down into the Holy City across the Judean wilderness and the Dead

Altstadt Jerusalem zu den Mosahvot des Baron von Rothschild', in *Judentum zwischen Tradition und Moderne*, eds Gerd Biegel and Michael Graetz (Heidelberg: Universitätsverlag Winter, 2002), 73–8.

[97] Letter attributed to Harte written to Harmon, 15 September 1926, 4, *YAAd*.

Figure 3.15 *Jerusalem YMCA Building, interior of auditorium wing. Photographed by Diego Rosman.*

Sea to the Hills of Moab and always have present an ever changing and inspiring view'.[98] Harte's reference to biblical places as he cited Judea, Moab and the Dead Sea introduced a theological element that would reveal 'where the feet of Jesus have trod'.[99] He expected Jews as well as Muslims to appreciate these views, which would stir memories related to their own holy geography. To enhance this reverence of the landscape, brass reliefs indicating the area's topography and major points of interest, designed by Raban and Gur-Arieh, were fixed on the wide railings of the tower's observation balcony.[100]

The tower was conceived as an element that would be accepted by all of Jerusalem's publics as familiar and as having both religious and civic meanings. As a belfry it had a Christian religious function; Harte thought of it as a memorial

[98] Harte to Ned(?), 22 January 1920, 1–2, *YA1918-27*.
[99] Harte to Jarvie, 7 June 1926, 1–2, *YA1918-27*.
[100] Raban to Adamson, 12 April 1932; Adamson to the Workshop for Industrial Arts, 4 August 1932; Raban to Adamson, 6 September 1932; Raban, probably to Adamson, undated; Adamson to Raban, undated; all letters, Jerusalem Municipal Archive, Box 64 (Ze'ev Raban).

Figure 3.16 *Jerusalem YMCA Building, tower. Photographed by Diego Rosman.*

to Jesus and named it 'The Jesus Tower'.[101] Accordingly, bells were installed at a great cost,[102] the twelve apostles were sculpted on the turrets, and symbols of the four evangelists were carved on the corners of the belfry level (Figures 3.17 and 3.18). They were prudently carved high, where they were less visible, rendering their Christian significance less apparent to members of the other faiths.

The sculptures in the tower were designed by the American architectural sculptor Maxfield H. Keck (1883–1943), who created them in the Art Deco style as reliefs and quasi-three-dimensional elements with strong angles, ziggurats, squares and polyhedrons.[103] His most prominent design for the tower is the five-metre-tall

---

[101] Harte to Jarvie, 7 June 1926, 1–2, *YA1918-27*.
[102] Jarvie's niece Amelia Jarvie donated the funds for the carillon. See General Secretary of the YMCA of the United States Frank W. Ramsey to Amelia Jarvie, 1 April 1932, Carillon file, 1932–3, Jerusalem YMCA Records, *KFYA*.
[103] Keck worked with Harmon on the Shelton Hotel and executed architectural sculpture for other important buildings, such as the new Waldorf-Astoria Hotel and the Riverside Church in

Figure 3.17 *Arthur Loomis Harmon, Jerusalem YMCA Building, apostle sculpture on observation balcony of the tower. Photographed by Diego Rosman.*

relief of a seraph at its centre, carved by Raban and Gur-Arieh according to a model that Keck supplied (Figure 3.19). This six-winged creature, resembling an angel, was inspired by the divine revelation to the prophet Isaiah when a seraph purified him by touching a burning coal to his lips.[104]

According to Harte, the seraph purifying Isaiah symbolised 'the holiness of God and of man's need for purification in order to [achieve] companionship with God'.[105] Purification was synonymous with the YMCA's ideology of improving human morals and ethics. In the designers' view, this transposition of the concept of atonement to the cultural realm could be more easily related to Muslim and

---

New York City, among others. See Inbal Ben-Asher Gitler, 'Reconstructing Religions: Jewish Place and Space in the Jerusalem YMCA Buildings, 1919–1933', *Zeitschrift für Religions- und Geistesgeschichte* 60, no. 1 (2008): 52–3.

[104] Bible, Isaiah 6: 6–7.
[105] Harte to McMillan, 15 October 1926, 1, *YAAd*.

Figure 3.18 *Arthur Loomis Harmon, Jerusalem YMCA Building, sculptures for the evangelist symbols at the belfry level (St John), 1926–33. © Jerusalem YMCA.*

Jewish publics than ideas grounded in theology. The designers were well aware of Judaism's and Islam's scriptural prohibition against sculpting human figures.[106] Thus – and in keeping with the dramatic description in Isaiah 6 – the seraph's eyes and groin were conveniently concealed by two pairs of wings in the hope that this would make this creature acceptable to all of the city's communities. The seraph's elongated figure is clad in symmetrical robes with vertical pleats. He is holding the burning coal in his right hand and his larger wings form an arch with feathers stylised as a two-tiered scalloped half-circle, a common motif in Art Deco architectural sculpture.

The seraph motif can be found in Raban's Zionist art as well, for example, in Passover Haggadot that he illustrated in 1925.[107] His earlier representations of the seraph are significant, as they indicate that it was accepted as a divine symbol of

[106] Harte to McMillan, 15 October 1926, 1, *YAAd*.
[107] Goldman, *Ze'ev Raban*, 117, figs 154–5.

Figure 3.19 *Jerusalem YMCA Building, seraph relief on the tower. Photographed by Diego Rosman.*

holiness in Jewish-Zionist art. As I have shown elsewhere, designing a single masculine seraph deviated sharply from Christian iconographical tradition.[108] Thus, it is not surprising that these design decisions engendered vehement debates among the team building the YMCA, demonstrating the influence that planning for intercommunal and interreligious uses had on the design process. These arguments also highlighted the novelty of the building's conceptualisation. After much deliberation on the seraph's character, an exasperated Adamson finally wrote:

> I wish you folks in New York would read your Bibles occasionally. You over and over again refer to the Seraphim (sic) as the Angel or Cherubim. Please be informed that the best authorities agree that the Seraphim is not an angel nor is it a Cherubim. The Seraphim is (sic) definitely a creature of masculine character

[108] Ben-Asher Gitler, 'Reconstructing Religions', 53.

whereas angels and cherubims (sic) are not at all definitely masculine. This idea of masculinity should not be lost sight of in connection with our Seraphim (sic).[109]

As can be seen, issues of gender representation surfaced in this discussion. It is noteworthy that, contrary to the statements that the building would also be used by women, Adamson summarised his support of a masculine seraph by rhetorically asking: 'Don't you know that this is going to be a he-man Building and not a girls ['] seminary?' – indicating that despite the building's declared hospitality for all, the all-male team managing its design upheld the YMCA's customary gender segregation, at least conceptually.

Two additional sources served as inspiration to further enhance the tower's relationship to all of Jerusalem's publics as a civic and religious presence. While acknowledging dome-topped minarets, typical of Jerusalem's cityscape, as a source, Harte was afraid that Muslims would interpret their direct imitation as an attempt to compete with their own religious institutions.[110] Indeed, Muslim Palestinian political parties, such as Istiqlal, warned against YMCA attempts to draw Muslims toward Christianity, going so far as to dissuade them from attending the building's inauguration ceremony.[111] When examining possible Muslim precursors that could avoid too obvious imitation, the Mamluk-era White Mosque minaret (1318) in the town of Ramla, west of Jerusalem, which has a remarkable resemblance to the YMCA tower, comes to mind (Figure 3.20). Atypical in form and uncharacteristic of the region, it could have answered the designers' search for an understated relationship to local minarets. The White Mosque minaret, which has no dome, features accentuated buttresses.[112] Arched fenestration, vestibules, sparse ornamentation and a streamlined appearance further suggest that this minaret was an inspiration for the YMCA tower. Harte, who frequently travelled around the country, was surely familiar with the White Mosque, and Harmon might well have seen it in travel accounts.[113]

An American tower that closely resembles the one on the YMCA is that of the Nebraska State Capitol (1922–1932; Figure 3.21) in Lincoln, planned by Harmon's contemporary, Bertram Grosvenor Goodhue (1869–1924). As a fellow architect engaged in contemporary design, Harmon was probably familiar with this major American commission. In planning the Nebraska capitol, Goodhue combined American Beaux-Art classicism with Art Deco innovations, the latter evident in the layering and setting-back of volumes and the integration of hexagonal and pen-

---

[109] Adamson to McMillan, 29 May 1931, 1–2, *YAAd*.
[110] Harte to Harmon, 23 September 1926, 1, *YAAd*.
[111] 'Agudat HaNotsrim HaTzeyirim', *Davar*, 7 December 1932; 'Ma Tiva shel Agudat HaNotsrim HaTzeirim', *Doar Hayom*, 8 November 1932, 4; 'LiKrat Bo'o shel Allenby LeYisrael', *Doar Hayom*, 29 March 1933, 3.
[112] Ze'ev Vilnay, *Ramla – Hove Ve'Avar* (Jerusalem: Ariel, 1961), 22–7.
[113] See illustrations in ibid.

Figure 3.20 *Minaret of the White Mosque, Ramla, 1318. Photographed by Ilan Gad. Wiki Commons, https://commons.wikimedia.org/wiki/File:White_t1.jpg, retrieved 16 February 2020.*

Figure 3.21 *Bertram Grosvenor Goodhue, Tower of the Nebraska State Capitol, Lincoln, Nebraska, 1922–32. © Nebraska Capitol Collection.*

Figure 3.22 *Bertram Grosvenor Goodhue, Nebraska State Capitol, competition entry, 1920. © Nebraska Capitol Collection.*

tagonal elements. The Nebraska tower – roughly three times higher than the YMCA tower, is similar in its clasping buttresses, octagonal turrets and dome. Goodhue's 1920 winning competition entry was even more indicative of the resemblance between the two towers. In that plan, domes, which were omitted from the final design, topped the turrets (Figure 3.22).[114] A tower was not a common feature in the architecture of American capitols and the one in Lincoln ascribed a new civic meaning to this typology, derived perhaps from urban clock towers.[115] Harmon's adoption of this scheme for the Jerusalem YMCA was thus a further indication of the building's urban-civic functions.

The YMCA Building's arcaded portico was inspired by both modern and ancient

---

[114] This drawing was previously published in Elizabeth G. Grossman, 'Two Postwar Competitions: The Nebraska State Capitol and the Kansas City Liberty Memorial', *JSAH* 45 (1986): 251, fig. 6.
[115] Kidder Smith, *Source Book of American Architecture*, 352–3.

models. In addition to its formal relationship to American hotel architecture, as exemplified by the comparison to the Hotel Ponce de León, the arcade appropriated and evoked local and medieval architecture (Figure 3.4). It was built as a series of square units that carry domical vaults and bi-chrome voussoirs, characteristic of medieval Islamic architecture in Jerusalem's Old City.[116] The arcade was the most important element in the YMCA Building's numerous tiers of arched openings – located in the tower, the wings and the fourth floor – all of which linked it to local architecture in general and, more specifically, to Middle Eastern Muslim precedents. However, the arcade also connotes Christian architecture and was often referred to as a 'cloister' by the designers, even though it does not enclose a court.[117] The arcade's double-colonette module, as well as its vaulting and sculpted capitals, clearly reflect Romanesque cloisters. Harmon and Harte were both familiar with these not only through books and from their travels in Europe,[118] but also from the Cloisters Museum in New York City.[119] Historic European architectural styles thus made their way to Jerusalem through the conduit of the American planners' knowledge of them. The arcade's columns featured more than forty sculpted capitals, carved with plants and animals typical of the Holy Land. I discuss their meaning in the context of the YMCA Building in the section that follows.

The Arcade: A Guide to the Holy Land

Images of the flora and fauna of the region sculpted on the capitals produced a superb ensemble of Palestine, or Eretz Israel's, natural environment. I use both 'Palestine' and 'Eretz Israel' here since, as I demonstrate, the display of nature in the YMCA Building arcade was associated with Zionist ideas.

Harte wanted the arcade capitals to be 'useful in making the young people ... [in Palestine] know the history of their country and be at the same time a sort of illuminated Bible to many others'.[120] For these purposes, the capitals served as a

---

[116] For the use of these arches, see Miriam Rosen-Ayalon, 'Omanut HaBniya VeHa'yitur BiYerushalyim', in *Prakim BeToldon Yerushalayim Bi'Ymei HaBeinayim*, ed. Benyamin Ze'ev Kedar (Jerusalem: Yad Itzhak Ben-Zvi, 1979), 287–315.

[117] See, e.g., Harte to Davison, 20 October 1925, 3, *YA1918-27*; Harte to Harmon, 28 April 1928, 1–2, and Harte to Jarvie, 21 March 1928, 2, both documents Jerusalem General Correspondence, January–August 1928, Jerusalem YMCA Records, *KFYA*.

[118] Harmon visited France, likely more than once, as he built two World War I memorials there. See 'Arthur Harmon, Architect, Dead', *New York Times*, 18 October 1958, 21; Harte had worked with Anglo-Saxon war prisoners in Germany prior to coming to Palestine and travelled extensively in Europe.

[119] The Saint-Guilhem-le-Désert or Trie Cloisters were reconstructed and exhibited in 1925 at the Cloisters Museum, an annex of the Metropolitan Museum of Art, New York, whose construction in north Manhattan was also funded by John D. Rockefeller. See William H. Forsyth, 'Five Crucial People in the Building of the Cloisters', in *The Cloisters: Studies in Honor of the Fiftieth Anniversary*, ed. Elizabeth C. Parker (New York: Metropolitan Museum of Art and the International Center of Medieval Art, 1992), 51–2.

[120] Harte to Jarvie, 7 June 1926, 1, *YA1918-27*, 1.

botanical and zoological guide (Figure 3.23a, c–f).¹²¹ This approach is similar to the didactic role assigned to capitals in the Oxford Museum in Oxford, England (1855–60 by Deane and Woodward) and the Natural History Museum in London (1871–81 by Alfred Waterhouse), where natural history was depicted in the sculptural details of the buildings. Many of the YCMA capitals bear a clear stylistic resemblance to these British precedents: for example, the YMCA bird and vine capital (Fig. 3.23a) is similar to the one depicting birds in the Natural History Museum (Fig. 3.23b). Capitals with doves, grain or grapevines, as well as other flowers and animals sculpted at the YMCA, have a clear iconographic tradition in Christian art and symbolise the Holy Spirit and Communion (Figure 3.23a, c, d). Other capitals, however, depict indigenous 'specimens', such as flowering bulbs and trees, as well as wild animals, which are not necessarily associated with Scripture.¹²²

All the arcade capitals were sculpted by Raban, Gur-Arieh and members of their workshop, modelled on the small-scale drawings done by Dimmock in New York. It appears that here the artists were granted some freedom in execution, and that they therefore relied on Zionist art, where the theme of local plant and animal life was popular, especially at the Bezalel school, where Raban and Gur-Arieh studied and later taught.¹²³ Moreover, Jewish symbolic meaning was introduced by representing the biblical 'seven species': the capitals in the YMCA include images of barley and wheat, figured together to depict grain (Figure 3.23c); capitals devoted to grapes, figs, pomegranates and olives; and one of dates, which are represented by featuring a palm tree. This produce symbolised the Holy Land's fertility and was central to the Zionist idea of reconnecting to Eretz Israel by cultivating the land.¹²⁴ The idea of fertility is further expressed in four capitals that figure livestock, sculpted alongside faces of shepherds and shepherdesses (Figure 3.23e, f). These relate the renewal of husbandry, common in Raban's art and connoting the importance of livestock for all of Mandatory Palestine's communities. The 'nature guide' created in the arcade includes representations of agriculture that were derived from Zionist art yet related to all of Jerusalem's communities, since agriculture was a central source of income for all of them. Moreover, the capitals express the American idea of the Holy Land. As argued by historian John Davis, Orientalist painting depicting traditional agricultural practices in Palestine, which often included representations of the region's flora and fauna, was perceived by American Protestants as symbolising the tie between the biblical past and the

---

[121] Trevor Garnham, *Oxford Museum: Deane and Woodward* (London: Phaidon, 1992); Brian Hanson, *Architects and the 'Building World' from Chambers to Ruskin: Constructing Authority* (Cambridge: Cambridge University Press, 2003), 201–26.

[122] For the capitals' religious content, see Ben-Asher Gitler, 'Reconstructing Religions', 56–7.

[123] For flora and fauna imagery in Bezalel, see Shiloh-Cohen, ed., *Bezalel shel Schatz*, 203–4, figs 208–11; Alek Mishori, *Shuru, Habitu U'Re'u – Ikonot VeSmalim Hazuti'yim Ziyoni'yim BaTarbut HaYisraelit* (Tel Aviv: Am Oved, 2000), 240–71.

[124] For the Zionist interpretations of the seven species, see Mishori, *Shuru, Habitu U'Re'u*, 241–7; Daliah Manor, 'Biblical Zionism in Bezalel Art', *Israel Studies* 6, no. 1 (2001): 57.

Figure 3.23a *Jerusalem YMCA Building, arcade capital: doves and grapevines. Photographed by Diego Rosman.*

Figure 3.23b *Alfred Waterhouse and [Auguste?] Dujardin, Bird Capitals at the Natural History Museum, London, 1871–81. Photographed by the author.*

Figure 3.23c *Jerusalem YMCA Building, arcade capital: wheat/barley. Photographed by Diego Rosman.*

Figure 3.23d *Jerusalem YMCA Building, arcade capital: doves. Photographed by Diego Rosman.*

Figure 3.23e *Jerusalem YMCA Building, arcade capital: shepherdesses and shepherds. Photographed by Diego Rosman.*

Figure 3.23f *Jerusalem YMCA Building, arcade capital: shepherdesses and shepherds. Photographed by Diego Rosman.*

Figure 3.24 *Jerusalem YMCA Building, portal. Photographed by Diego Rosman.*

present.[125] The arcade's 'guide' to the Holy Land thus represented not only Zionist ideology and Christian theology, but an established American tradition as well, and it negotiated an agricultural and natural present in tandem with the Holy Land's past.

Forged in Stone, Stenciled on Walls: Multifaith Elements in the Design of the Building

On almost every level of the building's main façade, as well as in key interior spaces, inscriptions in Arabic, Hebrew, German and Aramaic were included among texts carved in English, which contributed to the building's intertextuality and intercommunality. There are selected verses from various sources hailing peace, Jerusalem, Christ, and more. Largely scriptural in origin, the verses define the building's duality as a space that integrates religious beliefs and secular culture. Christ is only alluded to in these inscriptions, and his name is never written, so as to accommodate the other religions. For example, the portal inscription reads: 'And His name shall be called Wonderful, counselor, the mighty God, the everlasting Father, the Prince of Peace' (Figure 3.24).[126] This verse from Isaiah 9: 5 is

---

[125] Davis, *The Landscape of Belief*, 139–40.
[126] Isaiah 9: 6.

Figure 3.25a *Jerusalem YMCA Building, façade inscription in Hebrew. Photographed by Diego Rosman.*

Figure 3.25b *Jerusalem YMCA Building, façade inscription in Arabic. Photographed by Diego Rosman.*

considered by Christians as a prophecy of the birth of Jesus, but the first part of the sentence, 'For unto us a child is born; unto us a son is given', was omitted from the text selected for this prominent space.[127]

Much thought was devoted to whether or not to include inscriptions in Arabic and Hebrew. In 1931, in the face of the ongoing political strife between Muslims and Jews, McMillan suggested consulting the communities in order to prevent 'a feeling that one faith or the other has been favored', and to consider the possibility of 'leav[ing] off the inscriptions entirely if it is going to cause trouble'.[128] Trouble notwithstanding, two inscriptions were finally carved on the building: part of the Jewish pledge of allegiance to One God, *Shema Yisrael*, was carved in Hebrew on the main façade's north cornice, reading: '*Adonai Eloheynu Adonai Echad*' ('The Lord our God is one Lord'; Figure 3.25A). On the south cornice part of the *Shahada*, the Muslim profession of faith, the first Pillar of Islam, was incised in Arabic: '*lā ilāhā illā-llāhu*' ('There is no God but God'; Figure 3.25B). Both verses were carved in low relief yet are large and legible even from the street. The words from *Shema Yisrael* form the most prominent expression of Judaism on the building, as do

---

[127] Harte to Harmon, 23 September 1926, 2, *YAAd*.
[128] McMillan to Ramsey, 26 October 1931, 1, *YAAd*.

Figure 3.26 *Jerusalem YMCA Building, multifaith chapel. Photographed by Diego Rosman.*

those of the *Shahada* with respect to Islam. The original sentences in Hebrew and Arabic include the words 'Israel' and 'Muhammad', respectively, but those words were omitted. As such, these phrases remain legible to their own publics, yet underscore the one Lord common to the three religions. Seemingly infrangible verses were thus the bases for extractions that create the building's intertextuality and underscore monotheism as a common, unifying element.

Another important space that was designed to represent all three religions and serve them equally was the multifaith chapel (Figure 3.26), a small low-ceiling room faced with natural stone in which there are several reliefs. Its floor has an incised decoration, and a carved wooden door serves as its entrance. The chapel's location in the basement of the tower is symbolic, suggesting that the tower's foundations are emerging from Jerusalem's ancient rock. Harte wanted to leave the rock foundation visible, but architect Fitz-Henry Faye Tucker, Harmon's representative who visited the building in 1928, advised against it owing to some complications with the excavation.[129] Harte accepted Tucker's advice and instead

---

[129] Tucker to Harmon, 16 January 1928, 4, *YAAd*.

placed an altar constructed of natural stones from Bethel in the eastern part of the chapel.[130] The stones were described, probably in accordance with Harte's directives, as left in their natural state to symbolise 'an altar, or cairn of remembrance, as the early Israelites used to commemorate notable incidents, a custom still practiced by the Arabs today'.[131] By alluding to ancient remains or archaeological sites, this interpretation strengthened the building's connection with the Gospels. For Harte, using stones from Bethel also evoked the biblical story of the altar made from local stones that Jacob built in Bethel following God's revelation: 'I had thought of building the altar with twelve unhewn stones from Bethel, the traditional site of Jacob's dream of the ladder from earth to Heaven,' he wrote.[132] It is interesting to note that Katinke, the contractor, credited himself with the idea of gathering stones from Bethel, although Harte probably called for it in his plans.[133]

The chapel's stone reliefs describe the story of reconciliation and forgiveness based on Matthew 5: 23–4.[134] The floor drawing, incised into the stone, describes the 'Syrophoenician Table' as symbolising the lesson in humility taught in Matthew 15: 26–8. Above the altar is the phrase 'For their sakes I sanctify Myself' (John 17: 19). The oak door was carved with a picture showing 'representative figures of all the nations with heads uplifted in praise to God as a necessary element in worship'. The quote beneath it, 'Whoso offereth praise glorifieth me', was taken from Psalm 50: 23.[135] All these texts can be read as underscoring interreligious tolerance and unity.

The idea of a multifaith chapel was quite novel at the time, and this is arguably one of the first spaces having such a function worldwide. Architectural historian John Crompton distinguishes multifaith chapels from earlier shared religious spaces, the latter the results of negotiations regarding revered historic sites. He identifies purposely built multifaith chapels as a modern phenomenon, dating the first one to 1988, but also noting modernist 'meditation spaces' as precursors.[136] Clearly, this overlooked example indicates a significantly earlier appearance of

---

[130] Ibid.
[131] *JYMCA Brochure* (1933), 28, KFYA.
[132] Genesis 28: 18 and 35: 7. See letter from Harte to Davison, 20 October 1925, 3. Thirty-two years after the building's completion, Dimmock recounted an interesting story about the altar in the building's chapel to Herbert L. Minard, then General Secretary of the Jerusalem YMCA. He wrote that during his visit to Jerusalem in 1932, while grading for the soccer field was taking place, an underground burial vault was discovered. Dimmock accompanied the agents of the Museum of Antiquities who came to inspect the site. The vault was dated as Roman, and the authorities confiscated jewellery and other artefacts of archaeological significance, telling Dimmock to 'destroy everything else'. Out of respect for the ancient remains, Dimmock placed the skull of who was presumed to have been the head of the excavated clan within the stones of the altar. See letter from Dimmock to Herbert L. Minard, 4 January 1965, 1–2. Jerusalem Municipal Archive, Box 2683 (YMCA).
[133] Katinka, *Me'az Ve'Ad Hena*, 265–6.
[134] *JYMCA Brochure* (1933), 28, KFYA.
[135] Ibid. 28–9.
[136] Andrew Crompton, 'The Architecture of Multifaith Spaces: God Leaves the Building', *The Journal of Architecture* 18, no. 4 (2013): 477.

this typology. In his discussion of multifaith spaces built at the end of the twentieth century and after, Crompton contends that architects tackle the issues of multiple symbolism by refraining from decorations almost completely.[137] The YMCA's multifaith chapel thus represents a modern space wherein the designers approached the requirements of catering to three religions very differently: rather than avoiding text and image, they tried to find both appropriate materials – forging the chapel from ancient stone – and appropriate inscriptions and visualisations.

The Christian messages in the building were blurred by this intertextuality, as well as by local architectural elements and visualisations of Palestine/Eretz Israel and the Old Testament. Initially, this message of multiculturalism was perceived as a success: a pleased Dimmock wrote, 'the community seems to be awake to the great symbolic value that our building will always have. The significance of the carvings and scriptural texts, the atmosphere we have created.'[138]

Many elements in the building's interior further contribute to the building's multiculturalism and religious pluralism. A full discussion of the features is beyond the scope of the present book, but they should be mentioned, if only briefly. These elements include the painted and stencilled walls of the auditorium, noted earlier, as well as those of other common spaces, such as the lobby; there are also oriental-style spaces, such as the cafeteria, which features a marble-tiled Ottoman-style fireplace (Figure 3.27). Furniture and even a ceiling were brought especially from Damascus, and American historicist and Art Deco styles characterise such spaces as the library and the swimming pool. Elements reminiscent of ancient reliefs and mosaics are integrated in the main entrance. These carefully designed interiors create a sophisticated atmosphere, which represents Jerusalem's communities, regional traditions, and American design. In addition to their cultural role, it is noteworthy that these interiors reflect two approaches to production. On the one hand, the making of many of the elements was grounded in European and American Arts and Crafts traditions, which were revived in Jerusalem by the British and by the Bezalel School of Art. On the other hand, significant components of the interiors and their furnishings were executed using up-to-date production processes and technologies, planned and carried out in accordance with the directives of the YMCA Building Bureau, as I noted earlier in connection with allocating production to the different Jerusalem communities. This process implies a modern, prefabricated design approach in supplying furnishings, stencils, patterns and utilities that were adapted to the unique requirements of the Jerusalem YMCA.[139]

---

[137] Ibid. 474–7.
[138] Dimmock to Ramsey, 4 September 1932, 2, Jerusalem General Correspondence, 1931–1932, *KFYA*.
[139] Ben-Asher Gitler, 'The Architecture of the Jerusalem YMCA', 208–27.

Figure 3.27 *Jerusalem YMCA Building, Ottoman-style fireplace in the lobby (present-day restaurant). Photographed by Diego Rosman.*

'A Building at the Cross-roads of the World'

> Dr. Harte had for years the vision of a building for a Jerusalem YMCA, but much more than an ordinary YMCA – a building at the cross-roads of the World, the core of Christian thought, which would be a beacon and an inspiration both in its beauty and in its use for future generations...[140]

In calling the Jerusalem YMCA 'A building at the cross-roads of the World', Harmon denoted it as the meeting point of the three monotheistic religions. It was a Eurocentric and Americentric expression in that it implied the exclusion of other faiths from this 'World'. It did, however, signify that locating the building in Jerusalem was the reason and goal for its consecration. Harmon's interpretation of the building's role reveals an additional, crucial aspect: that is, that in order for the building to become a 'beacon' for its users – a source to be admired – its functions were just as important as its appearance.

Emphasis on function is arguably one of the key denominators of American modernism. Harmon is especially renowned for planning functional, modern skyscrapers, rather than religious edifices, but he nevertheless invested the Jerusalem

---

[140] Harmon to Ramsey, 6 February 1930, 3, *YA1929-30n*.

YMCA with many important religious facilities – the belfry, a multifaith chapel and pilgrim hostel. Moreover, religious content in sculpture and inscriptions is in evidence throughout the building. These elements have many matrices derived from religious complexes, including those built in Jerusalem, but their forerunners were always intended to service *one* faith and often only *one denomination or sect*. In contrast, in the YMCA Building these functions were no longer devoted solely to the liturgy of a single religious community. Rather, they were incorporated into a multifaith functional space that also integrated secular education, entertainment and sports.

Ayla Lepine notes that in eclectic early twentieth-century sacred spaces in Britain and America, architects integrated 'a historicist approach to Gothic and Classical architectural and decorative elements, with a keen attentiveness to the spirit and intentions of new understandings of sacred space'.[141] This American historicist approach in the YMCA Building comprised Byzantine and Romanesque as well as Jewish and Muslim sources of inspiration. More important, however, are the 'new understandings' that the building's architecture creates, identified in the mutual integration of sacred and secular spaces. Lepine contends that the novel 'spirit and intentions' of buildings render these twentieth-century sacred spaces modern. The same can be said of the Jerusalem YMCA: its modernity was manifested in new spatial configurations, in addition to implementing modern construction technology and using a systematised design approach. In this context, the synthesis of Middle Eastern, medieval Christian and Art Deco elements is revealed not as a conservative or eclectic design strategy but, rather, as an approach that I term *figurative modernism*. This is a type of modernism that differs from its renown, *abstract* interwar architectural counterparts, as exemplified in the International Style. In the Jerusalem YMCA Building, figurative modernism contextualised architecture, and the 'international' was discarded in favour of an unequivocal association with place and identity. A process that can be traced in other early twentieth-century sacred spaces and in additional typologies, it reflects a more pronounced specificity of history, religion or ideology. In the architecture of the Jerusalem YMCA, this specificity created 'spaces' among beliefs, heritages and histories.

Acknowledging all of Jerusalem's sects was intended to create a sense of mutual belonging to the YMCA, but public reactions to the building and the activities within it were ambiguous, and several of the city's communities considered the modern culture it brought to Jerusalem controversial. Some did, indeed, participate in YMCA activities and frequented the building: in 1930 there were 370 listed members: 175 Protestants, 91 Greek Orthodox, 24 Jews and 24 'Muhammadans'.[142] Government officials constituted the greater part of the membership. By the mid-

---

[141] Ayla Lepine, 'Modern Gothic and the House of God: Revivalism and Monasticism in Two Twentieth-Century Anglican Chapels', *Visual Resources* 32, no. 1/2 (2016): 89.

[142] N. Lattof, 'Administrative Report for the Year 1930', 1930 or 1931, 6, Jerusalem Annual Reports, Oversized/General, *KFYA*.

Figure 3.28 *First soccer match at the Jerusalem YMCA, 1 April 1933.* © IGPO, digital ID D637-002.

1940s YMCA membership totalled 1,500: some 50 per cent Christians, 25 per cent Jews, and 25 per cent Muslims.[143] Thus, whereas the YMCA did, indeed, embrace diversity, its members during the years of the Mandate were mostly Protestant and the association had limited success in recruiting Jews and Muslims. Non-Christian members were usually secular, as these made up the public that would use facilities such as the YMCA's unisex swimming pool, theatre, movie presentations and soccer field (Figure 3.28). As previously noted, many in the Muslim community viewed the YMCA's activity as missionary, and Muslim newspapers such as *Al Islamiyya* and *Al Jam'aa* voiced their concerns.[144] Even among liberal Zionists, the YMCA was often perceived as a missionary agent rather than as a peace-promoting community centre.[145] The Jewish Orthodox community called upon its members to boycott the building and beware of its activities, which were condemned as heathen and contradictory to Jewish culture.[146] Nevertheless, the YMCA Building fulfilled important international functions during the Mandate

---

[143] Retrieved 27 April 2005, jerusalemymca.org/eng/history.html.
[144] 'Agudat Hanotzrim Hatze'irim', *Davar*, 7 December 1932, 1.
[145] See, e.g., Baruch Stopniker, 'Hachinuch Hazar be Eretz Yisrael', *Doar Hayom*, 18 September 1932, 3; 'Du Partzufiyut shel Agudat Hanotzrim Hatze'irim', *Davar*, 1 December 1932, 1.
[146] Propaganda leaflet, Jerusalem Municipal Archive, file 2683 (YMCA).

Figure 3.29 *United Nations Special Committee on Palestine (UNSCOP) meeting at the Jerusalem YMCA Building auditorium, 1947. Photographed by Hans Pinn. © IGPO, digital ID D767-109.*

period, and at the height of post-World War II tensions surrounding Palestine's future, the United Nations Special Committee on Palestine (UNSCOP) was convened in the building's auditorium on 15 May 1947 (Figure 3.29).

Today, Harmon's building is still functioning in nearly all its originally planned spheres and it continues to promote coexistence through its activities. Thus, despite the attendant difficulties and objections, Americans imagining Jerusalem, their fundraising, and their ideas of cultural evangelisation introduced a novel architectural and urban presence that was as inspiring as it was controversial.

CHAPTER FOUR

Constructing Palestinian Identity: The Palace Hotel

THE SYMBOL OF COSMOPOLIS: The Great Palace Hotel building which symbolizes the new Jerusalem, no longer an obscure hill town with only a religious significance, but a modern city.[1]

THE ABOVE DESCRIPTION captioned a photograph of the then recently completed Jerusalem Palace Hotel (1928–9; Figure 4.1), which appeared in a 1930 issue of the British newspaper *The Sphere: The Empire's Illustrated Weekly*. Newly renovated and reopened in 2014 as the Jerusalem Waldorf Astoria Hotel, the original Palace Hotel did indeed symbolize the new, modern, Jerusalem in the eyes of its patrons, its community, and visiting tourists.

A cursory browse in twenty-first century web search engines reveals that the name 'Palace' is still used for hundreds of hotels around the world – from San Francisco to New York and from Malta to Istanbul. In Mandatory Palestine alone there were four 'Palace' hotels in addition to the one in Jerusalem: Arab hotels in Jericho and Ramallah were named 'Palace' and Jewish inns in Haifa and Tel Aviv were named '*Armon*' – Hebrew for 'palace'. The name is intrinsically associated with opulence and luxury. Although they held the promise of making every tourist feel like a king or queen in his or her traditional royal home, 'Palace' hotels also offered modern amenities. Moreover, as they served as the face of the host city vis-á-vis its guests, hotels often represented local or national identities, reflected in the choice of architect, style and construction methodologies.

In this chapter I look at the Jerusalem Palace Hotel, the most important edifice constructed by the Muslim Palestinian community during the British Mandate, taking these practical and conceptual functions into account. The Supreme Muslim Council commissioned the hotel with the goal of asserting a Muslim presence in the city, and the Turkish architect Mehmet Nihat Nigisberk (1880–1945), also known as Mehmed Nihad (or Nihat) Bey, was responsible

[1] H. J. Shepstone, 'Cairo's Potential Rival: The New Jerusalem', *The Sphere*, 13 September 1930, 456.

Figure 4.1 *Mehmet Nihat Nigisberk, Palace Hotel, Jerusalem, 1928–9. ACM, https://www.loc.gov/pictures/item/2019696252/, retrieved 11 February 2020.*

for its design.² It was constructed by a Jewish/Christian-Palestinian contractor partnership and built by workers practising all of the city's faiths. Its lavish exterior and the modern touristic amenities it offered reflected the emergence of Palestinian public architecture as a manifestation of national identity. However, this modern hotel, although it expressed the Muslim Palestinian desire to make a major physical mark on Jerusalem's rapidly developing cityscape, functioned as such for only a short time: economic constraints and commercial limitations hindered its operation, and managerial difficulties brought about its leasing to a prominent Jewish tourism entrepreneur, after which it served primarily as leased office and commercial space. Despite these various problems, which persisted throughout the 1930s, the hotel was the venue for several events of key significance for the Muslim Palestinian community, which underscored its importance to its public and assigned its architecture a role in the formation of a Palestinian identity.

Hajj Amin Al Husayni: Between Islam and Palestinian Identity

Muhammad Amin Al Husayni (1895–1974), known as Hajj Amin Al Husayni, one of the most important leaders of the Muslim Palestinian community during the British Mandate, initiated the construction of the Palace Hotel and oversaw its realisation. As his politics were central to the building's erection and to formulating its significance for that community, they should be explained in context. As I noted in the Introduction, the construction of a Palestinian national identity was initially inclusive of Christians and Muslims.³ However, British policies effected religious separation, leading to the formation of separate identities.⁴ British authorities established the Supreme Muslim Council (SMC) in January 1922, and appointed Hajj Amin Al Husayni, who was a member of one of Palestine's wealthiest and most influential Muslim families, as both the head of the SMC and mufti of Jerusalem in charge of Muslim religious affairs. These acts contributed significantly to the separation between Muslims and Christians in the city.⁵ The British further established a central Awqaf, or Waqf – the Muslim Pious Endowments Directorate – which Hajj Amin presided over as well.⁶

Many scholars have written about Hajj Amin's personality and career – primarily

---

² Katinka mentioned the architect of the Palace Hotel by the name 'Nihat Bey'. See Katinka, *Me'Az Ve'Ad Hena*, 257. The origin of the surname 'Nigisberk' is unknown. Although there are variations in the different sources – 'Nigizberk, Niğizberk, and Nigisberg'– I decided to use 'Nigisberk' for this study, in reference to Cengizkan's research. See Ali Cengizkan, 'Mehmet Nihat Nigisberk'in Katkilary: Evkaf Idaresi ve Mimar Kemalettin', in *Mimar Kemalettin Ve Çağı: Mimarlık/Toplumsal Yaşsam/Politika*, ed. Ali Cengizkan (Ankara: TMMOB Mimalar Odasi, 2009), 177–208.
³ Khalidi, *Palestinian Identity*, (2009) 169; Kimmerling, 'The Formation of Palestinian Collective Identities', 66.
⁴ Robson, *Colonialism and Christianity in Mandate Palestine*, 44.
⁵ Tsimhoni, 'The Status of the Arab Christians', 166–92.
⁶ Reiter, 'Waqf BiNsibot Mishtanot', 352–3.

in the framework of histories of the Israeli–Palestinian conflict. As Nicholas Roberts observes, Hajj Amin's portrayals vary: Israeli historiographers describe him as a devout, patriotic, and at times ruthless Muslim Palestinian, the most powerful Arab leader in Mandatory Palestine;[7] Palestinian historians present the more ambiguous aspects of his role in constructing Palestinian identity, at times giving him less credit than he deserves.[8] For the purpose of the present study, it is important to regard Hajj Amin as both a political and a religious leader. I must emphasise that his leadership underwent transformations during his long public service. Historians have shown that during the first decade and a half of his career, roughly between 1920 and 1936, he was a 'cautious, pragmatic and traditional leader who cooperated with British officials while opposing Zionism',[9] but that his approach changed during the Arab revolt that began in 1936.[10]

Hajj Amin Al Husayni was raised in Jerusalem. He received a Muslim education and studied languages in Christian and Jewish schools. He briefly attended the famous religious Al Azhar University in Cairo, where he met Rashid Rida – a Muslim reformer who deepened his awareness of Palestinian politics.[11] During World War I, he served in the Ottoman army, emerging as a leader within a family that took on key positions in the new Mandatory administration in 1921: the Husaynis controlled the Arab Executive, which was established by the British to represent Palestinian national interests;[12] the family was also among the founders of the Muslim Christian Association (MCA), which contributed to creating a unified national identity for the Arab community prior to the eventual separation of Muslims and Christians.[13]

The Husayni family also held the title of Shaykh al Haramyn – in charge of the Haram al-Sharif. As I noted in Chapter One, the Haram includes the Dome of the Rock (*Qubbat al-Sakhrah*, built in 692 CE)[14] and the Al-Aqsa Mosque (*Al-Masjid al-Aqsa*, built in 705–15 CE).[15] The latter is one of the holiest of sites for Muslims, who believe that it was from that place that Muhammad made his Night Journey

[7] Kimmerling, 'The Formation of Palestinian Collective Identities', 48–81.
[8] Roberts, 'Rethinking the Status Quo', 24–5.
[9] Mattar, 'The Mufti of Jerusalem and the Politics of Palestine', 228.
[10] Pappe, 'Haj Amin and the Buraq Revolt', 6–16; Roberts, 'Rethinking the Status Quo', 344; Mattar, 'The Mufti of Jerusalem', 228.
[11] Roberts, 'Rethinking the Status Quo', 202–3.
[12] Weldon Matthews, 'Pan-Islam or Arab Nationalism? The Meaning of the 1931 Jerusalem Islamic Congress Reconsidered', *International Journal of Middle East Studies* 35, no. 1 (2003): 3–5; Mattar, 'The Mufti of Jerusalem', 230–2.
[13] Roberts, 'Rethinking the Status Quo', 233–4. For a discussion of these processes see Jacobson, *From Empire to Empire*, 148–77.
[14] For a description of the Haram al-Sharif, see Oleg Grabar, *Jerusalem* (Constructing the Study of Islamic Art, 4) (Aldershot and Burlington: Ashgate, 2005), 59–64, 203–215. For detailed dating and discussion of the Dome of the Rock, see ibid. 111–15; Nasser Rabbat, 'The Meaning of the Umayyad Dome of the Rock', *Muqarnas* 6 (1989): 12–21.
[15] For detailed dating and discussion of this mosque, see Rafi Grafman and Miriam Rosen-Ayalon, 'The Two Great Syrian Umayyad Mosques: Jerusalem and Damascus', *Muqarnas* 6 (1999): 1–7, 11–12; Grabar, *Jerusalem*, 139–42.

– the *Miraj* – the event commemorated in the Archaeological Museum's reliefs I discussed in Chapter Two. Jewish tradition holds that the Haram was the site of Solomon's Temple.[16]

One of Hajj Amin's most important actions in his determination to promote Palestinian identity was the restoration of the Al-Aqsa Mosque. As we shall see, that restoration was central to the unfolding of the Palace Hotel project. Hajj Amin also used the Al-Aqsa restoration to strengthen Palestinian contacts with the Arab world, and the Husaynis had an important role in maintaining them. Members of the family were among the initiators of the international Arab congresses convened in Palestine beginning in 1913,[17] and they continued fostering ties with Turkey after World War I. The Husaynis's relations with Turkey began during Ottoman rule, during which they held important offices in the administration of Palestine.[18] These connections were not easily broken, as can be seen from the family's pro-Turkish sentiments, which they expressed on several important occasions during the Mandate.[19]

As head of the SMC, Hajj Amin became the most influential member of his family. The SMC was in charge of all Muslim religious affairs in Palestine, which were inseparable from political issues, so he was a key personage in both spheres. These politics involved the competition for land and the volatile disputes over the holy sites in Jerusalem, which were connected to the conflict with the Zionists and to how the Palestinians regarded and opposed the British Mandate. During the 1920s, Hajj Amin expanded the religious and political functions of the SMC in order to augment its influence. These actions were engendered not only by religious and political motives, but also by the well-known and well-documented rivalry between the Al-Husayni and the Nashashibi families – the latter a notable family that equalled the Husaynis in power and controlled the Jerusalem Municipality.[20] One strategy for strengthening the SMC was through extensive urban development, so Hajj Amin established a network of Muslim private schools, an orphanage, pharmacies, a Muslim library, a museum of Muslim antiquities, and more.[21]

The SMC's wide-ranging initiatives, which included religious, educational and commercial investments, reveal urban practices that engaged traditional and religious spaces alongside modern ones. Roberts identifies a process wherein during the 1920s political identity-forming activities gradually gained prominence over

---

[16] Rivka Gonen, *Contested Holiness: Jewish, Muslim, and Christian Perspectives on the Temple Mount in Jerusalem* (New York: KTAV, 2003); Rabbat, 'The Meaning of the Umayyad Dome of the Rock', 12–21; Isaac Kalimi, 'The Land of Moriah, Mount Moriah, and the Site of Solomon's Temple in Biblical Historiography', *Harvard Theological Review* 83, no. 4 (1990): 345–62.
[17] Matthews, 'Pan-Islam or Arab Nationalism?' 3–4; Roberts, 'Rethinking the Status Quo', 236–7.
[18] Mattar, 'The Mufti of Jerusalem', 228.
[19] Roberts, 'Rethinking the Status Quo', 262–4; Awad Halabi, 'Liminal Loyalties: Ottomanism and Palestinian Responses to the Turkish War of Independence, 1919–22', *Journal of Palestine Studies* 41, no. 3 (2012): 19–37.
[20] Alsberg, 'HaMa'avak Al Rashut Iriyat Yerushalayim Bitkufat HaMandat', 302–54.
[21] Roberts, 'Rethinking the Status Quo', 299–300.

those of a religious nature.²² In this context, the Palace Hotel project should be understood as one designed to enhance the image of the SMC as an organisation that promoted Arab Palestinians as a national entity. In his dual role as president of the SMC and chairman of the Waqf Directorate, Hajj Amin merged these two institutions, making the directorate subordinate to the SMC. This merger gave the SMC's projects religious legitimacy. According to Yizhak Reiter, the Jerusalem Waqf's approach to the urban assets and public institutions that were under its charge changed during the Mandate, and it began emphasising development, rather than maintenance, as had been the case earlier.²³ Waqf plots in Jerusalem were turned into profit-generating real estate, including those in the neighbourhood of Mamilla, where the Palace Hotel was built.²⁴ Thus, the administrative and functional relationship between the Waqf and the SMC assigned the Palace Hotel – a tourism-business venture – a dual significance, both secular and religious, and increased its cultural role in the Muslim community. This aspect was further underscored by hiring the Turkish Muslim architect Nigisberk, who, as I noted above, was working on the restoration of the Al-Aqsa Mosque.

Between Old and New: Restoration of the Al-Aqsa Mosque and the Building of the Palace Hotel

On 24 February 1924, the commission established to oversee the restoration of the Al-Aqsa Mosque submitted a report specifying the work to be done on one of Islam's most important holy sites.²⁵ The person listed second among the members of the commission was M. Nihad, probably referring to Mehmet Nihat Nigisberk, who had travelled from Turkey to Jerusalem with his boss, Ahmet Kemalettin Bey (1870–1927), to participate in the restoration.²⁶ Kemalettin was among Turkey's most well-known architects, as well as a pioneering architectural historian and teacher. In 1909 he was appointed chief architect of the Ottoman Ministry of Vakifs (Turkish for Waqfs),²⁷ and he continued in that capacity during the republican period until his untimely death in 1927.²⁸ An important aspect of Kemalettin's Ottoman-era work for the Ministry of Vakifs was the planning and execution of restoration projects of Islamic monuments all across the Ottoman Empire. All through World War I, his office continued working on these projects, which were designed to create an image of a strong wartime administration and gain support

---

²² Ibid. 299–300.
²³ Reiter, 'Waqf BiNsibot Mishtanot', 358.
²⁴ Ibid. 354–60.
²⁵ This report is appended to Yildirim Yavuz, 'The Restoration Project of the Masjid Al-Aqsa by Mimar Kemalettin (1922–26)', *Muqarnas* 13 (1996): 163–4.
²⁶ Cengizkan, 'Mehmet Nihat Nigisberk'in Katkilary', 177–208.
²⁷ Yavuz, 'The Restoration Project of the Masjid Al-Aqsa', 149.
²⁸ Paolo Girardelli, 'Re-Thinking Architect Kemalettin', *ABE Journal Architecture Beyond Europe* 2 (2012), https://journals.openedition.org/abe/575.

for the empire in regions still under Ottoman rule.[29] The Al-Aqsa Mosque, along with the entire Haram al-Sharif, was included in these restoration plans.[30] As suggested by Yildirim Yavuz, Kemalettin probably visited Jerusalem as early as in the early 1910s, as he published a detailed description of the Haram al-Sharif in 1912 in connection with the Ottoman restoration plans.[31]

Nigisberk worked under Kemalettin at the Ministry of Vakifs and was entrusted with important projects in Turkey and across the empire.[32] As I noted, when Kemalettin travelled to Jerusalem in 1914 to further the restoration plans for the Dome of the Rock and the Al-Aqsa Mosque, Nigisberk joined him.[33] However, in 1915 the latter was dispatched to Medina, Saudi Arabia, to plan a new Islamic University – a project that was probably carried out in the framework of the major Ottoman undertaking of restoring the holy mosque in Mecca.[34] A year later, Nigisberk was invited by Cemal Pasha, governor of Syria, to oversee the restoration of the Takiyya Madrasa complex in Damascus. He was appointed by the Ottoman Ministry of Vakifs as the chief architect of the Pious Foundations in the Syria-Arabia region, and restored two additional religious complexes in Damascus: the Selimiye Mosque and the Süleymaniye Madrasa and Imaret.[35]

Nigisberk returned to Istanbul in 1917 to recover from malaria, a mere six months before the Ottomans surrendered Damascus. There, he resumed work for the Ministry of Vakifs and held several key positions in its Architecture and Construction Department,[36] which remained in place even after the formal establishment of the Republic of Turkey in 1923.

Thus, Kemalettin and Nigisberk, in addition to visiting Jerusalem prior to embarking on the Al-Aqsa restoration project, gained valuable experience as conservation-restoration architects and as designers of new buildings in various locales in the Middle East. In 1922 Kemalettin was invited to Jerusalem by the SMC to commence restoration of the Al-Aqsa Mosque, and Nigisberk joined his team.[37] The two were in Jerusalem from 1922 to 1925, after which they returned to Ankara to plan buildings for the newly created republic, leaving behind a team headed by the architect Rushdi Bey Ahmad[38] to continue the work on Al-Aqsa.

[29] Hans Theunissen, 'War, Propaganda and Architecture: Cemal Pasha's Restoration of Islamic Architecture in Damascus during World War I', in *Jihad and Islam in World War I*, ed. Erik-Jan Zürcher (Leiden: Leiden University Press, 2016), 223–4.
[30] Ibid. 223–4
[31] Yavuz, 'The Restoration Project of the Masjid Al-Aqsa', 149.
[32] These projects are listed in full in Cengizkan, 'Mehmet Nihat Nigisberk'in Katkilary', 180.
[33] Ibid. 180.
[34] Theunissen, 'War, Propaganda and Architecture', 224; Cengizkan, 'Mehmet Nihat Nigisberk'in Katkilary', 182.
[35] Cengizkan, 'Mehmet Nihat Nigisberk'in Katkilary', 180.
[36] Theunissen, 'War, Propaganda and Architecture', 244; Cengizkan, 'Mehmet Nihat Nigisberk'in Katkilary', 180.
[37] Yavuz, 'The Restoration Project of the Masjid Al-Aqsa', 149; Cengizkan, 'Mehmet Nihat Nigisberk'in Katkilary', 180.
[38] Beatrice St. Laurent and András Riedlmayer, 'Restorations of Jerusalem and the Dome of the Rock and Their Political Significance, 1537–1928', *Muqarnas* 10 (1993): 83.

In 1927, following Kemalettin's untimely death, the SMC invited Nigisberk to continue work on the mosque, and the repairs were completed that year.[39] It is not known whether Ahmad continued to head the project, and it was probably at this time that Hajj Amin commissioned Nigisberk to design the Palace Hotel.

Continuing the appointment of Turkish Vakif architects for the restoration of the Al-Aqsa Mosque after the imposition of the Mandate is significant, as it manifested Muslim ownership of the buildings of the Haram al-Sharif. It was also likely a reaction to the British plans and restoration work, viewed by the Palestinians as an unwanted intrusion in matters regarding their religious and national icons.[40] As both Nigisberk and Kemalettin continued to work for the now-Republican Ministry of Vakifs,[41] the connection to Hajj Amin might have been formed through the countries' respective Waqfs/Vakifs, as well as the Husayni family's ties with the Ottoman administration and the Turkish one that succeeded it. Moreover, Hajj Amin's nephew, Muhammad Rushdi Imam Husayni, studied engineering in Istanbul under Kemalettin,[42] so the architect's connection to Palestine, and specifically to Hajj Amin, was unbroken.

The Palestinian reception of the newly established Turkish Republic may also have had a role in the choice of a Turkish architect for the Palace Hotel. As noted, Kemalettin and Nigisberk's involvement in SMC projects began in 1922, which was a time when Arab Palestinians professed strong pro-Turkish sentiments.[43] Although they soon experienced disillusionment in regard to their hopes that the Turks would aid them in resisting the British and the Zionists,[44] Hajj Amin and the SMC nonetheless valued this professional international Muslim collaboration.

As I discussed earlier, the restoration of the Al-Aqsa Mosque was initiated by Hajj Amin acting in all his offices – as Shaykh al Haramyn, as the mufti of Jerusalem, and as the head of the SMC. Moreover, he used the project to promote his own image vis-à-vis the Arab world, as well as to cultivate more power within Palestinian society.[45] He was intimately involved in the restoration project – a fact supported by Kemalettin's recounting that he reported directly to the 'President of

---

[39] Dating of the restoration's completion is based on Yavuz, 'The Restoration Project of the Masjid Al-Aqsa', 151.

[40] St. Laurent and Riedlmayer, 'Restorations of Jerusalem', 83; Roberts, 'Rethinking the Status Quo', 293; for the British restorations of the Dome of the Rock, see Ben-Asher Gitler, 'C. R. Ashbee's Jerusalem Years', 33–6; Hysler-Rubin, 'Arts & Crafts and the Great City', 356.

[41] Bilge Imamoglu, 'Architectural Production in State Offices: An Inquiry into the Professionalization of Architecture in Early Republican Turkey' (PhD diss., Delft University of Technology, 2010), 217–18; Girardelli, 'Re-Thinking Architect Kemalettin'.

[42] Yildirim Yavuz, 'Influence of Late Ottoman Architecture in Arab Provinces: The Case of the "Palace Hotel" in Jerusalem', *Proceedings of the 11th International Conference on Turkish Arts* (University of Utrecht, 1999), 3.

[43] Halabi, 'Liminal Loyalties', 19–37.

[44] In 1922 Hajj Amin's second cousin, Musa Kazim Al Husayni, participated in the Palestinian delegation to Istanbul, see ibid. 19–37.

[45] Roberts, 'Rethinking the Status Quo', 193; Kimmerling, 'The Formation of Palestinian Collective Identities', 68.

the Supreme Council of the Islamic State of Palestine',[46] and by the fact that Hajj Amin himself headed two of the delegations that the SMC sent to Arab countries to secure financial support for the restoration.[47] The delegations raised significant sums by appealing to Arab leaders and wealthy families, presenting the restoration project as essential to protecting the Haram al-Sharif from a Jewish takeover and British control.[48] The funds raised led to an additional link between the mosque and the Palace Hotel, as the excess budget from the restoration partially funded the Palace's 73,500 Palestinian-lira construction budget (roughly equivalent to $30,000 at the time).[49]

This reallocation of funds is significant, as it demonstrates that the Palace Hotel initiative was perceived by the Muslim community as having national and communal importance. It further exemplifies the convergence of the religious and secular spheres in the SMC's urban interventions, which also had its challenges. The controversy that developed with regard to the Palace Hotel site is a telling example of these demurrals. Across the street from the projected hotel site was the Muslim Mamilla Cemetery (pictured in the Introduction, Figure I.3), whose graves extended into the plot that the Waqf allocated for the hotel. For the SMC, the importance of participating in the rapid growth of this developing section of western Jerusalem overshadowed the significance of the burial site. It wanted to make its own mark in this area, where new hotels, consulates, the Jerusalem YMCA, the Zionist Executive Buildings, and more, were being erected. The SMC decided to relocate the graves, which provoked strong objections from the Muslim community. Three of Hajj Amin's political opponents prosecuted the SMC and him personally.[50] According to *Davar*, members of the Palestinian community appealed to religious courts in Egypt to prevent the graves' relocation, but to no avail.[51] The hotel's contractor, Baruch Katinka, about whom I talk further on, wrote that Hajj Amin asked him to covertly transfer the remains of any graves unearthed by his workers during construction to a special 'communal' burial site, as he was afraid that his enemy, Ragheb al Nashashibi, the mayor of Jerusalem, would halt construction should these exhumations be revealed.[52] The Palestinian newspaper *Al Jamaa Al Arabia* published the SMC's response to the criticism over its building in a cemetery in which it defended its actions by boasting of its nationwide revenue-generating developments for the benefit of the Muslim

---

[46] Yavuz, 'The Restoration Project of the Masjid Al-Aqsa', 160.
[47] Roberts, 'Rethinking the Status Quo', 293.
[48] Ibid. 293.
[49] Roberts, 'Rethinking the Status Quo', 300; Reiter, 'Waqf BiNsibot Mishtanot', 360. Reports of the hotel's construction costs vary. Nigisberk reports that it cost £69,659, and the contractors were paid £68,000. See Mehmet Nihat, 'Palas Otel, Kudüs', *Arkitekt* 3 (1931): 76, and Contract with 'Awad, 1928, file 20/44/,6/28/13, CHIR.
[50] Reiter, 'Waqf BiNsibot Mishtanot', 360.
[51] 'The Waqf is Building a Modern Hotel', *Davar*, 12 January 1928, 1.
[52] Katinka, *Me'Az Ve'Ad Hena*, 258.

community.⁵³ By the time the hotel opened, the criticism had subsided, and the Palestinian newspaper *Maraat Al Sharak* merely noted that the building was constructed 'upon antique remains belonging to the Eternal Muslim Council for Generations',⁵⁴ omitting the fact that it was referring to human remains. The debate surrounding the old graveyard underscores the fragile boundaries between the secular and religious domains, which the SMC attempted to balance in order to facilitate Muslim competition with the significant urban developments carried out by rival communities. It also demonstrates the immense power held by the SMC, and by Hajj Amin, who managed to successfully arbitrate the religious protests they encountered through the council's control of the Muslim religious administration.⁵⁵

The historical circumstances of the coming-into-being of the Palace Hotel thus reveal two important phenomena directly related to its architecture: first, its ties with Turkey and, second, the fact that religiosity both remained strong and significant among Muslim Palestinians during the British Mandate. This evidence contradicts suggestions made by historians such as Rashid Khalidi, who identified the period following World War I as a time when 'Ottomanism and religion were seriously diminished'.⁵⁶ The discourses and interactions involved in the construction of the hotel indicate that rather than being abandoned, Ottomanism was rearticulated by forming a relationship with the new Republic of Turkey, thus preserving sentiments, political connections and working relationships. The significance of the allocation of the Muslim Palestinian public's most important commissions to Turkish architects within this new 'Middle Eastern order' cannot be underestimated. The second phenomenon – religiosity – did not weaken, but was maintained through the mutuality and interdependence of the Muslim entities' religious and secular activities: two Muslim Palestinian projects – the restoration of the Al-Aqsa Mosque and the building the Palace Hotel – demonstrate that religion was harnessed alongside secular modernising approaches to create a national identity.

Plan and Design as Emblems of Nationality

The design of the Palace Hotel represents the importation of Turkish concepts in creating a national architecture. In the analysis that follows, I explore the way that these concepts were implemented by using Jerusalem's ancient religious Muslim monuments as sources of inspiration for the hotel and by establishing them as spatial and visual signifiers of emerging Palestinian nationalism.

Tourism in Palestine increased significantly during the British Mandate up

---

⁵³ Reiter, 'Waqf BiNsibot Mishtanot', 360–1.
⁵⁴ 'Palace Hotel', *Maraat Al Sharak*, 25 December 1929, 4.
⁵⁵ Reiter, 'Waqf BiNsibot Mishtanot', 360–1.
⁵⁶ Khalidi, *Palestinian Identity*, 158.

until the outbreak of World War II.⁵⁷ Tourists were no longer mostly pilgrims, as was the case during the nineteenth century, and most of them came from different social strata. In Jerusalem this led to an increase in the number of hotels, as well as to their diversity.⁵⁸ In the context of these changes, the Palace Hotel was intended for wealthy Muslim tourists and pilgrims.⁵⁹ Its area was 2200 square metres. It had 123 rooms, which could accommodate 200 travellers, hot and cold running water, electric lighting, elevators, central heating, restaurants and several meeting rooms.⁶⁰ Apart from these modern amenities, its design spoke of elegance and opulence, geared toward a wealthy clientele.

The plot on which the Palace Hotel was built was originally intended for a four-storey apartment building for which Kemalettin had made preliminary plans while he was working on the Al-Aqsa restoration project in 1925, which were sketched by Nigisberk.⁶¹ In his description of the Palace Hotel, published in the Turkish journal *Arkitekt* in 1931, Nigisberk wrote that foundations for the apartment building were laid and four or five shops were built, but construction was then halted.⁶² He gave no reason for the postponement of the project until sometime in the spring or summer of 1927, which might have been due to Jerusalem's mayoral campaign, which began in 1926 and lasted until the elections in April 1927. These elections were a crucial factor in the rivalry between the Nashashibis and the Husaynis and the campaign required significant efforts on the part of Hajj Amin.⁶³ It is also possible that the delay was caused by the major earthquake that shook Jerusalem in July 1927. It is also unclear when or why Hajj Amin decided to repurpose the intended structure from a residence to a hotel. When considering all the factors – increased tourism, intercommunal competition over urban space, and intracommunal political tensions – it is reasonable to assume that catering to international Arab tourists, rather than to locals (by erecting an additional apartment building), was intended to augment Hajj Amin's political power.

The hotel's preeminence was apparent from its prime location on the corner of Mamilla Road (present-day Agron Street) and Julian's Way (present-day King David Street). It was located only 400 metres from the site of the King David Hotel, which was being planned at the time,⁶⁴ and the Jerusalem YMCA, then under construction. It was nearer to the Old City than the latter two buildings,

---

57 Noam Shoval and Kobi Cohen-Hattab, 'Urban Hotel Development Patterns in the Face of Political Shifts', *Annals of Tourism Research* 28, no. 4 (2001): 915–16.
58 Doron Bar and Kobi Cohen-Hattab, 'A New Kind of Pilgrimage: The Modern Tourist Pilgrim of Nineteenth Century and Early Twentieth Century Palestine', *Middle Eastern Studies* 39, no. 2 (2003): 131–48.
59 Shoval and Cohen-Hattab, 'Urban Hotel Development Patterns', 915–16.
60 Nihat, 'Palas Otel, Kudüs', 76. Similar specifications are mentioned in an ad from the *Palestine Weekly*, 1 August 1930, cited in David Kroyanker, *Malon Palace: Hachzarat Atara Le'Yoshna* (Jerusalem: Jerusalem Municipality, 1981), 78.
61 Yavuz, 'Influence of Late Ottoman Architecture in Arab Provinces', 3.
62 Nihat, 'Palas Otel, Kudüs', 75.
63 Alsberg, 'HaMa'avak Al Rashut Iriyat Yerushalayim BiTkufat HaMandat', 302–54.
64 Kroyanker, *Adrichalut Bi'Yerushalayim: HaBny'ia BiTkufat HaMandat HaBriti*, 224–7, 238–42.

and hence closer to the commercial centre. The perimeter of the lot was delineated by Mamilla Road to the north, which separated the building from the Muslim cemetery, and Julian's Way marked the eastern boundary. A triangular plot was thus formed between these two main thoroughfares and an additional secondary road (present-day Ben-Shimon Street).

The hotel's ground plan was dictated by this obtuse triangle but was cut off by a diagonal wall at its southwestern corner. To the northeast, the building was designed as a circular segment and the ground plan was adapted to the junction of the main streets. Thus, the building was shaped as a quadrilateral with one circular corner. Its western façade was originally open at the centre toward the secondary street, providing access for deliveries in the back.

The hotel was originally planned for five storeys but, owing to budget limitations, there were actually only four,[65] which surrounded a courtyard where there was a single-storey restaurant (Figures 4.2 and 4.3). In accordance with up-to-date urban hotel design, more than twenty shops, facing the street, were included as rentable retail space on the perimeter of the ground floor. These were mostly separated from the hotel's interior spaces, effecting a modern business model, which generated revenue apart from the returns from tourism.

The main entrance to the hotel was in the circular segment facing the junction of Mamilla Road and Julian's Way (Figure 4.1). A wide hallway led from the entrance to an octagonally shaped main lobby with a central staircase (Figures 4.4 and 4.5). This octagonal space spanned all four storeys, ending in an octagonal skylight (Figure 4.6). Two main hallways extended from this front lobby, connecting it with the parlour and other public areas. The kitchen and other service rooms were located along the partially open western façade. Beyond the front lobby was a reception hall, which led to the spacious restaurant (Figure 4.7; see also Figure 4.17) and the courtyard. The roofs were flat, although aerial photos indicate that the restaurant's roof was slightly pitched. The hotel's upper storeys featured halls extending from the main staircases (Figure 4.3), with rooms arranged on both sides. Larger rooms faced the street and some featured balconies. Those above the curved main entrance were planned as six trapezoid spaces, forming a gently angled circumference.

The façade in its entirety revealed the building's internal plan, which was a series of adjacent rooms. Designed in the tradition of grand hotels, it had a taller first floor (derived from Neo-Renaissance designs) and three floors of equal height above it.[66] Identical rows of alternating windows and balconies, separated by pilasters, stretched across each of the three upper storeys (Figure 4.8). The exterior circular shape of the main entrance reflected the internal division into six angled walls, there were three balconies supported by corbels above the entrance, and a low, open parapet extended over the entire roof.

[65] Nihat, 'Palas Otel, Kudüs', 80.
[66] Pevsner, *A History of Building Types*, 184–5.

CONSTRUCTING PALESTINIAN IDENTITY

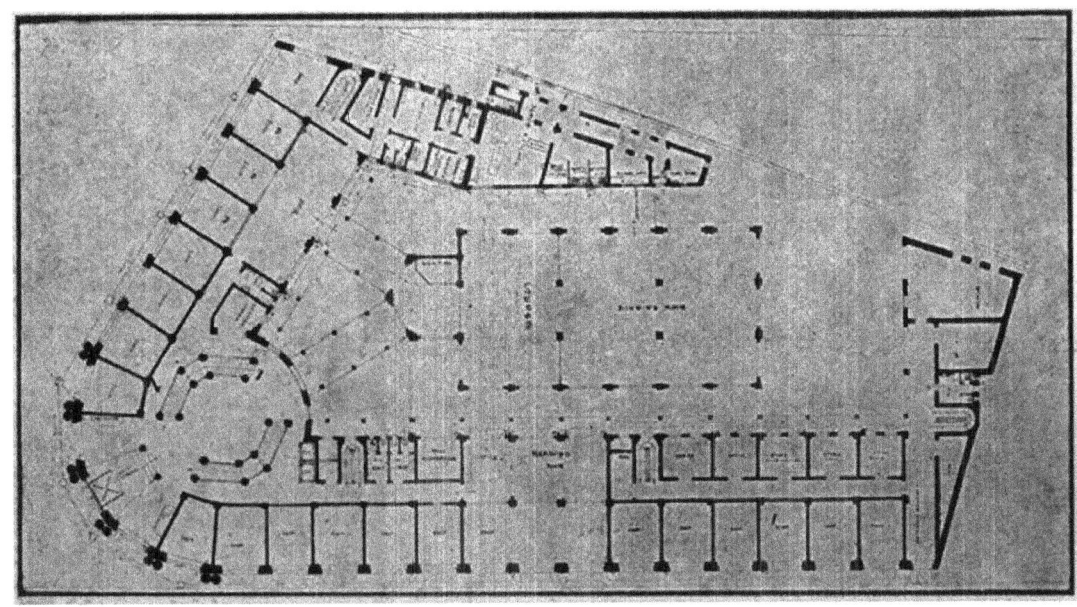

Figure 4.2 *Mehmet Nihat Nigisberk, Palace Hotel, ground plan of first floor, 1928–9. Mehmet Nihat, 'Palas Otel, Kudüs', Arkitekt 3 (1931): 76.*

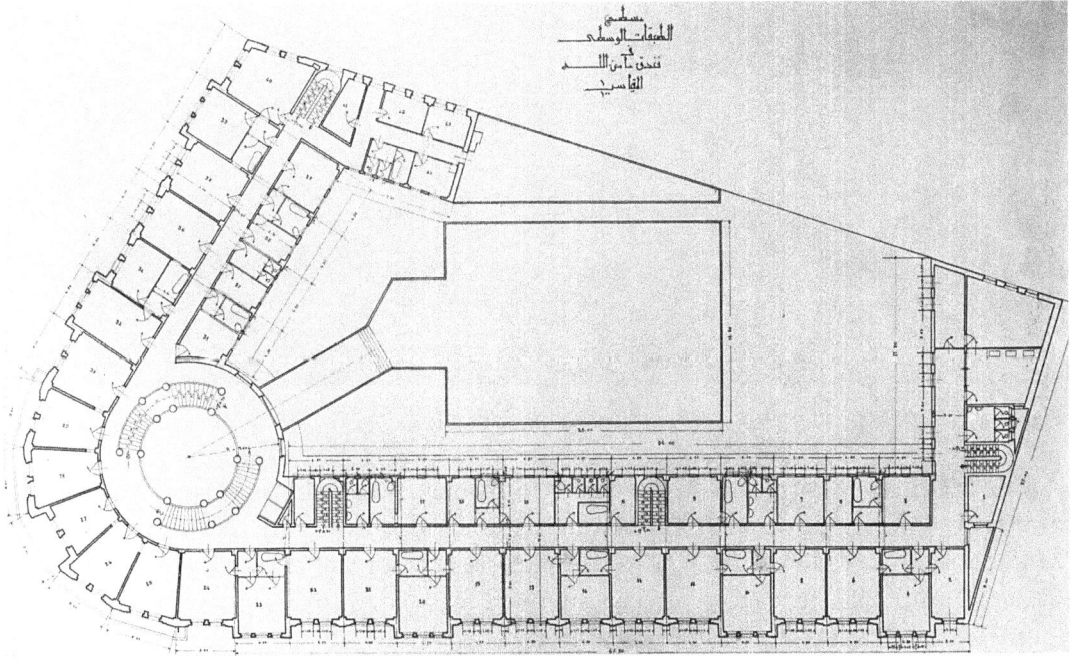

Figure 4.3 *Mehmet Nihat Nigisberk, Palace Hotel, typical floor plan, storeys 2–4, 1928–9. © NKU.*

Figure 4.4 *Mehmet Nihat Nigisberk, Palace Hotel, lobby, 1928–9. © CZA, NZO\634449.*

The building's plan and design reflected European (and American) late nineteenth- and early twentieth-century hotels, and the exportation and adaptation of these models to the Middle East.[67] The impact of turn-of-the-century models on the Palace Hotel was further reflected in the basic Beaux-Arts organisation of the elements of the façade, which featured rows of shops, upper-storey balconies and windows, and dictated the building's proximity to the street. Grand city hotels

---

[67] For a discussion and examples of these phenomena, see Kroyanker, *Adrichalut Bi'Yerushalayim: HaBny'ia BiTkufat HaMandat HaBriti*, 224–7, 238–42; Daniella Ohad Smith, 'Hotel Design in British Mandate Palestine: Modernism and the Zionist Vision', *Journal of Israel History* 29, no. 1 (2010): 101–2.

Figure 4.5 *Mehmet Nihat Nigisberk, Palace Hotel, lobby following conservation. Photographed by Diego Rosman.*

Figure 4.6 *Palace Hotel, skylight following conservation. Photographed by Diego Rosman.*

Figure 4.7 *Mehmet Nihat Nigisberk, Palace Hotel, restaurant, 1928–9. Mehmet Nihat, 'Palas Otel, Kudüs',* Arkitekt *3 (1931): 89.*

Figure 4.8 *Palace Hotel, north façade. Photographed by Diego Rosman.*

of this period usually referenced historic styles such as Neo-Renaissance, Neo-Baroque, or eclectic combinations of both. In the Palace Hotel, this historicism centred on a different set of architectural-historical references based on the principles of the Turkish First National Style, which used architecture to represent national ideologies, and on Jerusalem's ancient religious Muslim monuments.

Yavuz contends that the decorative and formal scheme of the Palace Hotel's exterior was clearly associated with early twentieth-century Turkish revivalism, which emerged in the wake of the Young Turk Revolt of 1908 and continued into the early years of the republic.[68] Also known as the 'First National Style' or the 'National Architecture Renaissance', it was characterised by integrating traditional Ottoman architectural elements into new building types that were constructed using modern technologies, such as reinforced concrete, steel and prefabricated components. The revivalist Ottoman architectural elements included hemispherical domes, wide roof overhangs, and pointed and semicircular arches, as well as mouldings or carvings inspired by Ottoman geometric and foliated patterns.[69] The style was widely implemented in public buildings that adopted Beaux-Arts plans. These structures, which included banks, office buildings, hotels, and more, also reflected Beaux-Arts principles in their façades. According to Sibel Bozdoğan, Turkish revivalism presented 'the first "modern" discourse in Turkish architectural culture, [being] the first systematic engagement of Turkish architects with new building types, construction techniques, and design principles'.[70] Bozdoğan emphasises that in the modern sense, this was also the first attempt to define a national style grounded in the country's history and carried out in the service of modern ideologies of nation building.[71]

Nigisberk, whose education and practice developed during the rise of the First National Style, had already implemented it in his public buildings, such as the First Vakif Han — an Ottoman Ministry of Vakifs office building — built around 1909–14 in Istanbul (Figure 4.9). His implementation of this style in the Palace Hotel raises several questions: How were the principles of Turkish revivalism reiterated in its design? How were they integrated with local sources of inspiration? Finally, how did Nigisberk, presumably with the involvement of his patron, Hajj Amin, combine these into an expression of national Palestinian identity in a secular commercial hotel?

As he was a student and subordinate of Kemalettin, Nigisberk's design can be understood within the formulation set by his senior for a Turkish revival in modern architecture – an approach shared by other leading contemporary Turkish

---

[68] Yavuz, 'Influence of Late Ottoman Architecture in Arab Provinces', 1–3; Sibel Bozdoğan, 'Reading Ottoman Architecture through Modernist Lenses: Nationalist Historiography and the "New Architecture" in the Early Republic', *Muqarnas* 24 (2007): 213; Imamoglu, 'Architectural Production in State Offices', 38.

[69] Sibel Bozdoğan, *Modernism and Nation Building: Turkish Architectural Culture in the Early Republic* (Seattle and London: University of Washington Press, 2001), 16–18.

[70] Ibid. 20.

[71] Ibid. 20.

Figure 4.9 *Mehmet Nihat Nigisberk, First Vakif Han, Istanbul, 1909–14.* © NKU.

architects.[72] Kemalettin defined his approach, to which he remained steadfast throughout his career, in 1908:

> We need to design our buildings suitable for modern everyday life and construct them with modern materials, but in harmony with our national character and in line with the principles and rules of Turkish architectural style in construction and decoration.[73]

The choice of 'principles and rules' from Turkish architecture afforded architects a broad range of elements from different eras and sites representing Ottoman architecture. The integration of these with modern plans and typologies continued to be a feature of Kemalist architecture. To a certain extent, this was a reappropriation of Orientalist notions, which implied, among other things, multiple combinations of sources and profound changes in their functional designations and in their meanings. However, as noted by Bozdoğan, Vakif architects, who had a broad knowledge of the histories of architecture of the Middle East, intentionally distinguished Turkish architecture from its Arab, Persian and Western counter-

---

[72] Bozdoğan, 'Reading Ottoman Architecture through Modernist Lenses', 199–222.
[73] Inci Basa, 'From Praise to Condemnation: Ottoman Revivalism and the Production of Space in Early Republican Ankara', *Journal of Urban History* 41, no. 4 (2015): 715.

parts.⁷⁴ Toward this end, they sanctioned both religious and secular architectural traditions for creating national identity in the face of the Western stylistic dominance that Anatolia experienced at the turn of the twentieth century.⁷⁵ Hence, Orientalist notions were revealed in the use of diverse sources, so long as they were interpreted as allowing for the creation of a Turkish national architecture. These practices reveal the challenges faced by architects in defining a national style at a time of dramatic political transformations, as well as the complex interpretations of East versus West, which were also evident in other arenas.⁷⁶

There were similar design challenges in planning the Palace Hotel. Nigisberk indeed used modern construction technologies harmonised – to use Kemalettin's expression – with historicist design elements. Modern construction technologies included reinforced concrete beams, modern metal railings and fenestration, as well as custom prefabricated building blocks.⁷⁷

In the case of the Palace Hotel, it is difficult and even misleading to attempt to distinguish Turkish design elements from the broader Middle Eastern vocabulary employed by the architect. Nigisberk used several of the region's typical arches integrated with more modern Art Deco arches and simple square windows. There were wide pointed arches as well as narrow, slightly ogee pointed ones– some of which indeed represented elements of the Turkish First National Style, yet were also common in the Mamluk and Ottoman architecture of Jerusalem and Palestine.⁷⁸ Thus, Kemalettin's call for the use of a 'Turkish style' to represent 'national character', was interpreted by Nigisberk and rearticulated to express the Muslim architectural traditions of Jerusalem and, in a broader sense, of the region. As far as materials were concerned, the details of the design and the hotel's stone facing reflected the integration of traditional building techniques.

This discursive process created between Turkey, the former imperial centre, and Jerusalem, the periphery, becomes even more apparent when we look at the Palace Hotel in relation to contemporary buildings in Istanbul, the historic capital of the Ottoman Empire, and Ankara, the capital of the new republic. Nigisberk's First Vakif Han can serve as an example (Figure 4.9). In a commercial sense, the building was similar to the Jerusalem hotel, being a Vakif revenue-producing office building. In plan and design the Palace Hotel had a similar arrangement of linear storeys and a taller ground floor. As in the Vakif Han, the Palace Hotel had narrow- and wide-pointed arched windows, as well as square ones. Window treatment was similar to that used by Nigisberk in Istanbul, as it displayed protruding extradoses and framed spandrels on the upper floors. The differences in the façades and the

---

74 Bozdoğan, 'Reading Ottoman Architecture through Modernist Lenses', 202–8.
75 Basa, 'From Praise to Condemnation', 714–15.
76 For a discussion of discourses on Orientalism in the early Turkish Republic, see Emmanuel Szurek, '"Go West": Variations on Kemalist Orientalism', in *After Orientalism: Critical Perspectives on Western Agency and Eastern Re-appropriations*, eds François Pouillon and Jean-Claude Vatin (Leiden and Boston: Brill, 2015), 103–20.
77 Katinka, *Me'Az Ve'Ad Hena*, 259; Nihat, 'Palas Otel, Kudüs', 76.
78 For examples, see Rosen-Ayalon, 'Omanut HaBniya VeHa'yitur BiYerushalyim', 287–315.

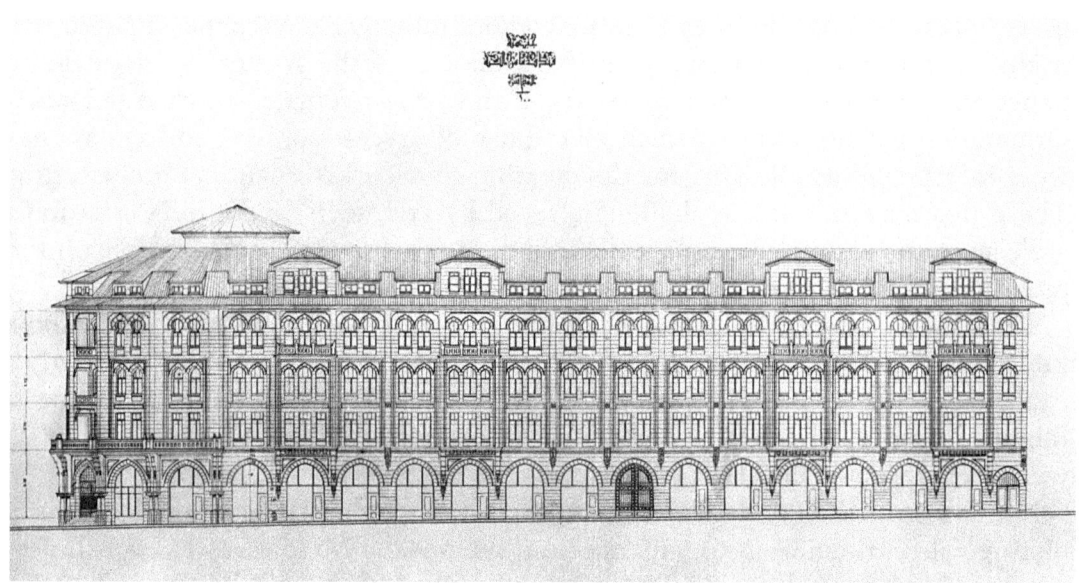

Figure 4.10 *Mehmet Nihat Nigisberk, Palace Hotel, north elevation, 1928–9. © NKU.*

roof structure are also significant, as they reveal that for the Jerusalem building, Nigisberk discarded the long protruding balcony and the pitched roof overhang that crowned the First Vakif Han. An early elevation drawing of the Palace Hotel (Figure 4.10) indicates that Nigisberk originally envisioned a series of pitched roofs above slightly protruding balconies, a wide pitched roof above the entrance, and a narrow rake across the entire building. These elements were typical of Turkish timber-frame houses, a typology that was an important source of inspiration for the Turkish revival style, as it added a local, secular dimension to a form inspired primarily by religious architecture.[79] Aware of the very Turkish character of these elements, Nigisberk probably considered them too foreign for Jerusalem and thus ruled them out; the building as executed had no pitched roofs or rakes.

The design of the Palace Hotel can also be compared to the Ankara Palas Hotel (1924–7), which was planned by Kemalettin and the architect Vedat Bey, who collaborated on several projects in Ankara and were considered the two leading architects of the revival style (Figure 4.11). The Ankara Palas hotel was an important project in the development of the new Turkish capital and was an excellent example of Turkish revivalism as implemented in a modern luxury urban hotel.[80] It was similar to the Jerusalem Palace Hotel in some of its design principles and details, such as the taller arcaded ground floor, the balconies with stone carved balustrades, and a wide main entrance. However, the Ankara Palas Hotel also possessed elements not exported to Palestine: a central dome and a pitched roof, as well as two pitched-roof towers, again derived from Ottoman domestic archi-

---

[79] Bozdoğan, 'Reading Ottoman Architecture through Modernist Lenses', 212–13.
[80] Basa, 'From Praise to Condemnation', 718.

Figure 4.11 *Ahmet Kemalettin Bey and Vedat Bey, Ankara Palas Hotel, Ankara, 1924–7.*
© Postcard and Engraving Collection, Suna Kıraç Library/Koç University.

tecture. When considered together, the elements imported from contemporary Turkish projects, with which Nigisberk was surely familiar, reflect a sophisticated approach to transposing architecture from one Middle Eastern country to another. It evidences, first, a continued reliance on the architecture of the recent imperial centre: four centuries of Ottoman rule in Palestine had left their mark, and the use of Ottoman models in this *sanjak*'s (Ottoman province's) architecture was prevalent. Palestine boasted numerous Ottoman architectural imports, among them the distinct form of the Ottoman mosque, discussed earlier in relation to the Jerusalem YMCA's precedents. Nigisberk's reliance on traditional Ottoman forms would thus have been acceptable and could have been interpreted as a continuation of centuries of architectural culture. Second, the recent Turkish engagement with these traditional forms to create a national style was rearticulated by Nigisberk so as to reflect the variant requirements of his Jerusalem patrons. In Jerusalem, Nigisberk made use of select local architectural elements that expressed Muslim Palestinian identity, just as in Turkey Ottoman monuments were harnessed for the revival style. In all likelihood, he drew Jerusalem's local elements from the Dome of the Rock and the Al-Aqsa Mosque. Politically, using these monuments as a source of inspiration manifested Muslim ownership of the Haram and reflected the Al Husayni family's custodianship. From an architectural perspective, Nigisberk's first-hand knowledge of Jerusalem's Islamic monuments

Figure 4.12a *Palace Hotel, detail of main entry capitals. Photographed by Diego Rosman.*

Figure 4.12b *Palace Hotel, north façade balcony. Photographed by Diego Rosman.*

Figure 4.13a *Palace Hotel, pilaster detail. Photographed by Diego Rosman.*

Figure 4.13b *Al Aqsa Mosque, detail of carved wooden beam (on display at the Rockefeller Museum, Jerusalem). Photographed by Diego Rosman.*

Figure 4.14a *Palace Hotel, octagonal rosette on pilaster. Photographed by Diego Rosman.*

Figure 4.14b *Al Aqsa Mosque, Salah al-Din Minbar, detail of wood carving on the right panel, Jerusalem, 1168–74. © Victoria and Albert Museum, London.*

paved the way for appropriating them in order to create a Palestinian identity when designing the Palace Hotel.

How were elements from the Dome of the Rock and the Al-Aqsa Mosque used in the design of the Palace Hotel? For example, whereas the Palace's arabesques bear a similarity to Turkish models in their locations and proportions, one can also identify important differences: they are circular interlacing palmettes and half palmettes, which are different from the Turkish feathery-leaf *saz* and lotus motifs in contemporary buildings in Ankara and Istanbul. The details of the motifs employed in the Palace Hotel (Figures 4.12A and B, 4.13A and 4.14A) have an affinity not to the former, but to the woodwork of the Al-Aqsa Mosque (Figure 4.13B). The famed Salah al-Din Minbar in the Al-Aqsa Mosque (Figure 4.14B), an Ayyubid masterpiece that symbolises the celebrated conqueror's 1187 victory over the Crusaders and his conquest of Jerusalem also comes to mind as a possible source of inspiration for the carved foliated palmettes and rosettes in the Palace Hotel (Figures 4.13A and 4.14A). These are similar to the polygons on the minbar and the details within them (Figure 4.14B).[81] It is possible that in choosing the

---

[81] For a detailed discussion of the minbar, see Walid H. Abweini *et al.*, 'Reconstructing Salah Al-Din Minbar of Al-Aqsa Mosque: Challenges and Results', *International Journal of Conservation Science* 4, no. 3 (2013): 307–16.

minbar or similar local sources of inspiration as models, the designer and patron might have been trying to ensure that the new building would reflect the significance of Muslim hegemony in Jerusalem. This adaptation of decorative elements from the Haram was selective, yet their resemblance to the carved elements in the Palace Hotel was significant and could not have been coincidental.

Another aspect of the design of the Palace Hotel that reflects Jerusalem's Muslim architectural heritage was the octagonal shape of the main lobby, which was created by the arrangement of the pillars and the shape of the staircase and ceiling, as seen in the plan (Figure 4.2) and in the photographs in Figures 4.4–4.6. I suggest that, similar to Turkish architects' insistence on using Ottoman and Turkish models, here Nigisberk searched for a clear historic Palestinian precedent. In such a paradigm, the use of the octagon would have been intended to evoke the structure of the Dome of the Rock. This famous monument could be drawn upon for creating a Palestinian identity in architecture, and referencing it would have been complemented by the arabesque carvings. However, rather than relating religious concepts, the octagon and the arabesques were intended to 'nationalise' the local religious heritage. This approach adopted the principles of the Turkish First National Style, wherein religious architectural forms and ornaments were secularised.[82] Nigisberk justified his implementation of this style in his 1931 article on the Palace Hotel. Replying to anticipated criticism, at a time when the adequacy of the revival style was being reassessed, he wrote:

> When my friends see these photos [of the Palace Hotel], they will righteously state that the time of stone ornamentation on the façades has ended. I had to do this due to the fact that Jerusalem is the city that envelopes within it the history of all civilizations and attracts tourists from all over the world with its possessions. I did not want to show much novelty in the architectural style of the building. My utmost aim was to determine our national architecture in this city of traditions by being faithful to the principles of our classical art.[83]

In these sentences Nigisberk clearly revealed that the purpose of the building's architecture was to represent a national identity. Whereas he seemed to have appropriated Jerusalem's monuments as part of the Ottoman heritage, his aim was to provide his Palestinian patron with a novel formulation of a Muslim Palestinian identity. Perhaps the most important declaration establishing this connection between Jerusalem's Muslim monuments and the Palace Hotel is the building's dedication (Figure 4.15), which was inscribed on a flat arched stone integrated into the parapet above the entrance. The carved inscription in *Thuluth* script reads: 'We are building like our forefathers have built, and we are doing like they have done.' Yair Wallach claims that this is a quote from the Umayyad poet al-Mutawakki al

---

[82] Bozdoğan, 'Reading Ottoman Architecture through Modernist Lenses', 210–12.
[83] Nihat, 'Palas Otel, Kudüs', 80.

Figure 4.15 *Palace Hotel, dedication plaque. Photographed by Diego Rosman.*

Laythī.[84] Another inscription, which runs across the lower part of the dedication arch, reads: 'This was built by the Supreme Arab Council in Falastin 1348/1929', 1348 being the Hijra year.[85] The latter dedication underscores the continuation of Muslim building in Jerusalem from the time of the 'forefathers' – the builders of the Haram al-Sharif and other important Muslim monuments in the city – to contemporary SMC projects. The dedication, taken from poetry associated with the first Muslim dynasty in Jerusalem, presented the modern hotel as part of a continuous Muslim history of the city, a history that transcended the different Muslim rulers of Jerusalem. It thus created Muslim Palestinian awareness of a shared past – an awareness that is one of the basic tenets of Palestinian national identity.[86] In the Palace Hotel this was mediated through architecture – as was the case in Turkish revivalism and locally in early Zionist architecture.[87] Nigisberk

---

[84] Yair Wallach, 'Readings in Conflict: Public Text in Modern Jerusalem, 1858–1948' (PhD diss., University of London, 2008), 202.

[85] Transliteration: (right side, from bottom to top) *nabnī kamā kānat awā'ilunā*; (left side, from bottom to top) *tabnī wa-nafʿalu miṯla-mā faʿalū sanat 1348 banā hāḏā al-nuzul al-maǧlis al-islāmī al-aʿlā bi-filasṭīn. sanat 1929*.

[86] Kimmerling, 'The Formation of Palestinian Collective Identities', 48–81.

[87] Bozdoğan, 'Reading Ottoman Architecture through Modernist Lenses', 199–222; Dolev, 'Architectural Orientalism in the Hebrew University', 217–34; Alona Nitzan-Shiftan, 'Contested Zionism – Alternative Modernism: Erich Mendelsohn and the Tel Aviv Chug in Mandate Palestine', *Architectural History* 39 (1996): 147–80.

thus imported the principles of late Ottoman and early republican approaches to Turkey's architectural heritage, adapting them as emblems from Jerusalem's Muslim architectural history to manifest local Muslim Palestinian identity.

The Hotel's Interior Design: Modern Amenities and Eclecticism

The hotel's interior design reflected the modern amenities it provided. Unlike its largely historicist exterior and conservative façade, its lavish interiors were an eclectic mix of Art Deco elements and historicism.

According to Yavuz, the interior design was done in collaboration with the Muslim Palestinian artist Jamal Badran (grandfather of renown Jordanian architect Rasem Badran).[88] The interiors can be partially reconstructed from the recent restoration and from contemporary photographs. The ground plan directed the guests' movement on a diagonal axis stretching from the street entrance through the soaring octagonal front lobby and on to the spacious reception hall, the restaurant and the courtyard. The entire lobby area was supported by round columns with trompe-l'oeil marble patterns (Figure 4.4; the patterns have not survived). Their flat capitals were incised with an arabesque-inspired strip of interlacing octagons and a lotus border beneath them; the ceilings were white and light fittings were set in the centre of diamond-shaped stucco decorations, echoing the palmette arabesques of the exterior carvings (Figure 4.16). Contemporary photographs show hemispherical and flower-shaped lamps. According to David Kroyanker, the galleries above the lobby had octagonal, Deco-style lamps.[89] The lobby floors were marble with a black pattern outlining major areas, and it featured Oriental carpets. Black metal banisters flanked the two imposing staircases. Their railings had a meander pattern and a rectangular grid, with a central rectangle framing an arabesque design. The lobby walls were painted with a dado, and a thin black line created a faux frieze below the ceiling. The black bordering of the floor and the walls together with the black grids and geometry of the banisters gave the lobby area a modern air with hints of Art Deco inspiration.

The ground floor's auxiliary spaces were no less luxurious. The restaurant had a parquet floor (Figure 4.7), and round, stucco-fluted columns with stalactite capitals, similar to those of the hotel's entrance exterior, supported its painted concrete ceiling beams. The space was well lit by large square windows, each topped by two, smaller, pointed-arch windows. Rods were placed under the upper windows, so that the lower ones were draped with sheer tie-back curtains. Carpets and Victorian-style upholstered chairs, a patterned stucco frieze, chandeliers and smaller light fittings – all of which descended from diamond-shaped stucco patterns similar to those in the lobby – completed the formal and extravagant appearance of this space. Photographs indicate that the restaurant's antique, Victorian-style

---

[88] Yavuz, 'Influence of Late Ottoman Architecture in Arab Provinces', 5.
[89] Kroyanker, *Malon Palace*, 10.

Figure 4.16 *Palace Hotel, detail of ceiling stucco decoration. Photographed by Diego Rosman.*

space was echoed in the design of the guestrooms.⁹⁰ The parlour was more modern in design, yet afforded a luxurious atmosphere through the use of wood panelling for dados, thinly framed wall sections, and leather armchairs; a wide painted frieze ran across the top of its interior wall, similar in design to the main staircase railings.⁹¹

The difference between the hotel's classical Beaux-Arts–Middle Eastern exterior and the more modern Art Deco lobby and parlour is significant. It indicates that both architect and patron sought to connect the building not only to the traditional urban 'grand hotel' typology, but also to modernity. This approach has been observed in other major hotels worldwide that were constructed during the 1920s and 1930s. Annabel Wharton, who wrote about the integration of Art Deco elements with traditional ones at the famous Waldorf Astoria Hotel in New York City, describes this phenomenon as the building's 'ambivalent location between the profitable efficiencies of modernity and its pretense to traditional luxury'.⁹² Whereas Nigisberk could not have been inspired by the New York hotel, as it was

---

⁹⁰ See Koç University Digital Collections: https://cdm21054.contentdm.oclc.org/digital/collection/p21054coll3/id/9282/rec/14, retrieved 21 December 2019.
⁹¹ Kroyanker, *Malon Palace*, 74 (photograph).
⁹² Annabel Wharton, 'Two Waldorf-Astorias: Spatial Economies as Totem and Fetish', *The Art Bulletin* 85, no. 3 (2003): 536.

only opened in 1931 – two years after the Palace Hotel – such similarities demonstrate the shared fashions and design approaches in planning interwar modern luxury hotels that were to cater to an international clientele.

Intercommunal Construction during a Time of Strife: 1928–9

As I noted in Chapter Three, the firm of ʿAwaḍ, Dunie & Katinka was established with a view toward building the Palace Hotel. At the beginning of 1927, a Christian-Palestinian contractor, Stello Elyās ʿAwaḍ, approached Baruch Katinka and suggested that they form a partnership in order to compete for the tender for the future hotel. After consulting with his partner, Tuvia Dunie, Katinka agreed. It was clear to all three contractors that Jews alone, without an Arab Palestinian, would not be awarded the contract for this Waqf-SMC funded project.[93] We have only a partial explanation of Muslim considerations in granting the contract to an intercommunal construction company. The first tender was issued in 1927, at which point the SMC hired two Muslim contractors – Muḥyī-ddīn Abus-S'uod and ʿAlī Ḥasan el-Maṣrī,[94] but on 8 October 1928, it sent a letter expressing dissatisfaction with the work.[95] This move was noted in a report in *Davar*, according to which initial construction of the Palace Hotel suffered from a lack of professionalism, which caused excess expenditures and forced the Waqf to publish the second tender to ensure proper management and execution of the project.[96] Although this report, published in a Zionist newspaper, appears to be biased in its emphasis of Arab mismanagement, such a failed beginning may indeed have caused Hajj Amin and the Waqf to make a selection based on professionalism and experience, rather than upon communal affinity. Moreover, Hajj Amin harboured a carefully concealed admiration for successful Zionist ventures in Palestine,[97] and this, too, may have had a role in his decision.

Katinka's memoirs, whose Hebrew title translates to *From Then until Here*, provide a telling description of the complex intercommunal cooperation that was in force during the hotel's construction. Katinka was the acting on-site contractor. He had been an engineer for the Ottoman railways during World War I and was thus probably the best choice for working with a Turkish architect on such a large-scale project. Katinka earned Hajj Amin's trust through diligent work, by meeting the very tight deadline for the hotel's completion, and by cooperating with him in concealing sensitive issues from Mayor Ragheb al Nashashibi, such as the graves found on site. He also successfully circumvented various attempts

---

[93] Katinka, *Me'Az Ve'Ad Hena*, 257. Zionist newspapers reported the contract with ʿAwaḍ, Dunie & Katinka in October 1928. See 'Binyan Malon ha-Waqf LeKablan Yehudi', *Davar*, 30 October 1928; 'Be'it HaMalon HaGadol Bi'Yerushalayim', *Doar Hayom*, 18 October 1928, 4.
[94] Letter from SMC, 20/39,6/28/13, 18 October 1928, *CHIR*.
[95] Ibid.
[96] 'Binyan Malon Ha Waqf LeKablan Yehudi', *Davar*, 30 October 1928, 4.
[97] Khalidi, *Palestinian Identity*, 167–8.

by Nashashibi to delay construction.[98] The mutual respect between Hajj Amin and the contractors is also evident from their ability to separate the building process from Palestinian politics. Not that politics were absent, and they clearly impacted construction: Katinka wrote that he and Dunie had many conversations with Hajj Amin about the Jewish–Arab conflict. Dunie was the brother-in-law of Chaim Weizmann, then president of the World Zionist Organization, with whom he was very close, and Hajj Amin was well aware of the relationship. According to Katinka, however, Dunie usually avoided being in the middle of such conversations with Hajj Amin, telling him that he and Weizmann have the following agreement: 'he [Weizmann] doesn't do construction and I don't do politics'.[99]

Only 'Awaḍ signed the contract for the construction of the hotel, probably in anticipation of protests against Jews managing the project.[100] It included a clause whereby the contractors were obligated to give preference to hiring Arab workers, and that should there be a day of rest, it would be Friday – the Muslim day of rest. Construction began in the winter of 1928, and the hotel was opened to the public on 5 December 1929.[101] The construction was thus remarkably fast, indicative of the sense of urgency in the face of Jewish, British and American projects. Katinka wrote that some 400 workers were hired, including 300 Arab stone carvers and builders and about 100 Jewish 'experts', specialising in concrete, iron and wood construction.[102]

Owing to the violent events in Palestine in the summer of 1929, tension at the building site increased and the Arab workers were 'eagerly waiting to begin rioting at the mufti's command'.[103] During the August riots and massacres that, as I noted, affected the YMCA project as well, work was halted for ten days. There was increased tension between Jewish and Arab builders when work resumed, and Katinka gave a detailed account of a conversation he had with Hajj Amin about the events. According to Katinka, the mufti's political assessment of intracommunal Arab politics was that any negotiation with the Zionists was doomed to failure, and that, unlike Jews, the Arabs would not agree to any arrangement that he, Hajj Amin, would attempt to negotiate on their behalf, and that such a move would cause him to be branded as a traitor. In any event, Katinka never compromised his own Zionist loyalties: in view of the intercommunal tensions and knowing that

---

[98] Katinka, *Me'Az Ve'Ad Hena*, 260–1.
[99] Ibid. 259.
[100] Contract with 'Awaḍ, 1928, file 20/44/,6/28/13, *CHIR* (the document is corrupted but an approximate date, prior to 11 October 1928, can be established as the contract states that the Waqf will transfer work on the building to 'Awaḍ on 11 October and that the latter is not responsible for work executed prior to 6 October 1928.
[101] File 20/55,6/29/13, *CHIR*. The hotel's opening was publicised in several newspapers: see, e.g., *Maraat Al Sharak*, 'Palace Hotel', 25 December 1929, 4; 'Jerusalem's New Hotel', *The Palestine Bulletin*, 23 December 1929, 4.
[102] Katinka, *Me'Az Ve'Ad Hena*, 258.
[103] Ibid. 260.

the hotel would be run by a Jew, he built two secret weapon storage rooms (known as 'slicks') on the premises.[104]

It is remarkable that the goal of building a luxury hotel at great speed was achieved during, and in spite of, one of the tensest periods of the British Mandate. This was a time viewed by historians as a watershed in Jewish–Arab–British relations, after which events took a decided turn for the worse.[105] Despite this deterioration, Katinka went on to build Hajj Amin's private villa in the upscale Arab Shaykh Jarrah neighbourhood.[106] They remained friends until Hajj Amin's exile in 1937, and he invited Katinka to the annual Nabi Mussah Festival every year and sent him condiments and pita at the end of every Passover holiday.[107]

The hotel's opening was celebrated as an intercommunal event. The Arab newspapers *Maraat Al Sharak* and *Filastin* reported that the governor of Jerusalem, Edward Keith-Roach, as well as many Zionists and Arab dignitaries, were present.[108] The *Palestine Bulletin*'s correspondent tried to extract a statement from the governor to the effect that 'here at last was a meeting place for people of all creeds and races'. The governor agreed, but refused to credit the SMC with being the first to offer such a site, saying that the British provided one at the Citadel's Arts and Crafts Exhibition.[109] For a brief moment, champagne was poured and glasses clinked in the hope that this very international and intercommunal project, which engaged Turks, Muslim Palestinians, Christian Palestinians, and Jews under British auspices, would be one of many such collaborations, and not the almost singular event it turned out to be.

Turmoil and Exile: The Palace's Functions in the 1930s

During the 1930s, the Palace Hotel underwent several upheavals, ceased to function as a hotel, and gradually became less used. However, during the early years of that decade it housed important functions as the representative urban icon of the Muslim Palestinian community.

Problems began for the hotel soon after it opened. In 1927, prior to construction, it was leased to George Barsky, a renown Jewish hotelier.[110] No explanation

---

[104] Ibid. 262. 'Slicks' were built by the Haganah – the largest Zionist military underground organisation in Palestine.

[105] Pappe, 'Haj Amin and the Buraq Revolt', 6–16; Segev and Watzman, *One Palestine, Complete*, 295–327; Mattar, 'The Mufti of Jerusalem', 230–4.

[106] Katinka, *Me'Az Ve'Ad Hena*, 260. For the circumstances and Mandatory development of the Shaykh Jarrah Neighborhood, see Mahdi Sabbagh, 'The Husayni Neighborhood in Jerusalem', *Jerusalem Quarterly* 72 (2017): 102–14.

[107] Katinka, *Me'Az Ve'Ad Hena*, 260–2.

[108] 'Palace Hotel', *Maraat Al Sharak*, 25 December 1929, 4; 'The Majlis (SMC) Hotel', *Filastin*, 25 December 1929, 3.

[109] 'Jerusalem's New Hotel', *The Palestine Bulletin*, 23 December 1929, 4.

[110] A file in CHIR mentions that the contract with Barsky was signed on 29 December 1927: see file 20/39,6/28/13, CHIR. For Barsky's bankruptcy, see 'In the Matter of the Bankruptcy of Mr. George Barsky, Jerusalem', *The Palestine Bulletin*, 9 March 1932, 4.

has come to light regarding the circumstances of this lease. It might have been an attempt to ensure professionalism, as Barsky was well connected with leading tourism agents in the United States and Europe, and hence potentially capable of bringing wealthy tourists to the hotel.[111] However, Barsky filed for bankruptcy in 1932, and the hotel closed, a failure that was due both to the financial crisis that Palestine was experiencing at the time and to the opening of the nearby King David Hotel in 1931. The new hotel, being larger and more extravagant than the Palace, succeeded in drawing wealthy tourists, thus emptying the latter of its target clientele.[112] An article in *Falastin* described the opening of the competing hotel as a Zionist scheme to undermine the Muslim tourism industry, a scheme that was aided by the British.[113] It thus appears that with the opening of the King David Hotel, and around the time of Barsky's bankruptcy, the Palace Hotel ceased to function as such, and was maintained by the Waqf as office space and as a venue for public gatherings.

The use of the hotel's spaces for these purposes was of no little consequence. Even before its closure, it was used by the Arab administration for various formal occasions.[114] More importantly, however, was the Muslim use as a major venue and accommodation for the delegates of the 1931 Jerusalem Islamic Congress, an international event of key political importance.[115] The congress, held on 6–16 December, was originally intended to promote the establishment of a Muslim university in Jerusalem, an initiative that was never realised.[116] In the framework of these plans, the Palace Hotel was to become one of the main buildings of the projected Al-Aqsa Mosque University.[117] A year later, the Waqf dedicated the building for use as several of the proposed institution's departments, as the university's new campus was planned on additional Waqf properties in Mamilla.[118] The plans for a university never actually materialised, but as late as 1935 the hotel continued to serve as a venue for political assemblies associated with the SMC, the Al

---

[111] '6000 Tourists in a Jewish Hotel', *Hatzafon*, 27 May 1927, 1.

[112] Reiter, 'Waqf BiNsibot Mishtanot', 360.

[113] Murqus 'Isa, 'The King David Hotel: One More Zionist Trap Intended to Put an End to Arab Economy', *Filastin*, 20 January 1931, 5.

[114] See, e.g., 'Arab Executive Gives Farewell Tea to Mrs. Luke', *The Palestine Bulletin*, 3 July 1930, 4.

[115] Martin S. Kramer, *Islam Assembled: The Advent of the Muslim Congresses* (New York: Columbia University Press, 1986), 221, n. 72; Matthews, 'Pan-Islam or Arab Nationalism?' 1–22; 'Ts'yirey HaVe'yida Chonim BeMalon Palace', *Doar Hayom*, 8 December 1931, 4. For Zionist concerns in regard to the congress, see a confidential report of a conversation between Nahum Sokolov of the Jewish Agency and [Arthur Charles C] Parkinson, assistant secretary at the Colonial Office, 31 December 1931, 4, 4v, 5. See also a confidential report of conversation with Selig Brodetsky of the Zionist Executive, 21 December 1931, 8–9. Both records: *NAGB* CO 733/198/3.

[116] *Report by His Majesty's Government in the United Kingdom of Great Britain and Northern Ireland to the Council of the League of Nations on the Administration of Palestine and Trans-Jordan for the Year 1931* (London: His Majesty's Stationary Office), 11. *NAGB* CO 10/1/308.

[117] Kramer, *Islam Assembled*, 123, 127–8, 133–4, 140.

[118] 'Malon Palace BiShvil HaMichlala HaMuslemit; Kitsva Shnatit Shel HaMo'atsa HaMuslamit LaMachlakah HaDatit', *Doar Hayom*, 1 December 1932, 1; Esther Nir, 'Hatochnit SheLo Nechsefa Me'Olam: Universita Palastinit began Ha'atzmaut', *Kol Ha'Ir*, 6 August 1999, 16–17.

Husseini family, and even the Jerusalem Municipality under Mayor Nashashibi.[119] Probably the most important event subsequent to the 1931 congress was the International Arab Exhibition, held in the summer of 1933. In the tradition of the great industrial exhibitions in Western countries, the Arab exhibition featured commerce, crafts and industry from all over the Muslim world, and the displays spanned all four storeys of the building.[120]

All these events, as well as the plans for a Muslim University, demonstrate that the hotel, despite its lease to Jewish hands and its ensuing commercial failure, remained a significant site of activity for the Muslim Palestinian community throughout the first half of the 1930s.

In 1935 the British leased the building for use as offices. It first housed the Department of Agriculture; in 1936 it became the home of the Peel Commission, the royal inquiry committee that, for the first time, would recommend the partition of Palestine (Figure 4.17).[121] It is perhaps ironic that this British Mandatory commission entrusted with examining the escalation of the Zionist–Arab conflict in Palestine, was hosted in the building so cherished by Hajj Amin, who vehemently objected to the commission's work and its propositions.[122] Nevertheless, as every public building in Jerusalem had political significance, conducting the commission's investigation in this key Arab facility demonstrated recognition of the Muslim Palestinian community and its achievements. Such an acknowledgement of its representative space overshadowed any objections and resistance that Hajj Amin and the Arab Palestinians had for the investigation itself.

Hajj Amin's final visits to the Palace Hotel were probably made in his capacity as president of the Higher Arab Committee and one of the leaders of the Arab revolt, as he was summoned to testify before the Peel Commission (Figure 4.18). In 1937, a few months after the commission returned to London, Hajj Amin escaped into exile and never came back to Jerusalem.

In his 2017 survey of Arab Palestinian buildings in Jerusalem, Palestinian sociologist Adnan Abdelrazek singled out the Palace Hotel as the most modern in the Middle East at the time of its opening.[123] I argue that although the hotel's significance is indeed firmly connected to its role in inscribing modern Palestinian urban practices in Jerusalem, its defining of a Muslim Palestinian identity through architecture was formative. As I have shown, the Palace Hotel was a secular project, but

---

[119] 'Arab Leaders Call General Protest Strike: Executive Meeting's Decision on Demonstration Friday', *The Palestine Post*, 9 October 1933, 1; 'New Arab Party Formed: Conference Held in Jerusalem', *The Palestine Post*, 28 March 1935, 5; an event held by the Jerusalem Municipality at the Palace Hotel in 1931 is recorded in a photograph, see *CZA* PHO\1353375.

[120] 'Arab Exhibition Opened', *The Palestine Post*, 9 July 1933, 5; 'HaTa'arucha Ha'Arvit', *Davar*, 8 August 1933, 1.

[121] 'The Destruction [reassignment] of the Waqf Hotel in Order to Rent It to the Department of Agriculture', *As-Sirat Al-Mustaqim*, 8 April 1935, 3; 'Offices Ready for Royal Commission', *The Palestine Post*, 5 November 1936, 5.

[122] Martin Gilbert, 'HaCha'yim HaKtsarim shel Ve'Adat Peel', *Zmanim* 1 (1979), 4–15; Mattar, 'The Mufti of Jerusalem', 235–6.

[123] Abdelrazek, *The Arab Architectural Renaissance*, 57, 58.

Figure 4.17 *Haim Weizmann testifying before the Peel Commission in the Palace Hotel restaurant, 1936. CZA, NZO\634447.*

Figure 4.18 *The Grand Mufti Hai Amin eff. el-Husseini, with attendants, leaving the offices of the Palestine Royal Commission [at the Palace Hotel] after testifying. 1937. ACM, https://www.loc.gov/pictures/item/2019709024/, retrieved 11 February 2020.*

Figure 4.19 *Hussni Kattawi, Jaljulia Mosque, Jaljulia, completed 2014. Photographed by Diego Rosman.*

it was related spatially and ideologically to religious activity as embodied in the traditions and policies of the Waqf. As such, it anticipated the transfer of historic design elements from the Haram's monuments to modern Muslim Palestinian building typologies, making the hotel's architecture a seminal experiment. The Haram a-Sharif has since continued to inspire Muslim Palestinian architecture: the Dome of the Rock, as well as elements of the more typical Al-Aqsa Mosque, have often been reiterated in contemporary architecture in Israel and in the Palestinian territories, for example, in the Jaljulia Mosque in Jaljulia, Israel, designed by Hussni Kattawi and completed in 2014 (Figure 4.19).

In considering hotel design, it is perhaps no coincidence that, following restoration and renovation, the Jerusalem Palace Hotel was reopened as a grand hotel belonging to the Waldorf Astoria franchise. At the beginning of the 1930s, both the Waldorf Astoria in New York and the Palace Hotel in Jerusalem represented luxury and modernity, as well as cultural and/or national identity. To this day, they remain 'symbol[s] of cosmopolis'[124] and so much more.

[124] Shepstone, 'Cairo's Potential Rival', 456.

CHAPTER FIVE

Constructing Zionist Identity: The Zionist Executive Building

THE SIXTEENTH OF May 1930 saw an event of key importance for the Jewish Zionist community of Jerusalem and all of Palestine – the inauguration of the newly completed building for the headquarters of the Jewish National Fund (JNF). The festive day was set for the Jewish holiday of Lag ba-Omer, which afforded the ceremony symbolic significance, as Lag ba-Omer was reinstated in the Yishuv as part of its emerging national identity.[1] The first constructed of the three wings of a building intended to house the Zionist institutions, it marked the most significant political presence of the Jewish Zionist community in Jerusalem's urban space. During the course of the next four years, two additional wings were added: one for the Palestine Zionist Executive, which was administratively replaced by the Jewish Agency in 1929, and one for Keren Ha'Yesod – the Foundation Fund of Palestine (known today as the United Israel Appeal). These three institutions presided over all the political and social aspects of the Zionist nation-building enterprise. The Zionist Executive Building (hereafter ZEB), or National Institutions House, as it was sometimes called, provided the space for their activities (Figure 5.1).

In this chapter I discuss this major undertaking, planned by the architect Yohanan Ratner. I argue that in designing the ZEB, Ratner took it upon himself to delineate a 'national style' for the Zionist project in Palestine, anticipating, and to no small extent determining, that modernism would serve this purpose. I reveal details about a construction project that was highly charged from both intercommunal and intracommunal perspectives, an enterprise that clearly reflected the interplay of cooperation and enmity that characterised the Palestinian labour market in all its spheres.

The establishment of the Jewish Agency on 14 August 1929, underscored the importance of the three institutions to be housed in the ZEB.[2] It was a political

---

[1] For the way the holiday evolved and its customs, see Yael Zerubavel, *Recovered Roots: Collective Memory and the Making of Israeli National Tradition* (Chicago: University of Chicago Press, 1995), 96–113.

[2] Dating based on a letter written on behalf of Sidney Webb, First Baron Passfield, secretary of state for the colonies, to the secretary-general of the League of Nations, 27 August 1930, *NAGB* CO 733/191/13.

Figure 5.1 Yohanan Ratner, Zionist Executive Building, Jerusalem, 1929–38. ACM, https://www.loc.gov/pictures/item/2019694026/, retrieved 11 February 2020.

act perceived as a concrete realisation of Zionist aspirations and as the implementation of Article 4 of the British Mandate for Palestine, which stated that the 'Zionist Organization should take steps ... to secure the co-operation of all Jews who are willing to assist in the establishment of the Jewish National Home'.[3] Thus, apart from their role of governing the Jewish community in Palestine, the three institutions represented the Zionist project to Jewish communities abroad, so as to secure their political and financial support. As JNF director Menachem Ussishkin declared when the first wing's cornerstone was laid in 1929: the new building would 'symbolize the unity of the nation, and project rays of light and salvation to millions of our brethren in the Diaspora'.[4]

There was an intention to house other international Zionist organisations such as WIZO (the Women's International Zionist Organization), Ezra Orthodox Jewish Youth Movement and Hadassah (the Women's Zionist Organization of America) in the ZEB,[5] but this did not materialise. Nevertheless, concentrating the major institutions that governed Jewish life in Palestine under one roof was a significant step. It reflected the Zionist perception that these institutions comprised the 'state in the making', anticipating its organisational structuring: they included political and nonpolitical institutions (some based on a democratic constituency and some not) and religious and secular bodies, as well as philanthropic organisations.[6] This institutional organisation was pluralist in its inclusion of Zionist and non-Zionist factions, which often had conflicting views and agendas regarding how to accomplish short- and long-term objectives in Palestine. In principle, the major Zionist bodies hoped to include all the Jewish communities in Palestine, and the ZEB's functions reflected these aspirations for multiparty participation and broad intracommunal impact. It was primarily ultra-Orthodox Jews who voiced objection to this joint intracommunal structure and cooperation.[7]

---

[3] 'Report of the Chairman of the Administrative Committee of the Jewish Agency for Palestine', 29 August 1930, 2. *NAGB* CO 733/191/13. See also 'Ne'umey Weizmann VeSokolov Be'Yeshivat HaPticha', *Davar*, 9 August 1929, 3; Smith, *Palestine and the Arab-Israeli Conflict*, 112–13. For a detailed report of the status of the Jewish Agency vis-à-vis the British Mandatory administration and the terms of its establishment, see 'Enlargement of the Jewish Agency for Palestine: Preparatory Note', 1929: 1–3. *NAGB* CO 733/164/5. See also 'The Position of the Jewish Agency', c. 1930, *NAGB* CO 733/191/13.

[4] 'Chag Even HaPina LeBeit HaKeren-HaKayemet: Osishkin Modi'a Al Gmar Rechishat 5,000 Dunam BaSharon BeKaspei Canada', *Davar*, 28 April 1929, 1.

[5] David Behrel to Jewish Agency, 28 May 1933, *CZA* S1/198; Leo Herrmann (General Secretary of Keren Ha'Yesod Jerusalem) to Jewish Agency, 13 April 1932, *CZA* S1/198.

[6] Joel S. Migdal, *Through the Lens of Israel: Explorations in State and Society* (Albany: State University of New York Press, 2001), 51–80.

[7] Levi Itzhak Hayerushalmi, 'HaCharedim MeHazionut VeHaCharedim LaZionut', *Moznaim* 6 (1997): 32–40; Shulamit Eliash, 'The Political Role of the Chief Rabbinate of Palestine during the Mandate: Its Character and Nature', *Jewish Social Studies* 47, no. 1 (1985): 36–7.

A Place for the ZEB: Locating the Institutions in Jerusalem

Following the imposition of the British Mandate, the leading Zionist institutions set up offices in various rented spaces in Jerusalem. The decision to locate them there, rather than in Tel Aviv, for example, was deliberate. As noted by several scholars, Jerusalem was treated with ambiguity within the Zionist project: on the one hand, it was revered as the historic capital of the biblical Jewish people and their religious and political centre, whereas, on the other hand, it was understood to be a mixed and contested city, posing many challenges and harbouring potential threats.[8] Locating the centre of Zionist governance in Jerusalem in spite of these realities asserted the Jewish community's presence and proclaimed its historic ties to the city. Moreover, Jerusalem was the centre of British administration, and the proximity was important for routine political activity. Jerusalem was also the locus of the Arab ruling elite, so building the Zionist institutions in the city would maintain the fragile balance among the political and religious entities functioning there.

In the second half of the 1920s, the need arose for permanent buildings for the Zionist institutions. Erection of these accommodations was a gradual process, which began in 1929 and lasted, in several phases, until 1939. Each of the institutions for which the buildings were intended moved into its respective wing upon its completion. The motivation for building new premises came from several causes and considerations. Politically, the Zionist project in Palestine experienced a profound economic crisis in 1926–7, and this sense of impending failure also impacted the Zionist Movement internationally.[9] This dire situation apparently served as an incentive for building, an act that would clearly manifest the Zionist institutions' political hegemony in the face of crisis. As I noted earlier, in 1927 a severe earthquake shook the country. Jerusalem suffered some loss of life; many buildings were destroyed; and the offices of Keren Ha'Yesod and the Zionist Executive were damaged.[10] Moreover, the institutions' expenditure on leased offices was significant, and from time to time they were forced to move.[11] Office space in these makeshift rentals was insufficient and could not accommodate all the necessary administrative functions. Hence, political, physical and economic considerations all led to the decision to build, and in 1927 a competition was held and plans for the ZEB were devised.

---

[8] Yossi Katz, 'Mekoma Shel HaYir Jerusalem BeMasechet Pe'ulotav Shel HaMimsad HaZioni BeShalhei Tkufat HaMandat', *Zion* (1996): 67–90; Golani, 'Hanhagat Ha'Yishuv VeShe'elat Jerusalem', 156–72; Elyakim Rubinstein, 'Yehudim Ve'Aravim Be'Yiryot Eretz-Israel (1926–1933) Yerushalayim Ve'Arim Acherot', *Cathedra: For the History of Eretz Israel and Its Yishuv* 51 (1989): 122–47.
[9] Pinchas Ofer, 'Achzava MeHesegei HaBayit HaLe'umi Ha'Yehudi Gorem LeTafnit BaMedini'yut HaBritit Be'Eretz-Israel Be-1930?' *Cathedra: For the History of Eretz Israel and Its Yishuv* 16 (1980): 125–32.
[10] 'Earthquake in Palestine', *The Times*, 12 July 1927, 14; 'Hedey Ha'Ra'ash', *Davar*, 18 July 1927, 1.
[11] See, e.g., 'Hananatz LeDirata HaChadasha' ('The Zionist Executive moves to a new apartment'), *Ha'Am*, 17 May 1931, 4.

The need for a new building was further confirmed in 1929, as the conflict between Arabs and Jews escalated significantly, and it clearly became advisable to relocate all the Jewish institutions to a relatively safe area of the city. The first wing of the ZEB was already under construction in the new Jewish neighbourhood of Rehavia in western Jerusalem, a neighbourhood relatively distant from the key sites of friction in the Old City.[12] David Werner Senator, a member of the Zionist Executive, addressed the urgency of continuing the project and moving the remaining institutions, which were still housed near the Old City walls:

> [T]he conditions under which we are working here [in temporary offices] are worse than are necessary owing to the insufficient office accommodation ... The conditions of security of the office of the Palestine Executive are very bad in the event of any disturbances. The present building is situated in a mixed section of the town not far from the Jaffa Gate and opposite the centre of traffic where all demonstrations have to pass. This has been proved again a few days ago when the Arab Delegation arrived and the masses of people who welcomed them passed our corner.[13]

Apart from compromised security noted by Senator, conflictual interaction with the British government that followed the August 1929 riots and massacres further underscored the need to inscribe Jewish presence in Jerusalem's urban space: as a result of that summer's violent events, the British radically changed their policy toward Jewish settlement in Palestine. They issued what came to be known as the first 'White Paper', which significantly limited Jewish immigration and land purchases.[14]

The effect that this new policy had on the desire to build can be clearly seen in a letter written by the building's supervising architects, the Jerusalem firm of Wilhelm Hecker and Eliezer Yellin. Probably relating to the construction of foundations for the two additional ZEB wings, the architects wrote to Senator that 'due to recent political events', they assume that the Zionist Executive will want to avoid creating an impression that construction has stopped.[15]

Thus, cramped space and security considerations were paramount in the decision to build and, at this specific point in time, mandated the project's continuation beyond the JNF wing, which was nearly complete.

---

[12] Segev and Watzman, *One Palestine, Complete*, 31. A piece in the *Palestine Post* makes a clear connection between the ZEB project and the '1929 Riots'. See 'Jewish Agency to Build Own Premises', *The Palestine Post*, 28 June 1933, 5.
[13] Senator to Oscar Wasserman, 8 June 1930, 1, *CZA* S1/198.
[14] Segev and Watzman, *One Palestine, Complete*, 332–7.
[15] Hecker and Yellin (on behalf of architect Ratner) to Senator, 3 November 1930, *CZA* S1/198; Garkovsky (JNF) to Jewish Agency, 30 July 1930, *CZA* S1/198.

Figure 5.2 *Yohanan Ratner, model for the Zionist Executive Building and Yeshurun Synagogue, c. 1927, Jerusalem, 1929–38. ABHC, Ratner Collection.*

Creating an Architectural Culture: The Competition

Financing for the ZEB came from loans from the Austrian Phoenix Insurance Company,[16] the Anglo-Palestine Bank and the Migdal Insurance Company.[17] These loans were secured gradually as the project progressed. Seed money became available in 1927 and a competition for planning the ZEB was announced.[18] According to Michael Ratner, the architect's son, the competition guidelines originally called for a larger complex, which was to include the ZEB and the Yeshurun Synagogue, which was later built across the street and can be seen in a photograph of Yohanan Ratner's original model (Figure 5.2).[19] The idea of creating this complex, intended to integrate the secular institutions governing the Yishuv and a synagogue, is in itself remarkable. It evolved from the Zionist institutions' commitment to developing Jewish religious institutions alongside national ones,[20] with the JNF involved in funding the purchase of land for Yeshurun Synagogue. Zionist leaders such as Ussishkin and Nahum Sokolov attended the cornerstone ceremony, and the former, alongside Zionist Executive member Yizhak Ben-Zvi (later Israel's second president) eventually prayed there.[21] It further indicates that, at that point in time, the Zionist project was committed to religiosity in the shaping of a

---

[16] 'LeBinyan Be'it HaMosadot HaLe'umi'yim Bi'Yerushalayim', *Davar*, 23 April 1928, 1; 'Tekes HaChagigca LeHanachat Even-Hapina LeBe'it HaKahakal', 28 April 1928, 1; Yehoshua Farbstein to Phoenix Insurance Company (Palestine Branch), 16 May 1932, *CZA* S1/198; Senator to Oscar Wasserman, 8 June 1930, 1, *CZA* S1/198.

[17] Eliezer (Siegfried) Hoofien to Senator, 4 June 1930, *CZA* S1/198; Letter from Keren Ha'Yesod to Jewish Agency, 11 May 1938, *CZA* KH4/7967; Deed of mortgage given by Migdal Insurance Company to Keren Ha'Yesod, 9 July 1939, *CZA* KH4/7968; Loan Capital prospectus – Migdal Insurance Company and Keren Ha'Yesod, 26 May 1939, *CZA* S1/199.

[18] David Kroyanker, 'Orientali Yoter MeHaMizrachi: Gilgule'ya Shel Sfat HaZitutim HaYerushalmit', *Zmanim* 96 (2006): 31.

[19] Interview with Michael Ratner, 26 July 2017.

[20] Reuven Gafni, *Tachat Kipat HaLe'om: Bate'yi Kneset ULe'umi'yut Be'Erets Israel BiTkufat HaMandat* (Sede Boker: Ben Gurion University of the Negev, 2017), 300.

[21] Ibid. 66–7.

national identity, as suggested by Reuven Gafni in his research dealing with synagogues in the Yishuv during the Mandate period.[22]

The ZEB competition had a very impressive response and more than thirty proposals were submitted.[23] There were entries by the foremost architects in Palestine, including Alexander Baerwald, who built the Technion Institute of Technology in Haifa, and Richard Kaufmann, the chief planner of the Zionist agricultural settlements in Palestine, who also planned the Rehavia neighbourhood. Leopold Krakauer, Dov (Baer) Kuczinski and Wilhelm Hecker of Hecker & Yellin also submitted designs.[24] Hecker placed fifth and, as I noted earlier, oversaw construction.

First place was awarded to Yohanan (Yevgheny-Eugen) Ratner (1891–1965). Ratner, soon to become a leading Zionist (and later Israeli) architect, had only two previous buildings to his credit, so was not well known. Israeli Prime Minister Itzhak Rabin described him in his obituary as a 'personality of many hues merged into completeness'.[25] Rabin was alluding to the remarkable achievements of this 'commander-architect-builder-teacher' – as one newspaper called Ratner.[26] Born in Odessa, Ukraine, in 1891, Ratner studied architecture at the Technische Hochschule in Karlsruhe, Germany, and immigrated to Palestine in 1923. He worked in construction and as a junior supervisor in the Zionist construction company Solel Boneh. He then joined the architecture faculty at the Technion, which opened its gates to students in 1924. At the time, the Technion was the only institution specialising in teaching engineering and architecture in Palestine. First serving as a teaching assistant to Alexander Baerwald, in 1932 he became dean of the Institute's Faculty of Architecture. At the same time, Ratner, who was a World War I veteran of the Russian army, took on command assignments in the Haganah, the Zionist military organisation. His outstanding military career continued alongside his architectural practice and teaching until he was well into his sixties.[27]

Ratner's winning entry for the ZEB competition was his professional breakthrough as an independent practising architect. The competition was among the

---

[22] Ibid. 300–8.
[23] The number of proposals varies in the different sources: Kroyanker, 'Orientali Yoter MeHaMizrach', 31, contends that there were 33, *Doar Hayom* counted 36 while the *Palestine Bulletin* cites '38 valid entries'. See 'Tots'ot HaTacharut LeBinyan HaMosadot HaLe'umi'yim Bi'Yerushalayim', *Doar Hayom*, 5 August 1928, 2; 'Design for Palestine Zionist Headquarters Selected', *Palestine Bulletin*, 5 August 1928, 1.
[24] 'Tots'ot HaTacharut LeBinyan HaMosadot HaLe'umi'yim Bi'Yerushalayim', 2; Kroyanker, 'Orientali Yoter MeHamizrach', 31.
[25] 'Manhigey HaMedina Ufshutey Am Livu et Aluf Yohanan Ratner BeDarko Ha'Acharona', *Ma'ariv*, 1 February 1965, 2.
[26] 'Yachas Livney Adam', *Ma'ariv*, 2 March 1965, 10.
[27] Silvina Sosnovsky, ed., *Yohanan Ratner: H'Adam, Ha'Architect Ve'Avodato* (Haifa: Technion, Israel Architecture Heritage Center, 1992), 7–8; Myra Warhaftig, *They Laid the Foundation: Lives and Works of German-Speaking Jewish Architects in Palestine 1918–1948*, trans. Andrea Lerner (Tübingen and New York: Wasmuth, 2007), 62–4.

first held in Palestine, and its prestige was ensured by including a juror from abroad – the Jewish Austrian architect Joseph Frank.[28] The jury also included a Dr Reiner, the Zionist architect Benjamin Chaikin, and representatives from the Jewish Agency and Keren Ha'Yesod.[29] Ratner later emphasised the significance of giving Zionist architects this equal opportunity to participate in the contest. In his view, the ZEB competition laid the basis for a progressive and democratic architectural tradition, and he considered that it played an important role in creating a Zionist architectural culture.[30] Michael Ratner contends that in reality the competition was not as democratic as his father later publicly described. He recounts that the more acclaimed architects who participated in the competition protested Ratner's win and that, as a result, the Yeshurun Synagogue was taken out of the commission and given to Alexander Friedman and Meir Rubin, who built it in 1934.[31] According to Michael Ratner, his father would not have won without the presence of Frank, who was modernist, foreign, and hence clearly impartial. Frank's presence encouraged the selection of entries on their merit, without regard for the submitting architects' reputations. Ussishkin also insisted upon respecting the judges' decision.[32] Ratner writes that after he won, Ussishkin said to him: 'I thoroughly dislike your plan, but should anyone attempt to take this commission away from you, don't worry – you were awarded the prize, so you shall build' (Figure 5.3).[33]

Documentation pertaining to the ZEB reveals that Hecker & Yellin – which was among the leading firms in Jerusalem – played a very significant role in the plan's development. From the project's inception and throughout the 1930s, the firm oversaw the entire project and planned many of the design details;[34] it was often cited alongside Ratner as the building's architects in the local press. At a certain point the Jewish Agency's building committee, referring to Hecker & Yellin's central role and influence on the project's routine execution, noted that Ratner's residence in the remote city of Haifa hindered his involvement in the venture.[35]

Little is known regarding the competition guidelines for the ZEB. These apparently dictated a two-storey office building with three wings, one for each of the

[28] Ratner, 'Hesegei Ha'Architectura Be'Israel Be'Esrim Shnot Ki'yum Agudat Ha'Enginirim VeHa'Architectim Be'Israel', *Handasa VeAdrichlut*, 21 (1963), in Sosnovsky, ed., *Yohanan Ratner*, 96.
[29] 'Tots'ot HaTacharut LeBinyan HaMosadot HaLe'umi'yim Bi'Yerushalayim', *Doar Hayom*, 5 August 1928, 2; 'Design for Palestine Zionist Headquarters Selected', *Palestine Bulletin*, 5 August, 1928, 1.
[30] Sosnovsky, ed., *Yohanan Ratner*, 96.
[31] 'Even Hapina LeBe'it Knesset Yeshurun', *Davar*, 8 May 1934, 1; Interview with Michael Ratner, 26 July 2017.
[32] Interview with Michael Ratner, 26 July 2017.
[33] Sosnovsky, ed., *Yohanan Ratner*, 96.
[34] Hecker & Yellin to Keren Ha'Yesod, 26 June 1935, *CZA* KH4/7966; Keren Ha'Yesod to Hecker & Yellin, 10 July 1935, *CZA* KH4/7966; Eng. Sverdlov (Director of the contracting firm, Misrad Kablani) to Keren Ha'Yesod, 16 January 1936.
[35] Minutes of the Building Committee, 3 March 1937, 2, *CZA* S1/198.

Figure 5.3 *Yohanan Ratner and JNF director Menachem Ussishkin, 1930s. Photograph courtesy of Michael Ratner.*

major institutions. Furthermore, it was not to be overshadowed by emerging four-storey buildings that were already being constructed nearby.[36] Ratner proposed a polygonal building surrounding an oval court (Figure 5.4). Contemporary critiques of his plan praised his placement of the larger mass of the building away from the street, hailing it as an original solution that eliminated competition in height with neighbouring buildings and removed it from the noise and bustle in the street.[37]

A Building for Three Institutions

In the following two sections, I discuss the building's plans and functions, analysing Ratner's engagement with the question of a Zionist national style and its expression in this representative edifice.

As I noted earlier, the new ZEB was built in Rehavia, the 'garden suburb' whose design was included in Ashbee's *Jerusalem 1920–1922* (see Figure 1.7). The ZEB plot in Rehavia was purchased by the JNF, and Keren Ha'Yesod and the Jewish

---

[36] Kroyanker, 'Orientali Yoter MeHamizrach', 31; Alexander Baerwald, 'The Jewish National House', *Jüdische Rundschau*, 76/77, 28 September 1928, cited in Sosnovsky, ed., *Yohanan Ratner*, 34.
[37] Sosnovsky, ed., *Yohanan Ratner*, 34; 'Jewish Whitehall in Palestine', *The Palestine Post*, 11 December 1934, 4.

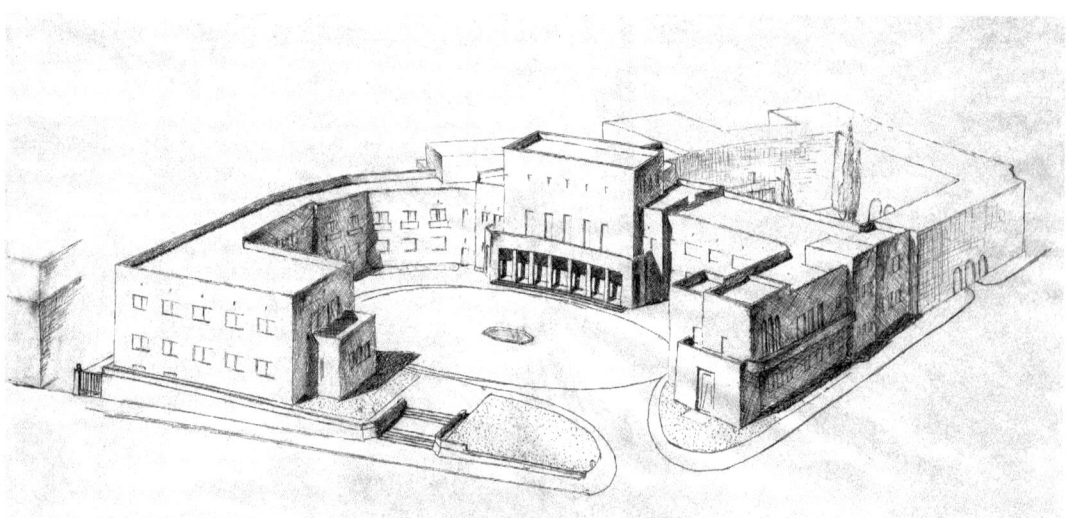

Figure 5.4 *Yohanan Ratner, Zionist Executive Building, isometric drawing, c. 1930. © CZA, S14\545-5M.*

Agency would lease their wings.[38] As a prominent new Jewish neighbourhood in the western part of Jerusalem, Rehavia was an ideal choice for the building's location. The ZEB was to be constructed on King George Avenue – a street that circumscribed Rehavia's eastern perimeter, which was quickly becoming a major thoroughfare and the site of several other construction projects. The ZEB was erected close to the Hebrew Gymnasium, built in 1928 by architect Fritz Kornberg. The adjacent Yeshurun Synagogue was also built facing King George Avenue, making this area the neighbourhood's civic centre. After the ZEB was completed, lodgings for the institutions' employees were planned in this thriving hub of Jewish life.[39]

The ZEB was divided into three unequal parts at their angles, with the central wing designated for the Jewish Agency and the Zionist Executive, the south wing for Keren Ha'Yesod, and the north for the JNF (Figure 5.5). Although some dating remains tentative, it is evident that the JNF wing was completed in 1930, the cornerstone for the Keren Ha'Yesod wing was laid in the autumn of 1932,[40] and the central wing was being built at the same time.[41] By December 1934, the three wings were completed.[42] The Jewish Agency, administratively treated as a

---

[38] 'Batim LaMosdot HaZioni'yim', *Davar*, 24 April 1929; Jewish Agency to JNF, 26 March 1935, CZA KH4/7966; G. Aboulafya, Memorandum regarding the Jewish Agency Building, 23 July 1933, CZA S1/198.
[39] 'LeShikun Pkidey Yerushalayim', *Doar Hayom*, 21 November 1935, 8.
[40] 'Hanachat Even-Hapina LeBinyan Keren Ha'Yesod', *Doar Hayom*, 18 October 1932, 3.
[41] Y. Markowitz (HaPo'el HaMizrachi Union – Jerusalem Branch) to Jewish Agency, 16 October 1932.
[42] 'Agaf LeBet HaMosadot Bi'Yerushalayim', *Davar*, 23 June 1932, 1; 'LeYeshivat HaVa'ad HaPo'el HaZioni', *Davar*, 21 March 1934, 1; 'Jewish Whitehall in Palestine', *The Palestine Post*, 11 December 1934, 4.

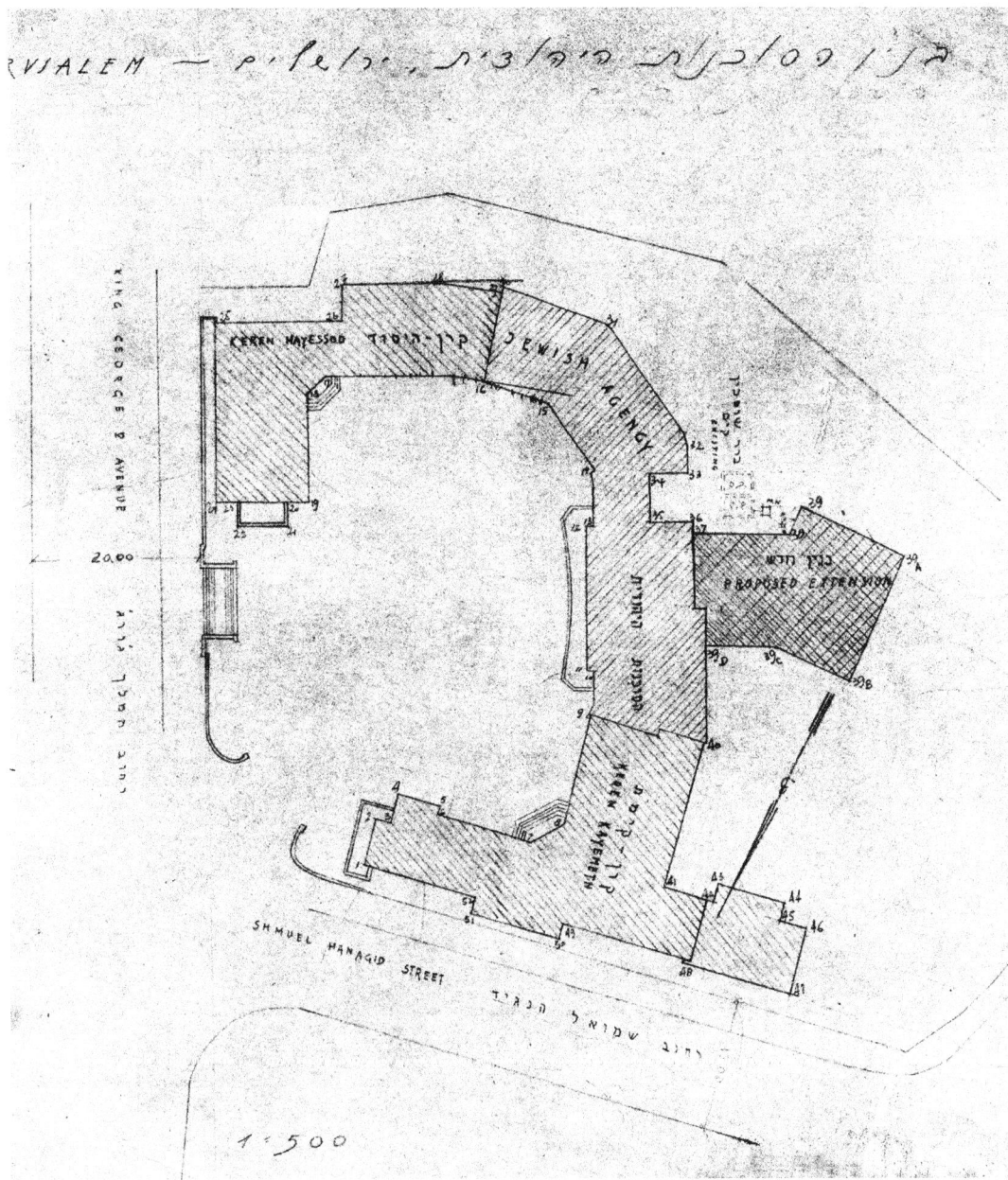

Figure 5.5 *Yohanan Ratner, Zionist Executive Building, plan showing division into wings (with proposed additions), 25 April 1937. © CZA, KH4/7960-1M.*

separate body, was assigned temporary rooms in the other wings until the central part of the building was finished.[43] The construction of an additional, fourth wing began almost immediately after the completion of the main tripartite building, in

---

[43] 'Agaf LeBet HaMosadot Bi'Yerushalayim', *Davar*, 23 June 1932, 1; 'Zionist Executive in New Premises', *The Palestine Post*, 5 May 1933, 2.

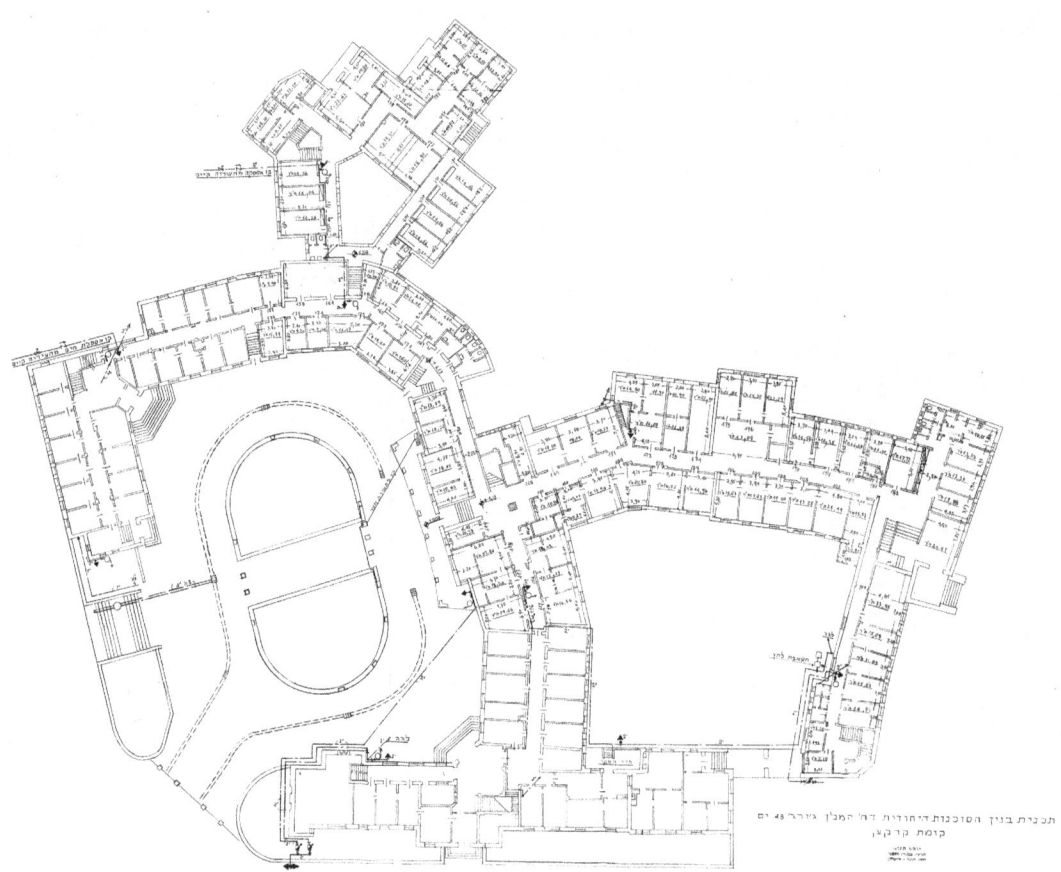

Figure 5.6 *Yohanan Ratner and Michael Ratner, Zionist Executive Building, final plan, after 1948. Courtesy of Michael Ratner.*

1934.[44] Another wing, having three rather than two storeys, was begun in 1937 and completed about 1939.[45] Built in the back part of the lot, where space was still available, it was connected to the western façade of the Jewish Agency wing (Figure 5.5). During the 1940s, the last wing was significantly enlarged, and at the present time it encloses a yard for maintenance and deliveries (Figure 5.6).[46] A general sketch of one such extension was included in an early isometric drawing by Ratner, which delineates this extension's street façade (Figure 5.7). A third floor was later added to the original three wings. The ZEB thus expanded gradually, as needs grew and as funding became available.

[44] Contract between Keren Ha'Yesod and Misrad Kablani Yerushalyim (the contractor) for additional wing dated 11 December 1934; Eliezer Kaplan to Keren Ha'Yesod, 14 December 1934. Both documents *CZA* KH4/7966. Additional correspondence regarding the addition is preserved in the same file.

[45] Contract between Keren Ha'Yesod and Misrad Kablani Yerushalyim (the contractor) for additional wing dated 11 July 1937, and ample correspondence regarding the addition. See also Minutes of the Building Committee, 2 February 1938. Both documents *CZA* KH4/7967.

[46] Reiser to Eisenberg, 24 June 1945, *CZA* S1/199.

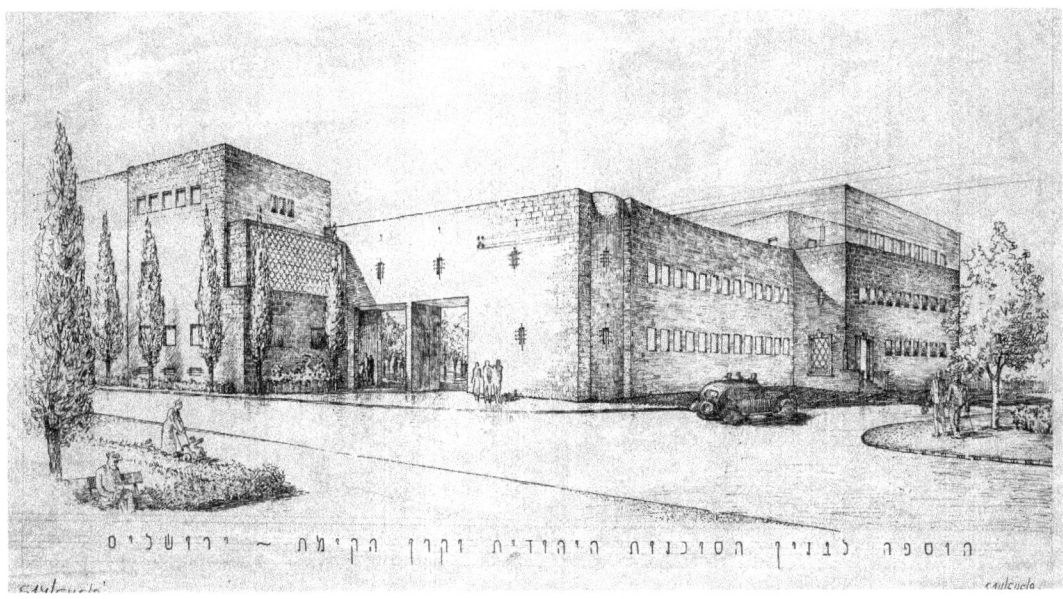

Figure 5.7 *Yohanan Ratner, Zionist Executive Building, elevation for new addition, 1929–38, Jerusalem. © CZA, S14\545-2M.*

The building's design is remarkably modernist. It is entirely stone-clad, in line with Jerusalem's ordinance, yet its volumes stand out in in their stark, unadorned simplicity (Figures 5.1 and 5.4). Its ground plan is asymmetrical, comprising seven sections surrounding a large oval-shaped entrance court (Figures 5.8 and 5.9). The building's northeast corner is open to the main street; originally a small vehicle access road began there and surrounded the oval, so that passengers could be dropped off near the various entrances. Apart from serving to separate the building from the main street, the court is also used for gatherings for important communal events. The JNF and Keren Ha'Yesod wings connect with the central – Jewish Agency – wing at right angles, and the Agency's wing is divided into three sections connected by obtuse angles (Figure 5.5). The ground plan for the original two storeys of this asymmetrical arrangement aligned offices along a central corridor. The second storey housed meeting rooms, and each wing had one or two larger offices for the director and senior staff. The building has a basement and flat roofs.

The plan reflects the division into three administrative entities; hence, the building's main façade, which faces King George Avenue, has three formal entrances – one serving each institution. The central entrance is reserved for the Jewish Agency (Figure 5.9), and the entrances to JNF and Keren Ha'Yesod are on the diagonal walls that are the wings' meeting points (Figures 5.10 and 5.11). The JNF also had an entrance on its north façade, facing present-day Keren Kayemet Street. All of the formal institutional entrances are spacious and are connected to a main staircase. The one to the Jewish Agency wing is the largest, forming part of its main corridor and staircase. In addition to these elements, the building reflects a modernist approach in its functionality. The ground plan was

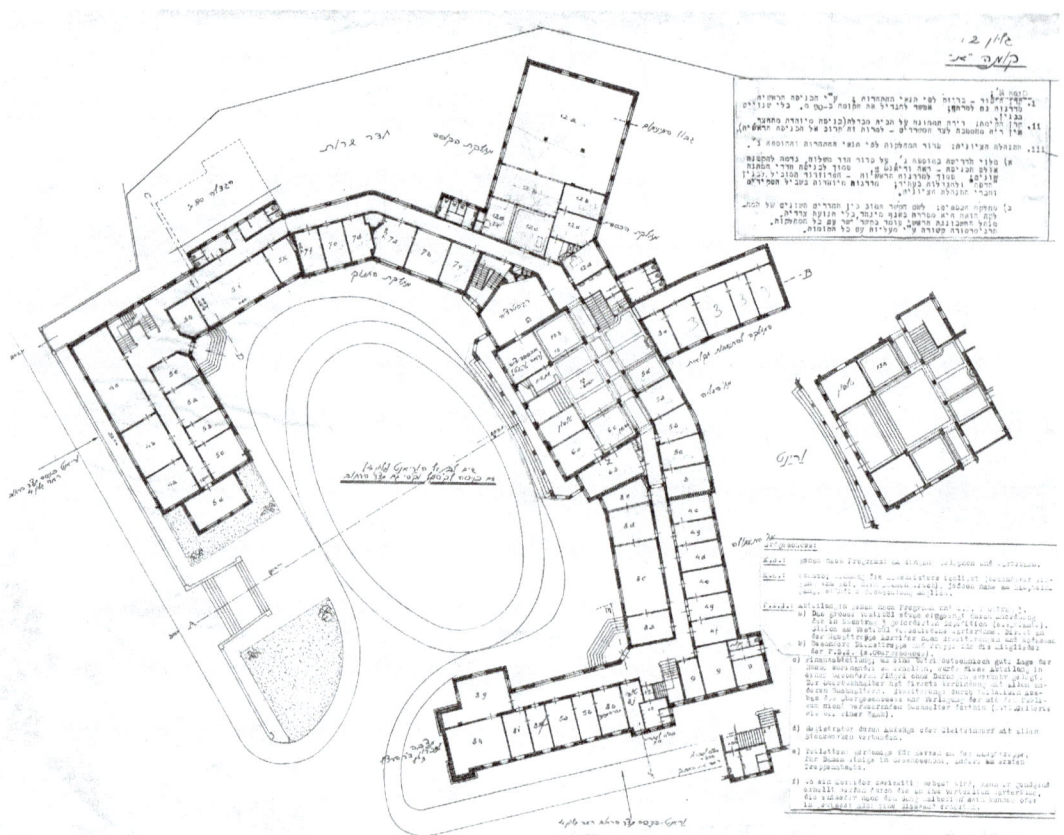

Figure 5.8 *Yohanan Ratner, Zionist Executive Building, plan including entrance court, Jerusalem, c. 1935.* © CZA, S14\545-8M.

Figure 5.9 *Yohanan Ratner, Zionist Executive Building, entrance court. Photographed by Diego Rosman.*

Figure 5.10 *Yohanan Ratner, Zionist Executive Building, entrance to Keren Ha'Yesod wing. Photographed by Diego Rosman.*

remarkably economical in its use of space, with most of it reserved for offices. The length of the different sections was dictated by the sizes of the offices and was thus not bound to symmetry. Apart from the entrance hallways, there were few formal spaces.

The central entrance façade is accentuated by a rectangular protruding volume that has a slightly higher roof; a simple colonnade, supporting a wide entry balcony, further defines its formal function. Each of the side wings ends in low, protruding sections, topped by a balcony accessed from the second floor. Whereas the Keren Ha'Yesod section is defined by a vertical wall with a window at its centre, the walls of the JNF section are slightly slanted. Fenestration of the entire building consists of rows of simple quadrilaterals in three or four basic sizes, repeated as horizontal and vertical rectangles, as well as squares. The windows are made of cast concrete frames incised into the walls, so they do not interfere with the stone facing. Exceptions are the ground- and first-floor lintels, each of which is faced with a row of vertical trapezoids. Apart from two small arched doors that open to the entrance court, all entryways are rectangular. Ratner's elevation sketch, probably made for the competition or shortly afterward, indicates that he originally planned three arched windows and a triple-arch entrance for the north façade (Figure 5.4). A balcony, which would have emphasised horizontality, was planned there, but was not built.

The building's modernist design is apparent in all planning aspects: stone facing

Figure 5.11 *Yohanan Ratner, Zionist Executive Building, entrance to JNF wing. Photographed by Diego Rosman.*

is smooth and simple; thin, horizontal windows combine with vertical ones; and the volumes forming the outer limits of the structure are asymmetrical. Balconies are unadorned and integrated into the building's volumes. An exception was made in the centre balcony, which displays one of the building's few decorative elements: a 'corbel' set at its centre 'supported' by a vertical stone, which probably represents an abstraction of a seven-lamp menorah, one of the symbols of the 'state in the making'. This balcony was intended as an elevated 'podium' from where speeches by Yishuv leaders or important guests could be delivered to crowds assembled in the front court (Figure 5.12).

Apart from its many offices, the building has several rooms that were originally dedicated to specific symbolic national functions that clearly demonstrated the

Figure 5.12 *Zionist Executive Building, balcony above the main entrance, 1934 [photo titled: 'Passing of Jerusalem Flag KKL-JNF School ceremony at National Institutions courtyard in Jerusalem']. Photographed by Zvi Oron (Oroshkess), 1929–38. © CZA, PHO\1356951.*

ZEB's role in creating the Zionist identity. A large meeting room adjacent to the main balcony was designed for the Assembly of Representatives, which was the Yishuv's de facto parliament. Figure 5.13 shows Chaim Weizmann, then president of the World Zionist Organization, speaking in this meeting room. At one time the JNF wing included a reconstruction of Herzl's study, called the 'Herzl Room' (Figure 5.14), which featured the original furnishings from the Vienna study of Theodor (Binyamin Ze'ev) Herzl, the father of political Zionism. This room embodied a physical space for Herzl's commemoration, complementing additional rites, such as 'Herzl Day', which acknowledges the deceased leader's historic achievements.[47] The plan in Figure 5.8, delineates a 'commemorative monument for Dr. Herzl R.I.P.' on the east wall of the JNF building, facing the main road entering the court, indicating that there was to be additional commemoration of Herzl in a visible location, but that was never constructed.

Another formal space is the JNF Golden Book Room (Figure 5.15). *The Golden Book* was a lavish, specially designed annual volume listing JNF donors. Devoted to these books and the donors named in them, the room, which has glass-enclosed

---

[47] The room was first opened in 1931. With the completion of the new JNF wing in 1937, the furniture was moved into a room specifically planned for this purpose, whose proportions and design were an exact replica of Herzl's room in Vienna. See 'Niftach Chadro shel Herzl', *Davar*, 6 July 1931, 1; S. Kutler, 'The Herzl Room in Jerusalem', *The Sentinel*, 28 June 1934, 8; 'Jewish Whitehall in Palestine', *The Palestine Post*, 11 December 1934, 4; 'Hannukat Cheder Herzl', *Davar*, 5 December 1937, 1; see also Segev and Watzman, *One Palestine, Complete*, 300.

Figure 5.13 *Dr Weizmann at a Jewish Agency meeting in the main board room of the Zionist Executive Building, 1945. © Weizmann Archive, Rehovot.*

Figure 5.14 *Zionist Executive Building, Herzl Room in the JNF wing, n.d. © Jewish National Fund Archive, D739-268.*

Figure 5.15 *Zionist Executive Building, Golden Books Room in the JNF wing. ACM, https://www.loc.gov/pictures/item/2019694066/, retrieved 11 February 2020.*

bookshelves and a large display table at its center, is adjacent to the JNF board room. In addition to honoring the donors, the room represents the JNF's crucial role in promoting Jewish settlement in Palestine.

In his memoirs, Israeli playwright and radio producer Yehuda Ha'Ezrachi, who was a resident of Rehavia neighbourhood and saw the new building as a youth, notes the significance that these rooms had for the community and how they served as emblems of the Jewish national home:

> In this tabernacle ... the original study of the father of political Zionism, Benyamin Ze'ev Herzl, was installed shortly after completion. [It was installed] in its original state: the bookstand, writing desk, the carpets, photographs and every wonderful souvenir, and the manuscript of *Der Judenstaat* was placed on a table under glass. The Golden Books were also displayed there in large glass-covered cases, each with its own unique binding...[48]

The rooms that commemorated the Zionist leader and Jewish donors worldwide further constituted spaces that suggested the ZEB's link with the Jewish diaspora,

[48] Yehuda Ha'Ezrachi, *Ir, Even ve Shamayim* (Tel Aviv: Ministry of Defense, 1968), 99.

and offered additional affirmation of the ZEB's role in unifying the Jewish People. All of these spaces reflected a simplicity of design, and their formality was expressed in the use of wood panelling (Figure 5.13), as well as the extra attention to such details as metal fittings, curtains and upholstery.

The Central Zionist Archive (CZA) also had its first permanent home in the ZEB.[49] Called the 'Berlin Archive' at the time, placing it in the building created the image of a progressive and democratic organisation, aware of its historic role in shaping the narrative of the political struggle over Palestine.[50] A 'secret archive' was included in the CZA,[51] the contents of which are unknown, but it is likely that it contained sensitive political documents. Security functions were also planned: in 1939 a bomb shelter was added;[52] a secret weapon storage room ('slick'), discovered only recently, was also included in the building.[53] The planning of both these spaces indicated increased attention to safety in the face of the escalating conflict.

Alongside its clear modernist iterations, some elements of the building can be defined as classicist.[54] This classicism is understated and is most apparent in its tripartite structure and elevated entrance façade, clearly seen, for example, in a sketch from 1932 (Figure 5.16). This design expressed hierarchy: emphasis on the central wing highlighted the Jewish Agency as the head of the other two organisations and separate entrances suggested each institution's relative independence. The central wing's elevated entrance also underscored this hierarchy, but the stratification was balanced and kept at bay by the building's unified design. This is significant, as this blurring of organisational boundaries reflected a sense of the unity of the Jewish People. Additional design details further demonstrated Ratner's integration of modernism and classical concepts: the portico was constructed with square pillars creating a seven-entrance colonnade, and above the balcony the windows have a pyramidal arrangement that enhances the centre.

Ratner complemented his modernist approach not only with classicism, but also with modest references to regionalism, which he created through a number of elements: first, he designed arched openings that, as I noted earlier, were reduced in number in later plans. Second, the JNF wing's eastern section – with its slanted wall and small, narrow windows – may be a reference to the walls of the Old City (Figure 5.17), as suggested by architectural historians Michael Levin and David Kroyanker.[55] In light of Ratner's use of arched entryways, this contention

---

[49] Keren Ha'Yesod to Jewish Agency, 12 April 1934, *CZA* KH4/7966.
[50] Segev and Watzman, *One Palestine, Complete*, 300.
[51] Jewish Agency to Keren Ha'Yesod, 4 July 1935, *CZA* KH4/7966.
[52] Plan for a bomb shelter, *CZA*, KH4/8467-1M, KH4/8467-2M, KH4/8467-5M.
[53] Nathan Roy, personal communication, July 2017. For the term slick, see Chapter 4, n. 104.
[54] Sosnovsky, ed., *Yohanan Ratner*, 24.
[55] Kroyanker, 'Orientali Yoter MeHaMizrach', 31; Kroyanker, *Adrichalut Bi'Yerushalayim: HaBni'ya BiTkufat HaMandat HaBriti*, 287; Michael Levin, 'Rashey Prakim LeMegamot Hatsmicha VeHaHitgabshut shel Omanut Ve'Adrichalut Mekomit', *Cathedra: For the History of Eretz Israel and Its Yishuv* 16 (1980): 200.

CONSTRUCTING ZIONIST IDENTITY

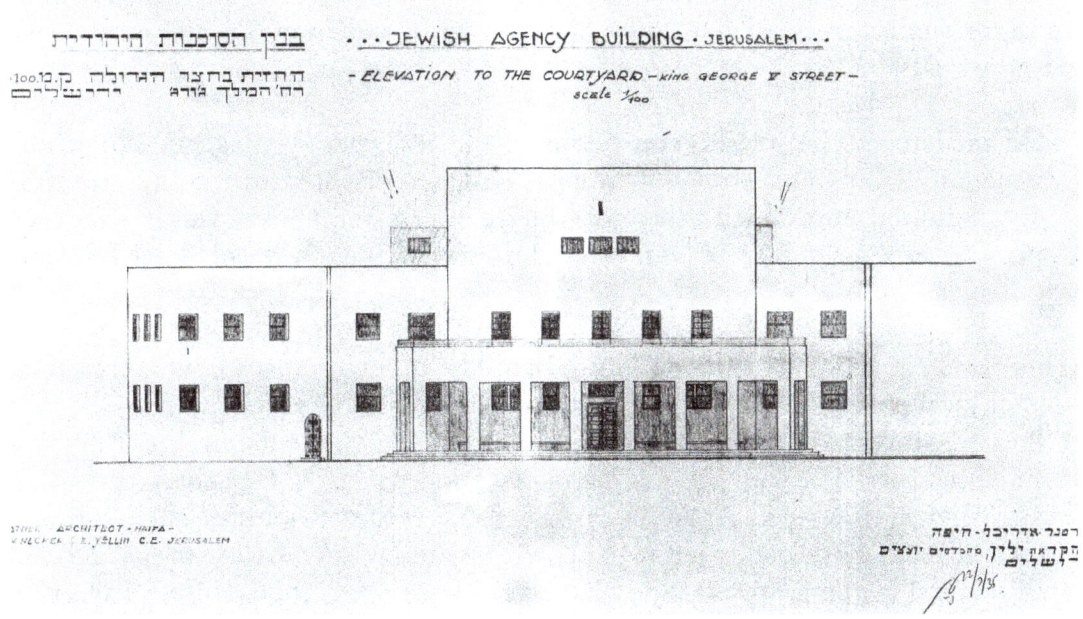

Figure 5.16 *Yohanan Ratner, Zionist Executive Building, main entrance elevation, 22 July 1932. © CZA, KH4/8468-14M.*

Figure 5.17 *Zionist Executive Building, JNF wing. Photographed by Diego Rosman.*

is plausible, although, as I note, the architect was rather critical of regionalism. A third regionalist aspect was suggested by the correspondent of the Zionist newspaper, the *Palestine Post*, who described the ZEB's street-facing court as:

> [A] modern edition of the courtyards of old Jerusalem Synagogues to which itinerant Rabbis and students from all corners of the Earth come. But this ... [building] hums with telegrams, bulging letter bags and even has its own printing press which grinds out printed matter incidental to this large business organization.[56]

This notion suggests that the building should be thought of as a novel interpretation of local precedents in the service of contemporary requirements.

Ratner's integration of classicist and regionalist elements in the ZEB was defined by Silvina Sosnovsky as 'restrained modernism'.[57] Her characterisation hints, perhaps, at early German modernist or expressionist sources, such as Bruno Taut's or Erich Mendelsohn's creations, with which Ratner, owing to his German architectural training, would surely have been familiar.[58] The architect's Western training, evident in the building's hierarchical structure, and the discourse he created with Jerusalem's traditions show that he explored the very concept of style. As I show, this questioning of the concept, even confrontation with it, was central to the evolvement of the ZEB's design.

The Question of Style and 'the Evolution of a National Architecture'

The ZEB, which was planned in 1927, was one of the first truly modernist civic-representational buildings in Palestine. The choice of functional modernism for the Zionist Movement's most representative building was not an obvious one. Zionist architecture of the 1920s was historicist, and the search for a local 'Hebrew' style took shape in Orientalist ornamentation and the use of local elements – domes or arches – eclectically integrated with other traditional components.[59] There were many submissions to the ZEB competition in this style, as well as several other modernist entries.[60]

For Ratner, receiving the ZEB commission intensified his engagement with two interrelated questions that were central to his architectural thought: first, what should the national style for Zionism and the emerging Hebrew nation be? He was in favour of modernism, thus eliciting the second question: how should

[56] 'Jewish Whitehall in Palestine', *The Palestine Post*, 11 December 1934, 4.
[57] Sosnovsky, ed., *Yohanan Ratner*, 24.
[58] I emphasise here a comparison to Mendelsohn's earlier work, including some sketches from the 1920s made for projects in Palestine. When he received commissions in Palestine, from 1934, Mendelsohn's work acquired important regional aspects alongside his modernism. See Nitzan-Shiftan, 'Contested Zionism – Alternative Modernism', 147–80.
[59] Michael Levin, 'Chamesh Gishot LaMizrach Be'Adrichalut Mekomit', *Zmanim* 96 (2006): 42–4.
[60] Kroyanker, 'Orientali Yoter MeHaMizrach', 80.

modernism be applied? In 1933, while the ZEB's newest wing was still under construction, he wrote an essay discussing architecture in Palestine in general and more specifically Zionist architecture, which was published in the local English-language periodical, *Palestine and Middle-East Economic Magazine*; the original, unedited, Hebrew manuscript has survived as well.[61] In this essay he professed his views on recent and contemporary local architecture, and his concepts serve to illuminate his plans for the ZEB.

Ratner contended that contemporary Zionist architecture could not be derived from the past, as there are no tangible remnants belonging to an ancient Hebrew 'original national style'.[62] Referencing the biblical descriptions of King Solomon's Temple, he asserted that no 'national style' ever existed.[63] He perceived the emulation of decorative elements from medieval Muslim architecture as the more 'serious experiment' in creating a national style, yet denounced it as outdated. He criticised the eclectic Orientalism of the early twentieth century 'Hebrew Style' in Tel Aviv, and complimented Zionist architects for discarding it. He disliked the Orientalism of 'the planners of the Hebrew University and the YMCA Building', which represent an importation of American culture and are 'devoid of character and as near to an Eastern style as Hollywood sets are . . .' (His coupling of the Hebrew University with American culture alongside the YMCA is interesting, considering the former building's British and Zionist planners.)[64] The one exception he made with regard to the appropriation of Muslim precedents was the work of his associate Alexander Baerwald, which he commended, as the latter employed the forms, volumes and proportions of Muslim architecture, rather than only its surfaces and decorative elements. However, Ratner wrote that even Baerwald's experimentation with the Oriental failed to meet the modern functions demanded of twentieth-century architecture.[65]

Reflecting on the styles and technologies of eras gone by, Ratner concluded that a national style does not evolve in a conscious manner; rather, it is engendered by the circumstances of place and culture and develops gradually and unintentionally.[66] He further contended that architecture, similar to technology, must be of its own time. This led him to propose modernism as the appropriate choice of style for Palestine, as well as for a Zionist national style. Opposing a conscious search for style, he predicted that a national style would materialise by referencing local environmental conditions, and that these should include climate-conscious planning, which addresses solar radiation and ventilation requirements.[67] In the ZEB,

[61] Yohanan Ratner, 'Architecture in Palestine', *Palestine and Middle-East Economic Magazine*, 7–8 (1933): 293–6, reprinted in Sosnovsky, ed., *Yohanan Ratner*; Yohanan Ratner, 'Signon Architektoni Le'umi', Yohanan Ratner Collection, Israel National Library, V 1370/12.
[62] Ratner, 'Signon Architektoni Leumi', 1.
[63] Ibid. 1.
[64] Ibid. 1–2.
[65] Ibid. 2.
[66] Ratner, 'Architecture in Palestine', 21E.
[67] Ibid. 24E.

these considerations are apparent in the deep-set windows, in the smaller windows facing east, and in the use of narrow horizontal openings, all of which serve to moderate incoming sunlight. When referring to local conditions, Ratner addressed not only climate, but also local building regulations.[68] In a 1936 article, he criticised the regulation dictating the use of stone cladding on all buildings in Jerusalem. In all likelihood, stone would probably not have been his first choice for the ZEB.[69] His emphasis on implementing modern technology in architecture resulted in the ZEB being built of reinforced concrete and modern materials, apparent in the building's volumes, proportions and flat roof, which, in a way, 'compensated' for the traditional appearance reflected in the stone facing.

Thus, according to Ratner, as an advocate of the modern style, a national style is derived from specific local conditions – both natural and regulatory, rather than from architectural traditions. A locality stripped of historicist references was, in his view, especially appropriate for a Zionist national style, as the Jewish people and their architects in Palestine emigrated from many countries and thus had diverse cultural backgrounds. Historicism, he contended, would result in a potential clash of styles that would be detrimental to good design. Modernism, on the other hand, 'brought about the creation of a common cultural language shared by all architects',[70] and in this lay its compelling advantage. Modernism could thus fulfil the central goal of Jewish rejuvenation and nation building – uniting the Jews of all the diasporas. As such, it provided Ratner with the architectural interpretation of the ZEB patrons' desire that the building represent Jewish unity. In addition to Ussishkin's speech, which I cited at the beginning of this chapter, at the cornerstone ceremony for the Keren Ha'Yesod wing, Sokolov, then president of the World Zionist Organization (WZO), stated that 'the new house will be a symbol of the unity of Israel and its allegiance to the land of Israel'.[71] The ZEB's modernism – manifested in its simple lines, understated formal entrances and almost complete lack of historical references – was thus intended to eradicate diasporic identities and limit evocations of Palestine's more recent past. Thus, the ZEB plan can be understood as an experiment in harnessing modernism for a Zionist style, anticipating the transformation that modernism effected on Jewish Zionist design of the 1930s. Indeed, by 1934, when the building's first three stages were complete, modernism had become the unrivalled design language and technological apparatus of the Yishuv. Apart from the role reserved for it by Ratner as an aesthetic agent of cultural unification, modernism manifested the Zionist community's identity as aligned with Western culture and progress.[72]

[68] Ibid. 26E.
[69] Yohanan Ratner, 'Hashpa'at Bhukey Banyan al Ha'Architektura Be'Eretz-Israel', *Habinyan BaMizrach HaKarov* 8 (1936), in Sosnovsky, ed., *Yohanan Ratner*, 80.
[70] Ratner, 'Signon Architektoni Leumi', 4.
[71] 'Hanachat Even-Hapina LeBinyan Keren Ha'Yesod', *Doar Hayom*, 18 October 1932, 3.
[72] For a discussion of Zionist adoption of Western identity via architectural culture, see Sigal Davidi, 'Ha'Adrichalut Ha'Chadasha Be'Yarid HaMizrach 1934: Havna'yat Zehut La'Yishuv Ha'Yehudi', *Israel* 24 (2016): 163–90.

Ratner's engagement with the way modernism should be applied in Palestine, and later Israel, was ongoing: is it solely an international style, he asked, 'or will national characteristics have their place in such a wide and general movement?'[73] In posing this question in the 1930s, he touched upon an issue that was gradually becoming seminal in architectural discourse.[74] In Palestine, Ratner identified two approaches to it: first, a direct application of modernism to local conditions in both form and technology, and, second, an enduring implementation of 'principles underlying the traditional Oriental style'[75] alongside modernism. Here he did not refer only to Zionist architecture and complimented Austen Harrison on his merging of the two.[76] Although careful not to commit himself to either of these two approaches, Ratner concluded that they were not in contradiction. His attempt to balance them in his architectural theory can serve as an explanation for his understated integration of local elements in the design of the ZEB. These elements, such as the two arched openings in the building's main (eastern) façade and the slanted walls of the northeastern corner (Figure 5.17), can thus be interpreted as the architect's reference to locality. The idea of a 'restrained modernism' proposed by Sosnovsky, which is expressed in the building's symmetrical main entrance (Figures 5.9 and 5.16) and the suggestive shape of a menorah at its centre, points to an approach similar to Harrison's as well. Both architects understood the balance of modernism and locality as an adherence to a certain classicism – achieved by selectively applying symmetry to the most representative parts of their buildings and by using abstracted ornamentation sparingly.

Ratner's theory included his concept of 'rational planning':[77] a building must first answer to 'function, hygiene and national economy', and it is only after these criteria have been met that its external character can be considered.[78] As Mira Warhaftig observes, the ZEB carries the full implementation of this Sullivan-derived 'form follows function' approach.[79] This is evident in the building's clear administrative organisation, attention to infrastructure, and the plan's strict adherence to budget.[80] Rational planning is first and foremost a functional approach yet, as demonstrated in Ratner's plan, the integration of traditional local structural elements does not contradict functionalism – it enhances it. 'Architecture,' Ratner wrote, 'is the physical manifestation of a nation and its ideologies.'[81] The

---

[73] Ratner, 'Architecture in Palestine', 24E.
[74] See, e.g., Kenneth Frampton's discussion of post-World War II architecture in his seminal essay 'Prospects for a Critical Regionalism', *Perspecta* 20 (1983): 147–62. See also Henry Russell-Hitchcock's discussion of the local characteristics of modern English architecture a few years later: Henry-Russell Hitchcock Jr, Catherine Bauer Wurster and Museum of Modern Art, *Modern Architecture in England* (New York: Museum of Modern Art, 1937), 38.
[75] Ratner, 'Architecture in Palestine', 25E.
[76] Ratner, 'Signon Architektoni Le'umi', 6.
[77] Ratner, 'Architecture in Palestine', 25E.
[78] Ratner, 'Signon Architektoni Le'umi', 6.
[79] Warhaftig, *They Laid the Foundation*, 300.
[80] See, e.g., from Keren Ha'Yesod to Jewish Agency, 8 July 1930, 1–2.
[81] Ratner, 'Architecture in Palestine', 20E.

architect's use of arches, the slanted wall, local stone, and possibly the court – all discernible in the ZEB's exterior – thus manifest culture and ideology, sanctioning locality and implementing it within the restraints of modernism.

'Were You Ashamed of Our Sun-tanned Skin?' – Building the ZEB

The ZEB construction project created intracommunal tension and also reflected Jewish Zionist attitudes toward intercommunal labour relations. In this section, I explore policies toward Jewish builders and reactions to them, as well as production realities and proposals that demanded hiring Arab builders despite Zionist ideologies advocating their exclusion.

Intracommunal tension relating to the project was generated by the complex relations between labour and ethnic, as well as religious, affiliations within the Jewish community. This was demonstrated, for example, in an open letter published in the daily newspaper *Doar Hayom* by Zachariah Gluska on 8 May 1929, two weeks after the cornerstone ceremony for the JNF wing was held. Gluska was chairman of the Yemenite Union and served as the Yemenite community's delegate to the Assembly of Representatives and other Zionist bodies. In his letter, Gluska vehemently protested the exclusion of the Yemenite community from the JNF ceremony. His grievances were directed at the heads of both the JNF and Keren Ha'Yesod:

> All parties and factions in Eretz-Israel were invited to the ceremony. The Yemenite Union did not receive an invitation as all the other [workers'] unions did.
>
> On the fourth day of Passover a festive meeting was held ... by Keren Ha'Yesod ... with important guests from abroad. Again [we] were not invited. The question should be raised as to why we were excluded? For what reason? Were you ashamed that the guests from abroad would see amongst you people with sun-tanned skin? Or perhaps you feared that the representatives of the Yemenite Union would tell the guests of the wrongdoings toward the Yemenite community in your National Home?[82]

Gluska concluded with a defiant declaration that the Yemenite spirit will not be broken and that their participation in nation-building will continue. This letter is testimony to the profound prejudiced sentiments attributed by the Yemenites to the Ashkenazi leadership of the Zionist Movement and reveals their keen sense of discrimination based on ethnic differences. This was but an additional aspect of the mutual suspicion that existed among Jewish sects, as well as the Yemenites' subalternity in the Yishuv and its hegemony.[83]

[82] Zachariah Gluska, 'She'ela Gluya', *Doar Hayom*, 8 May 1929, 3.
[83] Yael Guilat, 'The Yemeni Ideal in Israeli Culture and Arts', *Israel Studies* 6, no. 3 (2001): 27.

Intracommunal tensions with regard to the building project were also evident among the secular and religious workers' unions. These were engendered primarily by the latter's contestation with the hegemony of the Jewish community's leading union – the General Organization of Hebrew Workers in Eretz Israel – the Histadrut – which in itself was heterogeneous.[84] The religious Jewish community comprised, among other factions, ultra-Orthodox Jews and the Yemenites, as well as Sephardi, or Mizrahi, Jews. I use these terms here interchangeably, as they refer both to new Jewish immigrants from Arab countries as well as to the large, local Sephardi Jewish community in Palestine. Some of these sects were represented by Hapoel Hamizrahi, the religious Zionist Labor Movement's workers' union; others, such as workers from the Sephardi community, were not represented, as they did not join unions owing to political and ideological differences.[85] All of these factions perceived their treatment by the Histadrut, which represented the hegemonic, largely secular Ashkenazi community, as exclusionary.[86]

Thus, whereas the building project, similar to the Zionist institutions in charge of it, was intended to represent all Jews, the reality was that there were many instances of exclusion, which resulted from these political and ideological differences. These experiences were demonstrated first in formal gestures, or the absence of them, as in the case of Gluska's complaint. Another example was a protest letter sent to the Jewish Agency on 16 October 1932, complaining that the Jerusalem branch of Hapoel Hamizrahi was not invited to the cornerstone ceremony of the Jewish Agency wing: 'This is unprecedented!! Why indeed did you not see the need to invite us??'[87] – so wrote Y. Markowitz, the signee, concluding that Hapoel Hamizrahi nonetheless wishes for this 'house to become a center of the entire Israeli nation and will unite within it all the tribes of Israel, all its parties and factions, who together will build the Hebrew motherland in the spirit of the scriptures and their prophets'.[88]

The second aspect of these intracommunal conflicts was engendered by employment policy: one of the few extant contracts for building the ZEB specifically included a clause stating that only unionised Jewish labourers were to be employed on the project.[89] The problematic politics of such policies became

[84] Lockman, 'Land, Labor and the Logic of Zionism', 16.
[85] For a discussion of these disputes and rifts, see Yosef Gorny, 'Thoughts on Zionism as a Utopian Ideology', *Modern Judaism* 18, no. 3 (1998): 245–8; Smith, *Palestine and the Arab-Israeli Conflict*, 112–17. The political friction between Sephardi and Ashkenazi Jews in wider spheres and with relation to the Jewish–Arab conflict in Mandatory Palestine is discussed in Jacobson and Naor, *Oriental Neighbors*, 21–33.
[86] Isaac Breuer, 'HaPo'el Hacharedi Ba'Aretz', *She'arim*, 2 August 1936, 2. For a discussion of Breuer's political and religious ideology, see Israel-Vleeschhouwer, 'The Mandate System', 339–63; Monty Noam Penkower, 'A Lost Opportunity: Pre-world War II Efforts Towards Mizrachi–Agudas Israel Cooperation', *Journal of Israeli History* 17, no. 2 (1996): 221–46; Asher D. Biemann, 'Isaac Breuer: Zionist Against His Will?' *Modern Judaism* 20, no. 2 (2000): 129–46.
[87] Y. Markowitz to Jewish Agency, 16 October 1932, CZA S30/443.
[88] Ibid.
[89] This clause has survived only in one contract, but from additional correspondence and in light

apparent in, for example, a statement made by the Sephardi Executive's delegate to the Seventeenth Zionist Congress, who said that 'When considering the decision ... that the National Institutions will employ only unionized workers, we can understand why Sephardi workers suffer unemployment.'[90] General protests with regard to intracommunal exclusion were voiced constantly. In 1938, nearly a decade after the above complaint, a delegation of unemployed Mizrahi workers protested their exclusion from the construction of the ZEB's new wing.[91] The other side of these disputes lay in the actual professional stratification that existed in the Jewish labour market: European Jews had little to offer by way of much-needed construction workers,[92] and usually held planning and executive positions. Conversely, Jewish unskilled labourers were usually of Mizrahi origin, and the Jewish community in Palestine was well aware of this divide.[93]

In spite of these discourses and social realities, to say that the ZEB project's management and supervision was carried out entirely by Jews of European origin would be erroneous. As I noted earlier, the construction engineering/architectural firm of Hecker & Yellin presided over the project in more ways than just direct supervision of the construction process. Hecker was from Poland, whereas Yellin belonged to one of Palestine's foremost Sephardi families.[94] Other names that appear in project documents can perhaps hint at ethnic origins, but any deductions regarding the matter would be assumptive.

Additional aspects of the project's organisation are relevant to analysing its relationship to the construction labour market. The project's contractor was the Jewish firm Misrad Kablani, a Histadrut-affiliated construction company, which was among the biggest in the country during the 1930s, with offices in both Jerusalem and Tel

of the paramount importance of providing work for Jews in Palestine, it is safe to say that it was included in all contracts for the building's various stages. In the contract cited here, the sentence 'unionized by the General Organization of Hebrew Workers in Jerusalem' was added in handwriting, probably as a result of the employment problems discussed here and additional employment issues. See Contract between Keren Ha'Yesod and Misrad Kablani Yerushalayim [the contractor], 11 December 1934, CZA KH4/7966. For the organised structure of Jewish workers, see Lockman, *Comrades and Enemies*, 47–57.

[90] 'Tazkira shel Hitachdut HaSphardim LaCongress HaZioni HaTet-zayin', *Doar Hayom*, 22 July 1929.
[91] 'Min Hachayim Bi'Yerushalayim', *Hatzofe*, 27 February 1938, 3.
[92] Yoav Gelber, 'The Shaping of the "New Jew" in Eretz Israel', in *Major Changes within the Jewish People in the Wake of the Holocaust*, eds Yisrael Gutman and Avital Saf (Jerusalem: Yad Vashem, 1996), 447–8.
[93] For contemporary criticism of this issue, see B. Linkowsky, 'LeMatzav HaPo'el BiYerushalaim', *Davar*, 2 November 1928, 1. For a discussion of Jewish-European approaches toward Mizrahi Jews during the British Mandate period, see, e.g., Hayim Feierberg, 'Chevra Ironit BeMashber: Hivatzruta shel "HaBe'aya HaMizrachit" BeMerchav Tel Aviv VeYaffo Be'Et Me'ora'ot 1936', *Social Issue in Israel* 1 (2006): 178–81; Yehouda Shenhav, 'How did the Mizrahim "Become" Religious and Zionist? Zionism, Colonialism and the Religionization of the Arab Jew', *Israel Studies Forum* 19, no. 1 (2003): 73–87.
[94] Tidhar, *Entsiklopedyah LeHalutsei Ha'Yishuv U'Bonav*, vol. 12, 3998; vol. 2, 792. It should be noted that Yelin's mother was from Russia.

Aviv.⁹⁵ The Jerusalem branch was managed by an engineer named S. Sverdlov, who was directly in charge of the ZEB project.⁹⁶ Despite occasional arguments about monetary issues, work with Misrad Kablani ran smoothly. By 1937, when an additional set of rooms was to be added to the ZEB, David Ben-Gurion, Israel's first prime minister and, at the time, head of the Jewish Agency, personally authorised that the contract be given to Misrad Kablani without a tender.⁹⁷ Moreover, nearly all the subcontractors were Jewish.⁹⁸ As expected, Jewish dominance over the cement market in Palestine was evident here as well, and the building's reinforced concrete foundations were done by A. Gluckstein of Jerusalem.⁹⁹

The ZEB construction contract clause stating that only unionised Jewish labourers would be hired also had significant ramifications regarding hiring workers from the Arab Palestinian community. According to Zachary Lockman, Zionist ideologies and policies pertaining to the Arab and Jewish labour markets in Palestine were complex and were articulated differently depending on the situation.¹⁰⁰ As a highly representative edifice both ideologically and spatially, the ZEB project reflected those aspects of Zionist ideology that promoted Jewish work in all sectors of economic activity.¹⁰¹ Numerous factors, however, prevented the practical implementation of this ideology. As I discussed in Chapter Two, Arab labourers were paid lower wages and worked longer hours, making it difficult for Jews to compete with them.¹⁰² According to an article in the Zionist labour newspaper, *Davar*, special measures were taken in Jerusalem specifically to ensure the hiring of Jewish construction workers in light of this effective Arab competition.¹⁰³

In the face of these realities, Hebrew labour, one of the most sanctified values of political Zionism, was evident in the ZEB project to a relatively large degree and appears to have been strongly enforced. However, although the project was expected to be a trailblazer of the economic separatism between Jews and Arabs, its executives could not entirely avoid hiring Arab workers. As with other economic spheres in Palestine, which have been studied by such scholars as Lockman and Gershon Shafir,¹⁰⁴ despite efforts and propaganda, exclusive Jewish labour did not

---

⁹⁵ 'Hitpatchuto Shel HaMisrad HaKablani BeT'A [in Tel Aviv]', *Davar*, 15 April 1934, 1.
⁹⁶ See ample additional correspondence and contracts in *CZA* KH4/7966.
⁹⁷ Minutes of the Building Committee, 3 March 1937, 3, *CZA* S1/198.
⁹⁸ Contract between Paul Huerbet and Keren Ha'Yesod, 28 May 1935; contract between Isaac Schpitzen, n.d., both *CZA* KH4/7966. See also payment sheets with details of subcontractors and additional correspondence in *CZA* KH4/7966 and S1/199.
⁹⁹ JNF to Zionist Executive, 16 June 1930; A. Gluckstein to Technical Department of the Zionist Executive, 17 June 1930; Pinchas Ben-Eliezer (Hecker-Yellin) to Jewish Agency (?), 15 October 1930. All *CZA* S1/198.
¹⁰⁰ Lockman, 'Land, Labor and the Logic of Zionism', 9–38; Lockman, *Comrades and Enemies*, 68–72.
¹⁰¹ There is ample research discussing this ideology. See, e.g., Gelber, 'The Shaping of the "New Jew" in Eretz Israel', 443–61.
¹⁰² Lockman, *Comrades and Enemies*, 57.
¹⁰³ B. Linkowsky, 'LeMatsav HaPo'el BiYerushalaim', *Davar*, 2 November 1928, 1.
¹⁰⁴ Lockman, *Comrades and Enemies*, 47–57; Shafir, *Land, Labor, and the Origins of the Israeli-Palestinian Conflict*, 199–202, 215–17.

materialise fully in the ZEB construction project. In his memoirs, Ratner wrote that in the summer of 1929, in the wake of the violence between Arabs and Jews and the Hebron massacre, many of the Arab labourers did not show up for work, which is a clear indication that Arabs were included in the crew that was constructing the first wing.[105] Ratner himself clearly supported the principle of Jewish labour and addressed recurring shortages of Jewish workers in his business correspondence with Zionist institution executives.[106] This correspondence suggests that Arab workers probably participated in the project throughout its duration.

An important Zionist initiative that further evidences the complex politics with regard to the Arab labour market was the establishment of a 'Joint Bureau for Arab Relations' by the Jewish Agency and the Jewish National Council (JNC).[107] Created in June 1931, this bureau was intended chiefly to develop relationships with Muslim and Christian Palestinians. A confidential report that declared intentions to foster economic cooperation noted:

> It is suggested that the principle formulated as follows by the Joint Bureau should be adopted: 'there should be no declared boycott or organized exclusion of Arab workers or employees from Jewish undertakings, by which, however, it is not intended to justify any interference with the right of Jewish groups to organize themselves socially and economically on a purely Jewish basis if they so desire'.[108]

In September 1931, the *Palestine Bulletin* published key aspects of the Joint Bureau initiative based on a statement that Haim Arlosoroff, head of the political department of the Jewish Agency, made to the press. Although the bureau was apparently short-lived (just like Arlosoroff himself, whose unsolved murder may have been motivated by his pacifist actions),[109] the construction market, in which hiring only Jews was nearly impossible, likely benefited from this new conciliatory approach. The bureau's advocacy seems to have affected the ZEB project as well and provides a partial explanation for the constant presence of Arab workers on the project during the early 1930s.

An important aspect of Arab labour was the quarrying of stones. The stone industry operated with significant Jewish–Arab cooperation, rendering exclusive Jewish production virtually impossible. This amalgamation also ignited intracommunal tensions: for example, the Histadrut blamed Jewish Mizrahi excavators for

---

[105] Yohanan Ratner, *Chayay Ve'Ani*, trans. Rina Klinov (Jerusalem: Schocken, 1978), 230.
[106] Ratner to Keren Ha'Yesod Executive/Jewish Agency Technical Department, 12 March 1934, 1–2, *CZA* S30/443; Ratner to Reiser, 11 May 1930, *CZA* S1/198.
[107] 'General Report on the Constitution and Work of the Joint Bureau of Jewish Public Bodies in Palestine', 62. *NAGB* CO 733/207/8.
[108] Ibid. 62.
[109] Arlosoroff's murder on 17 June 1933, shocked the Yishuv, and has since been the subject of much public and academic debate. See, e.g., Zeev, 'The Struggle between the Revisionist Party and the Labor Movement: 1929–1933', *Modern Judaism* 8, no. 1 (1988): 22.

hiring Arab subcontractors, and thus 'conspiring' to uproot the Hebrew quarry industry.[110] Additional evidence of the imbrication of the Arab and Jewish stone-working enterprises was the establishment of a joint Arab–Jewish stone-grinding syndicate in 1929, even as hostilities were on the rise.[111] Hence, with regard to the ZEB, it seems highly unlikely that only Jews quarried stones. According to the *Palestine Post*, quarrying for the ZEB began at the Beit Safafa Arab quarry,[112] and judging by other press reports, it is quite likely that other Arab quarries were occasionally used.[113] Nevertheless, in 1931 *Davar* reported that the JNF building was built entirely with 'Hebrew excavation'.[114] Whereas such reports in the Hebrew news are not entirely reliable, they do demonstrate the immense importance attached to quarrying, which was perceived as the physical enactment of the abstract concept of nation-building. When not carried out by Jews, the task of quarrying was labelled *'avoda zara'* – a harsh biblical term meaning idolatry that was secularised and used to condemn hiring Arabs.[115]

Ratner noted that choosing a grey, rather than a pink, local stone for the building led to the establishment of the first Jewish quarry in the Kastel, west of Jerusalem,[116] which in fact followed upon an earlier Jewish quarry in Jerusalem, established in 1926 by Solel Boneh. Ratner's statement reifies the significant Jewish efforts invested in getting into this branch of the city's building industry.[117] The Kastel quarry introduced advanced technology that reduced the quantity of cement use during facing.[118] This quarry thus integrated tradition and innovation in building techniques, improving on the combination of stone and cement that, owing to the stone-facing ordinance, was required in Jerusalem's modernist architecture. For the ZEB, modernist in all aspects of design, this would have

---

[110] 'Machrimim Muv'hakim Chotrim Tachat Kibushey HaPo'el Ha'Ivri BeMikzoah Ha'even', *Davar*, 25 April 1937, 1. Complaints against Mizrahi excavators apparently had much earlier roots, and a similar dispute was reported as early as in 1924. See 'Hamizrachi VeHa'Avoda Ha'Ivrit', *Doar Hayom*, 24 September 1924. Many additional articles were published in *Davar* during the project's years. See also, e.g., 'Chotrim Tachat Kiyum HaChotzev Ha'Ivri', *Davar*, 5 April 1937, 1; 'Even mikir Tiza'ak', *Davar*, 30 April 1936, 1.

[111] 'BeCharoshet Ha'Even HaTchuna', *Davar*, 8 July 1929, 1.

[112] 'Jewish Whitehall in Palestine', *The Palestine Post*, 11 December 1934, 4.

[113] 'Ha'Yuchram HaChotzev Ha'Ivri?', *Davar*, 11 June 1931, 1; one of the buildings mentioned in this report, the Hebrew Teachers Seminary, had been the centre of a fierce protest as 'Arab stone' had been used for its construction. See 'Ha'Yibane HaSeminar Ha'Ivri Even lo Ivrit?', *Davar*, 25 February 1927, 1.

[114] 'Ha'Yuchram HaChotzev Ha'Ivri?', *Davar*, 11 June 1931, 1

[115] 'Ha'Yibane HaSeminar Ha'Ivri Even lo Ivrit?', *Davar*, 25 February 1927, 1; Hadassa Kantor, 'Current Trends in the Secularization of Hebrew', *Language in Society* 21, no. 4 (1992): 607.

[116] Sosnovsky, ed., *Yohanan Ratner*, 26, 96.

[117] 'LeHitpatchut Haroshet Ha'Even Ha'Ivrit', *Davar*, 30 July 1926, 1.

[118] 'Be'it Charoshet Meshuchlal Le'Even Le'Yad Yerushalayim', *Davar*, 22 October 1934, 1. In later stages of the building process, another Jewish quarry and stone-processing plant was established. This enterprise, called 'Even' (the Hebrew word for stone), was funded in part by the JNF and established by leading construction firms, among them Misrad Kablani; Sverlov was on its board of directors. Thus, it is logical to assume that this was another quarry and plant capable of supplying stones for the additional wings. See '"Even" – Mif'al Halutzi Chashuv', *Davar*, 20 April 1937, 1.

been extremely beneficial for speed and economy. It thus becomes clear that employment aspects of the construction process were intimately connected to the building's significance as one of the major Jewish enterprises in Palestine and as a symbol of Jewish unity. Employment issues revealed the complex intra-communal politics that impacted both the economic and the cultural aspects of architectural production. Moreover, employment in the ZEB project further demonstrated the ambiguous and complicated approaches toward the Muslim and Christian Palestinian communities and their participation in the construction industry.

'A Jewish Whitehall in Palestine'

While writing his memoirs, Ratner remembered his thoughts when he received the exciting news that he had won the ZEB competition:

> Should the building be erected ... it will be a creation that will justify my past decision ... that my life will not be guided by the coincidental events of this century, but by the aspiration toward artistic creation.[119]

As I noted earlier, the ZEB, Ratner's first major independent commission, was an ongoing project that gradually enlarged over time. The subsequent additions to the building demanded not only his services but also those of his son, Michael, who followed in his father's footsteps and became an architect.

That the building achieved its symbolic and representative function is clear from the fact that it was chosen as the venue for so many ceremonies, such as bringing the first fruits for the celebration of the Jewish holiday of Shavuot (Figure 5.18), Herzl Day, and more.[120] In the spring of 1937, the building was festively decorated for the coronation of British King George VI, and over the years Yishuv leaders have been commemorated there as well.[121] Of no lesser importance was the fact that the building became a site of political activism, at times violent. Mass Zionist demonstrations were held in the courtyard; Arabs attempted attacks, and the one car-bomb that exploded there during the 1948 war destroyed the second floor of the Keren Ha'Yesod wing, killing twelve people. Ultra-Orthodox protesters flung stones on occasion, and the Zionist right-wing Beitar Movement broke the entrance windows during one of their demonstrations.[122] Perhaps the most momentous political demonstration at the ZEB was the gathering of thou-

---

[119] Ratner, *Chayay Ve'Ani*, 228.
[120] 'Yom Herzl', *Davar*, 4 July 1934, 1. This is also described by Yehuda Ha'Ezrachi in *Ir, Even ve Shamayim*, 99.
[121] 'Floodlit Jerusalem', *The Palestine Post*, 13 May 1937, 5; 'Hayom – Levayato shel HaBaron Rothschild', *Davar*, 5 November 1934.
[122] 'Machar Mishpat nose HaPzazas SheNitpas Le'Yad HaSochnut', *Haboker*, 6 February 1989, 6; 'Al Hadar-beytar Ufri Hadar Shelo B'Yerushalayim', *Davar*, 16 February 1937, 1.

Figure 5.18 *Zionist Executive Building, kindergarten children at a Shavuot holiday ceremony in the entrance court, 1935. Photographed by Avraham Malevsky. © Jewish National Fund Archive, Glass40-13.*

sands to rejoice on 29 November 1947, when the United Nations voted in favour of establishing a Jewish State in Palestine.

'The Jewish Whitehall in Palestine' – so the ZEB was described in the *Palestine Post* in 1934.[123] Using the British government's building in London as a metaphor emphasised yet again not only the ZEB's function when erected, but also the projection that it would serve a Jewish government in the near future. Moreover, in its frugal, unadorned functionalism and understated, introverted symbolism, the ZEB provides the most significant and crucial evidence of the turn to modernism in Jewish Zionist visual culture for defining a national identity.

---

[123] 'Jewish Whitehall in Palestine', *The Palestine Post*, 11 December 1934, 4.

Conclusion: Buildings, Communities

THE TITLE OF this concluding chapter, which has a comma between the words 'buildings' and 'communities', is my way of contending that when one sets out to explore Jerusalem's architectural culture during the British Mandate (1917–48), one has to begin by asking to what degree does the act of building construct communities or set them apart. The separation of these two words also suggests that buildings invite reactions, either celebratory or condemnatory, from the communities that share their space. In this book, I have attempted to reveal those interactions, which involved planning practices, designing and constructing, as well as the relationship between architecture and urbanism.

My goals in this research were threefold: first, to explicate the architecture of four buildings that were and still are landmarks in Jerusalem's urban space; second, to demonstrate how these edifices, built during the British Mandate, constructed distinct communal and national identities; and third, to locate these case studies within the broader scope of early twentieth-century architecture. My intent in probing the last was to provide new insights regarding the development of international modernism and the ways in which the modern movement transformed historicism and engaged vernacular and local architectures. In the following pages, I elaborate on the way each building reflected these processes. I conclude with some thoughts about their presence in Jerusalem today.

British and American Projects

The Palestine Archaeological Museum and the Jerusalem YMCA were civic and public buildings whose architecture expressed British and American cultural authority. They represented British and American identities, as well as their Christianity. The design and construction and of both buildings were led by British and American architects and functionaries, who integrated modernist, historicist and local architectural traditions.

As a British initiative, the Archeological Museum manifested first and foremost the British perception of themselves as guardians of cultural heritage, as represented through archaeological evidence. It further reflected the British conviction that Palestine's publics – whether native or immigrant – required education by way of cultural institutions such as museums. This conviction was also apparent in their intensive engagement in planning Jerusalem's urban space. In this context, the museum was envisioned as part of the effort to modernise the city through its institutions. Both practices – the urban and the museological – reflected the deep appreciation that the British had for Jerusalem's histories and religions. Both the city plans and the museum created an image of the British as neutral custodians of Jerusalem and its communities, an image that set the mandatory situation apart from the colonial condition, making it a separate and distinct phenomenon. However, the introduction of these aspects of Western planning, science and culture to Jerusalem was grounded in colonial rule: the British controlled the urban space and manipulated the production of knowledge, realigning modern progress vis-à-vis ancient communal heritages and religions. The American involvement in the museum was in the persons of Rockefeller and Breasted, who had a profound impact on the building's design, as well as on the museum's curatorial practices.

The Americans, while lacking imperial legacies, nonetheless expressed cultural authority in their involvement in the Archaeological Museum and in bringing the YMCA's ecumenical multicultural approach to Jerusalem. The key roles that Americans played in developing Jerusalem's culture through these two institutions evinced America's rise as a significant power in the interwar period. American fortunes provided for a powerful urban presence in Jerusalem through architecture.

In earlier chapters, I indicated that both the YMCA and the Archaeological Museum introduced new building typologies to Palestine, reflecting the global spread of Western modern civic culture. One can argue that there were pilgrim hostels, and I discussed them as precedents for the YMCA Building; one can also reference the museum established by the Ottomans or even the Zionist Tower of David exhibitions as forerunners of the Archaeological Museum.[1] However, pilgrim hostels in Jerusalem did not function as modern intercommunal community centres, and no exhibition space was comparable to the Archaeological Museum in size, modern museum design, and research-based curatorship.

My premises in analysing these British and American buildings were that their plan, form and construction were grounded in Western architectural culture and that the architects and designers used this as a framework for relating to Jerusalem's and Palestine's communities by enlisting local architectural practices and traditions. Research revealed three guiding principles for this adaptive process. First, Mediterranean and Middle Eastern elements were utilised alongside modern Western components in planning spaces designated for modern functions: in the Archaeological Museum, the arcaded courtyard and domed exhibition halls serve as outstanding examples of this principle. In the Jerusalem YMCA, it is evident in the domed gymnasium and auditorium, as well as in the tower; the tower dome

---

[1] For a discussion of these exhibitions, see Graciela Trajtenberg, 'Be'in Burganut Le'Omanut Palestinit BiTkufat HaMandat', *Israeli Sociology* D, no. 1 (2002): 14–15.

resembled a minaret, yet its height, which exceeds by far the ancient towers of the Old City and those of more recent edifices, renders its modern technology explicit. This brings us to the second adaptation principle: merging modern construction technologies with traditional methods; reinforced concrete was used alongside locally excavated stone, its construction technologies and facing styles. Tiling, reliefs and mosaics were also utilised. The third principle relates to modern sculptural ornamentation of the buildings, which in Chapter Three I termed *figurative modernism*. This included the use of Art Deco elements identified in inscriptions and reliefs in the two buildings, as well as more classical approaches, which are apparent in the YMCA arcade capitals.

In the eclectic use of Middle Eastern and local elements, the buildings' architecture represents an enduring engagement with historicism. The Archaeological Museum was described by contemporary correspondents as 'a modern interpretation of ancient Arab Architecture',[2] as a 'merging of local character with the building's functional requirements',[3] and as 'a happy blend of Eastern and Western Architecture'.[4] In 1933 the YMCA was featured in the *Illustrated London News* alongside Harrison's Government House, a modernist 'concrete villa' designed by Zionist architect Dov Karmi, and an additional villa in the Rehavia neighbourhood, described as 'modern in style but built with primitive methods'.[5] These descriptions imply that to contemporary eyes, new architecture in Jerusalem was considered modern and up to date. Further, the buildings' hybrid styles and the architects' reliance on historic and vernacular Middle Eastern models were clearly acknowledged. Harrison used these models to express the region's multi-histories yet abstracted them in order to underscore multiculturalism and avoid overt manifestations of ownership assigned to a specific community or religion. He aligned abstracted historicism with modernism and blended Palestine's past cultures into a formal unity that suggested present and future coexistence.

In the Jerusalem YMCA Building, Harmon used historicism to represent the three monotheistic religions, as well as a local – both sacred and secular – architectural vocabulary. He deliberately imported to Jerusalem trends in the design of American hotels and negotiated changing concepts in the planning of sacred spaces. His utilisation of historicism was less abstract than Harrison's. This can be seen in the building's domes, tower and arcade, but his use of these forms alongside Art Deco elements in the context of a large-scale contemporary complex produced a novel formulation that balanced the building's historical and modernist components.

[2] Madeleine Miller, 'Al Ha'Atika BaMuse'on HeChadash', *Doar Hayom*, 28 January 1936, 2.
[3] 'Museum Ha'Atikot Bi'Yerushalayim', *Davar*, 25 February 1938, 1.
[4] 'Jerusalem's New Treasure House', *The Sphere*, 2 April 1938, 20.
[5] 'The New Jerusalem – Without Walls: The YMCA Building and Other Recent Developments', *Illustrated London News*, 15 April 1933, 526–7.

Palestinian and Zionist Projects

As I showed earlier, the construction of the Palace Hotel and the Zionist Executive Building (ZEB) were of the utmost importance for the Muslim Palestinian community and the Jewish Zionist community, respectively. The latter differed from the other three buildings I discuss in this book, in that it served only the Jewish community. The Palace Hotel also stands out as the one building among the four that had a clear commercial designation in addition to its ideological and political significance. The two communities erected these buildings in efforts to reinforce their claims to Jerusalem, which were central for constructing their respective identities. In effect, architecture played a crucial role in grounding these claims.

The architecture of the Palace Hotel integrated Muslim heritage with a modern building typology, and this was facilitated by implementing Turkish architectural theory and practice. Carried out by the architect Nigisberk in consultation with the building's patrons, the hotel's design demonstrated a complex exchange of ideas between Mandatory Jerusalem and the Turkish Republic. In my study of the hotel, I argued that the construction of Muslim Palestinian identity was achieved by selecting iconic historical sources of inspiration from the Haram al-Sharif. In selecting these highly sanctioned local precedents, the secular hotel transformed sacred symbolic spaces into manifestations of cultural heritage and political assets. As such, it contributed to the formation of Palestinian national identity and provided a response to parallel processes of identity formation in the Zionist community. Built in the tradition of the urban grand hotel, the Palace's style was historicist, but it included some elements of contemporary Art Deco design, which served as the aesthetic expression of the hotel's modern functions and construction technology.

Of the four buildings researched for this book, the ZEB – an office space – reflects the clearest adaptation of international modernism. This can be seen in Ratner's pure geometries, uninterrupted and uniform stone-setting, and remarkably sparse use of decorative elements. In his design approach, this emerging architect anticipated many of his contemporaries in Palestine. According to modernist concepts, Ratner's use of historic precedents in the building's volumes, entrances and shading devices was clearly subservient to function. His approach was comparable to Harrison's in the abstraction of traditional elements, but he took his abstractions a step further.

Engaging Modernism, Historicism and Local Traditions

A comparison of the four buildings indicates that although each architect used traditional elements, each had a different conception of historicism as a means for creating volume vis-à-vis its use as a decorative device. These differing approaches call for a more nuanced interpretation of how architects practising in the interwar years engaged historicism in the face of voices calling for its abandonment in light of rapidly changing design and construction technologies. They further demonstrate that historicism was no longer a totalising notion – a *gesamtkunstwerk* requiring representation in every aspect of the building. Moreover, in this multicultural and multifaith city, architects developed several strategies for the construction of identity and meaning. The inclusive cultural contents of the Palestine Archaeological Museum and the Jerusalem YMCA were expressed using components related to the histories and religions of the region, with an emphasis on Muslim architecture, which was the one Western architects most identified with the Middle East. As I noted above, Harrison's strategy implemented significant abstraction, whereas Harmon's was figurative and more explicit. Nigisberk's approach to the design of the Palace Hotel involved significant emphasis on façade treatment, which relied on Ottoman and Turkish historicist elements, which the architect integrated with local Muslim components. This approach connected Muslim Palestinian architecture with the larger sphere of Arab and Ottoman Middle Eastern architectural practice and production. Ratner's restrained use of historic elements implies his recognition of the inherent contradiction in appropriating local architectural heritage – usually identified as Muslim and rarely seen as distinctly Jewish – for the construction of Zionist identity. In order to resolve this contradiction, he adopted modernism, framed as *international* and implemented it as a *national* geographically specific style. This strategy is an early and remarkable example of the global transformations that characterised post-World War II international modernism. It anticipated modernism's central role in the architectural culture of new nations and the construction of their national identities through its adaptation, interpretation and diversification.[6]

It is noteworthy that in Jerusalem all these strategies employed selective processes and engendered lively debates with regard to the decorative and formal components of each building. Harrison considered different dome typologies; Harte, the YMCA secretary, feared direct imitation of minarets; Nigisberk carefully eliminated Turkish domestic elements in bringing revivalism to the Palace Hotel; and Ratner reduced the number of arches in his final design for the ZEB. All of these decisions suggest an intense engagement with questions of identity, as well as a constant reassessment of how Jerusalem's publics would receive the buildings.

Another important factor inherent in these processes is the differentiation between historicism and the use of Jerusalem and Palestine's vernacular architecture. Historicism relied on ancient and established precedents, such as Ottoman-style mosques, domes of iconic sacred buildings, famed palatial courtyards such as

---

[6] For examples in the Middle East, see Meltem Gürel, 'Modernization and the Role of Foreign Experts: W. M. Dudok's Projects for Izmir, Turkey', *Journal of the Society of Architectural Historians* 77, no. 2 (2018): 204–22; Nezar AlSayyad, 'Culture, Identity and Urbanism: A Historical Perspective from Colonialism and Globalization', in *Colonial Modern: Aesthetics of the Past-Rebellions for the Future*, eds Tom Avermaete, Serhat Karakayali and Marion Von Osten (London: Black Dog, and Berlin: Haus der Kulturen der Welt, 2010), 80–2.

the Alhambra, cloisters, stone-carved architectural details, and more. Vernacular inspiration was reflected in using locally derived arches and low and dwelling-type domes and facing the buildings with local stone. Historicist elements clearly overlap vernacular features in certain cases, yet the latter were often specific, recognisable and crucial in the construction of identity. Emphasis on vernacular architecture is apparent especially in Harrison's and Ratner's buildings. Harrison used domes derived from dwellings for the museum, whereas Ratner placed emphasis on climate-conscious planning as an expression of the ZEB's locality. Arches cannot be unequivocally identified as local, yet in all four buildings they were appropriated to display connection to place.

A word should be added with regard to locally excavated stone. It, too, was used to express locality, along with the conviction that stones provide tangible evidence of the city's past and inscribe traditional architecture on modern buildings. In all four buildings, stone was delegated to a largely aesthetic function, as most of the construction was based on concrete technologies. Thus, stone facing in effect stripped modernism of one of its foremost principles – the explicit use of new materials – in its interwar interpretation. It is important to remind ourselves once again that the use of stone was prescribed by a British city ordinance. This diligently enforced edict testifies that structures of power reasserted themselves in the mandatory situation and in some respects were no less authoritative and controlling than those of colonial rule.

The introduction of new typologies, technologies and formal approaches imported from the West, the reassessment of local and regional historicism, and a novel engagement with locality and vernacular traditions all spoke of an encounter that involved multiple processes of assimilation. Analysing these processes offers important insights regarding the adaptation of modernism not only in Jerusalem, but in the broader Middle Eastern, and even global, perspective. It reaffirms recent scholarship that has identified a cultural exchange between modernism and the architecture of the wider Mediterranean region – a region partially intersecting with that of the Middle East and Palestine.[7] However, the present research reveals additional matrices of these phenomena. This can be seen in the adoption of Art Deco as a modernist model – a phenomenon not exclusive to the Middle East.[8] Another aspect revealed here is the importation of American and Turkish architectural models in addition to the more widely acknowledged use of European and British examples. Identifying these compelling architectural practices provides an additional dimension to understanding processes of cultural exchange. It disturbs familiar characterisations of modernism, as well as accepted premises of architectural 'migrations'. The architecture of Mandatory Jerusalem thus adds novel perspectives to our understanding of the architecture of the first

---

[7] Nitzan-Shiftan, 'Contested Zionism – Alternative Modernism', 147–80; Lejeune and Sabatino eds, *Modern Architecture and the Mediterranean*.
[8] Michael Windover, 'Exchanging Looks: "Art Dekho" Movie Theatres in Bombay', *Architectural History* 52 (2009): 201–32.

half of the twentieth century and to its wide-ranging implications for the ensuing, post-World War II, architectural culture.[9]

Finally, design processes taking place in Jerusalem were evidence of alternative concepts of centre versus periphery. Architects and patrons regarded London or New York as *metropole*, yet looked toward Egypt for specific facilities; others regarded Istanbul or Ankara as their imperial centre-turned-periphery model, whereas Continental Europe, more so Germany in this case, was perceived as the locus of international modernism. In considering this plurality of centres, it is instructive to think about Jerusalem as a major spiritual centre of Judaism, Christianity and Islam: the city has historically evidenced famous local architecture and has always harboured spatial practices related to each of these religions. Hence, Jerusalem's unique character surely encouraged a broad outlook toward several centres of architectural production, as well as a thorough consideration of its buildings and monuments. As such, Jerusalem's architecture suggests a re-examination of how distinct sites of production should be relationally positioned. It demonstrates that in defining centre and periphery, several sets of criteria should be applied – criteria that should include material culture and spiritual assets, as well as the interactions among individuals and groups.

Communities

The production of representative architecture among groups competing for urban space was a key aspect in Jerusalem's political, cultural and commercial development. Architecture provided a nexus between communities, despite rivalry among them and contestation of British authority. The representative buildings discussed here thus had a major impact on intercommunal and intracommunal relations.

As we have seen, competition for location and prominence in Jerusalem was intense. A telling example can be found in a letter written by the American architect Dimmock, who, during his visit to Jerusalem, noted the YMCA builders' effort to overshadow the King David Hotel being built across the street and 'menacing' in its grandeur and speed of construction.[10] Dimmock confessed to one of the New York YMCA executives: 'I have not yet had a chance to see much of the city with the exception of the King David Hotel, which I swear at in a thoroughly

---

[9] For research of post-World War II modernism in the Middle East, see, e.g., Çelik, *Urban Forms and Colonial Confrontation*, 130–80; Monique Eleb, 'An Alternative to Functionalist Universalism: Ecochard, Candilis and ATBAT-Afrique', in *Anxious Modernisms: Experimentation in Postwar Architectural Culture*, eds Sarah Williams Goldhagen and Réjean Legault (Montreal: Canadian Centre for Architecture, Cambridge, MA: MIT Press, 2000), 55–71; Neta Feniger and Rachel Kallus, 'Israeli Planning in the Shah's Iran: A Forgotten Episode', *Planning Perspectives* 30, no. 2 (2015): 231–51.

[10] Ohad Smith, 'Hotel Design in British Mandate Palestine', 102–6; Shoval and Cohen-Hattab, 'Urban Hotel Development Patterns', 916.

un-YMCA manner every day.'[11] His expression is one of many that reflect the urgency of inscribing presence in the city's space, even by the Americans, who particularly strove to promote cohabitation and coexistence. On the other 'tracks' of this race to build, among others, I can again mention the Muslim assembly purposely convened on the day of the American Christian building's dedication so as to reduce attendance there;[12] and as I noted in Chapter Five, Ratner dismissively called the YMCA a 'Hollywood set'.[13]

The four buildings I deal with here were built between 1924 and 1935, a decade that witnessed profound political changes in Palestine and a serious turn for the worse in Jewish–Arab relations.[14] It was also a time when many projects were undertaken in the rapidly growing city, where, in the midst of ongoing political tensions, architecture and the construction business represented a site of intercommunal interaction, where individuals from every community developed creative and practical discourses with regard to the planning, design and execution of buildings.

For the Archaeological Museum, the British employed Harrison, one of their own, and British architects aided him in the planning. Any additional impact on the plans, as I noted above, came from the Americans. From a British perspective, this managerial policy was intended to prevent sectarian contestations that would have been triggered by selecting an architect identified with the Jews or the Arabs. Moreover, by not contracting local Jews and/or Arabs to oversee construction, the British again sought to reflect an impartial image. As we have seen, these policies aroused British criticism from home and did not appease the local communities. The construction itself was carried out by both Jews and Arabs, a policy clearly intended to promote coexistence, which was guarded by the British and scrutinised by the communities themselves.

In contrast, for the YMCA project the firm of ʿAwaḍ, Dunie & Katinka was chosen as the contractors in order to express the association's fostering of intercommunal cooperation. Moreover, YMCA executives initiated a critical discourse with Jerusalem's communities. Their consultations with local architects, as well as the constant reassessment of public reaction to the building's architecture, can thus be understood as a desire to create an image of liberal and inclusive American patronage of the building project and, through it, to enlist local support. Apart from the YMCA's construction process, its directors and its architect saw its architecture and curriculum as offering an opportunity for redefining the cohabitation of the various communities in the Holy City. From this aspect, the building was an early, perhaps pioneering, example of design and function that expressed

---

[11] Letter from Dimmock to McMillan, 8 September 1932, 3, Jerusalem General Correspondence, 1931–2, *KFYA*.
[12] Matthews, *Confronting an Empire*, 182.
[13] Ratner, 'Signon Architektoni Le'umi', Yohanan Ratner Collection, Israel National Library, V 1370/12, 1–2.
[14] Smith, *Palestine and the Arab-Israeli Conflict*, 111–12, 119–42.

the concept of diversity, which has become central to many late twentieth- and twenty-first-century cultures.

Both the Palace Hotel and the ZEB shaped intracommunal relations no less than their reaffirmation of their communal presence in the urban space. This could be seen in the intracommunal tensions between Ashkenazi and Sephardi Jews and religious and secular Jews that were ignited by the ZEB project. The same was observed in clan and political allegiances among the Muslims with relation to the building of the Palace Hotel. Both these projects were intercommunal in their execution, but in their architecture and use both the Palace Hotel and the ZEB reflected sectarian identities and were frequented mostly by members of their own publics.

For the Muslim Palestinian community, the 'Palace' was much more than a hotel: it was their new, modern representative building. Although secular, the hotel related spatially and ideologically to religious activity as embodied by the traditions and policies of the Awqaf. This reciprocity supports Jacobson's argument that Palestinian categories of community and religion were complex and flexible.[15] The evolvement of the hotel as an Awqaf project was intended to create broad intracommunal support in the face of internal political rivalries. In light of these rivalries and the Zionist–Arab conflict, the Jewish involvement in the management and execution of the project was remarkable and demonstrates an arguably unparalleled case of intercommunal cooperation. Such cooperation underscored the inherent contradiction between the desire to build advanced and impressive buildings speedily and Muslim politics, which adamantly opposed Zionism.

Of all four buildings discussed in this book, the ZEB least embraced cross-cultural iterations in its style and its building process and purpose. As I have shown, on the management level efforts were made to keep this project a Jewish one, efforts that may have been mitigated for a brief period with the establishment of the Zionist 'Joint Bureau for Arab Relations'. Moreover, the project was not exempt from the dynamics of construction in Palestine, which generated joint markets where exchange between Zionists and Arabs was routine. The attempts to reaffirm the principle of Jewish labour posited the ZEB as a project that aggravated intercommunal and intracommunal tensions. The exclusion of Sephardi, Yemenite and religious communities from both the ceremonial and occupational dimensions of the ZEB project reflected practices and discourses of ethnic and religious discrimination that were present in the political, economic and cultural spheres of the Yishuv. Thus, the construction of its most representative building, which was expected to unite Jewish subcultures, did not achieve this important goal.

All four buildings shaped these communities and were shaped by them. Tension, contestation and cooperation all surfaced in their construction and design pro-

[15] Jacobson, *From Empire to Empire*, 180.

cesses. Further, in light of their prominence as newly defined, powerful and symbolic spatial manifestations, their construction became an important platform for discourses and interactions. When completed, the buildings irrevocably changed Jerusalem's cityscape, and in form and meaning each edifice provided an unprecedented visual identity for its community in an era that proved to be crucial for all of them, both in Palestine and on the world stage.

Fish and Chips in Pita

On a hot summer day in June 2018, the English-language version of the local Israeli Jerusalem newspaper *Kol Ha'Ir* reported that a new fish bar serving fish and chips, the food 'most identified with British cuisine' has opened in the Jerusalem Mall.[16] Why serve fish and chips in Jerusalem? The owners contended that the incentive to serve the popular British dish in the city was that it was invented by a Jew.[17] 'We offer . . . mixed fish in pita, fish shwarma in pita, fish kebab in pita . . .'[18] – so said Dudu and Motti, the entrepreneurs, as they described a menu that imported the classic British dish and 'fused' it with its Middle Eastern counterparts.

In all likelihood, Dudu and Motti did not have the period of the British Mandate in mind. The immense impact that the British left upon Jerusalem's cityscape in their thirty-year rule of the city has been left largely to the scrutiny of scholars, diplomats and politicians. British presence has thus, somewhat ironically, shifted to the cultural realms of cuisine and popular music, and the Mandate's powerful presence, which was inscribed symbolically and concretely, is all but forgotten.

Jerusalem's urban space continues to be defined by its cross-culturalism, by its being an international, constantly fluctuating space. Cross-cultural, multicultural, multifaith and binational are some of the overlapping terms that can be used to describe Jerusalem today. They are terms that owe their existence to centuries of contestation, migration, displacement and coexistence: Orthodox Jews attempt to claim the urban hub of the Mahane Yehuda market in order to 'safeguard it from sin';[19] the United States moves its embassy to the eastern boundary of West Jerusalem amid Palestinian boycotting and protests from left-wing Israeli groups;[20]

---

[16] Sigal Klein, 'International Fish & Chips Day: A new bar in Jerusalem serves only the British dish – Introducing John Lee's', *Kol Ha'Yir*, 5 June 2018, retrieved 15 June 2018, https://www.kolhair.co.il/food/57775/.

[17] Ibid.

[18] Ibid.

[19] Yuval Nisani, 'HaCharedim Neged Mitcham HaBilu'yim BeShuk Machne Yehuda – Atzeret Mecha'a Gdola', *Kol H'a'Yir*, 11 June 2018, retrieved 15 June 2018, https://www.kolhair.co.il/jerusalem-news/58509/.

[20] Loveday Morris and Ruth Eglash, 'New U.S. Embassy in Jerusalem: A Stone Plaque and $400,000 in Renovations, for Now', *Washington Post*, 8 May 2018, retrieved 15 June 2018, https://www.washingtonpost.com/world/new-us-embassy-in-jerusalem-a-stone-plaque-and-400k-in-renovations-for-now/2018/05/07/0b01d0be-520f-11e8-a6d4-ca1d035642ce_story.html?noredirect=on&utm_term=.c1b7f94dcf59.

in East Jerusalem, an impassioned dispute is taking place among the Muslim Palestinian majority of that section of town – the Muqadis[21] – as to whether or not to participate in the elections for the Jerusalem municipality. This dispute was ignited by the urgency of improving the derelict conditions of life in the Palestinian neighbourhoods of the city caused by decades of neglect and mistreatment under Israeli rule of this contested space. The opposition to this idea, voiced on the Palestinian website *0202: Point of View from Jerusalem*, claims that 'participation in the [municipality] elections is a de facto recognition of the sovereignty of the [Israeli] occupation of Al-Quds [Jerusalem]'.[22]

The buildings that I discussed here, which were erected during the British Mandate were, in effect, symbols of earlier versions of these present realities. The circumstances of their making, as their design, reflect phenomena shared by mixed cities, contested spaces, cities under foreign rule, and sites of decolonisation. In such spaces, architecture's relation to its surroundings is as political as it is functional and aesthetic. In Jerusalem, this was evinced by architecture's role in the construction of new identities: a British Mandatory identity politically differentiated from the Imperial one; an American Protestant ecumenical identity in search of new directions for Christianity at the dawn of a new century; and emerging Zionist and Palestinian identities, entangled in the process of defining nationality. Each of these identities was interdependent and formed in relation to those of the other communities. This reciprocity dictated a search for a distinct representative architecture – a search guided by considering history, place, and international developments in construction and design.

In his study of the heyday of Ottoman Jerusalem, cited at the outset of the present volume, Lemire underscored 'complexity, nuances, and diversity' as characterising Jerusalem. He observed that 'historians ... have attempted for decades to catch Jerusalem's inhabitants ... with nets crudely sized to catch "communities", "ethnicities", "religions" and "homogeneous neighborhoods".'[23] Jerusalem's Mandate-era architectural culture similarly reveals that subtleties of intercommunal and intracommunal relationships in the city, its fragile politics and its entangled economies were already in place and even intensified during the Mandate years. The exploration of architectural culture – the visual and spatial embodiment of these complexities – shows that, indeed, delicate frameworks should be utilised when investigating various historical sociocultural phenomena in this city and in Palestine in general.

In a similar vein, historian David Nirenberg recently warned fellow scholars

---

[21] Muqadis is the term used by the Palestinians for members of their people living in Jerusalem.
[22] 'Normalizatsia Chadasha – Merkaz HaSkarim 'HaMachon HaPalestini LeDa'at Kahal' Shitef Peula im Ha'Oniversita Ha'Ivrit BeSeker al Odoteihem shel HaMakdasim [Ha'Yerushalmim Ha'Aravim] BeNoge'a LaBchirot Le'Yiri'yat HaKibush Be'Al-Quds HaKvusha', *0202: Point of View from Jerusalem* website, retrieved 15 June 2018, https://www.0202updates.org/0202-376-מבט-מירושלים-המזרחית/.
[23] Lemire, *Jerusalem 1900*, 165

against underestimating 'asymmetries of power' in the process of the search for the agency of every community they examine.[24] He explained that this 'warning' was his response to postcolonial scholars who, in their enthusiasm to 'demonstrate that "subalterns" could speak',[25] to some extent blurred the decidedly more powerful position of a conqueror or a force possessing economic or technological advantages when entering a region. All of the buildings researched here reflected the agency of their makers, and in the preceding chapters, I sought to avoid glossing over the asymmetries that were revealed in the architectural production. The Mandatory condition was a force to be reckoned with, and as I showed in Chapter One, the British implemented control strategies by planning, by dictating decision-making processes (even when seemingly democratic), and by intervening in the city's space. The Americans built their cultural and religious-cultural institution using their economic and technological advantages, as well as by taking advantage of the new asymmetries of global power. Zionists emigrating from Europe had the capital to purchase city plots and developed advanced, sought-after construction technologies. Palestinians reacted to these forces by increasing construction in key areas of the city that they controlled and by their significant participation in the construction labour market, but they were at a disadvantage in terms of modern technologies and management. These disadvantages, to a great extent, reflect the political situation in Palestine and Arab Palestinian strengths and weaknesses in the face of the Jewish immigrant-settler society.[26]

Over the years and as a result of the ensuing Arab–Israeli conflict, the Palestine Archaeological Museum – now the Rockefeller Museum – and the Palace Hotel changed hands more than once. The Rockefeller Museum was under Jordanian governance between 1948 and 1967 and is presently under Israeli control and an annex of the Israel Museum. The Palestinians contest its takeover (along with its artefacts and library), and as one of the most prominent cultural institutions in East Jerusalem (and in Israel/Palestine), its status will surely be under intense debate in any future negotiations. The Palace Hotel was confiscated by the Israeli government in 1948. It housed government ministries for many years, until it became part of the Hilton Hotels chain, which re-established it as a luxury hotel. Its nationalisation by Israel is also contested by the Palestinians. The YMCA Building and the Zionist Executive Building function to this day as originally intended: the YMCA remains the most significant American property in the city, serving mostly the Christian-Palestinian and Jewish communities, as well as tourists; the ZEB houses the Jewish Agency, the JNF and Keren Hayesod, which continue their Zionist activities – in their changing concepts and contents – and foster Israel's relations with global Jewry.

---

[24] David Nirenberg, *Anti-Judaism: The Western Tradition* (London and New York: Norton and Company, 2013), 8.
[25] Ibid. 8.
[26] Kimmerling, *Clash of Identities*, 76. The Pre-Mandate origins of this situation have been extensively researched. See, e.g., Khalidi, *Palestinian Identity*, 102–11.

Thus, the stories of these four buildings generate critical questions regarding the heritages that they represent, what they should be used for, and whether and how they should be preserved. Perhaps the most pertinent question that the present study should conclude with is: what can the histories of such representative architecture and its centrality to Jerusalem's communities contribute to our understanding of current spatial dilemmas and their contexts within present-day, conflicted, Jerusalem? Recent studies have proposed multiple contextualisations of Jerusalem's urban space within the Palestinian–Israeli conflict.[27] In their editorial in a special issue of the *Journal of Architecture* entitled 'Learning from Architecture and Conflict', Brigitte Piquard and Mark Swenarton discussed similar issues. They noted that unlike urban space, which has been studied extensively in relation to alleviating conflict, architecture's role, its potential to remedy spatial disputes and its capacity to encourage coexistence – has not been thoroughly researched, despite its immense significance and symbolic power.[28] With regard to Jerusalem, the important role of the major historic and religious landmarks has been discussed,[29] but important public or civic buildings, such as those researched here, are habitually overlooked in debates of this kind. I propose that by framing such buildings and their histories within current academic discourses and public debates, Jerusalem can be understood not only as a space of ancient religious monuments, but also as a site where architects negotiated and formulated responses to key early twentieth-century architectural developments. As Jerusalem's Mandate-era architecture reveals important aspects of intercommunal interactions, acknowledging this heritage as a milestone of local architectural culture might well produce new, alternative perspectives regarding the city's urban space and its practices.

As an Israeli who has lived in Jerusalem and frequents the city, I can sadly and soberly contend that I do not share the carefully harboured hope, implicit in Piquard and Swearton's editorial, that architecture can play a more prominent role in guiding the region toward peace. Nevertheless, I would like to think that

---

[27] Dan Rabinowitz and Daniel Monterescu, 'Reconfiguring the "Mixed Town": Urban Transformations of Ethnonational Relations in Palestine and Israel', *International Journal of Middle East Studies* 40, no. 2 (2008): 195–226; Jon Calame and Esther Charlesworth, *Divided Cities: Belfast, Beirut, Jerusalem, Mostar, and Nicosia* (Philadelphia: University of Pennsylvania Press, 2011), 83–102, 237–42; Esther Charlesworth and John Fien, 'Breaching the Urban Contract', *International Journal of Disaster Resilience in the Built Environment* 5, no. 2 (2014): 194–201; Wendy Pullan and Maximilian Gwiazda, 'Jerusalem's Holy Basin: Who Needs it?' *Palestine-Israel Journal of Politics, Economics, and Culture* 17, no. 1 (2011): 172–9; Monk, *An Aesthetic Occupation*, 129–32.

[28] Brigitte Piquard and Mark Swenarton, 'Learning from Architecture and Conflict', *The Journal of Architecture* 16, no. 1 (2011): 7. Several essays in this issue deal with urban space and architecture in Israel/Palestine.

[29] Monk, *An Aesthetic Occupation*, 172–9; Michael Dumper, *The Politics of Sacred Space: The Old City of Jerusalem in the Middle East Conflict* (Boulder: Lynne Rienner Publishers, 2002); Michael Dumper and Craig Larkin, 'The Politics of Heritage and the Limitations of International Agency in Contested Cities: A Study of the Role of UNESCO in Jerusalem's Old City', *Review of International Studies* 38, no. 1 (2012): 25–52.

the weft and warp that wove together the architectural production of the 1920s and 1930s will someday inspire and rekindle modes of cooperation and interaction among Jerusalem's communities and that these will, perhaps, provide even a partial foundation for a better future.

Bibliography

The Mandate System: Origins – Principles – Application. Geneva: League of Nations, 1945.
'The New Science Museum, South Kensington, designed by Sir Richard Allison.' *Architectural Review* 64 (1928): 23–5.
The Palestine Mandate 1, no. 3, June. Geneva: League of Nations Association of the US, 1930.
'Seamen's House, YMCA, NYC by Shreve, Lamb & Harmon.' *Architectural Record* 71 (1932): 321–4.
'Seamen's House, YMCA, NYC by Shreve, Lamb & Harmon.' *Architecture and Building* 64 (1932): 16–17.
'The Shelton: Arthur Loomis Harmon, Architect.' *Architecture* 49 (April 1924): 101–12.
Who was Who in America. Chicago: Marquis, 1960.
Abdelrazek, Adnan. *The Arab Architectural Renaissance in the Western Part of Occupied Jerusalem.* Limassol: Rimal Books, 2017.
Abt, Jeffrey. 'Toward a Historian's Laboratory: The Breasted-Rockefeller Museum Projects in Egypt, Palestine, and America.' *Journal of the American Research Center in Egypt* 33 (1996): 173–94.
Abu-Lughod, Janet. *Cairo: 1001 Years of the City Victorious.* Princeton, NJ: Princeton University Press, 1971.
——. *Rabat: Urban Apartheid in Morocco.* Princeton, NJ: Princeton University Press, 1980.
Abweini, Walid H., Rizeq N. Hammad, Abdel-Elah M. Abdeen and May M. Hourani. 'Reconstructing Salah Al-Din Minbar of Al-Aqsa Mosque: Challenges and Results.' *International Journal of Conservation Science* 4, no. 3 (2013): 307–16.
Adelson, Roger. *London and the Invention of the Middle East: Money, Power and War, 1902–1922.* New Haven: Yale University Press, 1995.
Allweil, Yael. *Homeland: Zionism as Housing Regime, 1860–2011.* Abingdon and New York: Routledge, 2017.
AlSayyad, Nezar. 'Culture, Identity and Urbanism: A Historical Perspective from Colonialism and Globalization.' In *Colonial Modern: Aesthetics of the Past-Rebellions for the Future*, edited by Tom Avermaete, Serhat Karakayali and Marion Von Osten, 77–87. London and Berlin: Black Dog and Haus der Kulturen der Welt, 2010.
——, ed. *The End of Tradition?* London: Routledge, 2003.
——. 'Hybrid Culture/Hybrid Urbanism: Pandora's Box of the Third Place.' In *Hybrid Urbanism: On the Identity Discourse and the Built Environment*, edited by Nezar AlSayyad, 1–19. Westport: Praeger, 2001.
——, ed., *Hybrid Urbanism: On the Identity Discourse and the Built Environment.* Westport: Praeger, 2001.
Alsberg, P. A. 'HaMa'avak al Rashut Iriyat Yerushalayim BiTkufat HaMandat.' In *Prakim Betoldot Yerushalayim Bazman Hachadash*, edited by Eli Shealtiel, 302–54. Jerusalem: Yad Ben-Zvi and Israel Ministry of Defense, 1981.
Altan Ergut, Elvan, and Belgin Turan Özkaya. 'Editors' Introduction: Culture, Diplomacy, Representation: "Ambivalent Architectures" from the Ottoman Empire to the Turkish Republic.' *New Perspectives on Turkey* 50 (2014): 5–8.
Amiri, Avner, and Annabel Wharton. 'Home in Jerusalem: The American Colony and Palestinian Suburban Architecture.' *Post-Medieval Archaeology* 45, no. 2 (2011): 237–65.

Amit, Vered. 'Community.' In *The Social Science Encyclopedia*, edited by Adam Kuper and Jessica Kuper, vol. 1. http://www.questia.com/read/109437237/the-social-science-encyclopedia.

Ariel, Yaakov, and Ruth Kark. 'Messianism, Holiness, Charisma, and Community: The American-Swedish Colony in Jerusalem, 1881–1933.' *Church History* 65, no. 4 (1996): 641–57.

Ashbee, Charles Robert, ed. *Jerusalem 1918–1920: Being the Records of the Pro-Jerusalem Council during the Period of the British Military Administration.* London: John Murray, 1921.

———, ed. *Jerusalem 1920–1922: Being the Records of the Pro-Jerusalem Council during the First Two Years of the Civil Administration.* London: John Murray, 1924.

———. *A Palestine Notebook: 1918–1923.* Garden City, NY: Doubleday, Page & Co., 1923.

———. *Where the Great City Stands: A Study in New Civics.* London: Essex House Press, 1917.

Azaryahu, Maoz. 'Hebrew, Arabic, English: The Politics of Multilingual Street Signs in Israeli Cities.' *Social & Cultural Geography* 13, no. 5 (2012): 461–79.

Baert, Barbara. 'New Observations on the Genesis of Girona (1050–1100). The Iconography of the Legend of the True Cross.' *Gesta* 38, no. 2 (1999): 115–27.

Bar, Doron, and Kobi Cohen-Hattab. 'A New Kind of Pilgrimage: The Modern Tourist Pilgrim of Nineteenth Century and Early Twentieth Century Palestine.' *Middle Eastern Studies* 39, no. 2 (2003): 131–48.

Bar-Yosef, Eitan. 'The Last Crusade? British Propaganda and the Palestine Campaign, 1917–18.' *Journal of Contemporary History* 36, no. 1 (2001): 87–109.

Basa, Inci. 'From Praise to Condemnation: Ottoman Revivalism and the Production of Space in Early Republican Ankara.' *Journal of Urban History* 41, no. 4 (2015): 711–38.

Basu, Paul, and Vinita Damodaran. 'Colonial Histories of Heritage: Legislative Migrations and the Politics of Preservation.' *Past & Present* 226, no. 10 (2015): 240–71.

Bayes, Walter. 'Sense and Sensibility. The New Head Offices of the Underground Railway, Westminster, London. Adams, Holden and Pierce.' *Architectural Review* 66 (1929): 225–41.

Ben-Arieh, Yehoshua. 'The Growth of Jerusalem in the Nineteenth Century.' *Annals of the Association of American Geographers* 65, no. 2 (1975): 252–69.

———. *Yir BeRe'yi Tkufa: Yerushalayim BaMe'a HaTesha-Esre.* Jerusalem: Yad Izhak Ben-Zvi, 1977.

———, and Moshe Davis. *Jerusalem in the Mind of the Western World, 1800–1948.* Westport, CT: Praeger, 1997.

Ben-Artzi, Yossi. *MiGermania Le'Eretz HaKodesh: Hityashvut HaTemplerim Be'Eretz Israel.* Jerusalem: Yad Yizhak Ben-Zvi, 1996.

Ben-Asher Gitler, Inbal. 'The Architecture of the Jerusalem YMCA Building (1919–1933): Constructing Multiculturalism.' PhD diss., Tel Aviv University, 2006.

———. 'C. R. Ashbee's Jerusalem Years: Arts and Crafts, Orientalism and British Regionalism.' *Assaph* 5 (2000): 29–52.

———. '"Marrying Modern Progress with Treasured Antiquity": Jerusalem City Plans during the British Mandate, 1917–1948.' *Traditional Dwellings and Settlements Review* 15, no. 1 (2003): 39–58.

———. 'Reconstructing Religions: Jewish Place and Space in the Jerusalem YMCA Building, 1919–1933.' *Zeitschrift für Religions- und Geistesgeschichte* 60, no. 1 (2008): 41–62.

Bennett, Tony. *Pasts Beyond Memory: Evolution, Museums, Colonialism.* London: Routledge, 2004.

Bernstein, Deborah. '"Ka'Asher Avoda Ivrit Eynena Omedet Al Haperek": Histadrut Ha'Ovdim LeNochach HaMigzar HaMemshalti HaMandatory.' In *Calcala Ve'Chevra Bi'Yemey HaMandat, 1918–1948,* edited by Avi Bareli and Nachum Karlinsky, 79–106. Be'er Sheva: Ben-Gurion Institute, 2003.

Bethell, Nicholas. *The Palestine Triangle: The Struggle between the British, the Jews and the Arabs 1935–48.* London: Andre Deutch, 1979.

Betts, Raymond F. *Uncertain Dimensions: Western Overseas Empires in the Twentieth Century.* Minneapolis: University of Minnesota Press, 1985.

Bhabha, Homi K. *The Location of Culture.* London and New York: Routledge, 2004.

Bianca, Stefano. *Urban Form in the Arab World.* London: Thames and Hudson, 2000.

Biemann, Asher D. 'Isaac Breuer: Zionist Against His Will?' *Modern Judaism* 20, no. 2 (2000): 129–46.

Biger, Gideon. 'HaHitparsut HaMerchavit shel Uchlusi'yat Yerushalayim BaMachatsit HaRishona shel Tkufat HaMandat.' *Cathedra: For the History of Eretz Israel and Its Yishuv* 39 (1986): 125–40.

Blau, Eve. 'Plenary Address, Society of Architectural Historians Annual Meeting, Richmond,

Virginia, April 18, 2002: "A Question of Discipline".' *Journal of the Society of Architectural Historians* 62, no. 1 (2003): 125–9.

Boas, Adrian J. *Jerusalem in the Time of the Crusades: Society, Landscape and Art in the Holy City under Frankish Rule*. London: Routledge, 2001.

Bozdoğan, Sibel. *Modernism and Nation Building: Turkish Architectural Culture in the Early Republic*. Seattle and London: University of Washington Press, 2001.

———. 'Reading Ottoman Architecture through Modernist Lenses: Nationalist Historiography and the "New Architecture" in the Early Republic.' *Muqarnas* 24 (2007): 199–222.

Braddell, Darcy. 'Academy Architecture, 1936: A Brief Review', *Architectural Review* 79 (1936): 273.

Bragdon, C. 'The Shelton Hotel, New York: Arthur Loomis Harmon, Architect.' *Architectural Record* 58 (July 1925): 1–18.

Bunton, Martin. '"Progressive Civilizations and Deep-Rooted Traditions": Land Laws, Development, and British Rule in Palestine in the 1920s.' In *Colonialism and the Modern World: Selected Studies*, edited by Gregory Blue, Martin Bunton and Ralph Croizier, 145–63. Armonk, NY, and London: M. E. Sharpe, 2002.

Calame, Jon, and Esther Charlesworth. *Divided Cities: Belfast, Beirut, Jerusalem, Mostar, and Nicosia*. Philadelphia: University of Pennsylvania Press, 2011.

Carmiel, Batia, Edina Meyer-Maril and Alec Mishori. *Arichim Me'atrim Yir: Keramika Bezalel BeBatey Tel Aviv 1923–1929*. Tel Aviv: Eretz Israel Museum, 1996.

Çelik, Zeynep. 'Defining Empire's Patrimony: Late Ottoman Perceptions of Antiquity.' In *Scramble for the Past: A Story of Archaeology in the Ottoman Empire, 1753–1914*, edited by Zainab Bahrani, Zeynep Çelik and Edhem Eldem, translated by Willard Wood, Leyla Tonguc Basmac and Doolie Sloman, 443–7. Istanbul: SALT, 2011.

———. *Urban Forms and Colonial Confrontations: Algiers under French Rule*. Berkeley: University of California Press, 1997.

Cengizkan, Ali. 'Mehmet Nihat Nigisberk'in Katkılary: Evkaf Idaresi ve Mimar Kemalettin.' In *Mimar Kemalettin Ve Çağı: Mimarlık, Toplumsal Yaşsam, Politika*, edited by Ali Cengizkan, 177–208. Ankara: TMMOB Mimalar Odasi, 2009.

Chaouni, Aziza. 'Depoliticizing Group GAMMA: Contesting Modernism in Morocco.' In *Third World Modernism: Architecture, Development, and Identity*, edited by Duanfang Lu, 57–83. Abingdon and New York: Routledge, 2011.

Charlesworth, Esther, and John Fien. 'Breaching the Urban Contract.' *International Journal of Disaster Resilience in the Built Environment* 5, no. 2 (2014): 194–201.

Christopher, Anthony J. 'Urban Segregation Levels in the British Overseas Empire and its Successors in the Twentieth Century.' *Transactions of the Institute of British Geographers* (1992): 95–107.

Clavel, Pierre. 'Ebenezer Howard and Patrick Geddes: Two Approaches to City Development.' In *From Garden City to Green City: The Legacy of Ebenezer Howard*, edited by Kermit C. Parsons and David Schuyler, 38–57. Baltimore: Johns Hopkins University Press, 2002.

Cody, Jeffrey W. *Exporting American Architecture, 1870–2000*. London: Routledge, 2003.

Cohen, Michael. *Palestine: Retreat from the Mandate: The Making of British Policy, 1936–45*. New York: Holmes & Meier, 1978.

Crawford, Alan. *C. R. Ashbee: Architect, Designer and Romantic Socialist*. New Haven: Yale University Press, 1985.

Crinson, Mark. *Empire Building: Orientalism and Victorian Architecture*. London and New York: Routledge, 1996.

———. *Rebuilding Babel: Modern Architecture and Internationalism*. London and New York: I. B. Tauris, 2017.

Crompton, Andrew. 'The Architecture of Multifaith Spaces: God Leaves the Building.' *The Journal of Architecture* 18, no. 4 (2013): 474–96.

Davidann, Jon Thares. *A World of Crisis and Progress: The American YMCA in Japan, 1890–1930*. Cranbury: Associated University Press, 1998.

Davidi, Sigal. 'Ha'Adrichalut Ha'Chadasha Be'Yarid HaMizrach 1934: Havna'yat Zehut La'Yishuv Ha'Yehudi.' *Israel* 24 (2016): 163–90.

Davis, John. *The Landscape of Belief*. Princeton, NJ: Princeton University Press, 1996.

Davis, Moshe. *America and the Holy Land* (With Eyes Toward Zion series, vol. 4). Westport: Praeger, 1995.

Deen, Y. M. 'Amidst a Grove of Olive Trees.' Paper presented at Chicago Literary Club, 2003.

DeNovo, John A. *American Interests and Policies in the Middle East, 1900–1939.* Minneapolis: University of Minnesota Press, 1963.
Dolev, Diana. 'Architectural Orientalism in the Hebrew University – the Patrick Geddes and Frank Mears Master-Plan.' *Assaph* 3 (1998): 217–34.
Dumper, Michael. *The Politics of Sacred Space: The Old City of Jerusalem in the Middle East Conflict.* Boulder: Lynne Rienner Publishers, 2002.
———, and Craig Larkin. 'The Politics of Heritage and the Limitations of International Agency in Contested Cities: A Study of the Role of UNESCO in Jerusalem's Old City.' *Review of International Studies* 38, no. 1 (2012): 25–52.
El-Eini, Roza. *Mandated Landscape: British Imperial Rule in Palestine 1929–1948.* London: Routledge, 2004.
El-Haj, Nadia Abu. 'Producing (Arti) Facts: Archaeology and Power during the British Mandate of Palestine.' *Israel Studies* 7, no. 2 (2002): 33–61.
Eleb, Monique. 'An Alternative to Functionalist Universalism: Ecochard, Candilis and ATBAT-Afrique.' In *Anxious Modernisms: Experimentation in Postwar Architectural Culture*, edited by Sarah Williams Goldhagen and Réjean Legault, 55–71. Montreal: Canadian Centre for Architecture, and Cambridge, MA: MIT Press, 2000.
Eliash, Shulamit. 'The Political Role of the Chief Rabbinate of Palestine during the Mandate: Its Character and Nature.' *Jewish Social Studies* 47, no. 1 (1985): 33–50.
Elkins, James, Zhivka Valiavicharska and Alice Kim. *Art and Globalization.* University Park: Pennsylvania State University Press, 2010.
Elliott, Bridget. 'Art Deco Worlds in a Tomb: Reanimating Egypt in Modern(ist) Visual Culture.' *South Central Review* 25, no. 1 (2008): 114–35.
Emberling, Geoff, ed. *Pioneers to the Past: American Archaeologists in the Middle East, 1919–1920 [in Conjunction with the Exhibition Pioneers to the Past: American Archaeologists in the Middle East, 1919–1920, Presented at the Oriental Institute Museum, 12 January to 29 August 2010].* Chicago: Oriental Institute of the University of Chicago, 2010.
Epstein-Pliouchtch, Marina, and Michael Levin, eds. *Richard Kaufmann VeHapro'yekt HaZioni.* Tel Aviv: Hakibbutz HaMe'uchad, 2016.
Farah, Rafiq A. *In Troubled Waters: A History of the Anglican Church in Jerusalem 1841–1998.* Leicester: Christians Aware, 2002.
Feierberg, Hayim. 'Chevra Ironit BeMashber: Hivatzruta shel "HaBe'aya HaMizrachit" BeMerchav Tel Aviv VeYaffo Be'Et Me'ora'ot 1936.' *Social Issues in Israel* 1 (2006): 171–207.
Feniger, Neta, and Rachel Kallus. 'Israeli Planning in the Shah's Iran: A Forgotten Episode.' *Planning Perspectives* 30, no. 2 (2015): 231–51.
Finnie, David H. *Pioneers East: The Early American Experience in the Middle East.* Cambridge, MA: Harvard University Press, 1967.
Fisher, Donald. 'The Role of Philanthropic Foundations in the Reproduction and Production of Hegemony: Rockefeller Foundations and the Social Sciences.' *Sociology* 17, no. 2 (1983): 206–33.
Forsyth, William H. 'Five Crucial People in the Building of the Cloisters.' In *The Cloisters: Studies in Honor of the Fiftieth Anniversary*, edited by Elizabeth C. Parker, 51–64. New York: Metropolitan Museum of Art and the International Center of Medieval Art, 1992.
Frampton, Kenneth. 'Prospects for a Critical Regionalism.' *Perspecta* 20 (1983): 147–62.
Frank, Raphael. *Al Otiyot Dfus VeGofanim.* Introduction by Jacques Adler, translation by Moshe Yarden. Berlin: Berthold, 1926.
Frantzman, Seth J., and Ruth Kark. 'The Catholic Church in Palestine/Israel: Real Estate in Terra Sancta.' *Middle Eastern Studies* 50, no. 3 (2014): 370–96.
Freestone, Robert. 'Greenbelts in City and Regional Planning.' In *From Garden City to Green City: The Legacy of Ebenezer Howard*, edited by Kermit C. Parsons and David Schuyler, 67–98. Baltimore: Johns Hopkins University Press, 2002.
Fromkin, David. *A Peace to End all Peace: The Fall of the Ottoman Empire and the Creation of the Modern Middle East.* New York: Avon Books, 1990.
Fuchs, Ron. 'Austen St. Barbe Harrison – Architekt Briti Be'Eretz HaKodesh.' PhD diss., Technion-Israel Institute of Technology, 1992.
———. 'The Palestinian Arab House and the Islamic Primitive Hut.' *Muqarnas* 15 (1998): 157–77.
———, and Gilbert Herbert. 'A Colonial Portrait of Jerusalem: British Architecture in Mandate-Era

Palestine.' In *Hybrid Urbanism: On the Identity Discourse and the Built Environment*, edited by Nezar AlSayyad, 83–109. Westport: Praeger, 2001.

———, and Gilbert Herbert. 'Representing Mandatory Palestine: Austen St. Barbe Harrison and the Representational Buildings of the British Mandate in Palestine, 1922–37.' *Architectural History* 43 (2000): 281–333.

Gafni, Reuven. *Tachat Kipat HaLe'om: Bate'yi Kneset ULe'umi'yut Be'Erets Israel BiTkufat HaMandat*. Sede Boker: Ben Gurion University of the Negev, 2017.

Garnham, Trevor. *Oxford Museum: Deane and Woodward*. London: Phaidon, 1992.

Gelber, Yoav. 'The Shaping of the "New Jew" in Eretz Israel.' In *Major Changes within the Jewish People in the Wake of the Holocaust*, edited by Yisrael Gutman and Avital Saf, 443–61. Jerusalem: Yad Vashem, 1996.

Gibson, Shimon. 'British Archaeological Institutions in Mandatory Palestine, 1917–1948.' *Palestine Exploration Quarterly* 131, no. 2 (1999): 115–43.

Gilbert, Martin. 'HaCha'yim Haktsarim shel Ve'adat Peel.' *Zmanim: A Historical Quarterly* 1 (1979): 4–15.

———. *Jerusalem in the Twentieth Century*. New York: John Wiley & Sons, 1996.

Gill, Eric. 'What is Lettering?' *Architectural Review* 73 (1933): 24–8.

Girardelli, Paolo. 'Re-Thinking Architect Kemalettin.' *ABE Journal: Architecture Beyond Europe* 2 (2012), https://journals.openedition.org/abe/575.

Golani, Motti. 'Hanhagat Ha'Yishuv VeShe'elat Yerushalayim BeMilchemet Ha'Atzma'ut (December 1947–May 1948).' *Cathedra: For the History of Eretz Israel and its Yishuv* 54 (1989): 156–72.

Goldman, Bat-Sheva Ida. *Ze'ev Raban: Symbolist Ivri*. Exhibition Catalogue. Tel Aviv: Tel Aviv Museum of Art, and Jerusalem: Yad Yizhak Ben-Zvi, 2001.

Gonen, Rivka. *Contested Holiness: Jewish, Muslim, and Christian Perspectives on the Temple Mount in Jerusalem*. New York: KTAV, 2003.

Goode, James F. *Negotiating for the Past: Archaeology, Nationalism, and Diplomacy in the Middle East, 1919–1941*. Austin: University of Texas Press, 2007.

Gorny, Yosef. 'Thoughts on Zionism as a Utopian Ideology.' *Modern Judaism* 18, no. 3 (1998): 241–51.

Grabar, Oleg. *Jerusalem* (Constructing the Study of Islamic Art, 4). Aldershot and Burlington, VT: Ashgate, 2005.

Grafman, Rafi, and Miriam Rosen-Ayalon. 'The Two Great Syrian Umayyad Mosques: Jerusalem and Damascus.' *Muqarnas* 6 (1999): 1–15.

Gravagnuolo, Benedetto. 'From Schinkel to Le Corbusier: The Myth of the Mediterranean in Modern Architecture.' In *Modern Architecture and the Mediterranean: Vernacular Dialogues and Contested Identities*, edited by Jean-François Lejeune and Michelangelo Sabatino, 15–40. Abingdon: Routledge, 2010.

Grossman, Elizabeth G. 'Two Postwar Competitions: The Nebraska State Capitol and the Kansas City Liberty Memorial.' *JSAH* 45 (1986): 244–69.

Gruber, Christiane. 'The Prophet Muhammad's Ascension (*Mi'Raj*) in Islamic Painting and Literature: Evidence from Cairo Collections.' *Bulletin of the American Research Center in Egypt* 185 (Summer 2004): 24–31.

Grubiak, Margaret M. 'The Danforth Chapel Program on the Public American Campus.' *Buildings & Landscapes: Journal of the Vernacular Architecture Forum* 19, no. 2 (2012): 77–96.

Guilat, Yael. 'The Yemeni Ideal in Israeli Culture and Arts.' *Israel Studies* 6, no. 3 (2001): 26–53.

Gupta, Akhil, and James Ferguson. 'Beyond "Culture": Space, Identity, and the Politics of Difference.' *Cultural Anthropology* 7, no. 1 (1992): 6–23.

Gürel, Meltem. 'Modernization and the Role of Foreign Experts: W. M. Dudok's Projects for Izmir, Turkey.' *Journal of the Society of Architectural Historians* 77, no. 2 (2018): 204–22.

Ha'Ezrachi, Yehuda. *Ir, Even ve Shamayim*. Tel Aviv: Ministry of Defense, 1968.

Habermas, Jürgen. *The Structural Transformation of the Public Sphere*. Cambridge, MA: MIT Press, 1989.

Halabi, Awad. 'Liminal Loyalties: Ottomanism and Palestinian Responses to the Turkish War of Independence, 1919–22.' *Journal of Palestine Studies* 41, no. 3 (2012): 19–37.

Hallote, Rachel. 'Before Albright: Charles Torrey, James Montgomery, and American Biblical Archaeology 1907–1922.' *Near Eastern Archaeology* 74, no. 3 (2011): 156–69.

Handler, Richard. 'Culture.' In *The Social Science Encyclopedia*, edited by Adam Kuper and Jessica Kuper, vol. 1. http://www.questia.com/read/109437237/the-social-science-encyclopedia.

Hanson, Brian. *Architects and the 'Building World' from Chambers to Ruskin: Constructing Authority*. Cambridge: Cambridge University Press, 2003.

Harvey, Charles E. 'Speer Versus Rockefeller and Mott, 1910–1935.' *Journal of Presbyterian History* 60, no. 4 (1982): 283–99.

Hathorn, Richard Y. *Greek Mythology*. Beirut: American University of Beirut, 1977.

Hayerushalmi, Levi Itzhak. 'HaCharedim MeHazionut VeHaCharedim LaZionut.' *Moznaim* 6 (1997): 32–40.

Heinze-Greenberg, Ita. 'An Artistic European Utopia at the Abyss of Time: The Mediterranean Academy Project, 1931–34.' *Architectural History* 45 (2002): 441–82.

Herbert, Gilbert. 'Crossroads: Imperial Priorities and Regional Perspectives in the Planning of Haifa, 1918–1939.' *Planning Perspective* 4, no. 3 (1989): 313–31.

———, and Silvina Sosnovsky. *Bauhaus on the Carmel and the Crossroads of Empire: Architecture and Planning in Haifa during the British Mandate*. Jerusalem: Yad Izhak Ben-Zvi, 1993.

———, and Silvina Sosnovsky. *Urban Developments in Down-Town Haifa during the British Mandate*. Haifa: Technion-Israel Institute of Technology, Faculty of Architecture and Town Planning, Documentation Unit of Architecture, 1984.

Hitchcock Jr, Henry-Russell, Catherine Bauer Wurster and Museum of Modern Art. *Modern Architecture in England*. New York: Museum of Modern Art, 1937.

Holliday, Clifford. 'Jerusalem City Plan by Henry Kendall (1948).' *RIBA Journal* (August 1948): 496.

Holmes, Nigel. 'Eric Gill: Cut in Stone.' *Visual Communication Quarterly* 15, no. 1–2 (2008): 44–9.

Hopkins, Charles Howard. *History of the Y.M.C.A. in North America*. New York: Association Press, 1951.

———. *John R. Mott, 1865–1955: A Biography*. Geneva: World Council of Churches, 1979.

Houghton-Evans, W. 'Schemata in British New Town Planning.' In *Shaping an Urban World*, edited by Gordon E. Cherry, 101–28. London: Mansell, 1980.

Hutchison, William R. *Errand to the World: American Protestant Thought and Foreign Missions*. Chicago: University of Chicago Press, 1987.

Hyman, Benjamin. 'British Planners in Palestine, 1918–1936.' PhD diss., London School of Economics and Political Science, 1994.

Hysler-Rubin, Noah. 'Arts & Crafts and the Great City: Charles Robert Ashbee in Jerusalem.' *Planning Perspectives* 21, no. 4 (2006): 347–68.

Imamoglu, Bilge. 'Architectural Production in State Offices: An Inquiry into the Professionalization of Architecture in Early Republican Turkey.' PhD diss., Delft University of Technology, 2010.

Irving, Robert. *Indian Summer: Luytens, Baker and Imperial Delhi*. New Haven: Yale University Press, 1981.

Isenstadt, Sandy, and Kishwar Rizvi. *Modernism and the Middle East: Architecture and Politics in the Twentieth Century*. Seattle and London: University of Washington Press, 2008.

Israel-Vleeschhouwer, Amos. 'The Mandate System as a Messianic Alternative in the Ultra-Religious Jurisprudence of Rabbi Dr Isaac Breuer.' *Israel Law Review* 49, no. 3 (2016): 339–63.

Jacobson, Abigail. 'A City Living through Crisis: Jerusalem during World War I.' *British Journal of Middle Eastern Studies* 36, no. 1 (2009): 73–92.

———. *From Empire to Empire: Jerusalem between Ottoman and British Rule*. Syracuse: Syracuse University Press, 2011.

———, and Moshe Naor. *Oriental Neighbors: Middle Eastern Jews and Arabs in Mandatory Palestine*. Waltham: Brandeis University Press, 2016.

Kaçel, Elâ. 'This is not an American House: Good Sense Modernism in 1950s Turkey.' In *Third World Modernism: Architecture, Development, and Identity*, edited by Duanfang Lu, 165–86. Abingdon and New York: Routledge, 2011.

Kalimi, Isaac. 'The Land of Moriah, Mount Moriah, and the Site of Solomon's Temple in Biblical Historiography.' *Harvard Theological Review* 83, no. 4 (1990): 345–62.

Kantor, Hadassa. 'Current Trends in the Secularization of Hebrew.' *Language in Society* 21, no. 4 (1992): 603–9.

Kark, Ruth. *American Consuls in the Holy Land, 1832–1914*. Jerusalem: Hebrew University's Magnes Press and Detroit: Wayne State University Press, 1994.

———, and Shimon Landman. 'HaYetsi'a HaMuslemit MiChutz LaChomot BeShalhey HaTkufa

Ha'Ottomanit.' In *Prakim Betoldot Yerushalayim Bazman Hachadash*, edited by Eli Shealtiel, 174–211. Jerusalem: Yad Ben-Zvi and Israel Ministry of Defense, 1981.

———, and Michal Oren-Nordheim. 'Colonial Cities in Palestine?' *Israel Affairs* 3, no. 2 (1996): 50–94.

——— and Michal Oren-Nordheim. *Jerusalem and its Environs: Quarters, Neighborhoods, Villages, 1800–1948*. Jerusalem: Hebrew University's Magnes Press, and Detroit: Wayne State University Press, 2001.

———, and Michal Oren-Nordheim. *Yerushalayim ve'Svivoteyiha: Reva'im, Shechunot ve'Kfarim, 1800–1948*. Jerusalem: Akademon, 1995.

Karl, Barry D., and Stanley N. Katz. 'Foundations and Ruling Class Elites.' *Daedalus* 116, no. 1 (1987): 1–40.

Karmi-Melamed, Ada, and Dan Price. *Architecture in Palestine during the British Mandate, 1917–1948*. Jerusalem: The Israel Museum, 2014.

Karol, Eitan. 'Naked and Unashamed: Holden in Bloomsbury.' *Past and Future* 4 (2008): 6–7.

Katinka, Baruch. *Me'az Ve'Ad Hena*. Jerusalem: Kiryat Sefer, 1964.

Katz, Itamar, and Ruth Kark. 'The Greek Orthodox Patriarchate of Jerusalem and its Congregation: Dissent over Real Estate.' *International Journal of Middle East Studies* 37, no. 4 (2005): 509–34.

Katz, Yossi. 'Mekoma Shel HaYir Jerusalem BeMasechet Pe'ulotav Shel HaMimsad HaZioni BeShalhei Tkufat HaMandat.' *Zion* (1996): 67–90.

Kay, Lily E. 'Rethinking Institutions: Philanthropy as an Historiographic Problem of Knowledge and Power.' *Minerva* 35, no. 3 (1997): 283–93.

Kenaan Kedar, Nurith. *HaKeramika Ha'Armanit shel Yerushalayim, Shlosha Dorot 1919–2000*. Tel Aviv: Eretz Israel Museum, 2002.

Kendall, Henry. *Jerusalem: The City Plan. Preservation and Development during the British Mandate 1918–1948*. London: His Majesty's Stationery Office, 1948.

———. *Town Planning in Uganda: A Brief Description of the Efforts Made by Government to Control Development of Urban Areas from 1915 to 1955*. London: The Crown Agents, 1955.

Kent, Susan Kingsley. *Aftershocks: Politics and Trauma in Britain, 1918–1931*. Basingstoke and New York: Palgrave Macmillan, 2009.

Khalidi, Rashid. *Palestinian Identity: The Construction of Modern National Consciousness*. New York: Columbia University Press, 1997.

———. *Palestinian Identity: The Construction of Modern National Consciousness*. New York: Columbia University Press, 2009. ProQuest Ebook Central, https://ebookcentral.proquest.com/lib/leip/detail.action?docID=895137.

Kidder Smith, George Everard. *Source Book of American Architecture: 500 Notable Buildings from the 10th Century to the Present*. New York: Princeton Architectural Press, 1996.

Kimmerling, Baruch. *Clash of Identities: Explorations in Israeli and Palestinian Societies*. New York: Columbia University Press, 2012.

———. 'The Formation of Palestinian Collective Identities: The Ottoman and Mandatory Periods.' *Middle Eastern Studies* 36, no. 2 (2000): 48–81.

———. 'A Model for Analysis of Reciprocal Relations between the Jewish and Arab Communities in the Mandatory Palestine.' *Plural Societies* 14 (1983): 45–68.

King, Anthony D. 'Colonial Cities: Global Pivots of Change.' In *Colonial Cities*, edited by Robert Ross and Gerard J. Telkamp, 7–32. Dordrecht: Martinus Nijhoff, 1985.

———. *Colonial Urban Development: Culture, Social Power, and Environment*. London: Routledge & Kegan Paul, 1976.

———. 'Exporting Planning: The Colonial and Neo-Colonial Experience.' In *Shaping an Urban World*, edited by Gordon E. Cherry, 203–26. London: Mansell, 1980.

Köroğlu, Nil. 'XIX. Yüzyil Ve XX. Yüzyil Başil Eminönü'nde Osmanli Büro Hanlari.' PhD diss., Yildiz Technical University, 2004.

Kramer, Martin S. *Islam Assembled: The Advent of the Muslim Congresses*. New York: Columbia University Press, 1986.

Kroyanker, David. *Adrichal Z. S. Harmat: Shishim Shnot Yetsira*. Jerusalem: HaMoreshet HaBnuya; Center for Social Policies in Israel, 1990.

———. *Adrichalut Bi'Yerushalayim: HaBni'ya Ba'Yir Ha'Atika*. Jerusalem: Keter, 1993.

———. *Adrichalut Bi'Yerushalayim: HaBni'ya BiTkufat HaMandat HaBriti*. Jerusalem: Keter, 1989.

———. *Adrichalut Bi'Yerushalayim: HaBni'ya Ha'Eropit-Notsrit MiChuts LaChomot, 1855–1918.* Jerusalem: Keter, 1991.

———. *Malon Palace: Hachzarat Atara Le'Yoshna.* Jerusalem: Jerusalem Municipality, 1981.

———. 'Orientali Yoter MeHaMizrach: Gilgule'yha Shel Sfat HaZitutim HaYerushalmit.' *Zmanim* 96 (2006): 28–37.

Kühnel, Bianca. 'Ti'aruch Knesi'yat Ha'Ali'ya Be'Har Haze'itim.' In *Prakim BeToldon Yerushalayim Bi'Ymei HaBeinayim*, edited by Benyamin Ze'ev Kedar, 327–37. Jerusalem: Yad Izhak Ben-Zvi, 1979.

Kumar, Margaret. 'Postcolonial Theory and Crossculturalism: Collaborative "Signposts" of Discursive Practices.' *The Journal of Educational Enquiry* 1, no. 2 (2000): 82–92.

Kuper, Adam. *Culture: The Anthropologists' Account.* Cambridge, MA: Harvard University Press, 2000.

Lamprakos, Michele. 'Le Corbusier and Algiers: The Plan Obus as Colonial Urbanism.' In *Forms of Dominance: On the Architecture and Urbanism of the Colonial Enterprise*, edited by Nezar AlSayyad, 183–216. Aldershot: Avebury, 1992.

Latourette, Kenneth S. *World Service: A History of the Foreign Work and World Service of the Young Men's Christian Associations of the United States and Canada.* New York: Association Press, 1957.

Leach, Andrew. *What is Architectural History?* Cambridge: Polity Press, 2010.

Lejeune, Jean-François, and Michelangelo Sabatino, eds. *Modern Architecture and the Mediterranean: Vernacular Dialogues and Contested Identities.* Abingdon and New York: Routledge, 2009.

Lemire, Vincent. *Jerusalem 1900: The Holy City in the Age of Possibilities.* Translated and edited by Catherine Tihanyi and Lys Ann Weiss. Chicago: University of Chicago Press, 2017.

Lepine, Ayla. 'Modern Gothic and the House of God: Revivalism and Monasticism in Two Twentieth-Century Anglican Chapels.' *Visual Resources* 32, no. 1/2 (2016): 76–101.

Levin, Michael. 'Chamesh Gishot LaMizrach Be'Adrichalut Mekomit.' *Zmanim* 96 (2006): 38–47.

———. 'Rashey Prakin LeMegamot Hatsmicha VeHaHitgabshut shel Omanut Ve'Adrichalut Mekomit.' *Cathedra: For the History of Eretz Israel and Its Yishuv* 16 (1980): 194–204.

Lockman, Zachary. *Comrades and Enemies: Arab and Jewish Workers in Palestine, 1906–1948.* Berkeley: University of California Press, 1996.

———. *Contending Visions of the Middle East: The History and Politics of Orientalism.* Cambridge: Cambridge University Press, 2004.

———. 'Land, Labor and the Logic of Zionism: A Critical Engagement with Gershon Shafir.' *Settler Colonial Studies* 2, no. 1 (2012): 9–38.

———. 'Railway Workers and Relational History: Arabs and Jews in British-Ruled Palestine.' *Comparative Studies in Society and History* 35, no. 3 (1993): 601–27.

Loomba, Ania. *Colonialism/Postcolonialism.* London: Routledge, 1998.

Loomis Harmon, Arthur. 'The Allerton Houses.' *Architecture* 47, no. 1 (1923): 41–4.

Lupkin, Paula. *Manhood Factories: YMCA Architecture and the Making of Modern Urban Culture.* Minneapolis: University of Minnesota Press, 2010.

———. 'YMCA Architecture, Evangelical Equipment for the American City, 1867–1920.' PhD diss., University of Pennsylvania, 1996.

MacCarthy, Fiona. *Eric Gill.* London: Faber & Faber, 2011.

McClellan, Andrew. *The Art Museum from Boullée to Bilbao.* Berkeley and London: University of California Press, 2008.

Manor, Daliah. 'Biblical Zionism in Bezalel Art.' *Israel Studies* 6, no. 1 (2001): 55–75.

Mattar, Philip. 'The Mufti of Jerusalem and the Politics of Palestine.' *Middle East Journal* 42, no. 2 (Spring, 1988): 227–40.

Matthews, Weldon. *Confronting an Empire, Constructing a Nation: Arab Nationalists and Popular Politics in Mandate Palestine.* London: I. B. Tauris, 2006.

———. 'Pan-Islam or Arab Nationalism? The Meaning of the 1931 Jerusalem Islamic Congress Reconsidered.' *International Journal of Middle East Studies* 35, no. 1 (2003): 1–22.

Mayer, Tamar. 'Jerusalem In and Out of Focus: The City in Zionist Ideology.' In *Jerusalem: Idea and Reality*, edited by Tamar Mayer and Suleiman A. Mourad, 224–44. London and New York: Routledge, 2008.

Mazza, Roberto. *Jerusalem: From the Ottomans to the British.* New York: Tauris Academic Studies, 2014.

Meller, Helen. *Patrick Geddes: Social Evolutionist and City Planner.* London: Routledge, 1990.
Metcalf, Thomas. *Ideologies of the Raj.* Cambridge: Cambridge University Press, 1994.
Metzer, Jacob. 'Jewish Immigration to Palestine in the Long 1920s: An Exploratory Examination.' *Journal of Israeli History* 27, no. 2 (2008): 221–51.
Meyer, Edina. 'Die Dormition auf dem Berge Zion in Jerusalem, eine Denkmalskirche Kaiser Wilhelms II. im Heiligen Land.' *Architectura* 14, no. 2 (1984): 149–70.
Meyer-Maril, Edina. 'Binyan Augusta-Victoria al Har-Hazeytim.' *Ariel*, no. 122–3 (1997): 51–62.
———. 'Synagogenbau in Palästina zwischen Tradition und Moderne. Vom jüdischen Viertel in der Altstadt Jerusalem zu den Mosahvot des Baron von Rothschild.' In *Judentum zwischen Tradition und Moderne*, edited by Gerd Biegel and Michael Graetz, 73–8. Heidelberg: Universitätsverlag Winter, 2002.
Migdal, Joel S. *Through the Lens of Israel: Explorations in State and Society.* Albany: State University of New York Press, 2001.
Miller, Mervyn. 'The Origins of the Garden City Neighborhood.' In *From Garden City to Green City: The Legacy of Ebenezer Howard*, edited by Kermit C. Parsons and David Schuyler, 99–130. Baltimore: John Hopkins University Press, 2002.
Miller, Rory, ed. *Britain, Palestine and Empire: The Mandate Years.* Farnham: Routledge, 2016.
Minerbi, Sergio I. 'Pe'Yilut Memshelet Italia LeHasagat HaBe'alut al 'Cheder HaSe'uda Ha'Achrona' BeHar Zion.' *Cathedra: For the History of Eretz Israel and Its Yishuv* 25 (1982): 37–64.
Mishori, Alek. *Shuru, Habitu U'Re'u – Ikonot VeSmalim Hazuti'yim Ziyoni'yim BaTarbut Ha'Yisra'elit.* Tel Aviv: Am Oved, 2000.
Mitchell, Katharyne. 'Different Diasporas and the Hype of Hybridity.' *Environment and Planning D: Society and Space* 15, no. 5 (1997): 533–53.
Monk, Daniel Bertrand. *An Aesthetic Occupation: The Immediacy of Architecture and the Palestine Conflict.* Durham, NC: Duke University Press, 2002.
Montgomery, James A. 'The Story of the School in Jerusalem.' *The Annual of the American Schools of Oriental Research* (1924): 1–9.
Murre-van den Berg, Heleen. '"Our Jerusalem": Bertha Spafford Vester and Christianity in Palestine during the British Mandate.' In *Britain, Palestine, and Empire: The Mandate Years*, edited by Rory Miller, 67–84. Farnham: Ashgate, 2010.
Nashif, Taysir. 'Palestinian Arab and Jewish Leadership in the Mandate Period.' *Journal of Palestine Studies* 6, no. 4 (1977): 113–21.
———. 'Social Background Characteristics as Determinants of Political Behavior of the Arab Political Leadership of Palestine under the British Mandate.' *Journal of Third World Studies* 26, no. 2 (2009): 161–73.
Nihat, Mehmet. 'Palas Otel, Kudüs.' *Arkitekt* 3 (1931): 75–81.
Nirenberg, David. *Anti-Judaism: The Western Tradition.* London and New York: Norton, 2013.
Nitzan-Shiftan, Alona. 'Contested Zionism – Alternative Modernism: Erich Mendelsohn and the Tel Aviv Chug in Mandate Palestine.' *Architectural History* 39 (1996): 147–80.
Northedge, F. S. '1917–1919: The Implications for Britain.' *Journal of Contemporary History* 3, no. 4 (1968): 191–209.
Ofer, Pinchas. 'Achzava MeHesegei HaBayit HaLe'umi Ha'Yehudi Gorem LeTafnit BaMedini'yut HaBritit Be'Eretz-Israel Be-1930?' *Cathedra: For the History of Eretz Israel and Its Yishuv* 16 (1980): 125–32.
Ohad Smith, Daniella. 'Hotel Design in British Mandate Palestine: Modernism and the Zionist Vision.' *Journal of Israel History* 29, no. 1 (2010): 99–123.
Omolo-Okalebo, Fredrick, Tigran Haas, Inga Britt Werner and Hannington Sengendo. 'Planning of Kampala City, 1906–1962: The Planning Ideas, Values, and their Physical Expression.' *Journal of Planning History* 9, no. 3 (2010): 151–69.
Pappe, Ilan. 'Haj Amin and the Buraq Revolt.' *Jerusalem Quarterly File* 18, no. 18 (2003): 6–16.
Parmar, Inderjeet. '"To Relate Knowledge and Action": The Impact of the Rockefeller Foundation on Foreign Policy Thinking during America's Rise to Globalism 1939–1945.' *Minerva* 40, no. 3 (2002): 235–63.
Penkower, Monty Noam. 'A Lost Opportunity: Pre-world War II Efforts Towards Mizrachi-Agudas Israel Cooperation.' *Journal of Israeli History* 17, no. 2 (1996): 221–46.
Petersen, Andrew. *A Gazetteer of Buildings in Muslim Palestine (Part 1).* Oxford: Oxford University Press, 2001.

Pevsner, Nikolaus. *A History of Building Types.* London: Thames and Hudson, 1976.
Piquard, Brigitte, and Mark Swenarton. 'Learning from Architecture and Conflict.' *The Journal of Architecture* 16, no. 1 (2011): 1–13.
Porath, Yehoshua, and Yaacov Shavit, eds. *HaHistoryia shel Eretz Israel: HaMandat VeHabayit HaLe'umi, 1917–1947.* Jerusalem: Keter and Yad Itzhak Ben Zvi, 1998.
Pullan, Wendy, and Maximilian Gwiazda. 'Jerusalem's Holy Basin: Who Needs it?' *Palestine-Israel Journal of Politics, Economics, and Culture* 17, no. 1 (2011): 172–9.
Rabbat, Nasser. 'The Meaning of the Umayyad Dome of the Rock.' *Muqarnas* 6 (1989): 12–21.
Rabinow, Paul. 'Colonialism, Modernity: The French in Morocco.' In *Forms of Dominance: On the Architecture and Urbanism of the Colonial Enterprise*, edited by Nezar AlSayyad, 167–82. Aldershot: Averbury, 1992.
Rabinowitz, Dan, and Daniel Monterescu. 'Reconfiguring the "Mixed Town": Urban Transformations of Ethnonational Relations in Palestine and Israel.' *International Journal of Middle East Studies* 40, no. 2 (2008): 195–226.
Rajagopalan, Mrinalini. 'A Medieval Monument and its Modern Myths of Iconoclasm: The Enduring Contestations over the Qutb Complex in Delhi, India.' In *Reuse Value: Spolia and Appropriation in Art and Architecture from Constantine to Sherrie Levine*, edited by Richard Brilliant and Dale Kinney, 199–222. Abingdon and New York: Routledge, 2016.
Ratner, Yohanan. *Chayay Ve'Ani.* Translated by Rina Klinov. Jerusalem: Schocken, 1978.
Reich, Ronny, and Ayala Sussman. 'LeToldot Muse'on Rockefeller BiYerushalayim.' In *Sefer Ze'ev Vilnai*, edited by Eli Schiller, vol. 2, 83–91. Jerusalem: Ariel, 1984.
———. 'Al Otiot Ivriot She'Yitsev Eric Gill.' *Cathedra: For the History of Eretz Israel and Its Yishuv* 95 (April 2000): 172–7.
Reiter, Yitzhak. 'Waqf BiNsibot Mishtanot.' In *Kalkala VeChevra Bi'Ymei HaMandat, 1918–1948*, edited by Avi Bra'eli and Nahum Kralinski, 349–66. Be'er Sheba: Ben-Gurion University of the Negev Press, 2003.
Roberts, Nicholas E. 'Rethinking the Status Quo: The British and Islam in Palestine, 1917–1929.' PhD diss., New York University, 2010.
Robson, Laura. *Colonialism and Christianity in Mandate Palestine.* Austin: University of Texas Press, 2011.
Rosen-Ayalon, Miriam. 'Omanut HaBniya VeHa'yitur BiYerushalyim.' In *Prakim BeToldon Yerushalayim Bi'Ymei HaBeinayim*, edited by Binyamin Ze'ev Kedar, 287–315. Jerusalem: Yad Itzhak Ben-Zvi, 1979.
Roy, Ananya, '"The Reverse Side of the World": Identity, Space and Power.' In *Hybrid Urbanism: On the Identity Discourse and the Built Environment*, edited by Nezar AlSayyad, 229–46. Westport: Praeger, 2001.
Rubinstein, Elyakim. 'Yehudim Ve'Aravim Be'Yiryot Eretz-Israel (1926–1933) Yerushalayim Ve'Arim Acherot.' *Cathedra: For the History of Eretz Israel and Its Yishuv* 51 (1989): 122–47.
Sabbagh, Mahdi. 'The Husayni Neighborhood in Jerusalem.' *Jerusalem Quarterly* 72 (2017): 102–14.
Schiller, Eli. 'Ha'Yir Ha'Atika KaYom.' *Ariel* 57–8 (1988): 70–92 (special issue titled *Yerushalayim: Ha'Yir Ha'Atika*, edited by Eli Schiller and Gideon Biger).
Scholch, Alexander. 'Britain in Palestine, 1838–1882: The Roots of the Balfour Policy.' *Journal of Palestine Studies* 22, no. 1 (1992): 39–56.
Schur, Natan. *Toldot Ako.* Tel Aviv: Dvir, 1990.
Scott, William B., and Peter M. Rutkoff. *New York Modern: The Arts and the City.* Baltimore: Johns Hopkins University Press, 2001.
Sefer, Akin. 'New Approaches to the History of Palestine: Relational History and the Ottoman Past.' *New Perspectives on Turkey* 48 (2013): 129–40.
Segev, Tom, and Haim Watzman. *One Palestine, Complete: Jews and Arabs under the British Mandate.* Translated by Haim Watzman. New York: Metropolitan Books, 2000.
Sela, Avraham. 'Chevra VeMosdot BeKerev Arvi'yei Palestine BiTkufat HaMandat: Tmura He'ader Ni'ut VeKrisa.' In *Kalkala VeChevra Bi'Ymei HaMandat, 1918–1948*, edited by Avi Bra'eli and Nahum Kralinski, 291–348. Be'er Sheba: Ben-Gurion University of the Negev, 2003.
Shafir, Gershon. *Land, Labor, and the Origins of the Israeli-Palestinian Conflict, 1882–1914.* Berkeley: University of California Press, 1996.
Shalev, Michael. *Labour and the Political Economy in Israel.* Oxford: Oxford University Press, 1992. http://www.questia.com/read/48984458/labour-and-the-political-economy-in-israel.

Shalev-Khalifa, Nirit, and Yair Wallach. 'Ke'Even Kechel al Rekah Nof Ha'Even HaTzehavhav.' *Et-Mol* (2011): 36–8.

Sharabi, Mohamed. 'Stadt- und Stadtarchitektur im Nahen Osten zur Kolonialzeit: Das Beispiel Kairo.' *Architectura* 15, no. 1 (1985): 47–68.

Shaw, Wendy M. K. *Possessors and Possessed: Museums, Archaeology, and the Visualization of History in the Late Ottoman Empire.* Berkeley: University of California Press, 2003.

Shenhav, Yehouda. 'How did the Mizrahim "Become" Religious and Zionist?: Zionism, Colonialism and the Religionization of the Arab Jew.' *Israel Studies Forum* 19, no. 1 (2003): 73–87.

Shewring, Walter. *Letters of Eric Gill.* London: Cape, 1947.

Shiloh-Cohen, Nurit, ed. *Bezalel shel Schatz, 1906–1929.* Exhibition Catalogue. Jerusalem: Israel Museum, 1983.

Shoval, Noam, and Kobi Cohen-Hattab. 'Urban Hotel Development Patterns in the Face of Political Shifts.' *Annals of Tourism Research* 28, no. 4 (2001): 908–25.

Smith, Charles D. *Palestine and the Arab-Israeli Conflict: A History with Documents.* 5th ed. Boston, MA: Bedford/St Martins, 2004.

Sosnovsky, Silvina, ed. *Yohanan Ratner: H'Adam, Ha'Architect Ve'Avodato.* Haifa: Technion, Israel Architecture Heritage Center, 1992.

Speaight, Robert. *The Life of Eric Gill.* London: Methuen, 1966.

Spurr, David. *The Rhetoric of Empire: Colonial Discourse in Journalism, Travel Writing and Imperial Administration.* Durham, NC: Duke University Press, 1993.

St. Laurent, Beatrice, and András Riedlmayer. 'Restorations of Jerusalem and the Dome of the Rock and Their Political Significance, 1537–1928.' *Muqarnas* 10 (1993): 76–84.

Stendell, Uri. 'Mishpachot HaNichbadim BeKerev Aravi'yei Yerushlayim.' In *Sefer Ze'ev Vilnai*, edited by Eli Schiller, vol. 2, 67–72. Jerusalem: Ariel, 1984.

Stern, Robert A. M. 'PSFS: Beaux-Arts Theory and Rational Expressionism.' *Journal of the Society of Architectural Historians* 21, no. 2 (1962): 84–102.

Storrs, Ronald. *The Memoirs of Ronald Storrs.* New York: G. Putnam's Sons, 1937.

———. *Orientations.* London: Ivor Nicholson & Watson, 1937.

Sutcliffe, Anthony. *Towards the Planned City: Germany, Britain, the United States and France 1780–1914.* New York: St Martin's Press, 1981.

Szurek, Emmanuel. '"Go West": Variations on Kemalist Orientalism.' In *After Orientalism: Critical Perspectives on Western Agency and Eastern Re-appropriations*, edited by François Pouillon and Jean-Claude Vatin, 103–20. Leiden and Boston: Brill, 2015.

Tamari, Shmuel. 'Maqam Nebi Musa SheLeyad Jericho.' *Cathedra for the History of Eretz Israel and Its Yishuv* 11 (1979): 153–80.

Taragan, Hana. 'Historical Reference in Medieval Islamic Architecture: Baybars's Buildings in Palestine.' *Bulletin of the Israeli Academic Center in Cairo* 25 (2002): 31–4.

Tauranac, John. *The Empire State Building: The Making of a Landmark.* New York: Scribner, 1995.

Tejirian, Eleanor S., and Reeva Spector Simon, eds. *Altruism and Imperialism: Western Cultural and Religious Missions in the Middle East.* New York: Columbia University Press, 2002.

Theunissen, Hans. 'War, Propaganda and Architecture: Cemal Pasha's Restoration of Islamic Architecture in Damascus during World War I.' In *Jihad and Islam in World War I*, edited by Erik-Jan Zürcher, 223–73. Leiden: Leiden University Press, 2016.

Tidhar, David. *Entsiklopedyah LeChalutsey Ha'Yishuv UBonav.* http://www.tidhar.tourolib.org/tidhar/.

Trajtenberg, Graciela. 'Be'in Burganut Le'Omanut Palestinit BiTkufat HaMandat.' *Israeli Sociology* D, no. 1 (2002): 7–38.

Tsimhoni, Daphne. 'The Armenians and the Syrians: Ethno-religious Communities in Jerusalem.' *Middle Eastern Studies* 20, no. 3 (1984): 352–69.

———. 'The Status of the Arab Christians under the British Mandate in Palestine.' *Middle Eastern Studies* 20, no. 4 (1984): 166–92.

Tuchman, Barbara. *Bible and Sword: England and Palestine from the Bronze Age to Balfour.* New York: New York University Press, 1956.

Twain, Mark. *The Innocents Abroad, or The New Pilgrims' Progress*, vol. 2. New York: P. F. Collier & Son, 1911.

Tzahor, Zeev. 'The Struggle between the Revisionist Party and the Labor Movement: 1929–1933.' *Modern Judaism* 8, no. 1 (1988): 15–25.

Vilnay, Ze'ev. *Ramlah – Hove Ve'Avar.* Jerusalem: Ariel, 1961.
Vlack, Don. *Art Deco Architecture in New York, 1920–1940.* New York: Harper & Row, 1974.
Wallach, Yair, 'Readings in Conflict: Public Text in Modern Jerusalem, 1858–1948.' PhD diss., University of London, 2008.
Warhaftig, Myra. *They Laid the Foundation: Lives and Works of German-Speaking Jewish Architects in Palestine 1918–1948.* Translated by Andrea Lerner. Tübingen and New York: Wasmuth, 2007.
Welter, Volker. *Biopolis: Patrick Geddes and the City of Life.* Cambridge, MA: MIT Press, 2002.
Wharton, Annabel. 'Erasure: Eliminating the Space of Late Ancient Judaism.' In *From Dura to Sepphoris: Studies in Jewish Art and Society in Late Antiquity*, edited by Lee Israel Levine and Ze'ev Weiss, 195–214. Portsmouth, RI: Journal of Roman Archaeology, 2000.
———. *Selling Jerusalem: Relics, Replicas, Theme Parks.* Chicago: University of Chicago Press, 2006.
———. 'Two Waldorf-Astorias: Spatial Economies as Totem and Fetish.' *The Art Bulletin* 85, no. 3 (2003): 523–43.
Whitehead, Christopher. 'National Art Museums in Britain.' In *National Museums: New Studies from Around the World*, edited by Simon Knell, Peter Aronsson and Arne Bugge Amundsen, 105–22. Abingdon and New York: Routledge, 2014.
Williams Goldhagen, Sarah. 'Coda: Reconceptualizing the Modern'. In *Anxious Modernisms: Experimentation in Postwar Architectural Culture*, edited by Sarah Williams Goldhagen and Réjean Legault, 301–23. Montreal: Canadian Centre for Architecture, and Cambridge, MA: MIT Press, 2000.
Willis, Carol. *Form Follows Finance: Skyscrapers and Skylines in New York and Chicago.* New York: Princeton Architectural Press, 1995.
Windover, Michael. 'Exchanging Looks: "Art Dekho" Movie Theatres in Bombay.' *Architectural History* 52 (2009): 201–32.
Winterowd, W. Ross. 'Capitalism and Culture: John and John and Scripture; Andy and Adam, Herb, Matt, and Waldo.' *JAC* 27, no. 3 (2007): 539–62.
Wintle, Michael. 'Renaissance Maps and the Construction of the Idea of Europe.' *Journal of Historical Geography* 25 no. 2 (1999): 137–65.
Wright, Gwendolyn. *The Politics of Design in French Colonial Urbanism.* Chicago: University of Chicago Press, 1991.
Yacobi, Haim. 'The Architecture of Ethnic Logic: Exploring the Meaning of the Built Environment in the "Mixed" City of Lod–Israel.' *Geografiska Annaler: Series B, Human Geography* 84, no. 3–4 (2002): 171–87.
———. 'The Language of Modernity: Urban Design in Mandatory Lydda.' *The Jerusalem Quarterly* 42 (2010): 80–93.
Yavuz, Yildirim. 'Influence of Late Ottoman Architecture in Arab Provinces: The Case of the "Palace Hotel" in Jerusalem.' *Proceedings of the 11th International Conference on Turkish Arts*, University of Utrecht, 1999.
———. 'The Restoration Project of the Masjid Al-Aqsa by Mimar Kemalettin (1922–26).' *Muqarnas* 13 (1996): 149–64.
Yorke, Malcolm. *Eric Gill: Man of Flesh and Spirit.* London: Constable, 1990.
Zerubavel, Yael. *Recovered Roots: Collective Memory and the Making of Israeli National Tradition.* Chicago: University of Chicago Press, 1995.
Zweig, Ronald W. *Britain and Palestine during the Second World War.* Martlesham: Boydell Press, 1986.

Index

References to images are in *italics*

Aalto, Alvar, 6
'Abd al-Hamid II, Sultan, 26
Abdelrazek, Adnan, 176
abstraction, 78–9, 88, 217, 218
Acre, 120
Adamson, Arthur Quincy, 109–10, 111, 112–13, 129–30
Africa, 92–4
agriculture, 134
Ahmad, Rushdi Bey, 151, 152
Algiers (Algeria), 28, 48
Alhambra (Spain), 74–5, 76, 97, 219
Allahabad (India), 38
Allenby, Gen. Edmund, 12
Allerton Houses (New York City), 108
Allied School, 57, 60, 80
Allweil, Yael, 9
AlSayyad, Nezar, 52
America *see* United States of America
American Colony, 8, 13
American School of Oriental Research, 57, 60
ancient civilisations, 87–8
Anglo communities, 11
Anglo-Palestine Bank, 7, 186
Ankara (Turkey), 151, 163, 164–5, 167, 220
Anthemius of Tralles, 124
antiquities, 57–9
Antiquities Department *see* Department of Antiquities
Al Aqsa Mosque (Al-Masjid al-Aqsa), xvi, 1, 22, 149, 167–8
   and inspiration, 165, 167–8, 179
   and restoration, 150–3
   and wood carvings, *166*, *167*
Arab Revolt, 99, 173
arabesques, 167, 168
Arabs, *xvi*, 8, 34, 87
   and construction, 96, 98–9
   and housing, 48
   and nationalism, 45
   and Old City, 22
   and Palace Hotel, 18–19, 145, 168–70, 172, 173–4, 175–6, 217
   and Palestine Archaeological Museum, 100
   and stone, 210–12
   and violence, 111
   and ZEB, 206, 209–10
   see also Al Husayni, Hajj Amin; Muslims
arcades, *115*, 118, 132–4, *135*, 136
Archaeological Advisory Board, 57
archaeology, 25, 44, 47, 55, 57–60
   and architecture, 60–2
   and Art Deco, 88
arches, *xvi*, 1, 78, 219
architecture, 1–2, 4, 108–9, 219–20, 226–7
   and archaeology, 60–2
   and competition, 95–6
   and cross-culturalism, 16–19
   and hotels, *117*, 117, 133
   and identities, 224
   and Islam, 133
   and Jerusalem, 8–11
   and Palestine Archaeological Museum, 66, 68, 70, 74–5, 77–81, 84–6
   and religion, 118, *119*, 120, 122–3, 124, 141–2
   and Turkey, 161–5, 168
   and USA, 107–8, 117
   and vernacular, 218–19
   and ZEB, 186–9
   see also modernism
Arlosoroff, Haim, 210
Armenians, 22, 74, 97
Art Deco, 79, 108, 216, 219
   and Gill, 86, 88
   and Palace Hotel, 163, 170–1
   and USA, 130, *131*, 132
   and YMCA, 126–7, 128, 140
Art Institute of Chicago (USA), 63
Arts and Crafts movement, 33, 36, 140
Ashbee, Charles Robert, 20–1, 24, 25–6, 28
   and archaeology, 60

and crafts, 97
and urban planning, 33–42
and YMCA, 106–7
Ashkenazi Jews, 13, 206, 207, 222
Asia, 92–4
Assembly of Representatives, 197, *198*
Assyria, 88
Assyria–Babylonia (relief), 89, *90*
atonement, 127–8
auditoriums, 113–14, 120, *121*, 124, *125*
Auguste Victoria Endowment hospice, 118, *119*
'Awad, Dunie & Katinka, 97, 110–11, *112*
'Awad, Stello Elyās, 110, 111, 172, *173*
Awqaf *see* Waqf

Badram, Jamal, 170
Baerwald, Alexander, 187, 203
Baghdad (Iraq), 22
balconies, 114, 125, 156, 158, 164, *166*
 and ZEB, 195, 196, *197*
Balfour Declaration, 62
Bankers Trust Company Building (New York City), 108
Bar-Yosef, Eitan, 62
Barluzzi, Antonio, 15
Barsky, George, 174–5
Basu, Paul, 58
Beaux-Arts, 68, 74, 77, 79, 81, 85
 and Palace Hotel, 158, 161, 171
Ben-Gurion, David, 209
Ben-Zvi, Yizhak, 186
Bentwich, Norman, 6
Bethel, 139
Bezalel School of Art, 113, 134, 140
Bhabha, Homi, 52
Bible Society Building, 42
Bible, the, 58, 60, 88–9, 124–5, 136–7, 139
Bosworth, William Welles, 81, *82*
Boubet, Etienne, 118
Bozdoğan, Sibel, 161, 162–3
Breasted, James Henry, 18, 62–3, 64, 65, 215
 and archaeology, 88
 and Harrison, 66, 81
 and museums, 77
 and USA, 85
Brisacier, Abbé, 118
British Broadcasting Corporation (BBC) House (London), 88
British Empire, 11–12, 21, 30–3, 54
British Mandate, 1–2, 5, 7, 12, 223
 and Antiquities Ordinance, 57–8
 and Arabs, 14–15
 and architecture, 224, 225
 and Ashbee, 34–5, 37–8
 and Jewish settlement, 185
 and Kendall, 49
 and land, 18
 and Muslims, 147
 and neutrality, 96, 98
 and Palace Hotel, 174, 176
 and politics, 35–6
 and urban planning, 20–1, 23–6, 28–9, 51–2, 53–4
British Museum (London), 60
British School of Archaeology, 57
Brodie, John A., 30
building blocks, 163
Bute House, 60
Byzantine architecture, 142
Byzantium, 88, 89, 124
Byzantium (relief), *91*, 92

Cairo, 22, 30, 74, 148
 and archaeological museum, 81, *82*
Canaan (relief), 88, *90*
capitalism, 48
capitals, 133–4, *135*, 136, *166*
Carey, Graham, 87
ceilings, 70, 78, 140
Cemal Pasha, 151
cement, 112, 209
cemeteries, 38, 153–4
Cenacle, 75, 77
Central Zionist Archive (CZA), 200
ceramic tiles, 74–5, *76*, 97, 216
Chaikin, Benjamin, 110, 188
chapels, 138–40
Chermayeff, Serge, 87
Chicago House (Luxor), 62, 84
Chicago University Oriental Institute (USA), 63, 85
China, 109
Christianity, 1, 92, 134, 220
 and communities, 12–13
 and Old City, 22
 and Rockefeller, 64–5
 see also Christians; Jerusalem YMCA Building
Christians, 7, 49, 112, 143, 147, 148
 and architecture, 75
 and communities, 11, 14–15
 and inscriptions, 137
 and Protestantism, 101, 105
Church of the Ascension, 120
Church of the Holy Sepulcher, 22, 120, *122*
Churchill, Winston, 35
City Beautiful movement, 36
City Clock Tower, 26, *27*
City Hall, 42
classicism, 200, 202
clerestories, 70
cloisters, 133, 219
Cody, Jeffery, 107
Colonial Problem, The, 35
colonialism, 5, 28–9, 30–3, 48
 and archaeology, 58
 and segregation, 37, 38, 40
 and urban planning, 51–3

communities, 11–16, 103, 109–13, 220–3
Concannon, T. A. L., 96
concrete *see* reinforced concrete
Constantine, Emperor, 92
courtyards, 42, 156, 170, 215, 218
   and Palestine Archaeological Museum, 66, 68, 69, 70, 73, 74–5, 79, 81, 84, 86, 97
   and Zionist Executive Building, 193, *194*, 195, 196, 202, 212, *213*
crafts, 38, 39, 97
Crinson, Mark, 4–5
Crompton, John, 139, 140
Crusader-era architecture, 75, 79, 120
Crusades, 89
Crusades (relief), *91*, 92
culture, 10, 39–40, 50, 53
   and archaeology, 55, 57, 58
   and architecture, 16–19, 75, 77
   and urban planning, 33
   and YMCA, 105–6
   see also multiculturalism
Cunliff-Lister, Sir Philip, 98
Cunningham, Sir Alan Gordon, 45

Damascus (Syria), 22, 140, 151
Damascus Gate, 26
Damodaran, Vinita, 58
David, King, 75
Davis, John, 134
De Farro & Co., 97, 110–11
decolonisation, 21, 51, 52, 224
Delhi *see* New Delhi
Department of Agriculture, 176
Department of Antiquities, 44, 57, 58, 60, 65, 80
Deucalion, 90, 92
diaspora, 199–200, 204
Dimmock, Marion, 101, 134, 140, 220–1
Diskin, Shimon, 97
Diskin Orphanage, 7
Dome of the Rock (Qubbat al-Sakhrah), *xvi*, 1, 22, 97
   and inspiration, 165, 167, 168, 179
   and restorations, 110, 151
domes, 70, *71*, 74, 78, 218, *219*
   and Islam, 130
   and religious architecture, 120, 124
   and YMCA, 106–7, 114
Dunie, Tuvia, 110, 172, 173

earthquakes, 114, 155, 184
East Jerusalem, 16, 18
ecumenism, 106, 113
Egypt, 55, 62, 63, 65, 88; *see also* Cairo; Luxor
Egypt (relief), 88–9, *90*
El-Eini, Rosa, 21
Empire State Building (New York City), 108
environment, the, 203–4, 219
Europeans, 22–3, 92–4

excavations *see* archaeology
Ezra Orthodox Jewish Youth Movement, 183

fenestration *see* windows
Fertile Crescent (relief), 89
fertility, 134
fireplaces, 140, *141*
First National Style, 161, 163, 168
First Vakif Han (Istanbul), 161, *162*, 163–4
flora and fauna, 133–4, *135*, 136
Florida (USA), 118
Fogg Art Museum (Boston), 87
fonts, 86, 94–5
France, 28, 57, 118
Frank, Joseph, 188
Friedman, Alexander, 188
Fuchs, Ron, 62, 74, 79, 81
functionalism, 4, 205–6
furniture, 111–12, 140

Gafni, Reuven, 187
galleries, 68, 70, 72
Garden City movement, 36, 40–2
garden suburbs, 48
Garstang, John, 55, 57, 89
Geddes, Sir Patrick, 20, 32–3, 39
General Organization of Hebrew Workers in Eretz Israel (Histadrut), 207, 208–9, 210–11
General Post Office, 86
George VI of Great Britain, King, 212
German Colony, 13, 38
Germany, 118, 220
Giat, Abraham, 113
Gibson, Shimon, 62
Gill, Eric, 86–90, 92–5, 112
globalisation, 5
Gluska, Zachariah, 206, 207
Golden Book, The, 197, 199
Goode, James, 63
Goodhue, Bertram Grosvenor, 85, 130
Government Printer, 86
Gray, Eileen, 6
Great Britain, 13, 35–6, 45–6
   and archaeology, 57–9, 59–60
   and museums, 75, 77–8
   and Palestine Archaeological Museum, 63–4, 65, 100, 214–15, 221
   and YMCA, 103, 104
   see also British Empire; British Mandate
Great Depression, 75
Greece–Macedonia (relief), 90, *91*, 92
Greek Orthodox Patriarchate, 18, 106
greenbelts, 38, 39, 44, 52
Gur-Arieh, Meir, 96, 97, 112–13, 125, 127, 134
gymnasiums, 113, 114, 120, *121*

Habermas, Jürgen, 103
Hadassah (Women's Zionist Organization of America), 183

Ha'Ezrachi, Yehuda, 199
Haganah, 187
Hagia Sophia Church (Istanbul), 124
Haifa, 7, 42, 145, 187
Hankey, Maurice, 35
Hapoel Hamizrahi, 207
Haram al-Sharif (Noble Sanctuary), 19, 22, 59, 92, 148–9
   and archaeological museum, 100
   and inspiration, 179
   see also Al-Aqsa Mosque
Harmat, Zoltán Shimshon, 42
Harmon, Arthur Loomis, 18, 101, 108–9, 111, 114, *115*
   and historicism, 216, 218
   and religious architecture, 118, 120, 124, 141–2
Harrison, Austen St Barbe, 18, 66, 68, 70, 95–6
   and crafts, 97
   and design development, 81, *83*, 84–6
   and domes, 219
   and functionality, 80–1
   and Gill, 87–8
   and historicism, 216, 218
   and inspirations, 74–5, 77–8
   and Ratner, 205
   and YMCA, 110
Harte, Dr Archibald Clinton, 104, 105–6, 109–10, 111
   and capitals, 133–4
   and chapel, 138–9
   and hotels, 117
   and tower, 124–6, 127, 130
Hebrew Gymnasium, 190
Hebrew Society for the Excavation of Palestine and Its Antiquities, 100
Hebrew University of Jerusalem, 7, 8, 100, 110, 203
Hebron massacre, 210
Hecker, Wilhelm, 185, 187, 208
Hecker & Yellin, 188, 208
Helen, Saint, 92
Herbert, Gilbert, 74, 79
Herzl, Theodor (Binyamin Ze'ev), 197, 199
Higher Arab Committee, 176
Histadrut see General Organization of Hebrew Workers in Eretz Israel
historicism, 5, 18, 19, 77–8, 108, 216, 217–20
   and Palestine Archaeological Museum, 66, 74, 86
   and Palace Hotel, 161–3, 170
   and YMCA, 140, 142
   and Zionism, 202, 204
Holden, Charles, 79
Holliday, Albert Clifford, 20, 42–4, 48, 49, 110
Holy Land see Palestine
Hopkins, Charles Howard, 103
hospices, 118, *119*, 215

hotel architecture, 117–18, *117*, 133; see also Palace Hotel
housing, 42, 44, 48
Howe, George, 85
Hurva Synagogue, 120, *123*, 124
Al Husayni, Hajj Amin, 19, 147–50, 152, 176, *178*
   and Katinka, 172, 173, 174
   and Palace Hotel, 153, 154, 155
Husaynis (family), 14, 176
hybrid spaces, 52–3, 216
hygiene, 26
Hyman, Benjamin, 21, 30, 44

identity, 10–11, 224
   and Arabs, 14–15, 217
   and Yishuv, 181, 186–7
India, 25, 33, 37, 79; see also New Delhi
industry, 44, 46–7
inscriptions
   and Palestine Archaeological Museum, 86, 94–5, 96–7
   and Palace Hotel, 168–9
   and YMCA, 136–8, 142
interior design, 111–12, 140, 170–2
International Arab Exhibition (1933), 176
internationalism, 4–5
Iraq, 22, 55
Isaiah, 127, 128, 136
Isidorus of Miletus, 124
Islam, 1, 127–8, 133, 220
   and mosques, 120, *122*, 124, 130
   see also Arabs; Muslims
Islam (relief), 91, *92*
Israel (relief), 89, *91*
Israel Museum, 225
Istanbul (Turkey), 59, 124, 161–2, 220
   and Nigisberk, 145, 151–2, 163, 167
Istiqlal party, 130

Jacobson, Abigail, 9, 21
Jaffa Gate, 26, 27, 28, 106
Jaljulia Mosque (Jajulia), 179
Janjirieh Garden City, 41–2
Jarvie, James Newbegin, 105
Al Jazzâr Pasha Mosque (Acre), 120, *122*, 124
Jericho, 145
Jerusalem, 1–2, 5, 6–8, 16–18, 223–4
   and architecture, 8–11, 226–7
   and Ashbee, 33–42
   and Britain, 215
   and communities, 11–16, 220–3
   and Holliday, 42–4
   and Kendall, 45–50, *51*
   and urban planning, 20–6, 28–33, 51–4
   see also Jerusalem YMCA Building; Old City; Palace Hotel; Palestine Archaeological Museum; Zionist Executive Building
Jerusalem Islamic Congress (1931), 175

Jerusalem YMCA Building, 2, 3, 4, 8, 15, 18, *102*, 215–16
   and arcade, *115*, *116*, 132–4, *135*, *136*
   and auditorium, *121*, *125*
   and communities, 109–13, 221–2
   and construction, 113–14
   and functions, 143–4
   and gymnasium, *121*
   and historicism, 218
   and inspirations, 117–18, 120, 124–30, *132–3*
   and membership, 142–3
   and modern day, 225
   and multifaith elements, 136–40, 141–2
   and Palace Hotel, 155
   and planning, 104–9
   and Ratner, 203
   and USA, 103–4
Jesus Christ, 125, 126, 137
Jewish Agency, 181, 183, 188, 210
   and ZEB, 189–91, 192, 195, 200, 207
Jewish National Council (JNC), 210
Jewish National Fund (JNF), 181, 183, 186
   and ZEB, 189–90, 193, 195, *196*, 197, *198*, 199–200, *201*
Jews, xvi, 1, 12, 13, 15–16
   and architecture, 75
   and Ashbee, 34
   and Balfour Declaration, 62
   and construction, 96–9
   and Gill, 87
   and inscriptions, 137–8
   and Kendall, 49
   and land, 18
   and Old City, 22
   and Palace Hotel, 172, 173–4
   and Palestine Archaeological Museum, 100
   and sculpture, 113
   and stone, 210–12
   and violence, 111
   and YMCA, 112, 143
   and ZEB, 206–10
   see also Ashkenazi Jews; communities; Sephardi Jews; Yishuv
Jordan, 97, 225
Judaism, 1, 220
   and flora and fauna, 134
   and sculpture, 127–9
   and synagogues, 120, *123*, 124
   see also Jews
Julian's Way, 106, 155–6
Julliard School of Music (New York City), 108

Kampala (Uganda), 39, *40*
Karl, Barry, 64–5
Karm-el-Sheik (Abraham's Vineyard), 63–4
Karmi, Dov, 216
Katinka, Baruch, 110, 153, 172–4
Kattawi, Hussni, 179

Katz, Stanley, 64–5
Kauffmann, Richard, 41, 187
Keck, Maxfield H., 126
Keith-Roach, Edward, 174
Kemalettin Bey, Ahmet, 110, 150–3, 155, 162, 163
Kendall, Henry, 20, 21, 23, 25, 26, 28
   Town Planning in Uganda, 39
   and urban planning, 45–50, *51*
Kenyon, Sir Fredric, 60, 80
Keren Ha'Yesod (Foundation Fund of Palestine), 181, 184, 188, 189–90, 193, 195
Khalidi, Rashid, 14, 154
Khartoum (Sudan), 30
Kimmerling, Baruch, 9
King David Hotel, 110, 155, 175, 220–1
Kornberg, Fritz, 190
Krakauer, Leopold, 187
Kroyanker, David, 170, 200
Kuczinski, Dov (Baer), 187
Kutahia (Turkey), 97

Lag ba-Omer, 181
Lamprakos, Michele, 48
land, 18, 37
language, 136–8
Last Supper, 75
Le Corbusier, 6, 85
   Plan Obus, 48
League of Nations, 35, 54, 57, 58
Leibnitz, Robert, 118
Lemire, Vincent, 9, 224
Lepine, Ayla, 142
Lescaze, William, 85
Levin, Michael, 200
Lishansky, Batia, 113
Lloyd George, David, 35
Lockman, Zachary, 9, 209
London, 220
Lutyens, Edwin L., 30
Luxor (Egypt), 62, 84

MacCarthy, Fiona, 87
McLean, William H., 6, 20, 29–33, 26
McMillan, Neil, Jr, 107–8, 111, 137
Maghribi community, 12
Mamilla, 150, 153–4, 155–6
Mamluk Maqam Nabi Musa, 74
Mauger, Paul Victor Edison, 96
Mayers, Murray & Phillip, 84, 85
Mecca (Saudi Arabia), 151
media, 99–100
Medina (Saudi Arabia), 151
Mediterranean vernacular, 85–6, 219
Mendelsohn, Eric, 85, 86, 87, 202
Mesopotamia, 88
metal railings, 163
Metropolitan Museum of Art (New York City), 108

Migdal Insurance Company, 186
minarets, 78, 130
Misrad Kablani, 208–9
missions, 103–4, 108, 109
Mizrahi *see* Sephardi Jews
modernism, 1, 4–6, 108, 216, 217–20
   and Harrison, 79, 86
   and YMCA, 141–2
   and ZEB, 193, 195–6, 200, 202–3, 204–6
Monk, Daniel
   An Aesthetic Occupation, 9–10
monuments, 25, 30
Morocco, 38
mosaic, 140, 216
Moses, 89, 95
mosques, 8, 120, *122*, 124, 130, *131*, 218
   and Jaljulia, 179
   see also Al-Aqsa Mosque
motifs, 167–8
Mott, John R., 104, 105
Mount of Olives, 38, 64
Mount Scopus, 64
Muhammad (Prophet), 92, 138, 148
multiculturalism, 10, 52, 109–13, 223–4
multifaith elements, 136–40
Museum of Modern Art (New York City), 85
museums, 57, 59–62, 75, 77–8; *see also*
   Palestine Archaeological Museum
Muslims, 1, 7, 11, 75, 101, 222
   and communities, 12, 14–15
   and Harte, 125, 130
   and inscriptions, 137–8
   and Kendall, 49
   and Palace Hotel, 147–8
   and reliefs, 92
   and YMCA, 112, 143
al-Mutawakki al-Laythī, 168–9

Naor, Moshe, 9
al Nashashibi, Ragheb, 153, 172–3, 176
Nashashibis (family), 14, 149, 155
Nashif, Taysir, 9
National Institutions House *see* Zionist
   Executive Building
nationalism, 14, 35, 45, 62, 63, 168
Natural History Museum (London), 134
Nebraska State Capitol (NE), 130, *131*, 132
neighbourhoods, 8, 16, 39, 47, 49–50, 224
   and Ashbee, 36, 37, 40–2
   and Holliday, 44
   and Mandate, 7, 52
   and Old City, 22
   see also American Colony; German Colony;
   Janjirieh Garden City; Mamilla; Rehavia;
   Shaykh Jarrah
Neo-Baroque, 161
Neo-Renaissance, 108, 161
neocolonialism, 5
New Delhi (India), 28, 30, *31*, 38

New York City (USA), 36, 108–9, 171–2, 220
Nigisberk, Mehmet Nihat (Mehmed Nihad
   Bey), 19, 110, 150, 151–2, 218
   and Palace Hotel, 145, 147, 155, 161–2, 163–5,
   167–70, 171–2, 217
Nikophoriah, 106
Nirenberg, David, 224–5
North Africa, 28, 37
Notre Dame de France hospice, 118, *119*

octagons, 66, 70, 168
Ohanessian, David, 97
Old City, 16, 22, 26, 33, 44
   and Ashbee, 36, 37, 38
   and demolitions, 26, 28
   and Kendall, 45, 46
   and Mandate, 53
   and McLean, 29, 30
   and Palestine Archaeological Museum, 64,
   65, 66
   and preservation, 23–4
   and urban planning, 51–2
   and ZEB, 200
   see also Jerusalem YMCA Building; Palace
   Hotel
Orientalism, 87, 107, 203
   and art, 134
   and ornamentation, 202
   and Turkey, 162, 163
Ormsby-Gore, William, 66
Orthodox Jews, 16, 183
Ottoman Bank, 7
Ottoman Empire, 1, 5, 6, 22, 215
   and archaeology, 57, 58–9
   and architecture, 161–5
   and British, 11, 12, 25–6
   and Ministry of Vakifs, 150–1, 152
   and mosques, 124
Oxford Museum (Oxford), 134

Palace Hotel, 2, 3, 4, 8, 18–19, 145, *146*, 147, 217
   and communities, 222
   and construction, 153–4, 172–4
   and design, 154–6, 158, 161–5, 167–70
   and façade, 156, *160*, *166*
   and floor plan, *157*
   and functions, 174–6, 179–80
   and historicism, 218
   and interior design, 170–2
   and lobby, 156, *158*, *159*, 168, 170
   and modern day, 225
   and Nigisberk, 110
   and restaurant, 156, *160*, 170–1
   and skylight, 156, *159*
Palas Hotel (Ankara), 164–5
Palestine, 1, 11–12, 45–6, 165
   and archaeology, 57, 58–9
   and flora and fauna, 133–4

Palestine (cont.)
  see also Acre; Bethel; Haifa; Jaljuliah; Jericho; Jerusalem; Ramallah; Samaria; Tel Aviv
Palestine Archaeological Museum, 2, 3, 4, 7, 18, 55, 56
  and architecture, 66, 68, 70, 74–5, 77–81, 84–6, 216, 225
  and Britain, 214–15, 221
  and central court, 69, 73
  and construction, xvi, 1, 95–9
  and ground plan, 67
  and historical approach, 99–100, 218
  and objectives, 57–8
  and reading room, 71, 75
  and Rockefeller, 62–5
  and sculpture, 86–90, 91, 92–5
  and south gallery, 68
Palestinians see Arabs
park system (Jerusalem), 36, 38–9, 40, 44, 46
pavilions, 73, 74
Peel Commission, 176, 177
Philistia (relief), 88, 89, 90
Phoenicia (relief), 89
Phoenix Insurance Company, 186
pilasters, 166–7
pilgrims, 113, 118, 155, 215
Piquard, Brigitte, 226
Plumer, Lord Herbert Charles O., 63, 66
politics, 95–6, 35–6, 37, 155
  and Arab labour, 209–10
  and archaeology, 55, 57
  and Palace Hotel, 173, 175–6
  and ZEB, 212–13
  and Zionism, 181, 183
Ponce de León Hotel (FL), 117, 117, 133
population distribution, 49, 50
preservation, 23–5, 38–9, 47; see also restorations
Price, W., 96
Pro-Jerusalem Society, 24–5, 34, 36
Pyrrha, 90, 92

Raban, Ze'ev
  and Palestine Archaeological Museum, 95, 96, 97
  and YMCA, 112–13, 125, 127, 128–9, 134
Rabin, Itzhak, 187
Ramallah, 145
Ratner, Michael, 186, 188, 212
Ratner, Yohanan, 19, 211, 217, 218, 219
  and ZEB, 181, 187–9, 200, 202–6, 210, 212
regionalism, 200, 202
Rehavia, 41–2, 185, 189–90, 216
Reich, Ronny, 89, 94–5
Reiner, Dr Marcus, 95
reinforced concrete, xvi, 1, 25, 216, 219
  and Palace Hotel, 161, 163, 170, 173
  and Palestine Archaeological Museum, 70, 98

and YMCA, 114
and ZEB, 183, 195, 204, 209
Reiter, Yizhak, 150
reliefs, 86–90, 91, 92–4, 140, 216
religious architecture, 118, 119, 120, 122–3, 124, 141–2
Remus, 92
residential zones, 47–8, 49
restorations, 150–3
Richmond, Ernst, 110
Rida, Rashid, 148
road system (Jerusalem), 46
Roberts, Nicholas, 148, 149–50
Rockefeller, John D., Jr, 18, 62–5, 66, 81, 215
  and construction, 98
  and USA, 85
  and YMCA, 105
Rockefeller, Nelson, 85
Rockefeller Museum see Palestine Archaeological Museum
Romanesque architecture, 133, 142
Rome (relief), 91, 92
Romulus, 92
Rubin, Meir, 188
Rühl, Frank, 95
Russian Patriarchy, 95

St Andrew's Church of Scotland, 7, 42, 110
St John's Opthalmic Hospital, 42
Samaria, 88, 89
sanitation, 26
sanjak, 165
sculpture, 112–13, 126–30, 133–4, 135, 136, 142; see also reliefs
Seamen's YMCA (New York City), 108
sectarianism, 15, 49, 50, 106
secularism, 4, 6, 103, 143, 222
segregation, 37, 38, 39–40
Senator, David Werner, 185
Sephardi Jews, 13, 207, 208, 222
seraphs, 127–30
Shafir, Gershon, 209
Shaw, Wendy, 59
Shaykh Jarrah, 174
Shelton Hotel (New York City), 108
signage, 86, 94
'slicks' (secret weapon storage), 174, 200
slums, 44
Sokolov, Nahum, 186, 204
Solel Boneh, 211
Solomon's Temple, 149, 203
Sosnovsky, Silvina, 202
Spain, 74–5, 76
sport, 113, 114, 143
Starkey, J. L., 99
Stern, Robert, 85
stone, xvi, 1, 70, 210–12, 219
  and Palace Hotel, 163

and YMCA, 114, 138–9
and ZEB, 193, 204
Storrs, Ronald, 23, 24, 25, 32–3
Suez Canal, 32
Sukenik, Eliezer, 95
Süleyman the Magnificent, Sultan, 25
Supreme Muslim Council (SMC), 100, 153–4, 172
  and Al Husayni, 145, 147, 149–50, 152–3
Sussman, Ayala, 89, 94–5
Swenarton, Mark, 226
Swinton, George S. C., 30
synagogues, 120, *123*, 124, 186, 188, 190
Syria *see* Damascus

Tanzimat, 6
Taut, Bruno, 202
Technion Institute of Technology (Haifa), 187
Tel Aviv, 97, 145, 184, 203
Temple Mount *see* Haram al-Sharif
Terra Santa College, 7, 15
Tiferet Yisrael Synagogue, 120, *123*, 124
tourism, 113, 154–5, 175
Tower of David ('Citadel'), 59, 215
towers, 78, 114, 118, 124–30, 132
tradition, 6, 38, 39, 217–20
Tree of Knowledge, 92–4
True Cross, 92
Tucker, Fitz-Henry Faye, 138–9
Turkey, 149, 152, 154, 161–5, 168; *see also* Ankara; Istanbul; Kutahia, Ottoman Empire
Turkish Archaeological Museum, 59
Twain, Mark, 101

Uganda, 39, *40*
unions, 96, 112, 206–7
United Nations (UN), 46, 144, 213
United States of America (USA), 2, 13, 134, 136
  and archaeology, 57
  and architecture, 107–8, 117, 225
  and museums, 77, 85
  and Palestine Archaeological Museum, 65, 214, 215, 221
  and Protestantism, 101, 105
  and towers, 130, *131*, 132
  and YMCA Building, 103–4
  see also American Colony; New York City
Ussishkin, Menachem, 183, 186, 188, *189*

Vedat Bey, 164
vernacular architecture, 85–6, 218–19
verse *see* inscriptions
violence, 45, 99, 185, 212
voussoirs, 78

Wailing Wall, 22
Waldorf Astoria Hotel (Israel) *see* Palace Hotel

Waldorf Astoria Hotel (New York City), 171–2, 180
Wallach, Yair, 168–9
Waqf (Muslim Pious Endowments Directorate), 8, 14, 172, 175, 179, 222
  and Al Husayni, 147, 150, 153
Warhaftig, Mira, 205
Wauchope, Sir Arthur, 30, 98
Way House (Palestine Antiquities Museum), 60–2
Weizmann, Chaim, 173, *177*, 197, *198*
West Jerusalem, 16–17, 18
Wharton, Annabel, 171
White Mosque (Ramla), 130, *131*
Whitehead, Christopher, 100
Wilson, Woodrow, 104
windows, 70, 78
  and Palace Hotel, 156, 163
  and YMCA, 114, 120
  and ZEB, 195, 196, 204
wings, 80–1
  and YMCA, 106–7, 114, 120
  and ZEB, 190–2
WIZO (Women's International Zionist Organization), 183
women, 130, 183
Workshop for Industrial Arts, 112–13
World War I, 1, 4, 11, 13, 31, 187
  and allies, 24
  and Greek Orthodox Patriarchy, 106
  and nationalism, 35
  and Turkey, 149, 150, 154, 172
  and YMCA, 103
World War II, 45, 144, 148, 155, 218, 220
World Zionist Organization (WZO), 197, 204
Wright, Frank Lloyd, 6

Yapp, Sir Arthur, 104
Yashpan, Yehoshuah, 113
Yavuz, Yildirim, 151, 161, 170
Yellin, Eliezer, 185, 208
Yemenites, 206, 207
Yeshurun Synagogue, 186, 188, 190
Yishuv, 8, 16, 181, 186–7, 212
YMCA Building Bureau, 109, 140
Young Men's Christian Association (YMCA), 101, 103; *see also* Jerusalem YMCA Building

Zionism, 15–16, 45, 225
Zionist Executive Building (ZEB), 2, *3*, 4, 8, 19, 181, *182*, 183–5, 217
  and architecture, 186–9
  and communities, 222
  and construction, 206–12
  and entrance court, *194*
  and institutions, 189–93, 195–7, 199–200, 202

Zionist Executive Building (ZEB) (*cont.*)
    and JNF wing, *201*
    and modern day, 225
    and modernism, 218
    and politics, 212–13
    and style, 202–6

Zionists *see* Jews

zoning system, 36–9, 44, 46–50

EU representative:
Easy Access System Europe
Mustamäe tee 50, 10621 Tallinn, Estonia
Gpsr.requests@easproject.com